Natural Masques
Gender and Identity in Fielding's Plays and Novels

Jill Campbell

Stanford University Press
Stanford, California 1995

Stanford University Press
Stanford, California

© 1995 by the Board of Trustees of the Leland Stanford Junior University
Printed in the United States of America

Published with the assistance of the Frederick W. Hilles Publications Fund at
Yale University

CIP data are at the end of the book

Stanford University Press publications are distributed exclusively by
Stanford University Press within the United States, Canada, and Mexico;
they are distributed exclusively by Cambridge University Press throughout
the rest of the world

for Lynn Campbell,
1955–84,
sister and guide still

Acknowledgments

As I have worked on this book, I have sometimes felt like one of the travelers in *Joseph Andrews*: able to pay the bill and move forward from some halting place along the way only because of the generous intervention of a passerby. Like the peddler who eventually teaches Joseph who he is, some of these passersby have returned to provide me with parts of my story I didn't even know I lacked. The academic world can feel as small as the England of Henry Fielding's novels; it has been one of the great pleasures of the endeavor of writing this book to come to know, in person or in correspondence, some of the people whose thinking I have most admired in print.

Looking for my first faculty position, I found not only a job but an acquaintance with several of those people. Laura Brown remembered my writing sample and gave me my first opportunity for publication; I am grateful for her inspiring example as well as the support she has offered over the years. Rereading Terry Castle's work on Fielding I always find I am even more indebted to it than I had realized. She has generously affirmed something of promise in my own work, as well as providing me with invaluable guidance at several points in this book's progress. Years ago, as I read the Wesleyan edition of *Joseph Andrews* at Cross Campus Library, I discovered that the tall stranger sharing a table with me was W. B. Coley, one of the editors of the Wesleyan Fielding project; he has since shared his vast knowledge of Fielding and of the period with me. I am grateful to the American Society for Eighteenth-Century Studies for holding annual conferences, at which I had the good fortune to meet such fine intellectual companions as J. Paul Hunter and Kristina Straub. I am delighted to have crossed paths repeatedly with Felicity

Nussbaum: I appreciate her interest in my work as well as her willingness to share her own.

Had I never met Ronald Paulson and Patricia Meyer Spacks, my work would nonetheless rely on the definitive contributions they have each made to eighteenth-century studies. Imagine the extent of my debt—and my good fortune—to have two such extraordinary literary historians as my dissertation advisers. John Guillory, David Marshall, and Claude Rawson offered valuable responses to early versions of the first portion of this book. Later portions of the book also developed in conversation with generous and discerning readers: among them, Nancy Armstrong, Judith Frank, Richard Halpern, and Cathy Shuman. My continuing debt to Ronald Paulson's support and example appears all too graphically, perhaps, in the illustrations I have chosen for Chapter 1; it is a premise of the text of this book as well.

My parents, Mary and Warren Campbell, have given faith and understanding, never stinting. The arrival of my son, Forrester Hammer, delayed the publication of this book and made it more joyful. Langdon Hammer's wit and wisdom, love and patience, provocation, sympathy, and material aid have seen this book through its many forms. In a real sense, it is his book too.

Early stages in the research and writing of this book were supported by a Wimsatt Scholarship and a Whiting Fellowship; and a Morse Fellowship allowed its completion. Part of Chapter 1 was originally published in *The New Eighteenth Century: Theory, Politics, English Literature,* ed. Nussbaum and Brown. A version of Chapter 4 was published in *ELH* 55 (1988) and is used here by permission of The Johns Hopkins University Press, Baltimore/London. Parts of Chapters 5 and 6 were published in *Genre* 23 (1990), published by the University of Oklahoma. I thank these publications for permission to reprint. I would also like to thank Mrs. Frank Sussler, curator of the print collection at the Lewis Walpole Library, for her assistance in locating illustrations for this book; and I thank her and curators at the British Museum and at the Beinecke Rare Book and Manuscript Collection, Yale University, for permission to reproduce those illustrations.

Contents

Introduction   1

PART I. FIELDING'S PLAYS   17

1. "When Men Women Turn": The Drama of
Gender Reversals   19

PART II. 'JOSEPH ANDREWS'   61

2. The Meaning of a Male Pamela:
Genre and Gender   67
3. "The Natural Amphitheatre": Dramatic Satire,
the Novel, and Milton's Christian Epic   90
4. "The Exact Picture of His Mother":
Misrecognitions, Mortal Loss, and Joseph's
Promise of Reunion   109

PART III. 'TOM JONES' AND
'THE JACOBITE'S JOURNAL'   131

5. Male Pretenders and Female Rebels:
Whig Responses to the '45   137
6. *Tom Jones*, Jacobitism, and Gender: History and
Fiction at the Ghosting Hour   160
7. "The Same Birchen Argument":
Flogging, Satire, and the Jacobite's Ass   182

x   Contents

PART IV. 'AMELIA'   201

   8. "If This Was Real": Female Heroism in *Amelia*   203

   Epilogue: Death, Witches, and Bitches in
   The Journal of a Voyage to Lisbon   243

   Notes   251

   Bibliography   301

   Index   319

Figures

Figure 1. Hogarth, frontispiece of *The Works of Henry Fielding*, 1762.

Figure 2. Hogarth, frontispiece of *The Tragedy of Tragedies*, 1731.

Figure 3. John Ireland, "Farinelli, Cuzzoni, and Senesino," from *Hogarth Illustrated from his own Manuscripts*, 1798.

Figure 4. Hogarth, "Masquerades and Operas," 1724.

Figure 5. Hogarth, *The Rake's Progress*, plate 2, "The Rake's Levee," 1735.

Figure 6. Hogarth, "Masquerade Ticket," 1727.

Figure 7. John Ireland, "Heidegger in a Rage," from *Hogarth Illustrated from his own Manuscripts*, 1798.

Figure 8. Hogarth, "Characters and Caricaturas," 1743.

Figure 9. Detail of Figure 8, "Characters and Caricaturas."

Figure 10. "*Tandem Triumphans*. The Victory Obtain'd over the Rebels, at Culloden, by the Duke of Cumberland," 1746.

Figure 11. Frontispiece of the first twelve numbers of *The Jacobite's Journal*, 1747 (attributed to Hogarth).

Figure 12. "The True Contrast—The Royal British Hero—The Fright'ned Italian Bravo," 1749.

Figure 13. "The agreable Contrast between the *British Hero*, and the Italian Fugitive," 1746.

Figure 14. "THE AGREABLE CONTRAST. Shews that a Greyhound is
      more agreeable . . . ," 1746.

Figure 15. Prince Charles disguised as Betty Burke.

Figure 16. "Lord Lovat a Spinning," 1746.

Figure 17. "Scotch Female Gallantry," 1746.

Figures appear following pp. 54 and 142.

Natural Masques

Gender and Identity in Fielding's Plays and Novels

Introduction

The great mystery of literary history, of course, as of other kinds of history, is the process by which change occurs—the dramatic or minute negotiations by which a century that begins, say, with attention to satiric and mock-epic verse, written in heroic couplets, may end with *Lyrical Ballads*, or a century that begins with variously defined prose narrative forms may end with a firmly established tradition of "the novel." At a turning point in the plot of *Tom Jones*, Fielding chastens any confidence we might feel in our own powers to trace the circumstances of change: "there are many little Circumstances," he remarks, "too often omitted by injudicious Historians, from which Events of the utmost Importance arise. The World may indeed be considered as a vast Machine, in which the great Wheels are originally set in Motion by those which are very minute, and almost imperceptible to any but the strongest Eyes."[1] At the same time, the events of Fielding's own life and writing career tempt us to try to apply those powers of historical analysis, for they present us with several strikingly concentrated instances of dramatic change in the lineaments of political, literary, and personal identity.

The same man who came to the attention of the London public in the 1730's as an inspired Opposition satirist—who in fact was credited with precipitating the passage of the Stage Licensing Act in 1737 by so effectively attacking Walpole's administration on the stage—was to serve in the final years of his life "as the government's most dutiful and effective apologist."[2] First known as a prolific and successful playwright, most memorably (as in *Tom Thumb*) in burlesque and satiric forms, Fielding is now remembered for his later contributions to the emerging genre of the novel: that is, for *Joseph*

Andrews, Tom Jones, and *Amelia,* the last of which specifically replays and revises the central scenario of *Tom Thumb*'s burlesque—the absurd spectacle of a woman in the role of a hero—by seriously elaborating an ideal of female heroism. This last novel has been described as deeply influenced by Samuel Richardson, the writer whose *Pamela* Fielding had so devastatingly ridiculed in his first, parodic experiment in prose fiction.[3] The events of Fielding's personal life, too, ironically recast his early ridicule of *Pamela*: he was destined, after his first wife's death, to marry her maid.

The inconsistencies and contradictions, the ironic reversals in the course of Fielding's pursuits, were not lost on his contemporaries, who jeered at the gentleman's decision to "marry his own cook-wench," and who commented skeptically on Fielding's "present State of Transformation" when the former literary hack and reputed libertine dispensed law, order, and morality in the last years of his life as justice of the peace for Westminster.[4] Observers more sympathetic to Fielding—literary critics and biographers looking back on his life and works—have sometimes expressed embarrassment about the various "transformations" wrought within him, straining to explain, in particular, what seem his political tergiversations.[5] For the differences in Fielding's positions and practices that appear over time suggest the possibility of incoherencies within his character at any one time, internal fissures or contradictions that might generate such rapid change. Some critics have in fact embraced this possibility, celebrating Fielding's willingness to sustain "unresolved dualities" or to "wrestle central contradictions . . . only to a standoff" as one source for the richness and interest of his work.[6]

Yet in seeking to explain one of the great literary-historical puzzles of the eighteenth century—the "rise" of the English novel—critics have typically treated this complex phenomenon, Fielding, as singular and monolithic, intent upon pairing him with Richardson and developing polarized contrasts that locate all the differences between the two authors rather than within the character or works of either.[7] Thus, in critical discussions based on impressions of the two men's contrasting lives, Fielding plays the part not only of the classically educated gentleman to Richardson's middle-class tradesman, but of worldliness, licentious appetite, and robust health to Richardson's sheltered piety and hypochondria.[8] In more sophisticated critical discussions, the structure of unifying definition by contrast remains in place, as Fielding's debts to epic and satiric forms differentiate his novels from those of Richardson, or his reliance on "external characterization" sharply distinguishes his narrative approach from Richardson's psychological one.[9] The opening remarks of Martin C. Battestin's introduction to *Joseph Andrews* suggest both how inborn the critical dualism of Richardson and Fielding has come to seem, and how crucial a function that dualism serves in appearing to offer insight into the genesis of the English novel. "In the early 1740's," Battestin explains,

after years of gestation . . . the English novel came all at once into being as an art form, its two main directions—inward, toward the individual personality, and outward, toward the panorama of society—arising from the conflicting temperaments and literary motives of two very different men, Samuel Richardson and Henry Fielding. It could hardly be called a marriage, but from the rude and often hilarious conjunction of Richardson's feminine sensibilities and Fielding's robust masculinity, the modern novel was born.[10]

Battestin incorporates several of the commonplace contrasts I have mentioned into his energetic evocation of Richardson and Fielding's historic confrontation; but, significantly, he also organizes those contrasts around a primary axis of gendered terms: the distinction between "inward" and "outward" directions of interest, as between sensibility and robustness, is finally the difference between "feminine" and "masculine" natures.

In claiming an almost biological status for the Richardson-Fielding opposition—in giving the relation between their novels the mythic cast of the ancient, if complex, relation between the sexes—Battestin draws on a long critical tradition. As Angela J. Smallwood has observed, Fielding's "masculine image" has been advanced unquestioningly both by traditional male critics eager to identify with and praise him, and (more recently) by feminist critics eager to dismiss him, even as "Richardson's work is commonly credited with a feminine ethos, and sometimes even a feminist one."[11] In Battestin's remarks on the two novelists, this familiar gendering of their characters and works serves the particular function of allowing him to develop an extended genealogical metaphor for the emergence of the English novel: by the time that we learn that it has been "born," we have met its two parents, appropriately masculine and feminine, though not officially united in "marriage." Although this metaphor is offered as a playful rhetorical flourish, it expresses two intuitions about the literary-historical phenomenon of the novel's rise—intuitions that are commonly expressed or implied, but generally thwarted or misapplied. The first is that dramatic literary-historical change, such as that seen in the eighteenth century in the appearance and development of the novel form, must somehow emerge from the confrontation of opposed or conflicting traditions or forces—thus the canonical gesture toward the *double* origin of the newly *singular* and consolidated genre of the novel in the neatly opposed works of Richardson and Fielding.[12] Second, the eagerness with which critics have regularly assigned gender terms to the two halves of this double origin seems to express an intuition that, in the case of the novel's rise in particular, this confrontation, this dramatic negotiation, must have something to do with the categories of gender.

Even as critics have relied on the intuitively satisfying idea that the novel form somehow emerges from the confrontation of opposed figures, when they have developed any extended account of the novel's "rise," they have tended to hypostasize those two figures, to insulate each from any real engagement with what the other represents, and to settle, rather quickly, on the traditions and impulses expressed in one or the other's work as the true explanatory center of the novel's origins.[13] And even as critics have so often evoked the terms of gender to describe the conditions and consequences of the novel's emergence, they have tended to rigidify those terms and to locate them outside the content of early novels themselves, allegorizing the dynamic interplay of ideas of feminine and masculine identity as the separate contributions of two authors with different figurative sexes. Recent literary historians of the English novel have become more reflective than earlier ones about their own use of gendered terms, no longer unselfconsciously referring to the novel's "founding fathers" as "a man's man" and "in all seriousness, one of our great women."[14] More important, they have, to varying extents, begun to emphasize the crucial participation of the novel form itself in the evolving construction of gender terms.

Thus Ian Watt and Nancy Armstrong, with quite different theoretical frameworks, have both argued that the eighteenth-century novel played a central role in formulating a new ideal of female nature, one that radically altered earlier conceptions of the relations between the sexes. Other critics (for example, J. Paul Hunter and Peter J. Carlton) have commented on how particular novels respond to the declining viability of the epic hero as a male ideal, or to a shift between Restoration and Whig models of masculinity.[15] Significantly, however, the studies of these two pairs of critics center on Richardson in the first case and on Fielding in the second: the novels of the "feminine" or even "feminist" Richardson are seen as actively engaged in the redefinition of female identity, while those of the manly and classically educated Fielding, seen as contending with the growing disjunction between inherited heroic models and contemporary society, seek to create new definitions of male roles. The effect is not only to extend the tradition of separate accounts of the novel's early developments, focused on either Richardson or Fielding, but to establish two separate histories of gender's changing construction over time, histories dominated, in the eighteenth century, by the emergence of the "new feminine ideal" *or* by changing models of male "heroism." The works of Henry Fielding, as I argue throughout this book, challenge us to bring these separate histories of the two genders together. In doing so, they also challenge us to bring together the two kinds of historical subject matter emphasized, often in isolation, by different literary critics—that of the political construction of gender and domesticity and that of more traditionally "political" matters such as war, governance, and kings.

Within the discipline of history, Joan Wallach Scott has argued eloquently for the importance of overcoming the invisible analytical boundaries that have divided social history into these apparently distinct subjects of study.[16] Indeed, such a compartmentalizing approach unhinges the very strength of "gender" as a concept, severely limiting its potential usefulness as a category of analysis, since (as Scott and others observe) the notion of "gender" has to do precisely with systematic and relational phenomena. Scott begins by defining gender as "the social organization of sexual difference"; Judith Butler invokes Scott's understanding of gender as "a shifting and contextual phenomenon," not "a substantive being, but a relative point of convergence among culturally and historically specific sets of relations"; and Donna Haraway summarizes Anglo-American feminists' use of the term to designate "a system of social, symbolic, and psychic relations, in which men and women are differentially positioned."[17] All these formulations employ the term "gender" to suggest the fundamentally social and historical rather than natural and universal status of experiences of sexual difference (although Scott, Butler, and Haraway are each anxious to insist that such a use of "gender" need not depend upon its binary coupling with a category called "sex" which then remains purely anatomical, "prediscursive," unconstructed).[18] In emphasizing the relational quality of gender, all these formulations also suggest that men's and women's positions in a changing gender system must be considered together—and, further, that since gender pervades all aspects of social life, its several dimensions ("social, symbolic, and psychic") are necessarily implicated in each other.

Part of what is so difficult about broaching an analysis of any historical system of gendered relations is that that "system" inheres, one might say, not so much in several "dimensions" as on several ontological planes. For Scott, gender conducts its business both on material and rhetorical planes: she proceeds from the paired propositions that "gender is a constitutive element of social relationships based on perceived differences between the sexes" and that "gender is a primary way of signifying relationships of power." Sandra Harding calls the second, rhetorical use of gender terms "symbolic," and broadens its possible range of applications, commenting that "dualistic gender metaphors" are regularly assigned "to various perceived dichotomies that rarely have anything to do with sex differences." Indeed, as Haraway notes, the etymology of "gender" links it to the very notion of categorization or classification, so that it is "at the heart of constructions and classifications of systems of difference" of all kinds.[19]

At the same time, the language of gender is not just a way of talking about things other than itself.[20] Harding goes on immediately to name two other processes involved in the production of "gendered social life": the use of gender dualisms as a central means of organizing social relationships, institutions, and practices; and the construction through gender dualisms of individual "personal identity." Gender structures economic and political life in the public world; it is a premise of private, psychic experience, shaping what it means to be a "self." Butler asks: "To what extent do *regulatory practices* of gender formation and division constitute identity, the internal coherence of the subject, indeed, the self-identical status of the person? . . . How do the regulatory practices that govern gender also govern culturally intelligible notions of identity?"[21] A newborn child begins its life by being declared a "boy" or a "girl"; Fielding's contemporaries liked to refer jokingly to castrato singers (as well as to particularly effeminate beaux) as "things."

As Scott notes, any use of the term "gender" in a historical (or literary-historical) analysis is necessarily anachronistic, since "concern with gender as an analytic category has emerged only in the late twentieth century."[22] Fielding does not use the term "gender," except to talk about grammatical instances or errors. And yet Fielding's interest in the widely diverse phenomena we now use the term to denote appears everywhere in his work. In spinning out the familiar literary-historical narrative of a momentous encounter between Fielding's masculine temperament and Richardson's feminine one, critics have overlooked Fielding's own sustained, complicated, dynamic, and often blatant engagement with the nature and consequences of gender terms.

As we shall see, in the plays that first made him famous, Fielding enacted the tenuous existence of gendered identity, casting actors in female parts and actresses in male ones, and recurring frequently to thematic treatments of the disruption of gender roles. In his first novel, *Joseph Andrews*, Fielding chose to frame his parodic response to Richardson's *Pamela* by reversing the sexes of the two participants in Richardson's scenario of embattled chastity. In *Tom Jones*, he intertwined his overt polemical representation of the 1745 rebellion with a treatment of masculine and feminine characters that drew on the claims of Whig propaganda about female nature and the Jacobite threat to male control; and in *Amelia*, he advanced his own version of the new domestic heroine, pairing her, however, with a husband sadly suspended between old and new models of male identity. Even in his final work, *The Journal of a Voyage to Lisbon*, Fielding's rendering of his own experience of bodily decay, lost social power, and approaching death is steeped in the language and imagery of unstable and fraught relations between the sexes.

What is striking about Fielding's concern with matters of gender in this broad range of works, beyond the pure insistence of it, is in fact the way he consistently treats problems of male identity and of female identity together, as necessarily interlocking parts of a single economy or system. Whether he is complaining about the violation of traditional gender roles, as in his satire of women who dominate their husbands and of effeminate beaux, or wistfully suggesting that those traditional roles may transform men into mere puppets of wooden authority and women into disembodied ghosts, he treats the definition of one gendered identity as inextricably bound up with the definition of the other. In doing so, he calls attention to the way that changes in the largely public forums of male identity—the institutions of government, the economy, high literature—shape and are shaped by changes in the conventionally female realms of home, virtue, and feeling. Throughout his career, Fielding comments frequently on the economic and ideological structure of "separate spheres" that critics and historians have recognized as so crucial to the development of modern capitalism. At times, Fielding expresses outrage and disgust at any disturbance of that structure, and at others evokes some of its costs. Fielding does not characteristically conceal the stakes of that structure, however: the mutual dependence of its two parts on each other, the close and dynamic relationship between political and economic matters and sexual ones.

In their obsessive treatment of questions of gender, then, Fielding's works frequently foreground how prevailing political and sexual ideologies rely upon each other for their force—but also how they at times may come into conflict when they fail to mesh perfectly or are transformed by emergent social forces at uneven rates.[23] I argue that the interconnections between political, economic, literary, and sexual forms stressed by Fielding's works are not seamless or precisely synchronized in their responses to historical change. In fact, the tensions between these separate though deeply interwrought social forms may at times carry out or precipitate change, even as at other times they so powerfully conspire together. I argue further that such tensions and at least temporary disjunctions appear within individual character (in novels as in life), making character dynamic, even in the ways that it is constructed or determined by historical circumstance. I am interested, then, both in the inconsistencies and disjunctions within Fielding's views at any one time—his simultaneous evocation of conflicting literary traditions, disparate political allegiances, dissonant models of personal identity—and in the dramatic changes that take place in his choice of literary genre, his political stance, and his representation of conventional gender roles in the course of his relatively short career. This study does not provide an account of the origins of the novel; it does not consider, in any sustained way, the contributions of other writers, such as Richardson, to the literary forms Fielding adopted and adapted to his own ends. Instead, it concentrates on differences within rather than on structures of difference between—as an experiment in ex-

ploring the circumstances of change as they appear in minute and
intricately interacting motions in an individual writer's career.

To concentrate in such an extended way on the work of a single
writer, Henry Fielding, and to focus on a particular concern, that of
gender, within his work, is not, however, to see him in isolation
from the broader context of his contemporaries; for Fielding shared
with those contemporaries an urgent interest in how the changing
nature of governmental, economic, and literary institutions might
affect both the institutions governing relations between the sexes and
the private experience of gendered identity. The briefest sketch will
here only crudely recall some of the areas of change that we will return to in considering individual works in the chapters to follow.

Fielding began his career as a writer during the fiercely controversial ministry of Sir Robert Walpole. As J. H. Plumb and Isaac
Kramnick have demonstrated, Walpole's "prime ministry" itself
represented a crucial change in the nature of government in England:
his long and very powerful tenure as minister, and the various methods of governmental power he introduced, consolidated and extended the changes initiated by the 1688 revolution, shifting the
center of national government further from a focus on the imposing
figure of the royal leader to highly "administrative" and "bureaucratic" operations.[24] The new economic institutions of the Bank of
England and the national debt, described by P. G. M. Dickson as
part of a "financial revolution" in early eighteenth-century England,
required Englishmen to think of money, of value, and of the nature
of their national wealth in very different terms than they had; during
the same general period, what Neil McKendrick has called "the birth
of the consumer society" required them to place themselves within
the new institutions, practices, and values of an increasingly commercialized society.[25] In the specifically literary marketplace, new
forms of literary production and new structures of relations between author, bookseller, and public were rapidly emerging.[26] In the
1740's and 1750's, readers nervously or enthusiastically noted shifts
in the prevailing forms of literary expression, as the "midcentury"
poets turned away from the characteristically Augustan mode of satire to other poetic modes, and as the genre of the novel suddenly
caught the nation's attention.

In various ways, all these quite disparate but deeply interconnected changes unsettled, threw into question, or even transformed the way English people thought about the meaning of gender categories. The old aristocratic values associated with patriarchy, with military valor, and with the rights of the king had relied on a particular image of masculinity that lost its apparent centrality and relevance as the king's power came to seem less important than his first minister's. The dangers of national debt were often interpreted as the consequences of women's indulged vanity, and women's newfound power as independent consumers seemed to some to threaten their husbands' control. The disappearance of the "manly" practice of satire was lamented, at the same time that a large female readership for the new novel form appeared. The forces of change did not flow in only one direction, from the public realm of politics, economics, and literature to an otherwise constant private realm of sexuality, family relations, and gendered experience: the growing authority granted to the concept of "companionate marriage," to the ideal of maternal nurturance, and to the claims of reproductive heterosexuality over various homosocial bonds not only reflected changes in the political and economic spheres but made them possible. Indeed, building on the work of Michel Foucault, a number of critics and historians have located in the eighteenth century the emergence of modern discourses of both sexuality and gender.[27]

In the company of his contemporaries, Fielding thus appears far from idiosyncratic in the intent interest he afforded the status of conventional gender roles, or even in his somewhat obsessive recurrence to certain stock figures representing the dangerous disruption of those roles: the beau, the Amazonian woman, the castrato, the henpecked husband. Smallwood has demonstrated the widespread attention turned to "the woman question" in the first half of the eighteenth century,[28] but concerns with the nature and consequences of gender roles extended beyond such topical treatments of the relations between the sexes, and did not focus on questions of *women's* nature alone. The active contestation in this period over the proper natures of male and female identities and their relations to matters of government, the arts, medicine, education, and money, can be seen in the strange insistence with which certain topoi appear again and again in the works of early- and mid-eighteenth-century writers.

During the reign of King George II, many Opposition satirists (including Fielding) harped on the notion that George was utterly dominated by Queen Caroline—the nation's king just one more victim of "petticoat government." The ambiguous sexuality of Walpole's ally and Caroline's favorite, Lord Hervey, seemed somehow crucially emblematic of the government's present corruption, not only to Fielding, but to Pope, Pulteney, and others. (Later, Whig polemicists sounding the alarm against the dread consequences of a rebel victory in 1746 warned that the Jacobite ranks consisted of weak-willed men and their fierce, dominating warrior-wives.) In expressing outrage at the corrupt state of the arts as well as of government, satirists again and again produced, as their clinching piece of evidence, the popularity of that extreme, literalizing figure of marred masculinity, the castrato singer; while Pope, in representing his apocalyptic vision of the state of the nation, eventually placed Colley Cibber at the center of his *Dunciad*, depicting him as an empty vessel of regressive or failed masculinity, dependent on the powers of a grotesque but "mighty" female figure.[29] In his essays and "letters," Goldsmith at times depicted *himself* as feminized by his dependence on booksellers and the marketplace, the authorial equivalent of a woman who has only her body to sell.

These dark emblems of shattered gender ideals coexisted, however, with more hopeful or more simply exuberant experiments in imagining new definitions of the sexes' roles, or new kinds of relations between them. Midcentury poets such as Gray, Collins, Akenside, and the Wartons (as John Sitter has shown) conjured up images of powerful maternal figures who might not only protect and nurture them, but grant them poetic power.[30] On the stage, Gay's *Achilles* playfully dwelt on the spectacle of a cross-dressed epic hero, and his banned *Polly* was to represent the exploits of a woman in male disguise;[31] particular productions of his *Beggar's Opera*—as of some of Fielding's plays—foregrounded the play's caricatures of gendered identity by casting men in women's and women in men's roles.[32] Offstage, in the popular social arena of the masquerade, the actors and actresses of everyday life adopted the clothing not only of other professions, classes, or races, but of the other sex.[33] "Female Warrior" ballads, reaching the peak of their popularity in the eighteenth century, told the stories of real or imaginary women who had ventured out into the world of war or onto the high seas in their male masquerade.[34] In a more earnest vein, the emerging genre of the domestic novel bodied forth new species of heroism and of virtue that only a woman could attain.

This rapid catalog of examples at least serves to demonstrate the energy with which English men and women engaged in a process of reformulating the import of gendered identity in the course of the eighteenth century—as well as something of the nearly chaotic multiplicity of attitudes and moods in which they did so. I will be returning to several of these examples in the chapters to follow, using related contemporary materials—satiric epistles about the castrato Farinelli, medical debates about the effect of a woman's imagination upon her fetus, the debate about the basis of political authority epitomized in the writings of Locke and Filmer, Whig propaganda against the 1745 rebellion, educational tracts from the midcentury—to explore the range of implications of Fielding's own works. In the meantime, this catalog also serves to demonstrate how frequently complaints or speculations about the alteration of traditional gender roles explicitly connected that alteration to historical changes in the public institutions of government, culture, and the economy. Satirists complaining of the changes surrounding them often gestured toward long-standing "natural" male and female roles, grotesquely disrupted by these changes; but the manifest involvement of matters of gender in other kinds of change could not help but arouse the suspicion that this presumably most basic feature of personal identity was implicated in more recognizably "historical" institutions, external to the individual. This suspicion, the apprehension that male and female identity might be in some sense conventional, acquired, or historically determined, is expressed over and over again by Fielding from the beginning to the end of his career, though in a wide variety of moods. It is the specter evoked by the image with which I have named this book: "natural masques."

Fielding's first published work, *The Masquerade*, is set in the arena of self-consciously and admittedly assumed identities, telling the story of the poet's visit to "Count" Heidegger's masquerade assembly at the Haymarket. When the poet meets up with a lady in a velvet hood, however, their conversation quickly turns to merely assumed aspects of identity that prevail outside the masquerade-hall as well: the poet describes the repertoire of affected mannerisms that distinguishes the social type of the "beau," and the lady replies that such affectations among men, compromising their masculine authority, may result in the real transformation of both men and women. "For when Men Women turn—," she exclaims, "why then / May Women not be chang'd to Men?" This query seems to call up the next topic to which the poem turns its attention, the passing vision of a figure who further challenges the division between assumed and natural or real features of identity. The poet comments on the ugliness of this figure's "Vizard" and asks what would prompt anyone to invent such a horrible mask, only to be told that the man they view is the leader of the masquerade, Count Heidegger himself—and that "that horrid Phyz is / (*Puris naturalibus*) his Visage." Heidegger wears what the dedication to the poem calls his "natural Masque"—a face exaggerated to the point of "Burlesque" which he can nonetheless not remove.[35]

The image of Heidegger's face, simultaneously inborn and unnatural, is linked to a number of images that form a strong motif in Fielding's early works, including his plays, his essays in *The Champion*, and *Shamela*. These works return obsessively, with hilarity and with horror, to the idea that people and puppets may turn out to be interchangeable, that what seems spontaneous action may really be an illusion created by a machine, that the apparently most personal and essential aspects of identity may be revealed as artificial and contingent constructs. In general, in these pieces, Fielding offers scandalized or satiric renderings of the possibility that personal identity may be conventional or externally determined, and he gives special attention to the possibility that gender identity and the experience of sexual desire may be so. Repeatedly, he expresses a fear that sexual difference and desire may not inhere in organic features of the individual, but in conscious or unconscious impersonations. In the light of this fear, the phrase "natural masque" might evoke not only a horrifically alienated, even inanimate countenance, but also some ritualized, highly formal set of actions and verbal lines, which emerges as the sum of gendered identity—pointing toward Butler's definition of gender as merely "the repeated stylization of the body, a set of repeated acts within a highly rigid regulatory frame that congeal over time to produce the appearance of substance, of a natural sort of being."[36] Yet Fielding characteristically holds out a hope that the face and the phallus, in particular, may survive as repositories of authentic identity, feeling, and value. The literary mode of satire represents for Fielding in these works a method by which one might strip off the layer of acquired or affected identity and uncover something truer.

From *Joseph Andrews* on, Fielding conveys an increasingly ambivalent or vexed relation to satiric modes, and he also begins to suggest less purely negative ways of imagining the presence of assumed or acquired features within personal identity. We will see this, for example, in the thematics of adoption in that novel, a thematics that returns to play a crucial role in *Tom Jones* as well. In considering *Joseph Andrews*, we will concentrate on the ways that the conventions of literary genre and the acquired language of literary echo may enter into and determine personal character, shaping the nature of male or female identity and making even the private experience of emotion dependent on prior texts. In exploring the links that *Tom Jones* has with other Whig polemics against the 1745 rebellion, we will turn from the conventions of literary history to the social conventions of gender associated with Restoration and with Whig government, to see how they may appear in Fielding's construction of Tom's and Sophia's male and female characters. Fielding neither denies that the hero and heroine of *Tom Jones* are in some sense constructed by the "machinery" of history nor suggests that they are mere wooden puppets because of that. The surgically reconstructed face of his last novel's heroine, Amelia, provides an extreme image of Fielding's new willingness to accept the merging of the artificial and contingent and the natural within human character: as Terry Castle has observed, the removal of the mask Amelia has worn after her surgery is ecstatic "precisely because it makes no difference," establishing no distinction between her former natural face, her masked one, and the artificially altered one that now lies beneath.[37]

Fielding's growing acceptance of the place of the conventional and contingent within private character may be associated with his own increasing ties, in later life, to the prevailing social order.[38] I will be arguing as well that he gradually came to conceive of the imposition of external forces and frames of reference upon individual identity not as singular and simply reifying, but as multiple, overlapping, and conflictual, and therefore as potentially dynamic. In *Joseph Andrews*, he brings multiple literary sources—Milton's *Paradise Lost*, Richardson's *Pamela*, his own previous satiric and dramatic modes—into sharp generic conflict in a way that destabilizes the import and influence of each; and he repeatedly calls attention to the diverse and ambiguous effects that can be created by playing literary echoes off each other. In *Tom Jones*, Fielding places his main characters simultaneously in several frames of historical reference, reminding us how residual and emergent social forms and beliefs often coexist—and also how the various forums of social and political power possess semiautonomous and material, and therefore potentially dissonant, existences, even as they are deeply bound together.[39] Thus individual "character" may be the meeting place of conflicting as well as of conspiring historical forces—as indeed Fielding's own character was.

At times Fielding nonetheless expresses the fear that his own character may be so rigidly determined as to appear impersonal, even inanimate—and at others, the fear that his own character may be so mercurial, so fraught with shifting and various forces, as to prove ineffable, ephemeral, even spectral. We may see these opposing but interconnected possibilities in renderings of Fielding's face. In a contribution to *The Champion* that we will consider in Chapter 1, Fielding describes the features of his own face as so exaggerated that they, like Heidegger's, may be mistaken for a mask. In one of the very few portraits we have of Fielding, the frontispiece to the 1762 edition of Fielding's *Works*, Hogarth links his apparently naturalistic and respectful depiction of the man whose writings are there collected to the obliquely rendered features of the mask of comedy lying below, the curled mouth and large nose and chin of which seem to echo the features within the oval of the formal portrait's represented frame (see Fig. 1). Suggestively, however, this first mask is propped upon another mask, presumably that of tragedy, which is turned away from the reader's view, so that its features remain largely unknown.

An anecdote about the creation of the frontispiece reinforces this quiet hint within it that the famously strong and striking features of Fielding's face may somehow prove elusive, difficult to discern or recover. According to Murphy, when asked to create a frontispiece for the *Works* eight years after Fielding's death, Hogarth was at first unable to call up his "lost ideas" of the author's face, though Fielding had been a personal friend. Garrick later claimed that what finally recalled the features of Fielding's face to Hogarth's mind and permitted him to record them in this portrait was Garrick's own late-night visit to Hogarth's apartment, disguised as Fielding's ghost, in which guise he commanded Hogarth to "take thy pencil, and draw my picture!" Both Battestin and Paulson treat Garrick's account as a fanciful fabrication;[40] if so, it is a fabrication that fittingly carries on the dead author's own obsessive concerns, embedding this influential image of Fielding's face at once in the problematics of acting and impersonation and in the uncertainties of ghostly visitation.

Two years after his career in the theater had been abruptly terminated by the passage of the Stage Licensing Act, Fielding glanced back at one of the salient features of that career in the pages of *The Champion*, where he referred to himself as "an Author who dealt so much in Ghosts, that he is said to have spoiled the *Hay-market* Stage, by cutting it all into Trap-Doors."[41] Like the famous joke at the end of *Tom Thumb*, when Grizzle threatens to kill Tom's ghost, this reference amusingly mingles the spectral and the material. In his plays, as we shall see, Fielding associates one version of female identity, detached from both bodily desire and material means of power, with a ghostlike existence; later, in *Tom Jones*, the notion of the "ghosting-hour" comes to designate, in a more general way, that continuous historical condition of incomplete transition, of an always partially incoherent reality in which some features of the past persist alongside both the lineaments of the present moment and foreshadowings of the future. It is not despite but because of the material and multiple arenas of cultural, political, and economic change that such "ghostly" vestiges are real.

Fielding's later works do not seek to conceal the conflicts, the incoherencies of belief and identity, created by the process of historical change and by the individual's implication in multiple social institutions. Nor do they consistently seek to conceal the connections between those institutions. Instead, they often trace a dynamic process of direct interaction, of palpable and specific intervention, between the forms of power exercised in national politics, in personal life, and in literature. In doing so, they suggest alternatives to the assumption of a kind of magical "expressive" causality that has haunted much recent historicizing literary criticism, with its tendency to describe a hidden power (or spirit-of-the-age) exerting itself in strictly homologous or analogous forms within separate spheres that never come into open contact with each other.[42] The widely diverse body of writings left by Fielding encourages us, therefore, to find ways to conceive of literary works' involvement in an ongoing process of historical struggle and change.

PART I

FIELDING'S PLAYS

"When Men Women Turn"

The Drama of Gender Reversals

Having earned royal favor and the stature of a hero by preserving King Arthur's kingdom from the giants, Fielding's little Tom Thumb asks not for political power or monetary reward but for domestic bliss: "I ask but this, / To Sun my self in *Huncamunca*'s Eyes." The King grants Thumb the Princess Huncamunca, but Queen Dollalolla, in love with Thumb herself, objects. When Arthur remains firm, Dollalolla threatens violence, but he insists:

> Be she, or be she not—I'll to the Girl
> And pave thy Way, oh *Thumb*—Now, by our self,
> We were indeed a pretty King of Clouts,
> To truckle to her Will—For when by Force
> Or Art the Wife her Husband over-reaches,
> Give him the Peticoat, and her the Breeches.[1]

For the original audience of *Tom Thumb* (and of its 1731 adaptation, *The Tragedy of Tragedies*), King Arthur's blustering defense against "Petticoat Government" must have called to mind a specific scenario of female domination: England's own queen, Caroline, was widely rumored to govern the country indirectly through her control of King George.[2] At the same time, for the audience at many of the play's early performances, the dramatic scenario before them itself provided satiric commentary on this passage: the Thumb King Arthur here addresses was himself most often a "her" in breeches—a female actor typically filled Thumb's singularly heroic trousers—and in some cases the Princess Huncamunca Thumb is to wed was

a "him" in petticoats—a male actor occasionally took this role.[3] In
Tom Thumb, Fielding burlesques political and literary notions of
public heroism or "greatness" not only by mixing inflated with deflated diction and by shrinking his hero to a Lilliputian scale, but by
casting a woman as masculine hero.

Though critics have not addressed this obvious aspect of *Tom
Thumb's* satire,[4] Arthur's remark confirms that the theatrical device
of cross-gender casting signifies as more than farce in this play. In
the 26 widely varied plays Fielding wrote in the first decade of his
literary career, interest in problems of gender identity recurs again
and again, and Fielding repeatedly links the significance of gender,
particularly as revealed at the moment of inversion, to matters of
"government," both political and literary. He often uses gender as a
means of representing other issues, but also as a vexed issue with its
own political and literary consequences. Of course, it is the historical
meaning of "masculine" and "feminine" that he draws on when he
makes a female Tom Thumb serve to comment on the nature of that
hero, and much of his satiric use of gender works to protect or enforce certain historical notions of masculine authority. But at times
it also explores the costs of those systems of understanding male and
female roles. While his career as a playwright and stage manager
lasted, the genre of drama and its forum, the theater, provided Fielding with a particularly powerful—though ultimately restrictive—
means of imagining and representing issues of sexual difference and
its reversal, and of asserting connections between the dominant
structures of gender, governance, commercial society, and literature.

In the nondramatic works of his early career, some of which
we will consider in this chapter, Fielding frequently employs metaphors of the theater (and of costume, masking, and disguise) to
suggest that gendered identity may exist, finally, only in its outward
expression or performance rather than as a feature of inner identity.[5]
Recent theorists, such as Garber and Butler, have employed similar
metaphors, describing gender as irreducibly "theatrical" or "performative" in its nature.[6] While they use these metaphors with enthusiasm, Fielding does so, always, with great ambivalence.

In his plays, as elsewhere, Fielding often uses ridicule of a character's
compromised masculinity to associate that character with the compromising of traditional political, cultural, or social standards. He

uses familiar figures from the standard repertoire of contemporary topical satire to make the association. The figure of Lord Hervey, agent of Walpole and bisexual—Pope's "Sporus" and "Lord Fanny," Pulteney's "pretty, little *Master-Miss*,"[7] and an inexhaustible crux for many Opposition satirists—must serve once more to link political with sexual corruption in the role of Miss Stitch in *Pasquin*, as he does later in *Shamela* and *Joseph Andrews*. Fielding repeatedly uses the ambiguous gender as well as the foreign birth of the Italian castrato singers so popular in London at this time to represent the decline of the values of native theater.[8] That signature of Restoration comedy, the fop or beau,[9] appears frequently in Fielding's comedies as well, and what Fielding concentrates on in this familiar comic type is its disruptive signification in a system of gender oppositions. "I have known a beau with everything of a woman but the sex," observes Wisemore in *Love in Several Masques*, "and nothing of a man besides it"; complaining that his son is a beau, Mr. Bellamant of *The Modern Husband* exclaims, "Let him dress like a man, not affect the woman in his habit or gesture."[10]

The stock jokes about gender in Fielding's plays show not only satiric interest in men who abdicate, for one reason or another, their masculinity and all it is imagined to entail—the corrupt courtier, the castrato singer, the beau—but his apocalyptic vision of women's appropriation of that masculine power. "And if the Breed ben't quickly mended," warns the poet's muse at the end of a passage satirizing beaux in Fielding's first published work, *The Masquerade*,

> Your Empire shortly will be ended:
> Breeches our brawny Thighs shall grace,
> (Another *Amazonian* Race.)
> For when Men Women turn—why then
> May Women not be changed to Men? (5–6)[11]

Women's appropriation of male "empire," the threat of "petticoat government," is the most general and persistent topic of sexual satire in Fielding's plays. "We are all under petticoat government," Trapwit announces as the Cibberian "moral" to the second act of his comedy within *Pasquin* (II.i). In *The Grub-Street Opera*, which presents English royalty as a Welsh family of henpecked husband, domineering wife, and "puny" son, Puzzletext the parson comforts Sir Owen with the company his misery keeps: "Petticoat-government is a very lamentable thing indeed.—But it is the fate of many an honest gentleman" (I.i). And Fielding extends the problem even into the afterlife and the underworld: when a critic asks the author of the rehearsal play within *Eurydice*, "Why have you made the devil hen-pecked?" the author replies, "How could hell be better represented than by supposing the people under petticoat government?" King Arthur himself, with whose defense against petticoat government we began, is described in the Dramatis Personae of *The Tragedy of Tragedies* as "A passionate sort of King, Husband to Queen *Dollalolla*, of whom he stands a little in Fear."

Most of these scenarios of the "misrule" of female domination involve the government of a public realm as well as of a household, superimposing a domestic onto a political hierarchy of power: the henpecked husband is also the dubious ruler of the English people of King Arthur's or King George's reign, or of hell's ghostly "people." Domestic and political satire are for Fielding closely linked. Often the content of his political satire might be said to *consist* of linking it with domestic material—the intrusion of the domestic realm into the realm of public action and rule, or the domination of political by domestic or sexual power, is repeatedly the source both of Fielding's humor and of his serious critique. When Fielding presents inverted masculine and feminine power relations, he often seems to be representing through them an inversion in the priority of public over private concerns assumed to be the respective domains of men and of women.[12] In a period that saw itself as fallen hopelessly below past standards of public heroism—from the increasing bureaucratization of government under Walpole's ministry to the degraded grandeur of Grub Street genres[13]—the gender inversion of a female hero functions as one species of mock epic. The diminishment or corruption of the public world of heroism and power appears in its collapse into the female world of mere domestic squabble.

When Hogarth created a frontispiece for *The Tragedy of Tragedies* in 1731, he foregrounded this aspect of the play, choosing to illustrate Act II, scene vii, in which Glumdalca and Huncamunca quarrel violently and a mostly speechless Tom Thumb looks on (Fig. 2). He shows the two women facing off, threatening each other with the domestic objects of candle and fan, while the male hero, in military attire, stands by, reduced to the size of a doll beside the giantess, head lowered beneath his helmet's showy feather, arms crossed in an attitude of static helplessness. In the particular lines Hogarth depicts, the women exchange insults:

HUNCAMUNCA. Let me see nearer what this Beauty is,
     That captivates the Heart of Men by Scores.
     [*Holds a Candle to her Face.*]
     Oh! Heaven, thou art as ugly as the Devil.
GLUMDALCA. You'd give the best of Shoes within your Shop,
     To be but half so handsome.

The mock-epic humor of the scene works not only by ridiculing Tom for ceding heroic combat to women but by ridiculing women for engaging in such unladylike aggression; and, in the final lines quoted, a homely metaphor further deflates their feminine pretensions by associating their beauty with public, commercial exchange. In this scene and elsewhere, Fielding's uses of gender inversion do not employ a sense of the feminine domain simply as the negation of the masculine public world but as a domain of other kinds of values and powers that can itself be betrayed by a collapse into its opposite, whether that opposite is defined as the political and military realm of power or the commercial one of profit-seeking and exchange. Indeed, Fielding often associates women's appropriation of masculine powers with a confusion between these presumably separate zones within public life, so that women somehow become responsible for the reduction of the ideals of government to the low motives of commercial self-interest, the translation of heroic drama into metaphors of shopkeeping, and so on. Thus Fielding uses the terms of gender to articulate his response to the economic as well as the political developments of his time: the revolution in banking and the growing place of paper credit, the increasing cultural power of "fashion," the new importance of consumer goods.

In Fielding's earliest play, *Love in Several Masques* (1728), two female characters articulate more fully what the realm of the feminine is *supposed* to hold; and they also begin to suggest some of the interests served by the aligning of other oppositions with gender. Vermilia laments Lady Matchless's decision to throw over Wisemore for Lord Formal:

VERMILIA. O constancy! thou art a virtue.
LADY MATCHLESS. It is indeed. For virtues, like saints, are never canonised till after they are dead—which poor Constancy has been long ago.
VERMILIA. I am afraid it proved abortive, and died before it was born.
     But, if it ever had being, it was most certainly feminine; and, indeed,

the men have been so modest to allow all the virtues to be of our sex.

LADY MATCHLESS. O! we are extremely obliged to them; they have found out housewifery to belong to us too. In short, they throw their families and their honour into our care, because they are unwilling to have the trouble of preserving them themselves. (IV.xi)

The feminine alternative to masculine public life is familiarly imagined at times as the private life of "housewifery" and at other times, more imposingly, as the abstract, internal life of "virtue." Richardson's story of "Virtue Rewarded," for example, draws on the association of virtue with feminine identity and shows this alternative to masculine physical, social, and economic forces ultimately overpowering them. Vermilia and Lady Matchless remain skeptical: together they exquisitely delineate the system by which family, "housewifery," and private virtue are sorted into women's hands, and they recognize that they inherit this realm only through a male abdication of it—an abdication that serves, finally, masculine purposes, allowing men better to pursue their business in the realms of power they retain as their own. Vermilia and Lady Matchless recognize, too, the ghostly nature of the realm they are granted: that powers that devolve upon women must be saintly ones—personified and dead.

But if Fielding sympathetically, I think, exposes the hollowness of the power men grant to women when "they throw their families and their honour into our care," he often himself employs the association of women with internal life—not only the moral life of virtue but the psychological one of feeling. He counts on women to preserve that province apart from the masculine worlds both of politics and of profit, but he frequently suspects them of merely using their association with virtue and feeling to serve their own purposes of power and acquisition. "Virtue" becomes "vartue" in Fielding's *Shamela*, a high-blown word deflated by vulgar usage, reduced to Shamela's means for getting her man; and, once married, she overreaches her husband through an artful use of feminine feeling—feeling that is calculated and constituted for the effect of its representation. The rupture of gender categories involved in "petticoat government" implies for Fielding, then, not only the intrusion of domestic concerns into political or commercial ones, but also the betrayal of the space of interior feeling associated with femininity by a counterfeit or "sham" exterior version of it, fabricated for its effects in the public world of the male. Fielding's insistent representations of gender exchange at times play out his long-recognized interest in problems of internal and external, authentic and affected self. The frame materials of *Shamela* confirm that Fielding associates what Shamela stands for—her replacement of feminine feeling by the ambitious and profit-seeking art of false self-dramatization—with the conflation or exchange of gender roles: Lord Hervey receives the honors of *Shamela*'s dedication under the name of "Miss Fanny," a name that casts a slur on the female genitals[14] as well as on Hervey's fame as a "delicate Hermophrodite";[15] Dr. Woodward, another public figure of suspect sexuality, comes in for satiric abuse in the course of the dedication;[16] and even Sir Robert Walpole, so frequently satirized but rarely accused of effeminacy, figures in the second Puff to *Shamela*, bodied forth as a castrated Parson Williams and proposed as the appropriate subject for Shamela's biographer's "next Performance." These materials, the conventional stuff of Opposition satire, show Fielding characteristically linking images of compromised sexual and political categories, but they also serve to frame *Shamela* with Fielding's personal paradigm for the betrayal of authentic interiority: the drama of gender reversal.

Shamela's form of petticoat government depends upon feminine theatrics performed at home, and Fielding gives her connections to the public theaters of London as well.[17] When Fielding discusses affectation as the central problematic of character in "An Essay on the Knowledge of the Characters of Men," printed in his *Miscellanies* in 1743, he explicitly renders the problem in the terms of dramatic acting: "the Generality of Mankind mistake the Affectation for the Reality; for, as Affectation always over-acts her Part, it fares with her as with a Farcical Actor on the Stage, whose monstrous over-done Grimaces are sure to catch the Applause of an insensible Audience."[18] Fielding immediately identifies Affectation as both female and hypertheatrical, and the mixed sexuality of cross-dressing may be what evokes the term "monstrous" from Fielding in his description of Affectation's grimaces, for the image of "a farcical actor on the stage" raises the idea of the male players in female roles and female players in male roles that were an important element of English farce tradition.[19] The arguments of the anti-theatricalists—

which extended 150 years before Fielding and which contributed to the Stage Licensing Act that ended his dramatic career—had used cross-dressing as a paradigm for the moral dangers of the theater. They thus implicitly made gender the ultimate preserve of natural identity to be broached, in its most scandalous extremity, by theatrical impersonation; at the same time, they identified the theater as the forum in which the boundaries of gender might be tested.[20] Problems of gender and problems of affectation or impersonation were historically linked, then, in the controversial institution of the English theater, within which Fielding began his literary career.

As we saw in the scene from *Tom Thumb* discussed above, Fielding explored issues of gender identity and inversion in his plays not only by treating them thematically, or by recurring to topics of social satire involving gender, but also by actually staging the situation of gender impersonation—playing with, capitalizing upon, the dramatic possibilities of the theatrical device of cross-gender casting objected to by the anti-theatricalists. In addition to *Tom Thumb*, a number of Fielding's plays featured cross-gender casting in strategic roles: the playbills and advertisements announce Miss Jones as Tom Thumb; Charlotte Charke as Lord Place, and Mr. Strensham as Queen Ignorance, in *Pasquin*; Mrs. Charke as Mr. Hen in *The Historical Register*; Mr. Bridgewater as Mother Punchbowl the bawd in *The Covent Garden Tragedy*; Mrs. Nokes as Signior Opera, and Mr. Hicks as Joan the puppet, in *The Author's Farce*.[21] In this chapter we will be moving among a number of Fielding's plays (and some early poems and essays), exploring a series of related motifs involving gender that emerge into view when these works are seen together. We will focus particularly, however, on Fielding's employment of cross-gender casting, especially in *The Historical Register*, as a usefully explicit expression of his interest in gender; and we will find that even this literalizing representation of gender inversion opens up into a complex and ambivalent commentary by Fielding on the abstract system of oppositions associated with gender, which are dramatically disrupted by these roles.

The forum of the theater provided Fielding with an especially powerful means to comment on some of the economic and political developments of his time and their implications for the meaning of gender; for the theatricalization of culture represented by the increasingly powerful force of "fashion," with its dual emphasis on costume and imitation, made the theater a special site of cultural contention. At times, Fielding frames his interest in gender in explicitly topical terms, linking it to particular historical changes and openly professing a particular political vantage upon those changes. At other times, he casts his interest in gender in terms of seemingly timeless philosophical questions about personal identity and desire. We will attend to both these treatments of gender, and to possible unacknowledged connections between them. In several of his own uses of theatrical cross-dressing in Haymarket productions of his plays, Fielding made the drama of transvestism the physical context for his exploration of troubled relations between interior and exterior selves, private qualities and public actions: not only raising the problematic disjunction between them represented by Affectation, but raising also the threat of an exchange or collapse of the two into each other that turns both personal feeling and public action into mere dramatic acting.

Fielding's *The Historical Register for the Year 1736*, performed at the Little Theatre in the Haymarket in May 1737, places us and a small onstage audience of author, critic, and lord at a rehearsal of Medley's new play. This new play consists of a series of brief satiric scenes that are to provide an "historical register" of the events—political, social, and theatrical—of the preceding year. Medley's first scene is spare: a thinly veiled political satire of Sir Robert Walpole and his cohorts, displaced from the island of England to the island of Corsica, portrays the party in power as ignorant and interested only in money, and Walpole, "my first and greatest politician," as a behind-the-scenes power who "never speaks at all" (I.i).[22]

Medley's second scene is more complex. At its center is the stage enactment of an auction, which Medley calls the best scene in the whole performance (II.i). He tells Sourwit the critic, "I intend to sell such things as was never sold in any auction before, nor ever will again," and explains, "Sir, this scene is writ in allegory, and though I have endeavoured to make it as plain as possible, yet all allegory will require a strict attention to be understood, sir." The casting of Medley's auctioneer—a satiric portrait of London's popular auctioneer of the time, Mr. Christopher Cock, here called Mr. Hen—must be attended to if we are to understand the allegory of the scene: the role of Mr. Cock/Hen was filled by the noted male impersonator and eccentric, Colley Cibber's daughter, Mrs. Charlotte Charke. Fielding's cross-gender casting of Mr. Hen creates a dramatic context for the selling of "such things as was never sold in any auction before" that interprets both that selling and sexual inversions in a particular way; but before the auction has even begun, the terms of such an interpretation have been established by the short dramatic prologue to the auction, a conversation among the ladies who will attend. We will look at some of the systems of satiric associations this short prologue economically conveys before turning to the auction scene itself.

"Now you shall have a council of ladies" or "female politicians," Medley promises as his second scene opens, but the "affairs of great importance" they are discussing when the curtain is drawn replace the politics of Medley's first scene with matters of social and sexual fashion—an interchangeability, as we have seen, characteristic of Fielding's satiric humor.

> The LADIES *all speak together.*
> ALL LADIES. Was you at the Opera, madam, last night?
> SECOND LADY. Who can miss an opera while Farinello stays?
> THIRD LADY. Sure he is the charmingest creature!
> FOURTH LADY. He's everything in the world one could wish!
> FIRST LADY. Almost everything one could wish!
> SECOND LADY. They say there's a lady in the city has a child by him.
> ALL LADIES. Ha, ha, ha!
> FIRST LADY. Well, it must be charming to have a child by him.
> THIRD LADY. Madam, I met a lady in a visit the other day with three! . . .
> All Farinellos, all in wax.
> FIRST LADY. Oh Gemini! Who makes them? I'll send and bespeak half a
> dozen tomorrow morning. (II.i)

The stage direction and first line open the scene with a caricature of the univocal control fashion exerts over all the ladies' words: the same voice, the voice of fashionable society, speaks through all of them. They all seem to have attended the opera the night before— "Who can miss an opera . . ."—but they discuss not the music or performance but its lead singer—". . . while Farinello stays?" And they discuss Farinelli (that is, Carlo Broschi, the great Italian singer in Porpora's opera at the King's Theater between 1734 and 1737)[23] not as musical performer but as an object of desire: "Sure he is the charmingest creature," "He's everything in the world one could wish."

When the First Lady qualifies this statement with an "almost," she acknowledges the irony of female society's selection of Farinelli as popular sex symbol or romantic idol: the sweet extraordinary voice of Farinelli that is said to have ravished the heart of every woman in his audience manifested precisely his inability to ravish a woman physically, the puzzle of his sexuality, his victimization and election to that strange foreign elite of castrato singers. Although castration has removed the singer's testicles rather than his penis, that removal leaves his penis impotent and developmentally infantile, so that his penis is neither sexually functional nor capable of sustaining all the symbolic attributes and powers of the "phallus." Yet it is the same First Lady who complicates the view of Farinelli's disabled penis as simply a qualification to his desirability when she declares, "it must be charming to have a child by him."[24] The ladies cry, "ha, ha, ha!" at the rumor that Farinelli has fathered a child, and their choric laughter expresses their recognition that the rumor presents a contradiction in terms. Yet the First Lady's comment and their universal willingness to resume discussion of the rumor *as if* it were truth express some simultaneous wish for this contradiction—they take it up enthusiastically the way we take up a novel that offers us some imaginative resolution, however fictive and temporary, of conflict or contradiction in our beliefs and desires.

Fielding's "female politicians" weren't alone in their titillated interest: the Italian castrato singers that began to perform in London in 1707 served widely as a cultural text upon which the ambivalences and pressures of the period's sexual ideology could be played out, both in the form of the tremendous popular vogue the castrati enjoyed and in the form of the tireless satiric abuse they sustained. Even without children, the castrati presented their audiences with a contradiction in terms;[25] and their treatment elsewhere, both by Fielding and by other satirists of the 1730's, helps us understand all that is at stake in the simple jokes of this prologue, and how it prepares us for the auction scene to follow.

The satiric reactions to the disruption a castrato creates along the boundary between masculine and feminine identity reveal some of the larger systems of oppositions normally stabilized by alignment with gender terms. Because the castrato's exception to masculine identity consists ultimately in the facts about his genitals, the castrati provided an occasion to isolate, and to literalize, to make explicit, the cultural significances of the phallus itself: in considering the nature of the castrato's loss, the satirists at times assume the phallus as the guarantor of everything from moral discourse to English currency to Englishness. And, in the real or imagined responses of women to them, the castrati provided a rare opening in the normally monolithic entity of masculinity in which to explore—whether with wishfulness, fear, or denunciation—complexities or contradictions in women's relation to the phallus. While some of the satiric material concentrated its ridicule on the castrati themselves, much of it, like this scene from *The Historical Register*, turned its satiric attention on the women interested in them, competing to articulate what it would mean for a woman to prefer a man without the sexual use of his penis.[26]

Contemporary depictions of Farinelli's body, whether graphic or verbal, tend to emphasize its peculiar gracelessness, which they link more or less directly to that body's most remarkable, though unseen, feature. Portraits such as the one John Ireland attributed to Hogarth represent Farinelli as knock-kneed, tall, and malproportioned (Fig. 3).[27] Lamenting that a man who offered such "ecstasy to the ear" presented only an "offence to the eye," the author of *Reflections on Theatrical Expression in Tragedy* (1755) compares Farinelli's manner of moving to that of "a cow, heavy with calf," rising up "at the command of the milkwoman's foot"; and then metonymically extends his association between the castrato's body and a reproductive female one when he likens Farinelli's arms, resting on his hips, to the handles of "an old-fashioned caudle-cup."[28] And yet by the time Fielding presented the ladies' discussion of Farinelli in *The Historical Register* in 1737, two pamphlets, appearing in London in 1735 and 1736, had humorously argued for the greater erotic desirability of a castrated man.

The first of these, entitled *The Happy Courtezan: Or, the Prude demolished*, took the form of "AN EPISTLE From the Celebrated Mrs. C-----P-----. TO THE Angelick Signior *Far--n--li*," with its "celebrated" author being (at least in the poem's fiction) Teresia Constantia Phillips, the notorious courtesan who appears in the shadowy background of *Shamela*.[29] Early in her epistle, "Phillips" adamantly rejects the male fantasy (present in *Pamela*, *Fanny Hill*, and many other novels) that a woman's sexual desire is necessarily adjoined to dread, pain, and awe, and with it, she at least playfully rejects the phallic ideal of a lover in favor of Farinelli.

> Man, like his Brother Brute, the shaggy Bear,
> Where he attempts to stroke, is sure to tear. . . .

Discord and Thunder, mingle when he speaks,
And stunning Noise the Ears thin Membrane breaks.

How fit for Dalliance and for soft Embrace,
Is Man, that carries Terror in his Face? . . .
Can we with Pleasure, what we dread enjoy,
That very Dread does Love itself destroy.

How much do those display their want of Sense,
Who scoff at Eunuchs, and dislike a Thing,
For being but disburthen'd of its Sting?[30]

In the first stanza quoted, masculine Discord and Noise stand in for the penis, deflowering the female ear, and in the last, the sweet-voiced and "sting"-less Eunuch emerges as the ideal object of a feminine desire unmixed with terror or pain. Fielding had used a similar set of images in 1733 in his epilogue to *The Intriguing Chambermaid*, where he complains that the popularity of "Italian warblers" has brought about the decline of native theater. He ironically approves his female audience's choice:

—But though our angry poets rail in spite,
Ladies, I own, I think your judgments right:
Satire, perhaps, may wound some pretty thing;
Those soft Italian warblers have no sting.
Though your soft hearts the tuneful charm may win
You're still secure to find no harm within.
Wisely from those rude places you abstain,
Where satire gives the wounded hearer pain.
'Tis hard to pay them who our faults reveal,
As boys are forced to buy the rods they feel.
No, let 'em starve, who dare to lash the age,
And, as you've left the pulpit, leave the stage.

Fielding, like the "Con Phillips" of *The Happy Courtezan*, compares the uncastrated penis to a wounding sting, a "harm within," and a violent rod, but his irony attempts to recuperate the masculine discord and noise that "Phillips" rejects as the harsh but moral voice of satire: phallic satire "gives the wounded hearer pain" but only in order to reveal our faults; the rod "lashes" us that we may learn. Thus Fielding presents the rejection of phallic masculinity as a moral "softness" or evasion, a desertion of the pulpit. At the same time he renders a man's penis violent, alienating, an inhuman tool. By the time he was to write his first novel, Fielding would attempt to imagine an escape from the pair of alternatives this epilogue implies; in Chapter 3 we will explore how *Joseph Andrews* mediates between Fielding's discomfort with and his allegiance to the aggression of both satire and purely phallic masculinity. In his plays' repeated satire of castrati,[31] however, the power the castrato lacks represents an instructive rather than destructive aggression, and the ladies' enthusiasm for him expresses the general degeneracy of the age.

In *The Intriguing Chambermaid*'s epilogue, Fielding associates this degeneracy particularly with the reduction of moral discourse to a consumer transaction: satire's instruction is passed over in favor of "tuneful charms" because " 'Tis hard to pay them who our faults reveal." When, in *The Author's Farce* (1730), Fielding recreated Pope's vision of the reign of Mother Dullness on the stage,[32] he characteristically combined Pope's satire of a court's misrule and the inverted literary and social values it promotes with his own insistent satire of inverted sexual identity and nonsensical female desire. In the play within this play, not only does the Goddess of Nonsense choose Signior Opera as the dunce-laureate of her underworld realm, but she has fallen in love with him, and plans to marry him until Mrs. Novel arrives and claims him as her own. When the Goddess of Nonsense chooses the castrato singer over the other competitors for her hand, he bursts into a passionate aria—not one, however, that frames his gratitude or love, but one that sets to music his belief that "In riches is centered all human delight," and "When you cry, he is rich, you cry a great man."[33] The Goddess repeats the latter line "in an ecstasy" and cries, "Bravissimo! I long to be your wife": like the ladies' choice in Fielding's epilogue, Nonsense's choice of Signior Opera, rejecting together the phallus and moral "sense," reduces both cultural value and personal desire to a highly charged monetary worth.

The enormous salaries and extravagant gifts commanded by several of the castrato singers performing in London at this time figured repeatedly in satires of them.[34] For example, when Hogarth incorporated the design of the print depicting an operatic trio (Fig. 3) into the more clearly satiric context of "Masquerades and Operas," he matched the figures of the three singers with those of three noblemen, pouring gold at the singers' feet and crying, "Pray accept 8000 £" (see banner, Fig. 4). Hogarth expresses a similar criticism of the singers and their fans in the alterations he made to the second scene of *The Rake's Progress*, "The Rake's Levee," in its engraved form: there, he adds three references to Farinelli in a sequence that moves diagonally across the lower left quadrant of the scene, from the musical score propped on the harpsichord naming the great castrato singer as the lead in *The Rape of the Sabine Women*, down a long scroll listing the extravagant gifts he has received, to a print depicting the ladies' wild adoration of him ("One God! one Farinelli!" [Fig. 5]). In the gathering pictured in "The Rake's Levee," which seems to substitute commercial relations for personal or familial ones, Hogarth, like Fielding, uses the figure of the castrato to link fashion's destabilizing of value with the disruption of gender categories and the triumph of foreign over native tastes and influences.

In the scene from *The Author's Farce*, after Nonsense responds to Opera's aria to money by offering herself as his wife, Mrs. Novel raises an objection to their marriage that makes explicit one more vexed subject for which the castrato may serve as text. Mrs. Novel claims Signior Opera as her own with the surprising announcement that "he knows I died for love, for I died in childbed" with his child. The important subjects of female desire, reproduction, and value intersect repeatedly in the figure of the castrato, who stands for trouble within each of them, and satire's variations on the simple joke of a castrato reproducing with which we began show that joke working through complex relations between the three subjects.

When Fielding included this joke in the scene of the "female politicians," it had already been spun out at some length in the second of the two pamphlets about Farinelli published in the years preceding *The Historical Register*. In Fielding's *Pasquin*, performed one year before *The Historical Register*, the country mayor's daughter shows off her taste and her knowledge of London by describing what she expects to see in town: "and then we shall see Faribelly, the strange man-woman they say is with child; and the fine pictures of Merlin's cave at the play-houses; and the rope-dancing and the tumbling" (II.i). Miss Mayoress only reveals, of course, her appetite for low entertainments, and she garbles Farinelli's name, but she does so in a way coherent with her version of the miracle of a castrato making a child. The author of *Reflections on Theatrical Expression in Tragedy*, as we have seen, ridicules Farinelli's body by associating it twice over with the reproductive female body; but in giving Miss Mayoress the story that Farinelli actually is pregnant, Fielding probably refers to a pamphlet that appeared the same year as *Pasquin*: "An Epistle to *John James H--dd-g--r*, Esq.; On the Report of *Signior F-r-n-lli*'s being with Child."[35] This pamphlet reiterates the theme of female

sexual desire for a eunuch, but it also imagines the revelation that
Farinelli's ambiguous gender actually disguises his true identity as a
woman, exposed by the disgrace of his pregnancy:

> What may we think? the Doubt has made me wild;
> Is the soft Warbler then a Wench with Child? . . .
> WHAT Words can speak the chaste CLARINDA's Woe!
> Who now must all her hop'd-for Bliss foregoe?
> Her lovely *Eunuch* to a Woman turn'd,
> For whose secure Embrace so long she's burn'd!
> She who's refus'd a thousand filthy Men,
> Must she still hug her beastly Lap-dog then? (3–4)

The pamphlet's exclamation, "Her lovely *Eunuch* to a woman
turn'd," recalls *The Masquerade*'s apocalyptic vision of gender instability: "For when Men Women turn—why then / May Women not
be changed to Men?" At the same time, the pamphlet, by turning
the castrato into a woman, explicitly reveals the threat of a woman's
sexual preference for another woman beneath the threatening oddity
of a woman's sexual preference for a eunuch. (It also includes a passage on male homosexual desire: a description of "Lord *Epicœne's*"
courting of what he thought was another man, Farinelli.) *The Happy
Courtezan* had linked Farinelli, with his ambiguous gender, to in-
terruptions of the class system ("Your glitt'ring Equipage the Ring
shall grace / And to no Man of Quality's give place"), to disruptions
of others' gender identities ("And he that would not start at Death,
or Fire, / Shall like a Girl at thy soft Trill expire"), and even to confusions of the categories of animate and inanimate beings ("Your
Voice shall cast all Mortals in a Trance, / Ev'n Things inanimate to
that shall Dance").[36] This second pamphlet ends by implying that the
stability of currency's value rests on the stability of gender categories: as long as a castrato stays at least "half a Man," his value in-
sures the value of his subscribers' investment, and only the proof of
his possession of a penis, even a castrated one, can provide that in-
surance. The pamphlet presents the abstract principle of the masculine basis of monetary value in crude and material form: the author recommends to opera subscribers that in the future they "serve
your Eunuchs as they serve the Pope / Before they sign, let every
Member grope." Each member of a jury of "good Matrons" is to
swear

> That she has seen and felt how Matters stand,
> With her own naked Eye and naked Hand.

Unless you take this Method for the future,
Your Silver Tickets may as well be Pewter (6–7)

The penis here submits to examination by palpation to sustain a system of monetary values, just as it submits to use as a lashing rod to sustain a system of moral values in Fielding's vision of satire, or as the Pope's penis must be grasped, according to the pamphleteer, before he can preside over a system of religious authority.[37] Of course the phallus to be witnessed by the opera subscribers is a specifically diminished one. Ironically, by focusing on the "half" of masculine identity the castrato maintains rather than the half he lacks, the pamphlet deepens the castrato's association with instability of value; by taking a castrated penis as its guarantor that silver will not turn to pewter, the pamphlet comments on the already deteriorated standard of its society, and by reenacting the replacement of the phallic man by the prized eunuch with the turning of that eunuch to a woman, it implies that once ambiguity has been introduced, value is open always to further deterioration. In an economy undergoing a financial revolution, newly dependent on the impalpable worth of paper credit and the invisible transactions of "stock-jobbing" and national debt,[38] the author warns investors to see and feel for themselves the object of value, here embodied in a penis, and he figures the collapse of value as the disastrous interruption of the opera season by the pregnancy of its supposed castrato lead singer—actually a male impersonator.

This pamphlet imaginatively links the significance of the figure of the castrato to the significance of the figure of a male impersonator, and I think that this interpretation of the fertile castrato informs Medley's scene in The Historical Register, even though the ladies go on to imagine the miracle of a castrato's reproduction in a different way, as the miracle of mechanical reproduction and market distribution. The children they imagine for Farinelli are the wax figures, sold at the New Exchange, that were the fashionable purchase of the moment. When the First Lady says she'll "bespeak half a dozen tomorrow morning," the Second outdoes her, planning to order "as many as I can cram into a coach with me." The women who have "all spoken together" in favor of Farinelli, substituting fashion's influence for sexual desire, blur together sexual reproduction and consumer transaction; their idol Farinelli fathers fashionable commodities that present multiple, identical images of life. One lady suspects that her husband will resent her acquisition of the "children"—"I'm afraid my husband won't let me keep them, for he hates I should be fond of anything but himself"—but another asserts the autonomy from male authority that the ladies' newfound power of purchasing can give them, and treats her devotion to commodities as a replacement for her maternal role within the family: "If my husband was to make any objection to my having 'em, I'd run away from him and take the dear babies [i.e., dolls] with me." Furthermore, if a "knowing" audience would have understood the "dear babies" to be dildos as well as dolls, the ladies' enthusiasm for them represents a specifically sexual rejection or replacement of men.[39] The lady who proposes running away with her wax "Farinellos" not only refuses the phallic moral enforcement of satire in favor of "tuneful charms"; she threatens to desert masculine systems of authority, sexuality, and lineage altogether.

In this scene, Fielding links the figure of the woman as a powerful consumer in a newly commodified society with the figure of the castrato performer, and he implicates the two of them in the issue of ambiguous gender and gender impersonation, the notion of inanimate objects representing or even impersonating life, the spectacle of prices being attached to what should be living things, and the specter of value's instability in such a scene—and all these concerns will carry over into the onstage auction.

"Gentlemen, you must make room," the prompter tells *The Historical Register*'s onstage audience, "for the curtain must be let down to prepare the auction room." While the curtain is down, Medley's stage *becomes* the auction room; when it rises, the public space the auction occupies is coextensive with the theatrical space of the play within *The Historical Register*. When Lord Dapper, one of the onstage viewers of Medley's work, finds himself carried away by the action and begins to bid on the lots offered, crossing from audience of a play to participant in an auction, we are reminded of the ways in which an auction is itself a kind of theatrical event. The fashionable pastime that Fielding chose to succeed the ladies' discussion of the opera is at once the scene of theatrical, social, and economic activity: it is a performance with material consequences, a theatrical event that sets prices and establishes values through the dramatics of the auctioneer's presentation of objects and the dynamics of audience reaction—the process Lord Dapper enters when he begins to bid. Fielding's frequent references to auctions in his work show his interest in this process of dramatic value-setting.[40] The value finally assigned to a lot at an auction marks the strength of the mediated desire it provokes in the audience, arrived at through the interplay of imitation and competition in the crowd, rather than the worth either of the labor involved in obtaining or creating it or of the uses to which it might be put. The auction attaches value in some sense not to the object but to its dramatic shell, to the representation of the object the auctioneer offers.

The auction did not emerge in England as a method of price-setting until the end of the seventeenth century, and it was in the eighteenth century that it first became institutionalized with the founding of the earliest auction house, Sotheby's, in 1744, followed by Christie's in 1766.[41] Christopher Cock has been called "the first auctioneer,"[42] and the events he presided over provided a new form of social occasion for the fashionable set in London: Cock's auctions made *buying* a social event, and the crowds that gathered at an auction for entertainment acted out the movement of price-setting through demand that was crucial to their emerging "consumer society," creating as well the spectatorship to consumption upon which that society depends.[43] The auction combined not only the social and the economic: it had a reputation in this period as a "cover" for the prosecution of "affairs of gallantry."[44] The husbands that try unsuccessfully to restrain their wives' passion for auctions in the period's literature fear both the expenditure and the sexual betrayal an auction might occasion. Like the opera with its ravishing castrato singers, the fashionable entertainment of the auction presents a complicated threat to one kind of masculine control.

When the ladies of the introductory conversation turn their attention from the opera to the auction they will attend, the First Lady links Mr. Hen, the auctioneer, to Farinelli, the castrato, when she exclaims, "Oh, dear Mr. Hen! . . . I never miss him," recalling the Second Lady's rhetorical question, "Who can miss an opera while Farinello stays?" In the play's original productions, the auctioneer's entrance enforced and rendered more substantial this slender verbal association of the two men: Charlotte Charke enters, in male dress, as "*Mr. Hen*, auctioneer, bowing," another figure of ambiguous gender. The castrato singer and the auctioneer are similarly public characters and objects of fashion's hyperbolic and platitudinous desire ("I never miss him"), and Fielding's alteration of the name of the real auctioneer he satirizes deepens the relation between them.

Not only does Fielding turn the male chicken in Cock's name into a female one, even as the auctioneer remains a "Mr.," but this simple alteration involves taking the penis out of the slang denotations of the auctioneer's name[45] and instead evoking connotations of "henpecking," the term of petticoat government derived from hen-house politics. The auctioneer, represented by a male impersonator and thus renamed, and the objects he sells, "such things as was never sold in any auction before," are versions of each other.

Hen, "in the pulpit," begins the auction:

Gentlemen and ladies, this is Lot 1: a most curious remnant of political honesty. . . . It will make you a very good cloak. You see it's both sides alike, so you may turn it as often as you will. Come—five pounds for this curious remnant. I assure you, several great men have made their birthday suits out of the same piece. It will wear forever and never be the worse for wearing.— Five pounds is bid. Nobody more than five pounds for this curious piece of political honesty? Five pound. No more? (*Knocks.*) Lord Both-Sides.—Lot 2. A most delicate piece of patriotism, gentlemen. Who bids? Ten pounds for this piece of patriotism?

The "allegory" Medley has rather grandly promised us in the auction scene turns out to inhere, ridiculously, in the objects sold at the auction themselves: the curiosities Hen offers are all allegorical objects, abstract personal qualities represented as pieces of clothing, cosmetics, liquid in a bottle, massive books. Hen takes bids not only on the public virtues of political honesty and patriotism but on modesty, courage, wit, a clear conscience, interest at court, the cardinal virtues, and Common Sense. Fielding here renders comically literal the externalizing of personal virtue with which Shamela makes her bid for profit ("I thought once of making a little Fortune by my Person. I now intend to make a great one by my Vartue"). The personified inner virtues that Vermilia and Lady Matchless identified as the cultural realm of the feminine here take the form most often of outer garments, to which the public affixes a price.

Although the humor of the scene depends on this nonsensical notion of auctioning off abstract personal qualities in the form of concrete objects, in his advertisements for many of the lots Hen acknowledges that what he offers for sale are not those qualities themselves but the profitable appearance of them. When he argues to raise the bids offered for patriotism, for example, Hen emphasizes that it is something that can be taken off or put on when its appearance is advantageous: "sir, I don't propose this for a town suit. This is only proper for the country. Consider, gentlemen, what a figure this will make at an election." He promises his inquiring audience that the "valuable commodity" of modesty that he offers in the form of "a beautiful powder" will "not change the color of the skin" but "serves mighty well to blush behind a fan with, or to wear under a lady's mask at a masquerade." Thus Fielding implies that Hen's farcical reduction of political honesty to the visible, palpable cloak sold in his auction is only an extension or literalization of the way in which the impalpable virtue of political honesty, like other virtues, has been reduced by the times to the advantageous appearance of such. This reduction, Fielding implies, leads to a confusion of the feminine and masculine realms of inner life and public action, to a kind of cross-dressing of one as the other—to Shamela's (profitable and powerful) affected sufferings and affected "vartue," the "cloak" of honesty, the impersonations of a Mr. Hen.

Fielding would satirize Christopher Cock again by supplying Cock's name in place of a general reference to auctions in his translation of Juvenal's Sixth Satire as "modernised in Burlesque Verse" (revised and published in the *Miscellanies*, 1743). The context of the reference in Juvenal's satire allows Fielding to associate Cock and his auction directly with the transgression of gender categories. The misogynist satire turns its attention for the moment from adultery and female willfulness to "fighting females, / Whom you would rather think to be males." As translated by Fielding, the poem asks, "Will they their sex entirely quit?" and warns:

> should your wife by auction sell,
> (You know the modern fashion well)
> Should Cock aloft his pulpit mount,
> And all her furniture recount,
> Sure you would scarce abstain from oaths,
> To hear, among your lady's clothes,
> Of those superb fine horseman's suits,
> And those magnificent jack-boots.
> And yet, as often as they please,
> Nothing is tenderer than these.
> A coach!—O gad! they cannot bear
> Such jolting!—John, go fetch a chair.
> Yet see, through Hyde Park how they ride!
> How masculine! almost astride![46]

While Cock remains Cock in this passage—he is not himself presented as a woman dressed as a man—what he sells from his pulpit
are the castoffs of women dressing as men. Fielding expands Juvenal's reference to an auction into a description of the "modern fashion" and its primo auctioneer, and this description leads to his free
rendering of Juvenal's complaint in the terms of "masculine"
women riding in Hyde Park. But, following Juvenal, he complicates his portrait of the masculine woman by saying she, contradic-
torily, can at times assert the special claims of high femininity: when
not riding astride, she may insist on her need for a more delicate
conveyance than a coach. The woman's demand for a chair in this
passage repeats an association of women with extravagant consumerism throughout the satire,[47] and Fielding's use of Juvenal to comment on modern women makes clearer a complication in the cross-
dressing of *The Historical Register*'s auction of virtues.

   While in many contexts women are consigned to the idealized
or at least etherealized realm of inner virtues, in the context of the
classical tradition of misogynist satire they are implicated in the material realm of the commodity more deeply than men. Laura Brown
comments, "For Pope, as for Juvenal, women embody the material
consequences of commodification much more directly than men."[48]
More directly than Pope does in "To a Lady," Fielding uses Juvenal's
satire to turn his attack on modern luxuries and commodification
against women. The Sixth Satire opens with a vision of a time before
either consumer goods or adultery: "Dame Chastity" dwelt on earth
when

> men no other house contain'd
> Than the wild thicket, or the den;
> When household goods, and beasts, and men,
> Together lay beneath one bough,
> Which man and wife would scarce do now (303)

Tellingly, Fielding chooses to close his translation of the satire—he
breaks off less than half of the way through Juvenal's poem—at the
point at which Juvenal returns to his opening thought and makes his
denunciation of women a denunciation of luxury, consumption,
and money. Juvenal goes on to consider women's crimes of lust and
violence, but Fielding stops here to conclude his version of the satire:

> Whence come these prodigies?
>   . . . I' th' mountain

The British dames were chaste, no crimes
The cottage stain'd in elder times;
When the laborious wife slept little,
Spun wool, and boil'd her husband's kettle. . . .
Money's the source of all our woes;
Money! whence luxury o'erflows,
And in a torrent, like the Nile,
Bears off the virtues of this isle. (341–43)

Fielding locates the virtue of chastity in the past economy of a "laborious wife" with her cottage industry, and, in associating the luxury and expenditure of the new economy with the women Juvenal's satire abuses, he acknowledges that England's developing capitalism had made women generally consumers rather than producers, and so figures for commodification itself.[49] If we look back to Hen's auction of virtues now, we can see how it uses the contradiction between two simultaneously maintained cultural realms of the feminine. Its absurd "allegory" of abstract qualities offered for sale as concrete objects ironically conjoins, in those objects, the sentimental association of women with inner life and the satiric association of them with material commodities. The auction shows one passed off for the other, and so makes women bear the brunt of its commentary on a society in which luxury has borne off virtues and the public world of action has been converted to a theater of goods. Mr. Hen, the cross-dressed auctioneer who calls for bids on items with names from one feminine realm and shapes from the other, stands as a figure for the way money and purchasing have entered into, and disrupted, the division of male and female roles. The influence of fashion upon women is one way both Fielding's translation of Juvenal and his auction scene in *The Historical Register* describe women's betrayal of the realm of virtues for that of commodities.

Even when Mr. Hen clarifies that it is merely the attractive semblance of patriotism or of modesty that he offers for sale, an elegant country "suit" or a "beautiful powder" rather than the virtues themselves, he finds he has no bidders: his audience rejects both of these qualities as unpurchaseable because "out of fashion." Once value attaches not to a virtue itself, but to the appearance of that virtue and the reception of that appearance by society, then its value will of course depend on the changing tastes of fashionable society. Several years after *The Historical Register*, Fielding would write in *The Champion*:

No Nation under the Sun can give more pregnant instances of this Force of Fashion on the Mind, than our own. Our Ancestors make as various a Figure in their Ways of thinking to a curious Reader of our History, as their Persons do in a Gallery of Family-Pictures. Particular Virtues and Vices have been as generally in Vogue at certain Seasons as the Fardingale, the Ruff, the Hoop, the broad Brim, the narrow Brim, or any other Singularities of Dress have been among us.[50]

As in Hen's auction scene, Fielding likens inner virtues in this passage to outer clothing, to "Singularities of Dress," and his description of "this Force of Fashion on the Mind" reveals a dimension to the exchange between internal and external realms beyond the problematics of affectation. Fielding suggests that not only are our private, inner qualities and feelings sometimes fabricated for the *sake* of the public, external world, or constituted in profit-seeking self-dramatization, but they may be *determined* by exterior forces as well, the creation of "fashion" rather than of our own nature. As Neil McKendrick has demonstrated, the first half of the eighteenth century saw the emergence in England of a commercialized society that made rapidly changing fashion more influential than tradition for the first time.[51] Fielding repeatedly suggests that the influence of fashion in his society extends not only to the elements of self-presentation, or even to the construction of this or that moral quality within the individual, but to the individual's own experience of personal impulse and desire.[52]

Often when Fielding satirizes fashion's determining influence, he imagines fashion as a specifically foreign force, a force from outside native English society responsible for its decadence. The "beautiful powder" of false modesty that Hen offers for sale "is true French, I assure you." Fielding regularly traces the effeminacy of the beau, the slavish observance of fashions in dress and manner, and even homosexuality to sources in France and Italy,[53] and he satirizes the castrato singers as much for being Italian as for falling short of virility: the two facts seem to him in some sense synonymous. The xenophobic cast to Fielding's complaints about fashion grounds those complaints in a specific and controversial historical development—that is, in England's sharply expanded importation of foreign goods and culture in this period.[54] At the same time, it provides Fielding with a metaphorically resonant image for what he presents as the large philosophical consequences of fashion's incursions upon the integral self. English importation of foreign taste seems to map on a geographic screen a process by which the self may import from foreign or exterior sources its inner life, the "Force of Fashion on the Mind."

For Fielding, the pervasiveness of this force threatens to empty the realm of authentic interior self, and even erodes the certainty with which a self possesses those presumably basic features of personal identity, gender and sexual desire.[55] When a contributor to *The Champion* describes a gathering of "FEMALE COXCOMBS," he claims to have at first mistaken them for "*pretty smock-fac'd curl'd-headed Boys.*" He was misled by their fashionable hairstyles, of which his friend explains, "they're call'd *Tetes de Mouton*, they're of *Foreign Extraction*, and tho' all the Heads you see there before you are downright *French*, yet you may easily distinguish by the matchless Symmetry of the Features and Mien of those fair Apostates to home-bred Fashion, that their *Faces*, in spite of all their Disguises, are *English*."[56] In this passage, as in numberless passages within Fielding's work, the author identifies the adoption of foreign fashion with both affectation and gender impersonation, but he leaves open here the hope of "home-bred Fashion" and the conviction that "*Faces*, in spite of all their Disguises," retain a native identity.

A trust in faces as an inalienable repository of natural and native identity is what maintains this comment as satiric corrective rather than existential anxiety. A different part of the body must serve a similar function in a satiric passage of Fielding's play *Eurydice* (1737). The author of the play-within elaborates on the familiar complaint that the fashionable popularity of the Italian opera is bringing about the decline of native theater:

AUTHOR. Sir, if they did not bring abundance of mad people together into their operas, they would not be able to subsist long at the extravagant prices they do, nor their singers to keep useless mistresses; which, by the way, is a very ingenious burlesque on our taste. . . . For an English people to support an extravagant Italian opera, of which they understand nor relish neither the sense nor the sound, is as heartily ridiculous and much of a piece with an eunuch's keeping a mistress.[57]

As we know from the preface to *Joseph Andrews*, the effect of the "ridiculous" marks affectation's operation, and the author likens the affectation of foreign taste in fashionable entertainments—turning pleasure into pretense—to a eunuch's affectation of sexual affairs—

socializing sexual desire into mere status symbol, or outward sign. But the author scapegoats the eunuch, with his unnaturally disabled phallus, as satiric perversity rather than existential paradigm, and so implies the norm of the intact phallus as the repository of authentic and native taste, pleasure, desire. At moments in Fielding's work, even the face and the phallus will threaten to become foreign artifacts, indistinguishable from affectation's monstrous acquisitions of identity. To avoid such a fate, Fielding implies, true virtue or true feeling may have to become disembodied; so that for him the subjects of impersonation, of feminine personifications, and of ghosts are strangely intertwined.

By offering virtues and other personal qualities for sale to bidders, Mr. Hen's auction caricatures the possibility that aspects of personal identity may be mere acquisitions. The last lot Hen offers receives no bids because, as Medley explains, like a face or like private parts, "everyone thinks he has it" already: Lot 10 consists of "a little Common Sense." Medley's satire, however, depends on the implication that in passing over the "very valuable commodity" of Common Sense, the crowd doesn't realize its own lack, and Fielding's original audience would be especially ready to catch this implication if they knew of Fielding's very popular play of the year before, *Pasquin*. Lot 10 is the first of Hen's lots that appears in capital letters as a personified entity, and the figure of Common Sense had appeared, not only personified but dramatized and enthroned, in Fustian's tragedy within *Pasquin*, as Queen Common-sense. Indeed, Fielding's presentation of Common Sense there had been memorialized just a month and a half before *The Historical Register*'s first performance, when Chesterfield and Lyttleton named their new Opposition newspaper after her, commenting in their first leader that they took the name from "an ingenious Dramatick Author [who] has consider'd Common Sense as so extraordinary a thing, that he has lately, with great wit and humour, not only personified it, but dignified it too with the title of a *Queen*."[58] So far from being something everyone already has, Common Sense is "so extraordinary a thing," according to Fielding's *Pasquin*, that when Queen Common-sense fights her battle against Queen Ignorance in the play's final scene, she has only one follower, a "poor drummer, who was lately turned out of an Irish regiment" and "was willing to learn a little of my trade before I died" (V.i).

Queen Ignorance boasts more followers. They include native representatives of law, physic, and religion who all honor the letter over the spirit of their professions—legal codes and fees over justice, pills over health, priestly power over gods. But Queen Ignorance herself and the bulk of her followers come from afar: a messenger announces to Queen Common-sense that "Queen Ignorance is landed in your realm, / With a vast power from Italy and France / Of singers, fiddlers, tumblers, and rope-dancers," and Queen Common-sense prepares to oppose "this foreign force" (IV.i).

This foreign force, as we might expect, is deeply implicated in gender confusions and inversions. It includes opera singers and welcomes "Squeekaronelly" to its fold; it sponsors Lord Hervey's play *The Modish Couple* (V.i);[59] and it extends its sponsorship of impersonation beyond gender to species when it welcomes "Two dogs that walk on their hind legs only, and personate human creatures so well, that they might be mistaken for them" and "A human creature that personates a dog so well, that he might almost be taken for one" (V.i).[60] Gender impersonation remains the central paradigm for Ignorance's inversions: played by Mr. Strensham in *Pasquin*'s original productions, the role of Queen Ignorance is one of Fielding's most obviously significant cross-gender casting choices. In *The Author's Farce*, as we have seen, Fielding imagines a Popean reign of Dullness as the scene of nonsensical female desire for a eunuch-husband; in *Pasquin*, he reimagines Pope's apocalyptic vision of Dullness's triumph as the triumph of cross-dressing.[61] Common-sense is a feminine personification, as Vermilia's and Lady Matchless's comments would have predicted, and she lacks any attendant, active force in the masculine military world. Ignorance, with all her followers, is a man masquerading as a queen.

A poet who approaches Queen Common-sense in the last stages of her battle identifies Ignorance as an impersonator by nature. He threatens Common-sense:

> I'll dedicate my play
> To Ignorance, and call her Common-sense:
> Yes, I will dress her in your pomp, and swear
> That Ignorance knows more than all the world. (V.i)

The force of Ignorance has dressed itself, according to this play, in feminine pomp in order to impose upon the England it seeks to conquer. The danger Fielding sees in his equation of virtues with clothing in both the *Champion* essay and the auction scene of *The Historical Register*—and the danger of Common-sense, for instance, appearing with any pomp at all—is that clothing and pomp, inherently transferable, immediately introduce the possibility of appropriation: any ways in which virtue manifests itself externally allow for its impersonation. Perhaps this is why Fielding must insist in "On the Knowledge of the Characters of Men" that "Nothing can, in Fact, be more foreign to the Nature of Virtue, than Ostentation," and why he there imagines Virtue as a *naked* woman.[62] But the dilemma that troubles that essay throughout looms obtrusively in this passage on Virtue's "naked beauty": if Virtue, unwilling to put on the "foreign" garb of ostentation, but "conscious of her innate Worth, and little desirous of exposing it to the publick View," must shrink from sight in her necessary nakedness, how is she to be effective, or even recognizable, in the world? We are left to choose between the invisible authenticity of Virtue and the dramatically visible but monstrous impersonations of Affectation.

Defeated, Common-sense is murdered at the end of *Pasquin*. As she dies, the Queen prophetically describes a world in which universal darkness covers all:

> Farewell, vain world! to Ignorance I give thee.
> Her leaden sceptre shall henceforward rule. . . .
> Henceforth all things shall topsy-turvy turn. . . .
> Statesmen—but oh! cold death will let me say
> No more—and you must guess et cætera.
> [*Dies.*

Unexpectedly, Queen Common-sense will return to provide, herself, the feminine "et cætera"[63] lacking from the topsy-turvy world of the transvestite Queen Ignorance. Firebrand the priest tries to pass off her death as feminine "self-murder," the self-canceling fulfillment of Pamela's and Dollalolla's threats. But Common-sense proves not completely canceled:

> [*Ghost of* COMMON-SENSE *rises to soft music.*
> . . .
> GHOST. Here, though a ghost, I will my power maintain,
>   And all the friends of Ignorance shall find
>   My ghost, at least, they cannot banish hence.
>   And all henceforth, who murder Common-sense,

Learn from these scenes that though success you boast,
You shall at last be haunted with her ghost.

Sneerwell the critic, a member of the onstage audience at the rehearsal of Fustian's play, tells Fustian as the ghost finishes her speech, "I am glad you make Common-sense get the better at last; I was under terrible apprehensions for your moral," but of course Queen Common-sense has triumphed only equivocally, losing her life but retaining some form of voice, gaining the special authority of ghostly speech. She reminds us of the feminized virtues Vermilia and Lady Matchless describe, which "are never canonised till after they are dead"—the ghostly, disembodied, retrospective nature of the realm of power men cede to women in "allowing all the virtues to be of our sex."[64] Under the humor of this surprise second ending to Fielding's version of the *Dunciad* lies, I think, some kind of serious attempt to imagine a way out of the dilemma presented by "On the Knowledge of the Characters of Men": Common-sense escapes the hopeless alternatives of invisible truth and visible impersonation by returning as an aftereffect, a lost presence, a haunting. To ward off any possibility of impersonation, apparently, she must be deprived not only of clothing but of her body.

In a number of his plays and essays, Fielding circles with humor and with intent fascination around the question of what kind of existence a ghost possesses: some of the most memorable moments of *The Author's Farce, Tom Thumb* and its revision as *The Tragedy of Tragedies, Eurydice*, and *The Covent Garden Tragedy* involve jokes that probe our half-formed answers to this question by defying them.[65] Becoming a ghost is in some sense what Fielding asks of the woman who is to represent Virtue's "modest backwardness" from "public view"; woman bears the representational burden for Fielding of his disappointment about the relation between internal and external selves, as, culturally, she must sustain the realm of private life, interior feeling, and personal identity apart from the public and commercial world of the male; inevitably, then, she must fail Fielding through her reliance on the "harlotry" of pomp, ostentation, or the drama of self-display if she is to be a part of this world. And yet he fears her alternative fate as a ghost as well, though he may seem to wish it on her.

Fielding's *Eurydice Hissed* (1737), performed as an afterpiece to *The Historical Register*, simultaneously tells the story of the damnation of Fielding's farce *Eurydice* and the history of the damnation of Walpole's 1733 excise bill, merging tales of stage and of state; but in the final lines of the play the damnation of the woman Eurydice surfaces as the third story that must be told. Pillage, the author of the damned farce, at once a figure for Fielding and for Walpole, crushed by his failure, begins to rave:

> I'm giddy. Ha! My head begins to swim,
> And see Eurydice all pale before me.
> Why dost thou haunt me thus? I did not damn thee.[66]

Having consigned her to her ghostly realm to sustain his sense of inner life, Fielding can't decide whether to lead woman out again (he's not sure whether she would come with him),[67] and he is haunted by her, afraid of her, if only for the claim of feeling she exerts on him, the power of his own guilt she evokes: "You shall at last be haunted by her ghost." In taking on a cultural understanding of gender and identity that divorces the private, inner life from the physical and public self, and grants to women that shadowy inner realm, Fielding finds himself with a mixed legacy, which he represents with all the vexed subtleties of his own ambivalence.[68] Women are rendered by this system of thought both conveniently powerless in public terms and conveniently receptive to all the values men "are unwilling to have the trouble of preserving themselves," values perhaps in conflict with the demands of public life, and yet ones they have some stake in preserving, even as ghost-presences. Yet Fielding seems to suspect that by using gender to divorce these realms, he has rendered both sexes genderless, inhuman in some way: either a ghost's spirit or a mechanically animated body. In insisting that Virtue remain invisible and not seize the raiments of outward authority or drama, Fielding exiles spirit to the underworld of ghostly abstraction—and also exiles outward authority to the lifeless materiality of puppetry or costume. Fielding's interest in puppets and other mechanical impersonations of life is as insistent as his interest in ghosts. A hint in *The Historical Register*'s auction scene at the kind of merging between flesh and foreign matter that most worries Fielding returns us to that scene—which will then lead us onward to a group of poems, pictures, popular anecdotes, and essays that all touch upon the idea of "natural Masques." In some of these works, Fielding himself seems in danger of wearing such a mask.

*

Ghostly Common Sense is the last lot Hen offers. The first, as we recall, is a public virtue, "a most curious remnant of political honesty." "Who puts it up, gentlemen?" Hen asks. "It will make you a very good cloak. You see it's both sides alike, so you may turn it as often as you will. Come—five pounds for this curious remnant." Hen's recommendation of the political honesty he offers as "a very good cloak" immediately establishes that what he offers is only an external facsimile of the name it goes by; and his comment that "it's both sides alike, so you may turn it as often as you will" creates a little allegory of the turning of outside to inside and inside to outside involved in the ontological conflations Hen plays upon in his auction. His next comment shows the costume of affected virtue not just disguising the real self but emerging as the only self that some people own, as costume becomes skin: "I assure you, several great men have made their birthday suits out of the same piece. It will wear forever and never be the worse for wearing.—Five pounds is bid. Nobody more than five pounds for this curious piece of political honesty?"

The primary meaning of "birthday suit" in the eighteenth century, that of an outfit worn on the King's birthday, obviously obtains here, but a sly inference enters as well: the "great men" of the court scene likely to wear such suits also make their bodies and souls out of the whole cloth of court politics—they possess no prior skin or self, Fielding implies. The slang sense of "birthday suit" as *no* suit, or as the under-suit of skin in which one is born,[69] provides a humorous and ironic subtext to the term's conventional sense, the opposite state of dress, the high and elaborate garb of public court celebration. Hen's use of the term collapses the two senses, drawing out its sense as a state of undress with his promise that "it will wear forever, and never be the worse for wearing" just like one's own skin, but also emphasizing the impersonal and acquired nature of ceremonial garb with his observation that "several great men have made their birthday suits out of the same piece." The kind of birthday suit Hen here advertises, one that can be made out of an affected virtue, disrupts the opposition between native self and foreign and acquired pomp, implicating a self at its very outset—the naked self, the newborn self—in impersonation.

The scene of Fielding's first published work calls upon all present to engage in impersonation: he chose as the subject for his first poetic satire the fashionable entertainment of the masquerade. As we know from Terry Castle's monumental study of masquerade, Fielding was not alone in being both fascinated and disturbed by the license for impersonation such an institution provides. In *The Masquerade* Fielding links the socially licensed carnival of costume contained within the masquerade hall to the more unsettling impersonations licensed by social roles outside the perimeter of the hall, particularly the gender inversions represented by the fashionable figures of the beau and the Amazon. *The Masquerade*'s warning about gender impersonation reminds us of the *Champion* essay on the "*curl'd-headed Boys*" that turn out to be women in French haircuts, but the passage immediately following it denies us the guarantee provided in that essay that "*Faces*, in spite of all their Disguises" peek out from within cultivated or foreign roles to assert a natural, native, human identity. As the muse finishes warning the poet about what happens "when Men Women turn," a passing figure arrests the poet's attention, and he asks about the figure's hideous mask: "How cou'd it come into his Gizard / T'invent so horrible a Vizard?" The muse explains that it came not into his "Gizard" but into "his Mother's Belly": "you must know, that horrid Phyz is / (*Puris naturalibus*) his Visage." The poet has mistaken face for disguise and exclaims, "Monstrous! that humane Nature can / Have form'd so strange Burlesque a Man" (6).

This passing figure turns out to be a figure central to the poem and to the scene it describes—the muse identifies him as "Count" John Heidegger, Master of the Revels at the masquerade, and dedicatee of the poem. In the dedication of *The Masquerade* to Heidegger, Fielding refers to his famously ugly face, a frequent subject of satire, said to be so hideous as to look like a monstrous vizard he had donned.[70] Though ugliness might seem an elemental or unanalyzable quality, Hogarth's graphic depictions of Heidegger and the popular anecdotes that circulated about him can help us explore some of the specific meanings of "ugliness" as his contemporaries discovered it, so definitively, in his face.

In Hogarth's two satires of the masquerade, the image of Heidegger's face appears as a tiny but presiding element. In each, that face appears strangely detachable, like an emblematic sign—or perhaps a commercial logo. In each, it hovers above the crowded scene. In "Masquerade Ticket" (published in the same year as Fielding's *The Masquerade*), Heidegger's face is outside the narrative action, showing up as a decorative doodle on the clock that hangs above the

hall in which time wastes (Fig. 6). Disembodied and placed at the
center of the picture frame's top edge, it works visually to triangulate
the reversal of bodily attributes in the male and female statues to the
picture's far left and right: a Priapus whose torso dwindles to a narrow stand, and a Venus whose accompanying Cupid provides the
illusion of a phallus at her groin. In "Masquerades and Operas"
(published four years earlier), the same face is attached to the upper
third of Heidegger's body, seen leaning out a window above the
busy street scene (Fig. 4). Its outlines are echoed in the face of the
statue of William Kent above the pretentious "Academy of Arts"
and in the flat grinning face of Dr. Faustus in the banner advertising
the low entertainment of the pantomime. Three versions of Heidegger's face, in three different sizes and presiding over three different "levels" of culture, thus form a motif across the top of the print;
its famous ugliness, in this context, seems tied to the way the human
face has come to circulate like a commercial counter, leveling all individual differences.

In some of the popular anecdotes about Heidegger's ugly face,
its "ugliness" again has to do with its failure as the outward sign of
a persuasively organic and individual human identity. That failure
may be played out in these anecdotes as either a sexual or a political
indeterminacy. In one story, Heidegger himself challenges the Earl
of Chesterfield to find a face as hideous as his own in all of London.
The Earl produces a woman who seems to exceed Heidegger until
he outdoes her by proving interchangeable with her, "clapping her
head-dress upon himself," when "he was universally allowed to
have won the wager." In a more elaborate anecdote, "the facetious
Duke of Montagu" literalizes Heidegger's face's supposed likeness
to an artificial mask: he has a plaster cast made from Heidegger's face
when he is drunk, dresses up a "counterfeit" Heidegger in the mask
made from that cast, and has him appear at one of Heidegger's masquerades, where the King is also in attendance and where this "false
Heidegger" repeatedly countermands Heidegger's orders to the mu-
sicians to play "God Save the King" with orders to play the anthem
of the King's own doubling rival, "Charley Over the Water." A hys-
terical Heidegger, finally confronted with his masked, subversive
double, threatens never to show his face in public again unless the
mask is melted "before his face" and its mold broken. In "Heidegger
in a Rage," a sketch illustrating the concluding scene of this anecdote, Heidegger's face is only made more grotesque by its efforts to

assert its human singularity and to convey authentic human emotion (Fig. 7).[71]

In his dedication to *The Masquerade* and in the passage dealing with Heidegger within the poem, Fielding emphasizes what is implicit in these various visual and verbal comparisons of Heidegger's face to a mask: the sense of the appropriateness of a distinctively alienated countenance to the "First Minister" of the masquerade. In his dedication to the poem, Fielding comments that this "natural Masque" of Heidegger's is a "Gift of Nature, by which you seem so adapted to the Post you enjoy." A "natural Masque" at once epitomizes the proceedings over which Heidegger presides and ironically challenges the status of those proceedings. A relative of the courtier in his ambiguous "birthday suit," the leader of the masquerade himself dissolves that distinction between self and costume, original and imitation, upon which the special realm of the masquerade-hall depends. He can't take off his mask; it travels with him when he leaves the hall.

The ontological uncertainties raised by the masquerade thus appear, concentrated, in the dubious surfaces of Heidegger's face, which the poet-speaker of *The Masquerade* treats as freakish or singularly monstrous; but the same conceit of face as mask would come to hand twenty years after the publication of this poem, when the authors of *Old England* set out to ridicule not Heidegger's face, but Fielding's own. In August of 1749, these authors claimed that Fielding's face was so "grotesque" that it was easily mistaken for "a Vizard"; later that year, they described the crowd at the Westminster election responding to Fielding's face as if it were a burlesque imitation rather than a human original. Fielding appeared, they say, with "such a Length of *Chin*, of *Nose*, and *Woefulness* of Countenance, as caused a loud Laugh at first sight among the Crowd."[72] According to Martin Battestin, a portraitist much friendlier to Fielding also depicted his God-given countenance as hovering between natural "character" and the exaggerated lineaments of "caricature": although the caption to Hogarth's "Characters and Caricaturas" alludes to a clear "Difference Betwixt *Character & Caricatura*" (referring the viewer to the preface of *Joseph Andrews* for "farther Explanation"), and although the lowest segment of the print is neatly divided into contrasting instances of the two types of representation, the two faces at the very center of the sheet, which Battestin identifies as the faces of Hogarth himself and of his friend Henry

Fielding, "seem to argue that there can be a fine and subtle line indeed between 'the exactest copying of Nature,' that *'Alma Mater,'*
and the exhibiting of 'Monsters, not Men' " (see Figs. 8 and 9).[73] The
realities of Fielding's own extraordinarily long nose and chin, it
seems, rival the presumably "preposterous" inventions of burlesque
writers, caricature artists, or mask makers for the farcical stage or
masquerade.

Fielding himself seems to allude to the unusual length of his
own nose in his portrait of Booth in *Amelia*, and, more suggestively,
in *The Champion*, to the surprising size of his chin.[74] The main essay
for *The Champion* of May 24, 1740, consists of a dream-vision,
which the fictional correspondent says was inspired by reading Lucian's *Dialogues of the Dead* and attending Rich's *Orpheus and Eurydice*
on the same day.[75] The dreamer finds himself "on the Banks of the
River *Styx*, where *Charon* was just arrived with his Boat from the
infernal Side of the River, and a great Number of Persons were
crowding in Order to get in." Following Lucian, he tells us that no
person was allowed to enter the underworld "unless stark naked."[76]
This requirement becomes the satiric premise for exposing the pre-
tenses and adopted characteristics of a rapid litany of standard types
(from beaux to politicians to Methodists). Fifth among them is a
"tall Man" in "an old Grey Coat," apparently representing Fielding
himself, who has been "sent hither once or twice before by the Pit"
and who receives only contempt from the "very grave" man who
follows him. While Mercury predictably demands that the latter
abandon his affected gravity before he enters the boat, what he demands of the Fielding figure is "half his Chin, which he utterly refused to comply with, insisting on it that it was all his own." As described here, the contours of Fielding's face, like Heidegger's, are so
exaggerated as to elicit confusion in the viewer about the distinction
between natural and assumed features: his flesh-and-blood chin
looks as though half of it may be made of wood or papier-mâché.

The self-mockery involved in this fancy is light; and the imagined contention over whether Fielding's chin is part of his "stark naked" self or not serves both to include him in the group of satiric
types reviewed in the essay and to separate him from them. Narratively, the contention leads to his physical separation from the others: because the dispute cannot be resolved, Mercury sends him back
to the world to "be d--mn'd again" rather than allowing him to join
the other members of the crowd in Charon's boat. This failure to

pass into the boat links the Fielding figure to a "Heroe" in the dream who won't give up his honor or integrity, and so is also forced to stay on shore. Suggestively, the female counterpart of this idealized male hero, a virtuous beauty who cannot be stripped by Mercury of either her beauty or her innocence, is allowed to proceed into the boat, where she shines among the crowd of variously contemptible characters there. Like Eurydice or Common-sense or the personified virtues that Lady Matchless and Vermilia discuss, the representative of female virtue belongs among the ghostly inhabitants of the underworld, whereas the representative of male virtue apparently cannot retain his true character and pass over to that dematerialized realm. Tonally, however, the dispute about Fielding's chin separates him from *both* of these idealized figures and places him within the roll call of ludicrous figures ticked off rapidly in the course of the essay. The subject of his dispute with Mercury is the authenticity of an outlandish physical feature rather than of a dignifying inner quality; and the uncertainty evoked by his chin about where the bounds of the body end and costume or mask begins connects him with the satiric types that precede and follow him in this roll call.

The first and third portraits of satiric types in the essay reiterate commonplace examples of gender inversion that we have seen in other *Champion* essays and elsewhere. Like the "female coxcombs" of the April 26, 1740, *Champion* essay, whose French hairdos make them appear to be boys, the first lady to undergo Mercury's inspection wears a "Tête de Mouton," which turns out to be a wig covering "a Crown shaved as close as a Friar's." "A fine young Gentleman," a beau, is third in line. He resists giving up his "laced Paduasoy," and when he does, the crowd discovers that his reluctance derives from more than "Affection for his Cloaths." Apparently, those clothes compensated for some embarrassing lack in the body beneath them—presumably for an absent, small, or dysfunctional penis. Between these two stock figures comes a sketch of a "beautiful young Creature" whose body also turns out to contain less than it promises: she appears "big with Child" but "pull[s] off her Cloaths and her big Belly together," explaining that "it was the Fashion for all young Ladies to appear with Child in the World she came from" (that is, prison, where "pleading one's belly" offered one strategy for avoiding execution). In *The Masquerade*, when the muse explains to the poet that Heidegger's countenance is no mask, she does so by distinguishing between artificial productions of the inventive "Gizard" and the natural, if "horrid," ones of a "Mother's

Figure 1. Hogarth, frontispiece of *The Works of Henry Fielding*, London, 1762. Courtesy of the Beinecke Rare Book and Manuscript Library, Yale University.

W. Hogarth inv.t   Ger Vander Gucht sculp.

Figure 2. Hogarth, frontispiece of *The Tragedy of Tragedies; or the Life and Death of Tom Thumb the Great*, London, 1731. Courtesy of the Beinecke Rare Book and Manuscript Library, Yale University.

FARINELLI, CUZZONI, AND SENESINO.

Published March 1796.

Figure 3. John Ireland, "Farinelli, Cuzzoni, and Senesino," from *Hogarth Illustrated from his own Manuscripts*, vol. 3, London, 1798. Courtesy of the Beinecke Rare Book and Manuscript Library, Yale University.

Figure 4. Hogarth, "Masquerades and Operas," 1724. In the banner advertising the opera, the nobleman kneeling at Cuzzoni's feet begs, "Pray accept 8000 £." Courtesy of the Print Collection, Lewis Walpole Library, Yale University.

Figure 5. Hogarth, *The Rake's Progress*, plate 2, "The Rake's Levee," 1735. Farinelli's name appears in the cast list on the score of "The Rape of the Sabines" on the harpsichord; a list of gifts to him fills the scroll behind the musician's chair; and a woman in the scene depicted on the print on the floor cries, "One God! one Farinelli!" Courtesy of the Print Collection, Lewis Walpole Library, Yale University.

Figure 6. Hogarth, "Masquerade Ticket," 1727. Courtesy of the British Museum.

Figure 7. John Ireland, "Heidegger in a Rage," from *Hogarth Illustrated from his own Manuscripts*, vol. 3, London, 1798. Courtesy of the Beinecke Rare Book and Manuscript Library, Yale University.

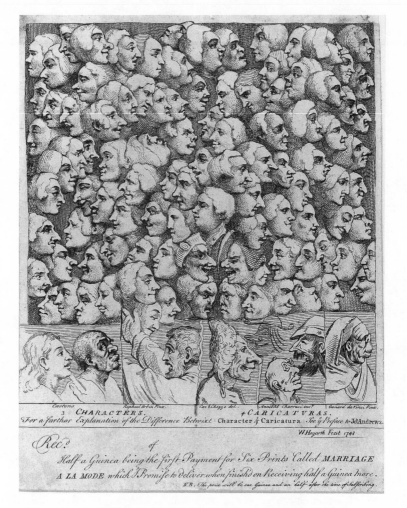

Figure 8. Hogarth, "Characters and Caricaturas," 1743. The line below the drawing suggests to the viewer: "For a farther Explanation of the Difference Betwixt *Character & Caricatura* See the Preface to *Joseph Andrews*." Courtesy of the Print Collection, Lewis Walpole Library, Yale University.

Figure 9. Detail of Figure 8, "Characters and Caricaturas," showing the two faces that Battestin interprets as those of Fielding (left) and of Hogarth himself (right).

Belly." Here, that touchstone and source of organic reality, the woman's pregnant belly, itself becomes an artful illusion; so that when the Fielding figure insists soon after that his chin is "all his own," he only participates in a general indeterminacy about the bounds of bodies and the bounds of personal identities that obtains throughout the scene. Although his body turns out to go farther and those of the others less far than a viewer might expect, the masklike status of Fielding's chin, like that of Heidegger's face, ties him closely to such figures as the impotent beau.

In *The Masquerade*, as we have seen, Fielding moves directly from the figure of the effeminate beau to that of Heidegger. Even more emphatically, the author of the second pamphlet on Farinelli (discussed above) links the figure of the Count not simply to an effeminate or an impotent man, but to a castrated one. He addresses his satiric epistle "on the Report of *Signior F-r-n-lli*'s being with Child" to this same "*John James H--dd-g--r*, Esq.," conjoining the figure of the Count, overseer of sexual misrule at the masquerade and owner of a natural mask for a face, with the figure of the castrato singer, there imagined as a male impersonator.[77] Heidegger represents the failing of Fielding's trust in faces as inalienable repositories of native identity, only the most striking among Fielding's many images of man as a puppet or as a creature whose face might as *well* be made "of Wood or Brass."[78] In the *Champion* essay of May 24, 1740, describing his trip to the River Styx, Fielding places a self-portrait within his gallery of such images. In a *Champion* essay published a week later, he questions the status not only of the face but of the phallus as an inalienable natural part. There, he imagines Priapus introducing himself as originally "*the Trunk of an old Fig-Tree, a very sorry Stick of Wood*," which might as easily have been made into a "JOINT-STOOL" as into a "DEITY."[79] If the deity of phallic power is only a stick of wood, what is there to keep it in the possession of men? The career of one male impersonator came to represent for Fielding the failure of the phallus to guarantee an organic masculine authority beyond the reach of appropriation. The specter of a constructed or acquired phallus—so shocking an object as to remain unnameable for Fielding—figures large in his most direct, extended, and violently defensive account of gender impersonation, which we will address here only briefly: *The Female Husband*.

The Female Husband (1746), based very loosely on an actual case tried before Fielding's first cousin, recounts the adventures of "Mrs.

Mary, alias Mr. George Hamilton," a lesbian and male impersonator who courts and actually marries several women in the guise of a man. In "Matters not Fit to be Mentioned," Terry Castle observes the element of exuberant admiration that exists alongside the tones of shock and revulsion with which Fielding relates Hamilton's exploits. She accounts for this tonal mixture as an expression of Fielding's "ambivalence regarding nature and theater, and his troubled absorption in the world of 'false' appearance," arguing that his interest in Hamilton, despite his revulsion, reveals his "countervailing, often enchanted awareness of the theatricality and artifice of human sexual roles."[80] This pamphlet, then, though a nondramatic work and written some nine years after the close of Fielding's theatrical career, has a close thematic link to the concerns and to the medium of his plays. It has, too, a closer historical link than Castle may have realized—not only because of Fielding's own use of gender impersonation in the theater, which she does not discuss, but because of one possible source for many of Fielding's elaborations on the outlines of Hamilton's story.[81] The fictional life he gives Mary Hamilton shares much with the real life story of Charlotte Charke, whom Fielding had known—and whom we have met already in the role of Mr. Hen in *The Historical Register*.[82] Fielding's treatment of her life as conflated with Mary Hamilton's can provide us, then, with a view into a final level of reference for the figure of Mr. Hen as he presides over the auction of virtues within the "allegory" of that scene, to which we have turned repeatedly in the course of this chapter.

Within the theater, Fielding played with and capitalized upon the dramatic possibilities gender impersonation offers, but Charlotte Charke's acting career carried over into her offstage life—she lived as a male impersonator outside the theater as well—and her life, superimposed onto Mary Hamilton's, seems to have raised for Fielding the difficulty of framing impersonation within a given theater, the difficulty of finding an arena on "the stage of life" in which impersonation may not effectively stand in for identity—an arena in which masks don't merge with faces and donning the breeches doesn't make one as good as male. In this pamphlet Fielding tells us that, for all intents and purposes, it matters not to the female husband's wives what her penis is made of, whether it is artificial and "affected" or real. After the consummation of Mary's first marriage, "the bride expressed herself so well satisfied with her choice, that being in company with another old lady, she exulted so much in her happiness, that her friend began to envy her."[83] When her second wife is questioned at Mary's trial as to whether "she imagined the Doctor had behaved to her as a husband ought to his wife? Her modesty confounded her a little at this question; but she at last answered she did imagine so" (50). In fact, this wife too has aroused suspicious envy in other women by "the extraordinary accounts which she had formerly given of her husband" (49).

At the same time, not everyone he meets is thoroughly impressed with "George" Hamilton's masculinity. A widow he courts early in his adventures sends him a sarcastic letter of rejection that describes her astonishment at receiving a written proposal from him: "I thought, when I took it, it might have been an Opera song, and which for certain reasons I should think, when your cold is gone, you might sing as well as *Farinelli*, from the great resemblance there is between your two persons" (35–36). We can see the Fielding of the dramatic satires of the 1730's at work inventing this letter for the widow; it is the satiric concerns we find there that shape her rebuff. The letter makes explicit for us the male counterpart to the female husband, appearing beside her within the same halo of anxiety she inhabits for Fielding: the detachability of masculine identity and power implied by the castrato prepares us for the appropriation of phallic identity represented by that "something of too vile, wicked and scandalous a nature, which was found in the Doctor's trunk" and which forms the basis of her conviction and the final unspeakable outrage in Fielding's account of her (49). Of course, this artificial phallus has its shortcomings, its inconvenient absences, but, as Fielding himself points out, so does a natural phallus—Fielding glosses a story of George's near-discovery through the unexpected amorous advances of his wife with an analogy to the failures of un-impersonated masculinity:

One of our English Poets remarks in the case of a more able husband than Mrs. *Hamilton* was, when his wife grew amorous in an unseasonable time.

> *The doctor understood the call,*
> *But had not always wherewithal.*

So it happened to our poor bridegroom, who having not at that time *the wherewithal* about her, was obliged to remain meerly passive, under all this torrent of kindness of his wife. (39)

Although the doctor in Prior's poem continuously possesses a penis, unlike the doctor in Fielding's narrative, that penis is not always prepared to manifest itself as the phallus with which it is supposedly identical—as, that is, an erect and potent sexual instrument. The phallus that was to safeguard normative masculinity from the disruptive implications of the figure of the castrato, and from his "burlesque" and "ridiculous" fate as an empty imitator of desire— that phallus which was to insure moral and rhetorical, financial and political order—we here find reduced to an erratic and undignified means, a *"wherewithal,"* which flickers in and out of the possession of even "a more able husband than Mrs. *Hamilton.*" And *"wherewithal"* in this passage serves to describe both the original and the constructed phallus: they are bracketed together here under one demeaning term, and belittled, together, in the face of the demands of female desire.

The Female Husband plays out some of the concerns that pervade Fielding's early work in one extreme version, literalizing in an unpleasant but often revealing way Fielding's fear that sexual difference and desire may not inhere in organic features of the individual, but may be successfully impersonated or approximated in artificial forms. The details with which Fielding embellishes Mary's story suggest the material interests at stake in retaining gender categories as inborn and unbreachable. As an effective female husband, Mary may disrupt systems of distributing not only sexual but financial power by gender. The scandalous motivation for her first marriage, Fielding tells us, is not lesbian love but "the conveniency which the old gentlewoman's fortune would produce in her present situation" (36–37)—as nominal husband Mary would legally control the fortune she wedded in her impersonated role.[84] In some sense, paradoxically, it is all the authority of every kind with which the penis has been entrusted in Fielding's works that makes it hard to distinguish from its "vile, wicked and scandalous" counterfeit: vested with so much authority, the phallus threatens detachment and dispossession, the possibility of appropriation. Other repositories of authority and power, other fetishized parts of sexual or political bodies, undergo a similar process. A *Champion* essay printed at the end of 1739 discusses the *"strange Lignifaction"* that spreads from the staffs of authority to the men who wield them, turning living flesh to wood and puppetry.[85]

When inborn visage and artificial vizard become indistinguishable, as personal identity merges with social, political, or professional role in the exclusive masculine realm of public life—Heidegger in the masquerade-hall, or the courtier in his pompous skin at court—not only does face become mask, but an acquired face comes to serve as well as a natural one. While the women who attend Hen's auction represent the collapse of the disembodied feminine realm of virtue into the alternative, negative realm of the material commodity, the male impersonator who presides over the auction reminds us of the susceptibility to impersonation of masculine identity as conceived in relation to those realms. The notorious offstage life of the woman who played Mr. Hen may have provided another layer to the onstage figure of Mr. Hen, deepening the audience's awareness of that susceptibility.[86] In any case, *The Female Husband* shows Fielding at once at his most violently defensive about the scandal of female appropriation of male identity and at his most explicit about the thorough appropriability of a masculine identity constituted by clothing and the force of the phallus. When the phallus, counted on to insure so much, becomes indistinguishable from an inanimate impersonation of life, like a "birthday suit" or like Virtue's treacherous "pomp," it becomes transferable—then the castrato appears too typical, and the male impersonator emerges as too powerful, too capable of convincingly wearing the breeches that the man, after all, only filled with something not really his own.

Fielding holds an ambivalent relation to the authority of breeches or staffs: he wants to clothe phallic identity in the outward authority of political, financial, and moral power but he is not blind to the ways in which, put to such uses, the phallus becomes part of the impersonal trappings of power, leaving the domain of personal identity and desire void and the trappings in precarious possession of their wearer. Though in the satire of his plays he cannot seem to move beyond imagining separate domains of masculine and feminine power, Fielding cannily and anxiously observes that such a geography of gender populates its world with ghosts and puppets. When he turned to writing novels in 1742, Fielding was not to abandon his interest in gender: *Joseph Andrews's* comic revision of *Pamela* relies upon its inversion of genders in its recreation of *Pamela's* central situation, and Joseph's implication in feminine positions remains crucial to the novel until the discovery of the key to his identity at its very end. In *Joseph Andrews*, however, Fielding would explore the use of novelistic rather than theatrical means of constructing character to create a figure whose double gender identity serves multiple functions. Through the character of Joseph, Fielding not only satirizes the disruption of gender roles, but attempts to imagine an escape from the system of oppositions aligned with those roles.

PART II

'JOSEPH ANDREWS'

Incredulous (and deeply displeased) at Joseph's resistance to her advances, Lady Booby emphatically articulates the expectation about chastity's irrelevance to male identity that underlies *Joseph Andrews*'s parodic perspective on *Pamela*: "Did ever Mortal hear of a Man's Virtue! Did ever the greatest, or the gravest Men pretend to any of this Kind! Will Magistrates who punish Lewdness, or Parsons, who preach against it, make any scruple of committing it? And can a Boy, a Stripling, have the Confidence to talk of his Virtue?" Joseph's response to her concluding question has been widely ridiculed:

"Madam," says *Joseph*, "that Boy is the Brother of *Pamela*, and would be ashamed, that the Chastity of his Family, which is preserved in her, should be stained in him. If there are such Men as your Ladyship mentions, I am sorry for it, and I wish they had an Opportunity of reading over those Letters, which my Father hath sent me of my Sister *Pamela's*, nor do I doubt but such an Example would amend them." (41)

Arthur Sherbo nominates Joseph's proud declaration of identity—"that Boy is the Brother of *Pamela*"—as "a likely candidate for the most priggish statement of the century," and J. Paul Hunter comments, "The rhetoric of 'that Boy' seems the oration of a fool."[1] Joseph's third-person, self-objectifying reference to himself as "that Boy" recalls Pamela's manner of referring to herself, and his confidence in the power of "example" and wish for the dissemination of his sister's letters make him a naive representative of the moral pretensions (and profit-seeking designs) of Richardson's work. We will return to these aspects of Fielding's satire, through the character of

Joseph, of *Pamela's* style and purposes. More central to Fielding's ridicule of *Pamela* seems the very notion of a brother-identity to Pamela's: the scenes between Lady Booby and Joseph, and this exchange in particular, ask us to imagine whether a family resemblance to Pamela can be transposed onto a man, or whether her character inheres entirely in feminine roles. I argue, however, that Fielding takes this question more seriously than critics have generally assumed. Furthermore, I believe that Joseph's implication in female character and roles, functioning initially and most obviously in Fielding's debunking of Richardson's definition of the novel, becomes crucial as well to the more positive imperative of *Joseph Andrews*: its struggle to provide its own constructive rendition of the novel form, as Fielding makes a transition from playwright to novelist in this, his first full-length published prose fiction.

Critics allude to the inherent absurdity of the transposition of Pamela's virtues onto a man when they conjure Joseph's initial ridiculousness simply by calling him a "male Pamela."[2] Bernard Schilling elaborates most fully on the nature of the absurdity: "The comic inversion of ascribing female qualities to a man is the easiest for Fielding to establish when he makes Joseph assume his sister's virtue. Like dressing a man in woman's clothes, it lowers his dignity and makes him ridiculous. . . . Fielding makes it all seem the more outlandish by a glowing description of Joseph's physical beauty." As Schilling describes it, then, the comedy of gender inversion in the opening of *Joseph Andrews* might be seen as a close novelistic extension of Fielding's theatrical uses of gender, quite continuous with the literal transvestism he employed to comic effect in the production of some of his plays—Mr. Strensham as Queen Ignorance in *Pasquin*, or Mr. Hicks as Joan in *The Author's Farce*, for example—and with the figurative transvestism of social roles he mocked repeatedly in his treatment of the beau, the domineering wife, the effeminate and corrupt politician, or the favored castrato singer. The "outlandish" or "preposterous inversion"[3] in which Fielding involves Joseph in the opening scenes of *Joseph Andrews* may make him, like the recurrent figure of the man implicated in femininity in Fielding's plays, a satiric representative of the inversion or collapse of literary, political, or moral categories as well as sexual ones.

What we learn at the end of the novel about Joseph, however, as Maurice Johnson points out, is that he is *not* in fact the brother of

Pamela, and we've learned much earlier, along the way, that he is not brother to her in spirit, either: "When the burlesque has subsided," Johnson comments, "Joseph turns out to be better than a male Pamela. He deserves respect in his own right."[4] Most readers agree that in the course of the novel Joseph develops from a ridiculous to a sympathetic figure, from a vehicle for parody to a more autonomous and positive character, and that the mode of the novel itself changes correspondingly.[5] Dick Taylor, Jr., argues most confidently that Joseph actually becomes a "hero" in the course of the novel, and even names a specific scene as the turning point in this transformation: Joseph emerges, he says, "from the episode in 2.12 no longer a male Pamela but the hero of *Joseph Andrews*, who becomes increasingly the Master of the Event." Taylor's choice of phrases in contrasting "a male Pamela" with "the *Master* of the Event" implies that Joseph's emergence as hero requires his increasing masculinization; though he never says this directly, his account of details of Joseph's growing status accords with this implication (later in the novel, for example, "Joseph exhibits proper manhood by beating up the captain").[6]

Joseph does leave behind both the familial and literary relation to Pamela that initially implicated him in feminine roles, but to the very end of the novel Fielding repeatedly and significantly places Joseph in positions that compromise or complicate his gender identification, allowing what Schilling imagines as his initial transvestism to cling to him in ways critics have not acknowledged. In the course of the novel, however, Fielding establishes increasingly complex and serious stakes for the issue of gender inversion, so that he is finally doing something quite different with Joseph from what he did with the figures of feminized men in his plays. In fact, he evolves an account of the new form in which he is working—playing off each other with real intricacy and ambivalence the disparate models provided for the novel by Richardson's epistolary novel, by his own dramatic satires, and by Milton's Christian epic—largely *through* his evolving treatment of Joseph's ambiguous gender identity.

For Fielding's negotiation of his new form, despite *Joseph Andrews*'s initial emphasis, is not conducted exclusively with Richardson: through the story of Joseph Andrews Fielding reflects as well on the epic tradition with which he has been associated and on the satiric and dramatic forms of his own earlier career. Fielding invokes the epic tradition in explaining his new kind of writing in his preface to the novel, but he uses Joseph's character to explore the limitations of conventional ideas of the literary hero he inherited from the epic. In Chapter 3 we will study how *Joseph Andrews* draws upon the model of the epic provided by Milton in particular. In his reworking of the idea of a hero Fielding at times calls up Milton's *Paradise Lost* as a background text for his own very different epic, meditating upon Milton's revision of the heroic as it passes into a Christian context (and into the English language); and drawing out the domestic nature of Milton's epic, its concentration on sexual relations, and its replacement of the traditional single male hero of the epic with a paired man and woman at the center of his work.

Fielding's reflection on satiric and dramatic forms, too, is shaped by an interest in gender. In some of the same scenes in which he recalls both the beauties and the potential bathos of the form Milton established, Fielding places under a harsh light the satiric forms of his own earlier career, representing verbal attack as a form of physical violence linked to masculine sexual aggression and to the patriarch's abuse of class power, and even playfully suggesting its association with Milton's fallen angels. As these scenes cluster around the figure of the Roasting-Squire, Chapter 3 will concentrate on the two chapters in book 3 that center on him. They are examples of the kind of textual node in which Fielding brings up against each other the forms of drama and satire that he had combined in his own brand of dramatic satires and the specific form of epic, the Christian epic, represented by Milton's *Paradise Lost*. The generic conflict he thereby creates changes the stakes he'd attached earlier to the situation of compromised gender.

Fielding uses gender oppositions in *Joseph Andrews* to examine the implications of literary forms—commenting indirectly on the novel's own movement from parody to a more complex, mixed mode—but also to meditate upon issues of power, violence, and (as we shall see in Chapter 4) mortal loss. As we study the elegiac strain in *Joseph Andrews* and its relation to notions of masculine and feminine identity, we will find that tracking the meaning of gender in Fielding's writings has brought us back across more familiar critical issues in his works: the effects of elaborate plotting and of external characterization, the problem of affectation, the difficulty of knowing other selves. Even in Chapter 2, as we survey the range of Joseph's connections to female identity, we will begin to see how the specifically literary traditions and conventions involved in matters of genre and literary form resonate with the traditions and conventions shaping social relationships in the world. Fielding repeatedly associates the forum of the theater, for example, with certain forms of erotic desire; he implicates both satiric and heroic modes in male abuses of physical or institutional power. Fielding's gradual creation of a distinctly gendered identity for Joseph unites textual with social frames of reference, as gender proves to be both a literary and a social construction.

When *Joseph Andrews* traces crossings between literary and social forms, it probes the conventional and allusive nature of human relationships and of personal experience in general. Critics have noted that *Joseph Andrews* (like *Tom Jones*) seems to ask what kind of access to other minds is possible when other selves are only known through language, or through external and often deceptive observation. It asks, too, whether real attachments and continuities between selves are possible in a world of derivative and conventionalized social relationships; and, for that matter, whether spontaneous personal expression may be achieved within the space of verbal convention and echo. What kind of integral and autonomous self may be said to exist in the dissonant interplay between conflicting "genres" of identity? Whereas in my chapters on *Tom Jones* I will be focusing on the multiplicity of historical forces or frameworks at work in defining individual identity at any one moment, here I will concentrate on a multiplicity of literary-historical influences at work together in the creation of Fielding's first novel, and in the creation of "character" within it. The conflicts between these diverse literary-historical sources and structures place Fielding's characters in the dynamic flux of history.

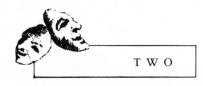

The Meaning of a Male Pamela

Genre and Gender

Even in the opening scenes of *Joseph Andrews*, Fielding's substitution of a man for a woman in Richardson's plot does not function as simply as it might seem to at first glance. The inversion it creates is comic and strikes us as a kind of parodic reduction of Richardson's high drama; but it also confronts us with the question of what has been reduced in the act of substitution—why what is virtue in one sex comes off as triviality in the other. If, as Schilling says, Joseph's assumption of his sister's virtue looks as ridiculous as "dressing a man in woman's clothes," Fielding reminds us of a surprising similarity between virtues and clothing by showing us chastity worn out of fashion, out of character, on the wrong occasion. In the auction scene in *The Historical Register* Fielding expressed a clearly satiric view on the externality and adventitiousness of virtues by presenting them for sale in the form of clothing and cosmetics, whose prices reflect fashion's whim. In the opening scene of *Joseph Andrews*, he only raises our awareness that a virtue's value depends on its bearer, implying that Pamela's virtue might itself be "assumed," but not clearly guiding our conclusions about whether virtue *should* look ridiculous when it appears as cross-dressing.[1]

A male Pamela reminds us of assumptions about gender roles by defying them, though we are free to laugh at him or reconsider them. More specifically, he makes visible the conventional analogizing of class and gender structures by standing in different relations to the two. When Fielding replaces Richardson's woman with a man in the position of sexually embattled servant, he not only displaces the defense of chastity from its traditional female preserve but also breaks the correspondence between socioeconomic and sexual disempowerment in Richardson's protagonist. Pamela could become a virtually mythic representative of the culturally disentitled because her age, gender, and class position all coincide in powerlessness; the mythologizing of her powerlessness serves complex ideological functions in Richardson's novel, a vehicle for both progressive and conservative suggestion.[2] The very associations between class and gender positions employed by critics when they liken Richardson to a woman writer are explored by Fielding when he replays Richardson's scenario in a different key, separating the part of masculinity from the position of social and economic power. The scenes between Lady Booby and Joseph especially foreground the tension between hierarchies of class and of gender in Fielding's narrative, expressed by the mistress Lady Booby as a titillating form of sexual tension:[3]

"La!" says she, in an affected Surprize, "what am I doing? I have trusted myself with a Man alone, naked in Bed; suppose you should have any wicked Intentions upon my Honour, how should I defend myself? . . . But then, say you, the World will never know any thing of the Matter, yet would not that be trusting to your Secrecy? Must not my Reputation be then in your power? Would you not then be my Master?" (30)

When Lady Booby voices astonishment at Joseph's reference to his own virtue in the second interview between them—"Your Virtue! Intolerable Confidence! Have you the Assurance to pretend, that when a Lady demeans herself to throw aside the Rules of Decency, . . . your Virtue should resist her Inclination?"—Joseph's defense oddly aligns his masculinity and his poverty. " 'Madam,' said *Joseph*, 'I can't see why her having no Virtue should be a Reason against my having any. Or why, because I am a Man, or because I am poor, my Virtue must be subservient to her Pleasures' " (41). Pamela must resist the assumption that because she is doubly powerless as a woman and a poor one her virtue should be subservient to her master's pleasures; Joseph must defend his right to control his own virtue against a more complicated pairing of assumptions—his disentitlement as a servant limits his power to act on his own virtue while his sexual entitlement as a man limits the dramatic *authority* of his desire to do so. Lady Booby had reminded Joseph in their first interview of the greater physical vulnerability of women, even socially superior women, to sexual attack ("how should I defend my-self?"), and her outrage at Joseph's resistance when she voluntarily invites sexual advances reflects a sense that the relative invulnerabil-ity of male chastity to coercion makes it less valued, less available as a privileged symbol of self-determination—the symbol on which Pamela's story centered.[4]

These early scenes of *Joseph Andrews* contain some suggestion of an inquiry into the deep cultural assumption (made explicit in Lady Matchless and Vermilia's remarks in *Love in Several Masques*) that the interior realm of private virtue belongs to woman, and that the greater physical (and social) power of a man makes any claim he might assert to personal or sexual virtue a misplaced pretense. These scenes do not foreclose the possibility that we should take a man's chastity more seriously than we do, or that a masculine version of private virtue might be conceived; but they also include the possi-bility that a man's claim to private virtue can *only* be modeled on a woman's and will necessarily involve him in a laughable kind of cross-dressing of identity.[5] After asserting his right to his own vir-tue, though poor and a man, Joseph immediately goes on to reject Lady Booby's incredulity about a boy's virtue by declaring that "that Boy is the Brother of *Pamela*"—his virtue taken from his sister's wardrobe. In the first book of *Joseph Andrews* Joseph is feminized by his economic vulnerability (the "defenseless" Lady Booby deprives him of his employment, has him stripped of his livery, and denies him the "character" that would have allowed him to find other em-ployment), by his appearance in the conventionally female role of embattled chastity, and by his reliance on his sister's example in con-ceiving the importance of his own virtue. With Pamela as the im-mediately proximate representative of femininity, Joseph's connec-tion with female identity in the novel's opening scenes works pre-dominantly to render him ridiculous.

But a connection between Joseph and female identity will prove crucial to the end of the novel as well, when Joseph has left his initial appearance as parodic reduction far behind him. In the scene that provides a comic resolution to the novel's plot, Gammar Andrews reveals the key to Joseph's obscured birth, history, and true family relations: he came into the Andrews family as a sick boy sub-stituted in the cradle by gypsies for a healthy girl. The long-ago ex-change of Joseph and Fanny that emerges in *Joseph Andrews'* rec-ognition scene reasserts as the identifying feature of Joseph's character the substitution of boy for girl that we were aware of in the novel's inaugural joke. Though he is not interested in the exchange of genders involved, Homer Obed Brown comments that this secret event in Joseph's past "might perhaps be allegorized as part of the shifting and substitutional nature of the relationship between Fielding's text and Richardson's,"[6] and we can give that allegory more specific content when we see it repeat the relation between Joseph and a female character in the novel's opening. It repeats it with a difference, however: the substitution has now come inside Fielding's own narrative, as plot device rather than as an allusive relation to a prior text, and it now places Joseph in a physical space previously occupied by a girl rather than in her feminine role.

The literalizing of the substitution removes it from its earlier parodic purpose and satiric reflection on Joseph's character—although, suggestively, Gammar Andrews implies that the gypsies left Joseph in Fanny's place because he was such "a poor sickly Boy, that did not seem to have an Hour to live" (337). The sickliness that motivated this exchange might be said to feminize Joseph the way his reliance on Pamela's example did. But in an aside, Gammar Andrews at once asserts the identity between the past and present Josephs and marks the change between them: "the poor Infant (which is our *Joseph* there, as stout as he now stands) lifted up its Eyes upon me so piteously, that to be sure, notwithstanding my Passion, I could not find in my heart to do it any mischief." Though the infant Joseph's self-protection through piteous appeal is reminiscent of Pamela's, the girl with whom he is associated through the exchange in the cradle turns out to hold a relation to the grown Joseph quite different from Pamela's in the novel's first book. At the beginning of the novel, Joseph has replaced a female character to whom he claims a genealogical tie and family resemblance, and with whom he is mimetically identified, modeling himself on her through the notion of moral "example"; the end of the novel reveals that Joseph has occupied the same space as a female character with whom he will eventually be erotically rather than mimetically united.

The ending of the novel cancels its opening's version of Joseph's relation to female identity not only through repetition with a difference but through the details of its plot resolution: the story of the gypsies' exchange is also what establishes that Joseph is *not* Pamela's brother (or Fanny's, for that matter). As Joseph is released from a genealogical relation to Richardson's heroine by the revelations of the novel's conclusion, so Fielding's work itself has gained a kind of autonomy from its predecessor in the course of the novel, finally insisting that an accurate identification of its main character can only be made within the perimeter of its own narrative.[7] And still, when the novel comes to providing its own history for the character of Joseph, it concludes by creating an alternative, narrative version of that same fluid relation to feminine identity in which Joseph first appeared—by making Joseph, again, a changeling of gender, though perhaps of another kind.

Before Joseph's history is revealed, a series of what Fielding calls "curious Night-Adventures" occur among those spending the night at Lady Booby's, and provide one last deferral of plot resolution. The content of these adventures prepares us for the importance of gender substitutions in the news that arrives in the morning, confirming that that feature of Joseph's history is not a narrative accident. The adventures occupy all of book 4, chapter 14, and begin with Beau Didapper's plan to impersonate Joseph and to seduce Fanny by taking Joseph's place in her bed. His plan goes awry immediately, however, when he enters Slipslop's bedroom rather than Fanny's; and when Slipslop cries out for help and Adams runs to her rescue, the confusions in identity that create the farcical upheaval of the chapter become confusions specifically of gender identity:

[Adams] made directly to the Bed in the dark, where laying hold of the Beau's Skin (for *Slipslop* had torn his Shirt almost off) and finding his Skin extremely soft, and hearing him in a low Voice begging *Slipslop* to let him go, he no longer doubted but this was the young Woman in danger of ravishing, and immediately falling on the Bed, and laying hold on *Slipslop's* Chin, where he found a rough Beard, his Belief was confirmed; he therefore rescued the Beau. (331–32)

This scene anticipates the interchanging of genders in a bed that will be revealed the next morning as the hidden secret of Joseph's identity; it also recalls the comic recasting of the embattled chastity story of the novel's opening, imagining a man rather than a woman as in need of rescue—but here only as the characters of the drama are misrecognized by Adams. When we place the revelation of the gypsies' replacement of Fanny with Joseph in the context of the night-adventures that precede it, we might broaden the allegory Brown finds in it, and see it as one emblematic moment in a sustained investigation of the "shifting and substitutional nature" of the relationship not only between Fielding's and Richardson's texts but also between the two sexes.

Lady Booby soon arrives on the scene of Adams, Slipslop, and Didapper's struggle and straightens out the story, sending Adams back to his room. But all paths lead to confusion on this night before the novel's plot is resolved, and Adams makes a wrong turn and enters Fanny's room—the room Didapper had been seeking to start with—and sleeps, oblivious, beside her for hours. All paths lead specifically, that is, to gender confusion: when awakened by a surprised Joseph in the morning, Adams protests repeatedly, "I know not whether she is a Man or Woman"; he insists that his male clothes have been "bewitched away too, and *Fanny's* brought into their place"; and he is only convinced of the truth of the situation when Joseph points out that "the Women's Apartments were on this side Mrs. *Slipslop's* Room, and the Men's on the other," and that "it was plain he had mistaken, by turning to the right instead of the left" (334–35). Gender structures even the physical space in which these characters reside, and in the comic entr'acte through which they must pass before Joseph's identity is revealed, the possibility of wrong turns in gender identification is underscored with all the literalizing insistence and extremity of farce.

The burlesque treatment of gender inversions and confusions in this scene may remind us of the farcical inversions and slapstick action centering on gender in Fielding's *Tom Thumb*, *Pasquin*, or *The Author's Farce*. Early in the novel, Joseph's assumption of feminine roles potentially grouped him with the effeminate men satirized repeatedly in Fielding's plays, but in this scene he stands notably on the sidelines of theatrical role-confusions—he is even instrumental in sorting out the last of the confusions.[8] It is Beau Didapper, instead, whose gender is comically compromised in this scene; and in several ways Didapper's character is imported so directly from the comic repertoire of Fielding's theatrical days as to make it appear incongruous in the pages of *Joseph Andrews*. Not only do Fielding's choice of a name for the beau, his references to him as a Hylas rather than a Hercules (303 and 333), and his description of his physical appearance place him among the sexually ambiguous beaux of Fielding's dramatic satires; but the echoes of Conyers Middleton's dedication of his *Life of Cicero* in Fielding's description of Didapper's "qualifications" identify him with Lord Hervey in particular, a frequent butt of the political/sexual satire in his plays (312–13, 313 n. 1).

While the world of Fielding's plays was filled with characters that suggested themselves as versions of one or more offstage actors, Beau Didapper, entering the novel quite late, seems oddly anomalous as the one character in *Joseph Andrews* with a pointed historical referent. His presence reminds us that in the largely political context of Fielding's plays, figures of compromised gender were usually clearly negative ones, implicated in compromises of political, moral, or literary categories as well. Beau Didapper's character also shadows Joseph's own—at least in broad outline. Both of them replay, in different ways, the story of Potiphar's wife: Fielding alerts us to that story as the source of Joseph's name when he begins to call him Joseph rather than Joey (29 and 47);[9] but he in fact recalls the biblical story in more detail (the woman's self-serving accusations of rape, the piece of the man's garment left behind serving as evidence) in Didapper's encounter with Slipslop than in Lady Booby's interviews with Joseph. Taking over the allusive context that had provided Joseph's very name, Beau Didapper might seem to present a dark mirror to the character of Joseph, as a satiric doubling of the theme of compromised gender.

To invoke Lord Hervey as the original of Beau Didapper has the effect of making Didapper a kind of self-conscious cliché of gender problems within the corpus of Fielding's own works, the easily recognizable sign of the negative possibilities of gender compromise; and Fielding's treatment of Didapper identifies him with both the theatrical forms and some of the recurrent satiric subjects of his early writings. Robert Alter notes that some of the Beau's actions "read like comic stage directions translated into the idiom of the novel." He observes that Fielding also "appl[ies] in new ways techniques he had learned in his years of writing for the theater" in the dialogue he writes for Lady Booby: in her defense of her virtue, "Lady Booby's hypocrisy confesses itself with such splendidly lucid theatricality that it is entirely appropriate for Fielding to include actual stage directions, properly italicized."[10] Within the novel, the theatricality of Lady Booby's manner of expression is acknowledged in Joseph's first letter to Pamela: "and she held my Hand, and talked exactly as a Lady does to her Sweetheart in a Stage-Play, which I have seen in *Covent-Garden*, while she wanted him to be no better than he should be" (31).

The theatrical thus appears within *Joseph Andrews* not only as a literary mode, but as a characterizing manner of self-expression, and even a style of sexuality for both Lady Booby and her "distant relation," Beau Didapper (303)—one that Joseph recognizes and specifically rejects. The little we learn of Didapper's sexuality establishes its similarity to the purely mimetic and mediated desire, concentrated upon display and "reputation," which Fielding had represented in the beaux and castrato-lovers of his dramatic satires (and which he touches upon in Wilson's story of his life as a London fop, 203–4). In his ironic description of Didapper's "Qualifications" he tells us that he was "no Hater of Women; for he always dangled after them; yet so little subject to Lust, that he had, among those who knew him best, the Character of great Moderation in his Pleasures" (312); and the Beau confirms this character when, after being routed from the wrong bed in his attempt at a sexual adventure, "he was far from being ashamed of his Amour, and rather endeavoured to insinuate that more than was really true had past between him and the fair *Slipslop*" (336).

Beau Didapper's plan to seduce Fanny, which sets all of the "curious Night-Adventures" in motion, relies on the fact that "he was an excellent Mimick." We have heard something of this earlier when he frightened the members of Adams's household with a display of his wit in announcing his party's arrival at Adams's cottage by "mimicking" with his cane "the rap of a *London* Footman at the Door" (312).[11] The role Didapper mimics at Adams's door is one Joseph has actually filled earlier in the novel—we meet him first, in action, as a London footman—and when we see Didapper practice mimicry for the second time, it is Joseph in particular that he impersonates: "he groped out the Bed with difficulty; for there was not a Glimpse of Light, and opening the Curtains, he whispered in *Joseph's* Voice (for he was an excellent Mimick), '*Fanny*, my Angel . . .'" (330). Through his emphasis on Beau Didapper's reliance on mimicry, especially as focused on Joseph, Fielding suggests one possible relation between the two male figures of compromised gender in this novel: that the Beau is just a poor dramatic impersonation of something more complicated in Joseph's character.

Didapper's doubling of aspects of Joseph's identity may function, then, not to reflect badly on Joseph but to split Fielding's initially ambiguous treatment of him into a pair of linked characters, one clearly satirically conceived and the other positive. Occurring on the brink of the revelation of Joseph's true identity, Beau Didapper's appearance seems to work to free Joseph of some of the dangers or satiric potential of his compromised gender position by embodying them in someone else, locating the negative version of mixed gender identity specifically in someone also implicated in play-acting. Didapper's very anomalousness within the novel provides a measure of how far Fielding has moved, in creating Joseph, from the satiric treatment of the effeminate man in his plays.

Much earlier in the novel, Fielding associated Joseph with another standard satiric figure from his plays: the Italian castrato singers so popular in the London opera at this time. The decision to associate his romantic hero with the figure of the castrato is surely a bold one, and in examining Fielding's treatment of that association we can begin to explore to what end he might create a hero of ambiguous gender to start with—what positive purposes such a design might hope to achieve—and by what means he works, gradually, to disengage his hero from the expected negative burden of such a role.[12]

At the beginning of *Joseph Andrews*, Abraham Adams first notices Joseph in church, where "his Voice gave him an Opportunity of distinguishing himself by singing Psalms" (22). Later in the novel, Joseph is recognized by the sound of his voice (see, for example, 154 and 295). We are told that Joseph distinguished himself particularly in music while in London, so that "he led the Opinion of all the other Footmen at an Opera, and they never condemned or applauded a single Song contrary to his Approbation or Dislike" (27). Lest the reader forget the focus of Fielding's satiric concern with the opera in his plays, soon after Joseph's success at the opera is reported, Slipslop reminds us of it, sharply responding to Lady Booby's censure of "lewdness" in her house: " 'If you will turn away every Footman,' said *Slipslop*, 'that is a lover of the Sport, you must soon open the Coach-Door yourself, or get a Sett of *Mophrodites* to wait upon you; and I am sure I hated the Sight of them even singing in an Opera' " (43). But the Joseph she calls "a strong healthy *luscious* Boy enough" (35) has already been more pointedly associated by the narrator with those "hermaphrodites" she abhors. In summarizing the brief and rather uneventful history of Joseph's life before the action of the novel opens, the narrator explained the vicissitudes of his employment in the Booby household:

the young *Andrews* was at first employed in what in the Country they call *keeping Birds*. His Office was to perform the Part the Antients assigned to the God *Priapus*, which Deity the Moderns call by the Name of *Jack-o'-Lent*: but his Voice being so extremely musical, that it rather allured the Birds than terrified them, he was soon transplanted from the Fields into the Dog-kennel, where he was placed under the Huntsman, and made what Sports-men term a *Whipper-in*. For this Place likewise the Sweetness of his Voice disqualified him: the Dogs preferring the Melody of his chiding to all the alluring Notes of the Huntsman. (21–22)

Fielding refers to the humble task Joseph is given of scaring off birds from the fields as "the Part of Priapus," introducing into the English landscape the image of this ancient figure, a daimon of fertility often represented as a grotesquely misshapen man with a huge and erect phallus, and sometimes represented simply as the phallus itself, "the other human attributes being incidental."[13] Joseph is found unfit for this part by the sweetness of his voice—like the castrati, he combines an alluringly sweet voice with a disqualification from phallic office.[14]

Why would Fielding want to link the man who will gradually emerge as the hero of his novel to the castrati he had so satirized in his plays? In those works the figure of the castrato serves not only as an object of ridicule but as an occasion to defend the very practice of ridicule: Fielding's satire of him involves an account of satire it-self, imagined as threatened directly by the castrato's popularity. The allusions to this satiric subject within *Joseph Andrews*, then, may function not just to adapt the humor of his dramatic satires to the novel form but to reexamine the nature of that humor, and to reflect on his old and new forms. As we saw in Chapter 1, Fielding had repeatedly associated the castrati's popularity with a moral decline, making explicit an assumption that moral rigor resides in a specifi-cally phallic authority, and that such rigor is enforced specifically by the instrument of satire. For example, in his epilogue to *The Intrigu-ing Chambermaid* (1733), he opposes the "soft Italian warblers" who "have no sting" and "no harm within" to satire, which "may wound some pretty thing" and "gives the wounded hearer pain." He con-cludes the epilogue by expressing sympathy with his female audi-ence's choice of opera over other forms of drama, but his sympathy and approval are only ironic: although he describes the phallic satire that "soft Italian warblers" lack as aggressive and wounding, as a lashing rod, he defends it as a necessary aggression in the service of moral correction, like the disciplines of the schoolmaster and the preacher. In *Joseph Andrews* Fielding allows himself to explore more openly some of the negative dimensions of phallic satire, the possibility that its aggression is at times primary and the moral purpose of its application not assured. Though Fielding pokes fun at Joseph's compromised gender identity in the passage quoted above by showing his failure in the part of phallic enforcement—his office of chasing the birds off—he also pokes fun at the image of a more adequate masculinity by choosing to imagine it in the figure of the grotesque Priapus, all phallus and no form.

Two books later, Fielding will give more extended and serious treatment to the negative dimensions of conventional masculine identity that Joseph may be created to evade: the Roasting-Squire who bursts upon the scene in book 3, chapter 6, and dominates the chapters that follow provides a dark embodiment of irresponsible satiric impulses allied with the misuse of masculine power. Associated, too, with drama, the Roasting-Squire requires us to understand *Joseph Andrews* as a complicated reflection not only on Richardson's *Pamela* but on Fielding's own most popular early works, his dramatic satires. By the time we meet the Roasting-Squire, however, Fielding's characterization of Joseph has evolved to make him a more viable alternative to the portrait of masculinity we find there; and before we turn in Chapter 3 to the problem represented by the Squire, we must trace the way Fielding gradually redefines Joseph's compromised gender. He begins by superimposing the figure of the castrato, familiar from his dramatic satires, onto Joseph, and then separates Joseph in certain ways from that figure to free him from its negative associations—he thus uses the old figure in a new way to explore some of the more positive possibilities represented by the castrato's escape from monolithic phallic identity.

Fielding's description of Joseph's physical appearance early in the novel offers a simple example of his construction of Joseph's gender in equivocal terms, but an example in which we can already see the value given to that equivocation becoming less strictly negative. Indeed, Fielding provides his description of Joseph's appearance when he does so that we may better understand the temptation Joseph is about to present to Lady Booby. Schilling comments that Fielding makes Joseph's assumption of feminine virtue "seem the more outlandish by a glowing description of Joseph's physical beauty," but as Fielding sketches the features of Joseph's body and face for us, we find that his particular form of physical beauty combines the feminine with the masculine.[15] Fielding introduces the special nature of Joseph's attraction by alluding to "the uncommon Variety of Charms, which united in this young Man's Person"; what is uncommon about them is that they bring together, in his person, beauties traditionally granted to each gender. The systematic way in which Fielding surveys the separate features of Joseph's appearance is itself reminiscent of descriptive techniques conventionally applied to women:[16]

[Joseph Andrews] was of the highest Degree of middle Stature. His Limbs were put together with great Elegance and no less Strength. His Legs and Thighs were formed in the exactest Proportion. His Shoulders were broad and brawny, but yet his Arms hung so easily, that he had all the Symptoms of Strength without the least clumsiness. His Hair was of a nut-brown Colour, and was displayed in wanton Ringlets down his Back. His Forehead was high, his Eyes dark, and as full of Sweetness as of Fire. His Nose a little inclined to the Roman. His Teeth white and even. His Lips full, red, and soft. His Beard was only rough on his Chin and upper Lip; but his Cheeks, in which his Blood glowed, were overspread with a thick Down. His Countenance had a Tenderness joined with a Sensibility inexpressible. (38)

The first sentence of the description establishes a rhythm of assertion followed by qualification which serves to characterize Joseph throughout the passage: his height is of the highest degree—of middle stature. Repeatedly, the syntax of the description creates hinges between assertions and their modification which either pair disparate characteristics, providing a balanced weighting of qualities associated with masculine and feminine beauty ("great Elegance and no less Strength," "as full of Sweetness as of Fire"), or insist on the distinction between a positive masculine characteristic assigned to Joseph and some negative extension of it ("His Shoulders were broad and brawny; but yet his Arms hung so easily, that he had all the Symptoms of Strength without the least clumsiness"). The description of Beau Didapper that Fielding will provide in book 4, chapter 9, not only mockingly echoes Middleton's praise of Hervey, but parallels, in its balanced weighting of qualities, the syntax of this earlier description of Joseph. The "moderation" achieved by the balanced weighting there is handled, however, as Fielding acknowledges, "negatively": "He had lived too much in the World to be bashful, and too much at Court to be proud . . . No Hater of Women; for he always dangled after them; yet so little subject to Lust, that he had, among those who knew him best, the Character of great Moderation in his Pleasures" (312). While Fielding emphasizes what's lacking from Didapper's body—he is four feet five inches tall, scarce of hair, "thin and pale," with "very narrow Shoulders, and no Calf"—the balance of qualities in Joseph is not achieved negatively, by absence. Though the description of Joseph immediately precedes the interview in which Joseph declares himself "the brother of Pamela," Fielding does not broaden his parody of a "male Pamela" in it by denying him the strength and brawn of a traditionally masculine body.

At the same time, though, Fielding carefully negotiates Joseph's particular relation to expectations about the masculine body. He emphasizes the presence of a "Tenderness" and a "Sensibility" in Joseph's countenance that is "inexpressible"; along with his male massiveness, there is something elusive here that is traditionally associated with female beauty.[17] Even Joseph's beard equivocates: it is rough below, but downy above, in a way that allows the flush of his blood to appear. Finally, if his facial hair presents us visually with some kind of vertical distribution of Joseph's complex sexual identity, Fielding's description of his "Ringlets" complicates Joseph's gender identification in another direction, in the relation between narrative foreground and the background of literary echo, where it again crosses into association with a woman.

The display of Joseph's hair in "wanton Ringlets down his Back" seems an apparently insignificant flourish in the description of his pretty-boy good looks, but the phrase "wanton Ringlets" connects Fielding's description of Joseph's physical appearance to the passage in *Paradise Lost* that first introduces a structuring principle of gender into the poem's cosmos. Traveling with Satan in his approach to the Garden of Eden, the reader of *Paradise Lost* first glimpses Adam and Eve when Satan does, in book IV. Milton presents him and us with the "two of far nobler shape erect and tall" among God's new creatures, saying that "the image of thir glorious Maker shone" in them both:[18]

> though both
> Not equal, as thir sex not equal seem'd;
> For contemplation hee and valor form'd,
> For softness shee and sweet attractive Grace,
> Hee for God only, shee for God in him:
> His fair large Front and Eye sublime declar'd
> Absolute rule; and Hyacinthine Locks

> Round from his parted forelock manly hung
> Clust'ring, but not beneath his shoulders broad:
> Shee as a veil down to the slender waist
> Her unadorned golden tresses wore
> Dishevell'd, but in wanton ringlets wav'd
>
> (IV.295–306)

Though Joseph's hair is just one of a number of features of his appearance that Fielding describes, the passage from *Paradise Lost* that he recalls by referring to Joseph's "wanton Ringlets" gives hairstyle a singular importance. Milton chooses it, rather than the more obvious differences of bodily parts or shape or size, to represent the difference in identity created by sex in the first man and woman.[19] But not only does Fielding echo Milton's reference to Eve's hair rather than to Adam's; he specifies that Joseph's hair hangs "down his Back," while Milton insists that Adam's "manly" locks hung "not beneath his shoulders broad." Elaborating on his physical emblem of the two sexes' different statuses, Milton glosses its figurative significance with a simile. Eve's hair

> in wanton ringlets wav'd
> As the Vine curls her tendrils, which impli'd
> Subjection, but requir'd with gentle sway,
> And by her yielded, by him best receiv'd,
> Yielded with coy submission, modest pride,
> And sweet reluctant amorous delay.
>
> (IV.306–11)

When, in placing Joseph against the backdrop of this first description of our first parents, Fielding aligns him with Eve, he implicates him, then, not just in feminine appearance but in the feminine position of "subjection" and "submission" which Milton says her curling, pendant locks fittingly picture. The adjective "sweet," repeated twice to characterize Eve in the seventeen-line passage, appears in the description of Joseph's eyes, as the "softness" given to Eve in contrast to Adam appears in Joseph's lips. Suggestively, Milton's account of Adam's and Eve's hair and of the primal nature of "hee" and "shee" ends on a note about female sexuality: the "sweet reluctant amorous delay" afforded by Eve's "coy submission" and "modest pride" brings the passage to a close. While the meanings "undisciplined," "natural," or "profuse" seem denoted by "wanton" in the description of Eve's long hair, as Milton interprets all that

that hair represents about female identity, the sexual meaning of "wanton" surfaces as well, and her hair comes to express the need created, even by Eve's gorgeous plenitude and luxuriance, for masculine "sway," a need shaping the sexual relations between the first man and woman.

In its relation to *Pamela*, Fielding's novel has from the first placed Joseph in a position held earlier by a woman, the position of a young servant defending her chastity; in its relation to the passage from *Paradise Lost*, the novel again places Joseph in a position held earlier by a woman, linking Joseph to Eve through a phrase that specifically figures both her subjection and her sexuality. The force of this gender-inverting allusion is complex: as it appears in the context of a description of Joseph's attractions, its force would not seem to fall so clearly against Joseph himself as the inversion of Richardson's scenario does. The interpretive tensions created by the crossing of gender categories within the allusion raise questions about the relevance of Milton's Eden to a modern "history" and about the authenticity of Richardson's version of gender difference, as well as about the character of Joseph. The incongruity with which Fielding alludes to Eve's "wanton ringlets" might remind us of the distance between Joseph's world and Adam and Eve's: Joseph exists in a historical world, one where power is structured by changing class distinctions as well as by the gender categories which represent stable, naturalized hierarchies of authority in timeless Eden. Replacing Pamela momentarily with Eve as Joseph's female counterpart, the allusion also historicizes notions of gender, shifting the content of Joseph's feminine sexual role from the eighteenth-century identification of woman with chastity to a more complex picture of feminine sexual luxuriance and compliance—a "modest pride" and "coy submission" that are not without desire.

As Ian Watt has argued, notions of female identity changed dramatically between the appearance of Milton's Eve and Richardson's Pamela. Indeed, following R. P. Utter and G. B. Needham, Watt asserts that the publication of *Pamela* itself "marks a very notable epiphany in the history of our culture: the emergence of a new, fully developed and immensely influential stereotype of the feminine role," an ideal of womanhood characterized by youth, inexperience, passivity, extreme mental and physical delicacy, and the absence of sexual passion. By conjuring the older tradition represented by Milton, which was "prone to lay more emphasis on the concupiscence of women than of men,"[20] Fielding reminds us that Richardson's portrait of female nature is not the only one (as he does also through the characters of Lady Booby and the more appealing Betty, the innkeepers' chambermaid). But his use of Milton within the parody of Richardson, suggesting a competing version of the feminine sexual role, also destabilizes Milton's own mythologized gender oppositions, not only reversing the characteristics assigned by Milton to the two sexes but explaining them in terms of fashion.

If we look back to an earlier passage in *Joseph Andrews*, we recognize that Joseph's ringlets, unlike Eve's, are not a natural outward expression or emanation of his inner identity. Though Joseph remains uncorrupted by vice while living in London, he is reshaped by fashion, having his hair cut, we are told, "after the newest Fashion" and learning to curl it in curling papers (27). Fashion has shaped the appearance of Fanny's hair too, and has shaped it in a way that makes it actually less like Eve's than Joseph's is. Although "Nature" has given Fanny "extremely lavish" hair, she too has had it cut; and on Sundays she arranges it in curls that, unlike Joseph's, reach only "down her Neck" in what Fielding calls "the modern Fashion" (152). Even the powerful physical attractions of Fielding's romantic hero and heroine are not entirely untouched by artifice, although Fielding emphasizes, for example, that in Fanny's skin "a Whiteness appeared which the finest *Italian* Paint would be unable to reach" and that "she had a natural Gentility, superior to the Acquisition of Art" (152–53).

Fielding concentrates the influence of fashion on his hero and heroine in the treatment of their hair, and the glancing allusion to *Paradise Lost* in his description of Joseph's hair recalls a context in which a natural difference in hair length is to express the whole order of relations between the sexes. The quiet echo of Milton early in the novel, with the discontinuities between its original and new contexts, suggests a contrast between the constructed nature of gender in Joseph's world and the stable, "natural" hierarchy of gender in Milton's Eden. We will see that this is not an isolated or entirely fragmentary echo: further echoes of *Paradise Lost* in *Joseph Andrews* sustain and develop a relation between the two works that provides one form of commentary on the later work's aims. Indeed, in these echoes, the very act of invoking Milton will assume a special force and significance within the novel.

The Eve of "wanton ringlets," despite her distance from Joseph's world, provides a more complex and appealing version of the feminine sexuality with which he is identified than the initial model of Pamela; and the allusion to her within a description of Joseph's physical charms begins the novel's movement beyond a strictly parodic treatment of him. As Joseph advances toward the chapters in which we will meet the Roasting-Squire (and encounter a cluster of Miltonic allusions) he passes through a number of situations that progressively reformulate his relation to the feminized man as a butt for Fielding's satire. In his travels, he will literally pass through a series of inns that house different scenarios from Fielding's satiric repertoire about domestic and sexual relations.

In book 1, Joseph sets out from Lady Booby's house, is severely beaten by highwaymen, and first comes to rest in the outside world (returning, according to his doctor, from the very threshold of death) in a stronghold of "petticoat government." As we have seen, Fielding had satirized the inversion of domestic power relations in a number of plays, including *The Tragedy of Tragedies*, *The Grub-Street Opera*, *Pasquin*, and *Eurydice*, and the innkeepers at the Dragon establish their familiar roles of browbeaten husband and domineering wife in their first piece of dialogue. " 'Well,' says he, 'my Dear, do as you will when you are up, you know I never contradict you.' 'No,' says she, 'if the Devil was to contradict me, I would make the House too hot to hold him' " (56). The name the two innkeepers share expresses the domination of their marriage by the woman: Mr. and Mrs. Tow-wouse are named with a slang word for the female genitals.[21] While staying in their inn, Joseph is physically weak and vulnerable, penniless, and at the mercy of Mrs. Tow-wouse's notions of charity (" 'Common Charity, a F--t!' says she, 'Common Charity teaches us to provide for ourselves, and our Families' "). Going out into the world, the "male Pamela" has turned up in the scene that King Arthur described with his maxim:

> when by Force
> Or Art the Wife her Husband over-reaches
> Give him the Peticoat, and her the Breeches.
> *The Tragedy of Tragedies* (I.iii)

And Joseph seems to be aligned within this scene with the ineffective husband, Mr. Tow-wouse, who wishes to do him well but has little will or way.

The next time we see Joseph he is at an inn quite decisively ruled by a husband. In this scene, however, Joseph appears grouped with the tyrannized wife. Again, Joseph is injured and helpless—this time Adams's horse has suddenly knelt, crushing his leg—and has retreated to the woman's realm of the kitchen, where he is tended by the innkeeper's wife (118–19). Her husband chastises her for attending to a mere footman's leg and proposes that Joseph "find a Surgeon to cut it off"; in the brawl that follows, the offended Adams exchanges blows with the host and hostess, while Joseph sits helplessly by, scarce able to "rise from his Chair" (120). Fielding's thrice-repeated emphasis on the hostess's rubbing, "with a warm Hand," of Joseph's leg, the strength of her husband's objection, and his nasty recommendation that the leg be cut off, all hint at a metonymic association of Joseph's leg with his genitals, his injury signifying as a figurative castration that keeps him out of the masculine physical struggle even after the hostess and Slipslop have joined in. Moving between the two inns, each representative of one extreme in domestic arrangements, Joseph passes through identification with several different satiric versions of the feminized man—from the weak-willed husband overreached by his aggressive wife to the dephallicized man adored and attended to by someone else's alienated wife. When we again meet up with Joseph at an inn, he will be more directly implicated in that role of the castrato opera singer recalled by the description of his bird-keeping in 1.2 and distantly evoked in this injury to his leg.

We enter the inn that is the scene of book 2, chapter 12, with Adams and Fanny, and share their surprise at the revelation of Joseph's presence there as well. In this chapter the three characters are reunited on the road for the first time. Both Dick Taylor and Maurice Johnson see this chapter as a crucial turning point in Joseph's development from a parodic to a serious and sympathetic character.[22] And yet the chapter does not begin by freeing Joseph from association with satiric figures. The preceding chapter has ended on a note that might prepare us for satiric allusions to opera. Meditating upon the "litigious Temper" in men, Adams rather gratuitously tells a story about two men, contending for the place of clerk, whose fierce competition in the singing of psalms at church eventually breaks forth into fighting (150–51); this story seems less arbitrary if we see it as modeled on one of the standard jokes in send-ups of the Italian opera—the bitter rivalry between the sopranos Faustina Bordoni and Francesca Cuzzoni (which led to their aggressively competitive singing while together on stage and even to an exchange of blows there).[23] Our introduction to Joseph in the chapter that follows recalls his association early in the novel with an even more frequent target in jokes about the Italian opera—for Joseph appears here singing an extended song with "one of the most melodious [voices] that ever was heard."

To be more precise, he doesn't *appear* here singing the song: if the bird-keeping passage somehow imagined him as deprived of his phallus, disqualified, like the castrato singers, for the part of Priapus by the sweetness of his voice, this chapter momentarily disembodies him altogether, returning him to his friends first *only* as a voice, overheard singing "from an inner Room." He is recognized by, and overwhelmingly present to, Fanny (who, like an opera fan, swoons) simply through the sound of his voice. Yet although the song he sings tells a story of passionate sexual desire and eventual fulfillment, Joseph's own body has been temporarily removed from that story. Fielding's dramatic satires ridiculed the notion of the castrato celebrities who sought romantic affairs for reputation's sake,[24] and the first stage of Joseph's reunion with Fanny acts out the absence of the phallus, and of real sensual contact, from the fashionable appearance of "Intrigues"—here generalized to the absence of the whole body.

The description of Fanny that leads up to it and the content of the song itself pose, in a variety of ways, the question of the place of "images" in the physical experience of sexual desire. Introducing his description of Fanny's physical beauties with a warning to readers of an "amorous Hue," Fielding alludes to the fates of Pygmalion and Narcissus as versions of the frustration he fears for us. The words of Joseph's song, given on the next page, return us to the reflection of Narcissus. The speaker of its pastoral love story first laments that he can't escape the remembrance of Chloe's beauties; then reasons with rapture that he is "thus of *Chloe* possest," as, "Nor she, nor no Tyrant's hard Power, / Her Image can tear from my Breast"; but next uncovers the limits of this consolation:

> But felt not *Narcissus* more Joy,
> With his Eyes he beheld his lov'd Charms?
> Yet what he beheld, the fond Boy
> More eagerly wish'd in his Arms.   (153)

Explaining the frustrations of fixing on the image rather than the substance of the loved one with the example of Narcissus, the speaker implies that there is something self-enclosed or even self-loving about such a fixation; and the insularity of Joseph's performance of the love song, alone in another room, evokes another side of this reflective relation—the self-enclosure of a desire to turn *oneself* into an image of love, like Wilson writing love-letters to himself to acquire the reputation of intrigues (203).[25] Joseph, however, has turned himself not exactly into an image, but into a disembodied voice: Joseph's absent presence when overheard at the inn takes the theatricality of this kind of desire to an odd, even paradoxical, extreme. His offstage performance is at once somehow stagey (the "inner Room" from which he sings might suggest the "inner stage" or "discovery space" of the theater) and decidedly untheatrical; the personal body that is flattened by the theater into an image is here so attenuated that it disappears. The effect of Joseph's song on Fanny recalls both classical allusions used by Fielding in the chapter's opening: its performance turns her momentarily into the Echo figure of Narcissus's story (" 'Bless us,' says Adams, 'you look extremely pale.' 'Pale! Mr. Adams,' says she, 'O Jesus!' "), and then into Pygmalion's statue. After her stunned repetition of Adams's last word, Fanny faints, unceremoniously falling "backwards in her Chair." It is only when Joseph enters the room and clasps her in his arms that, like Pygmalion's statue softening and blushing at his touch, she comes (back) to life with "Life and Blood returning into her cheeks" (154–55).[26]

For Joseph *has* suddenly appeared in the room—not as insular as he has seemed, he responds to Adams's call for help at Fanny's distress—and now enacts a physical passion so far from mere theatricality that he embraces and kisses Fanny "without considering who were present" as witnesses. Fanny and Joseph meet here in the flesh for the first time in the novel, and one effect of Joseph's disembodiment on the threshold of that meeting is to make his entrance almost an act of materialization, his passion given flesh in this scene, his body conjured more strongly as a physical presence after being pointedly withheld, except as it manifested itself in voice. The scene that Taylor and Johnson identify as a turning point in the presentation of Joseph does, among other things, establish his difference from the castrati with whom he'd been identified—at least with respect to the ironic relation they represent for Fielding between public passion and bodily reality, which this scene confronts by staging and then reversing it. Suggestively, we learn in the following chapter that the next morning Joseph finds "his Leg surprisingly recovered" (161).[27]

From this point in the novel on, Fielding is increasingly straightforward and firm about Joseph's physical strength and self-possession. He shows him carrying Fanny in his arms, beating a pack of hounds off Adams with his cudgel, drubbing (as Taylor notes) the Roasting-Squire's captain, defeating Beau Didapper's servant in a fistfight, and giving the Beau himself a box on the ear. In the first of these events, when Joseph carries Fanny down a hill in the dark, Fielding uses the occasion explicitly to distinguish Joseph from the beaux whose questionable gender Joseph's role as a male Pamela and his mixed masculine and feminine charms might at first have seemed to mirror. Fielding moralizes,

Learn hence, my fair Countrywomen, to consider your own Weakness, and the many Occasions on which the strength of a Man may be useful to you; and duly weighing this, take care, that you match not yourselves with the spindle-shanked Beaus and Petit Maîtres of the Age, who instead of being able like *Joseph Andrews*, to carry you in lusty Arms through the rugged ways and downhill Steeps of Life, will rather want to support their feeble Limbs with your Strength and Assistance. (194)

Joseph is here actually exhibited as the alternative to the gender role reversals in which he at first seemed to be implicated. Even before Joseph has met up with Fanny at the inn, the novel's "embattled chastity" theme has begun to shift its focus from Joseph to Fanny, a more conventional object of sexual aggression; and once they have been reunited, Joseph not only ceases to appear as a male Pamela, defending his own chastity, but takes up the proudly masculine role of the defender of that of a woman. Is the body that the reunion scene in 2.12 seems dramatically to award Joseph, after all the equivocations and negotiations about Joseph's gender that lead up to it, the simply and conventionally masculine one that the first portion of the novel had denied him? Does Joseph turn out to be "something entirely, almost diametrically different" from what he'd first appeared, as Hunter eloquently argues,[28] or does something of his initial appearance remain crucial to what he has to offer as the novel's central character?

The addresses to his reader that Fielding places on either side of Joseph's song and sudden materialization in book 2, chapter 12, suggest that the reunion scene plays out the ambiguities not only within theatrical modes of behavior but within the promise offered by Fielding's new form, the novel. Fielding's comments at both the beginning and the end of the scene tease us about what *our* relation to the actions and passions of the scene could be: "if it should happen to us or to thee to be struck with this Picture, we should be perhaps in as helpless a Condition as *Narcissus*; and might say to ourselves, *Quod petis est nusquam*." "But, O Reader, when this Nightingale, who was no other than *Joseph Andrews* himself, saw his beloved *Fanny* in the Situation we have described her, can'st thou conceive the Agitations of his Mind?" (152, 154). Within the scene, Adams's position as an onlooker might allegorize ours. Fielding comments that "Some Philosophers may perhaps doubt, whether he was not the happiest of the three; for the Goodness of his Heart enjoyed the Blessings which were exulting in the Breasts of both the other two, together with his own"; but he then debunks the thought as "Metaphysical Rubbish," and provides a sobering emblem of the reader's fate. Adams has flung the book of Aeschylus he's been studying into the fire when Fanny faints, and "as soon as the first Tumults of *Adams's* Rapture were over, he cast his Eyes towards the Fire, where *Æschylus* lay expiring; and immediately rescued the poor Remains, to-wit, the Sheepskin Covering of his dear Friend, which was the Work of his own Hands, and had been his inseparable Companion for upwards of thirty Years" (155).

Adams's relation to "the Work of his own Hands," "his inseparable Companion," suggests the attachments of Pygmalion and of Narcissus as much as Joseph's theatricality might; and the reduction of his book to sheepskin covers pictures a kind of emptying out of the reader's experience in the face of the demands of human events. In some ways, of course, a novel's characters are quite literally disembodied, while the drama functions precisely by giving its characters body. But then, the book Adams was reading was not a novel: it was a copy of the plays of the first tragic dramatist, itself referred to by that dramatist's name. This episode, described by Taylor and Johnson as a turning point in the presentation of Joseph's character—and which we read as a crisis in the depiction of Joseph's gender identity—also plays out with some urgency issues of literary representation and reception, bringing into a kind of associational circulation questions about theater, theatricality, opera, voice, and reading. In the present chapter, while focusing on Fielding's changing treatment of the problem of Joseph's gender, we have repeatedly come across a loose and sometimes mysterious network of connections between definitions of gender, alternative forms of sexual desire, and matters of generic convention and literary echo (as Didapper's inadequate masculinity and suspect forms of desire are linked by Fielding to the theater, as the castrato is placed in opposition to masculinized satire, as Richardson's new novel form and Milton's Christian epic offer competing accounts of female character). In the chapter below, we will focus more directly on a specific example of an interplay between genre, allusion, and contending definitions of gendered identity. Despite its warnings to the reader, the episode in 2.12 at the inn, and *Joseph Andrews* more generally, do not simply throw textually dependent forms of feeling and identity into the fire.

If Joseph has earlier rejected Lady Booby's theatrical expressions of sexual desire—and if, in the course of 2.12, he is carefully separated from a theatricalized desire centered on images—he nonetheless remains implicated, as Chapter 4 shows, in what we might term echoic emotion, or in desire and feeling that are dependent upon conventionalized acts of voice and upon prior texts. Indeed, before we arrive at Chapter 4, in the first section of Chapter 3 we will study Fielding's suggestion in *Joseph Andrews* that echo itself evokes the materiality of words, so that the opposition I have been using above between "images" and the physical reality of the body breaks down before the bodylike presence of words. What Fielding seems to highlight about echo in his direct narrative treatment of it in several scenes is the way that echo (unlike Didapper's "mimicry") can become dynamic rather than mechanical as it overlays recollections of *multiple* prior texts. The specific verbal echoes of Milton in the scenes analyzed in Chapter 3 can only be heard amid the simultaneous redounding of echoes from a variety of prior texts. The multiplicity of the texts recalled seems itself to be essential to the effect Fielding seeks in these scenes.

THREE

"The Natural Amphitheatre"

Dramatic Satire, the Novel, and Milton's Christian Epic

As Beau Didapper appears in a complicated, reflective relation to the character of Joseph Andrews—raising questions about the implications of Joseph's ambiguous gender identity, serving ultimately to distinguish him from one negative version of the "effeminate" man—the "Roasting-Squire" who appears in chapters 6 and 7 of book 3 of *Joseph Andrews* might seem to provide a dark, even diabolic reflection of Fielding himself as a man who makes others laugh by exposing the ridiculous. The context in which he appears, however, is carefully constructed to require us to make distinctions between kinds of laughter and, specifically, between various comic literary forms: those of drama, satire, and the lost comic epic that Fielding has described in his preface to the novel. The Roasting-Squire is associated with the first two forms—but then, so was Fielding for the first ten years of his literary career. The chapters involving the Roasting-Squire constitute a complex meditation on Fielding's own methods for creating laughter in his new form, the novel. This meditation emerges through the interaction between narrative action and literary echo in these chapters and through the expository treatment of generic questions in surrounding chapters. Milton's *Paradise Lost* comes to play an important role in Fielding's placement of the Squire's satire among alternative literary forms; and the Squire's masculinity is part of what is threatening in his intrusion.

The Squire is not a literary satirist but a man who subjects those around him to satiric ridicule. In some of the examples we will study below, verbal echoes or questions of generic placement arise in specifically literary contexts, constructing or negotiating relations between literary texts; in others, they appear as important structuring elements in the world of social relations. Drawing implicit connections between these literary and nonliterary functions of echo and of generic convention, Fielding allows us to see their complex and often ambiguous participation in matters of gender and of social class. Both verbal echo and the conventions of literary form might seem to highlight a text's status as derived, mediated, determined by forces outside it. Before turning to an analysis of the scenes involving the Roasting-Squire himself, we will consider Fielding's depiction within *Joseph Andrews* of the surprisingly diverse effects that can be created by echo, and then study his explicit and implicit commentary on satire, drama, and epic in the chapters leading up to the Roasting-Squire episode, where echoes of Milton will contribute to a disorienting confrontation between these three genres.[1] We will see that the complex resonances of specific echoes can make the relation between earlier literary or social texts, "generic" expectations, and the present scene as it unfolds far from straightforward, mechanical, or determining.

While in the scenes involving the Roasting-Squire Fielding relies on verbal echo to shape the meaning of narrative action, elsewhere in the novel he playfully uses narrative action to represent the dynamic process and the range of meanings of verbal echo. Consider the following exchange of words between Lady Booby and Slipslop:

"—And then for his Virtues; such Piety to his Parents, such tender Affection to his Sister, such Integrity in his Friendship, such Bravery, such Goodness, that if he had been born a Gentleman, his Wife would have possest the most invaluable Blessing." —"To be sure, Ma'am," says *Slipslop*. —"But as he is," answered the Lady, "if he had a thousand more good Qualities, it must render a Woman of Fashion contemptible even to be suspected of thinking of him, yes I should despise myself for such a Thought." "To be sure, Ma'am," said *Slipslop*. "And why to be sure?" reply'd the Lady, "thou art always one's Echo. Is he not more worthy of Affection than a dirty Country Clown, tho' born of a Family as old as the Flood, or an idle worthless Rake, or little puisny Beau of Quality?" (296)

Talking her way through some definition of Joseph's worth, Lady Booby employs Slipslop to play a part in the dialogue of her own ambivalence. Talking out the contradictions in her response to him, she at times relies on Slipslop's reflexive acquiescence ("To be sure") and at times reacts with annoyance to Slipslop's confirmation of her own words when her feelings have already diverged from them: "'And why to be sure?' reply'd the Lady, 'thou art always one's Echo.'" Indeed, in the first book of the novel, Slipslop provided a more exact, and exacting, echo to Lady Booby's words.

The Lady . . . desired to know what she meant by that extraordinary degree of Freedom in which she thought proper to indulge her Tongue. "Freedom!" says *Slipslop*, "I don't know what you call Freedom, Madam; Servants have Tongues as well as their Mistresses." "Yes, and saucy ones too," answered the Lady: "but I assure you I shall bear no such Impertinence." "Impertinence! I don't know that I am impertinent," says *Slipslop*. "Yes indeed you are," cries my Lady; "and unless you mend your Manners, this House is no Place for you." "Manners!" cries *Slipslop*, "I never was thought to want Manners *nor Modesty neither*; and for Places, there are more Places than one; and I know what I know." (43)

Voice is just what's at issue in this echo-exchange—whether servants may have tongues as well as their mistresses—and though Slipslop's voice seems dependent on Lady Booby's in this passage, returning to her the key noun of each of her statements, here her echoes of her mistress express not compliance but resistance: Slipslop repeats Lady Booby's words to dispute the meaning of her terms. The exchange ends with a mutual decision that Slipslop find herself another place; both women think better of this decision, and when Lady Booby patches things up she explains, "I can't help being surprised . . . that you will take the surest Method to offend me. I mean repeating my Words, which you know I have always detested" (44).

She detests it when it is put to certain uses, but it's also just what she employs Slipslop to do. In the last scene that pictures Slipslop and Lady Booby together before the novel ends, Fielding more rapidly sketches their relation: Lady Booby "then went up into her Chamber, sent for *Slipslop*, threw herself on the Bed, in the Agonies of Love, Rage, and Despair; nor could she conceal these boiling Passions longer, without bursting. . . . *Slipslop* well knowing how to humour her Mistress's Frenzy, proceeded to repeat, with Exaggeration if possible, all her Mistress had said" (326). With the dialogues between Lady Booby and Slipslop in books 1 and 4 Fielding frames the allusive passages in book 3 with narrative that thematizes the question of literary echo, dramatizing in the conversations of two characters how echo can reveal the ambivalences of a first speaker, or express the ambivalences of a second, and how it can be used as a verbal device to resist, to reduce, or to subvert an original meaning as well as to affirm, to please, and to reassure.

Tellingly, in the conversation with which we began, in which echo's effect oscillates—at times soothing Lady Booby, seconding her statements, at times aggravating her, forcing her to express the conflicting side of her feelings—the subject of discussion is Joseph, and Lady Booby goes on to explain the forces that make it difficult to respond to him as the "Tyranny of Custom." As we have seen, the character of Joseph provides a focus for ambivalence about gender roles, and about the tyrannical constraints of custom, for more than Lady Booby; and the narrative itself repeatedly employs echoes of other texts to work out the questions Joseph raises. In the character of Slipslop, Fielding has drawn into one corner of his picture a comical depiction of one of his methods of representation in the whole of the picture.

The "rather too corpulent" and highly corporeal Slipslop described in 1.6 seems an unlikely representative of the disembodied voice of mythological echo, but both her language and her actions in the novel make her a figure for the burlesque and deflating possibilities among echo's effects. Slipslop fills her speech with distorted repetitions of the "hard Words" she has learned and is so proud of knowing, like a spirit of domesticating deformation in words' iteration ("Barbarous Monster! how have I deserved that my Passion should be *resulted* and treated with *Ironing*?" [33]). Slipslop's name evokes her appearance and character, but the very sound of her name also suggests the comic "tick-tock" of a syllable and its hollow echo.

Slipslop's comic function in the novel is not only to repeat her mistress's words but to repeat her actions, in a burlesque key, downstairs. Johnson observes that the reader laughs because Lady Booby's "bid for Joseph is echoed by Mrs. Slipslop's cruder, below-stairs onslaught—in the sure-fire manner of stage comedy, where laughable antics draw forth increased laughter the second time around"; Alter, noting the parallel of character between "the would-be seductress and the frustrated female rapist," comments that Slipslop "is both a voice for and critic of the desires her mistress politely conceals, a living testimony to what lies on the other side of Lady Booby's facade of hypocrisy.'"[2] Both in her words and in her mirroring actions, then, Slipslop takes on the function of echo that John Hollander describes when he says, "Echo's power is thus one of being able to reveal the implicit, and if she is oracular it is in a way which demythologizes all the oracles.'"[3] Slipslop's ability to reveal what's hidden in her mistress's polite facade depends largely on that very corporeality which makes her an unlikely or unwieldy figure of echo, serving to reduce matters of rhetoric to those of flesh.

Her spirited exchanges with Lady Booby depend upon one of echo's more traditional effects, described by Hollander as "satiric fragmentation, in which the breaking apart of a longer word or phrase is literally and figuratively 'reductive.'"[4] In this regard, she embodies within the novel the technique of satiric fragmentation and reduction used by Fielding himself in some of the narrator's language. For example, his description of Beau Didapper closely echoes the description of Lord Hervey in Middleton's dedication to his *Life of Cicero*, fragmenting and distorting Middleton's words in ways that turn his praise into ridicule. More figuratively, one might say that the whole opening sequence of the novel works like a satirically fragmented echo of *Pamela*, effectively reducing its resonance. But the scenario in which Fielding represents verbal echo within his narrative suggests a more complex relation than we might at first suppose between first and second voices in the narrative itself. Slipslop's repetition of her lady's words in a variety of moods, and with a variety of effects, dramatizes the very different forces with which literary echoes may fall against the texts they answer. Her relation to Lady Booby is suggestive: the figure of echo appears here, demythologized, within the social and economic structures of class and employment, shaped by Slipslop's dependent position and voicing her alternation in that position between subservience and rebellion.

While acknowledging a model of echo as servility in the person of Slipslop, Fielding's narrative achieves more with its echoes than a simple alternation between abject, exaggerated repetition and a menial's defiance. It is in Fielding's recollections of Milton in *Joseph Andrews* that we find him mixing with real subtlety echo's abilities to affirm, to reduce and ridicule, and to expand or augment.[5] Hollander notes generally that "the Miltonic presence sounds heavily in the 1740's, and resounds where it has not been asked," and critics have noticed the importance of parallels and allusions to Milton's

Paradise Lost in Fielding's work in particular.[6] As we already began to see in Chapter 2, the allusions to *Paradise Lost* in *Joseph Andrews* reflect in complicated ways not only on Milton's attempt to create a Christian epic in the vernacular, and on the contemporary novelistic world that Joseph inhabits, but on the epistolary novel to which *Joseph Andrews* is more immediately responding; and the very ambivalence of Fielding's echoes of Milton represents one way they reflect on, and pose an alternative to, *Pamela*.

Part of *Joseph Andrews*'s critique of *Pamela* centers on Richardson's naive insistence on the value of moral patterns or models to be imitated strictly, straightforwardly. This critique of what Hunter calls "exemplary theory"[7] appears on a number of levels of *Joseph Andrews*: in the foolishness of Joseph's dependence on his sister's example ("O most adorable *Pamela*! most virtuous Sister, whose Example could alone enable me to withstand all the Temptations of Riches and Beauty, and to preserve my Virtue pure and chaste" [58]); in his reliance, early on, upon the amiable but inadequate guide, Adams, "a representative of the folly of following authority for authority's sake"[8]; even in the emphasis on imitation in the theatricalized erotic lives of some of the novel's characters, reminiscent of the "triangular desire" we traced among many of the characters satirized in Fielding's plays.[9] Fielding's use of literary echoes in *Joseph Andrews* extends his critique of Pamela-as-exemplum in a different way, placing beside Richardson's notions about moral models and strict imitation all the ambivalence and complexity of the "imitative" relations that echo can sustain. In Fielding's movement from the theater to fiction, a reader's form, allusion takes on some of the function staging devices had earlier served for him—to present contradictory messages simultaneously (King Arthur condemning "petticoat government" to a cross-dressed hero, or Joseph's Eve-like "wanton Ringlets"), to dramatize tensions between speech and context, to confront one level of intended meaning with the defiant materiality of actors' bodies or of words' past uses.[10]

The first chapter of book 3 of *Joseph Andrews*, "*Matter prefatory in Praise of* Biography," not only alerts us to the role Milton has to play in the narrative that will follow but prepares us generally for the importance of questions of genre in the rest of book 3. The chapter's rather free-floating discussion of genre eventually settles on the problem of defining satire. It begins, however, by first comparing historians and "Biographers," and then distinguishing the latter from "those Persons of surprising Genius, the Authors of immense Romances, or the modern Novel and *Atalantis* Writers; who without any Assistance from Nature or History, record Persons who never were, or will be, and Facts which never did nor possibly can happen." Though Fielding affects admiration of romance writers' creative powers, he eventually yokes a derogatory image from Voltaire with a phrase from *Paradise Lost* to suggest his real views of them: they are carried, he says, at "*an irregular Pace*" upon the unnatural "*Stilts*" they have assumed, "far out of the sight of the Reader, *Beyond the Realm of Chaos and old Night*" (187–88). The echo of Milton, though brief, seems to confer on his poem a special authority in this contention between genres: Fielding invokes Milton not to place his poem within the critical taxonomy he has been sketching, but rather to place that critical taxonomy within *Paradise Lost*'s own cosmology, effectively damning romance writers to the realm of its infernal reaches.[11]

When Fielding goes on to explain what he means by biography, and to apply the term to "the Work before us," he suggests an unexpected though distant consonance of his own work with Milton's poem. "Biographers," it emerges, speak more truth than historians because they represent true-to-life characters that need not be confined to any particular place or time: *Don Quixote*, for example, "is the History of the World in general, at least that Part which is polished by Laws, Arts and Sciences; and of that from the time it was first polished to this day; nay and forwards, as long as it shall so remain." Fielding declares his own "History" to be like *Don Quixote* in this way, asserting "once for all" that he describes "not Men, but Manners; not an Individual, but a Species," and that the lawyer he has portrayed, for example, "is not only alive, but hath been so these 4000 Years." Fielding sees his fiction, then, as providing an account of a species, or of human experience from the beginning. This makes his project, in its own way, something like Milton's in *Paradise Lost*—except that he marks the beginning of his "History of the World in general" differently, taking as Cervantes' and his own subject "that Part which is polished by Laws, Arts and Sciences." His is the history of a specifically civilized and postlapsarian world, dated from the moment "when the first mean selfish Creature appeared on the human Stage, who made Self the Centre of the whole Creation" (188–89).

While his work takes its authority from "Nature" and from "Life," its claim to generality and age-old reference will prove crucial for Fielding's negotiation of its relation to satire. Though Fielding had satirized contemporary individuals over and over in his popular dramatic satires, he here invokes the familiar distinction between general and particular satire, and insists that his intention is not "to *mimick* some little obscure Fellow," nor "to expose one pitiful Wretch, to the small and contemptible Circle of his Acquaintance; but to hold the Glass to thousands in their Closets, that they may contemplate their Deformity, and endeavour to reduce it, and thus by suffering private Mortification may avoid public Shame" (189; my emphasis). In fact, he not only disclaims any intention of particular satire, but denies that such should be dignified by the name of satire at all: "This places the Boundary between, and distinguishes the Satirist from the Libeller; for the former privately corrects the Fault for the Benefit of the Person, like a Parent; the latter publickly exposes the Person himself, as an Example to others, like an Executioner." Fielding thus disposes of certain potential problems with satire—the violence and humiliation inflicted by its moral judgments, for example—by simply casting out some of its most problematic forms and calling them something else, something that adamantly rejects them as improper ("Libel"). But this dismissal or disowning of satire's more problematic side serves only for the moment: the boundaries Fielding here establishes prove hard to hold (we recall, for one thing, the character of Beau Didapper), and a troubled contemplation of satire, violence, and public exposure will return in narrative form in chapter 6 of the book, mediated in a more extended way by the model of Milton's epic.

In the meantime, the very next chapter of book 3 opens with another reference to Milton—who had been directly referred to only once in the novel's first two books (92)—and the narrative situation of the first half of 3.2 might almost seem a gothic-comic rendering of the intrusion of past literary voices. When Fielding tells us that the travelers have had to stop because of the night's darkness, he confides that the cloudy, starless sky "was indeed, according to *Milton*, Darkness visible." The phrase again invokes the home of Milton's fallen angels, although the palpable darkness encountered by these innocent travelers does not seem especially congruent with that of hell. The effects of this darkness, however, are suggestive: it cuts the would-be reader off from his text—Adams "lamented the loss of his

dear *Æschylus*; but was a little comforted, when reminded, that if he
had it in his possession, he could not see to read"—and at the same
time unleashes a number of disembodied, misidentified voices. Adams and Joseph see lights and then Adams suddenly hears "several
Voices which he thought almost at his Elbow, tho' in fact they were
not so extremely near." The voices speak of murder and killing, and
Adams responds to them by repeating aloud a fragment in Latin
from the *Aeneid*. He is convinced that the murderous voices are
"Ghosts" or "Spirits" (and never does give over this suspicion entirely). The three hear battling, at a distance, in the dark; but when
they hasten away, Adams suffers a literal as well as bathetic fall, roll-
ing down a steep hill so rapidly that, could they have seen it, Fanny
and Joseph "would scarce have refrained laughing" (192–94). Their
experience of epic danger, too, soon suffers a bathetic deflation:
when the travelers arrive at the Wilsons', they learn that the "Mur-
derers" were just sheep-stealers, and that the twelve Persons they
heard them refer to murdering "were no other than twelve Sheep."
And there, at Joseph's father's house, the questions of genre, quotation, and literary parentage that were addressed in expository but
rather unsystematic form in 3.1, and that floated in fragmentary narrative form in this first half of 3.2, are given focus as Wilson ex-
amines Adams on the *Iliad* to test his identity as a clergyman.

Adams begins unpromisingly by failing to answer Wilson's
questions about Pope's translation of Homer and then seems eager
to derail the discussion from Homer to his beloved Aeschylus, but
when asked "what Part of the *Iliad* he thought most excellent," he
quickly and decisively sketches a literary genealogy and a hierarchy
among genres:

it is not without Reason therefore that the Philosopher, in the 22d Chapter
of his *Poeticks*, mentions [Homer] by no other Appellation than that of *The
Poet*: He was the Father of the Drama, as well as the Epic: Not of Tragedy
only, but of Comedy also; for his *Margites*, which is deplorably lost, bore,
says *Aristotle*, the same Analogy to Comedy, as his *Odyssey* and *Iliad* to Tragedy. To him therefore we owe *Aristophanes*, as well as *Euripides*, *Sophocles*,
and my poor *Æschylus*. (197–98)

This dialogue about literary models within the novel recalls Fielding's introduction to the novel and his account of the generic ancestors of his own work. In justifying the classification of his novel as
a "comic Epic-Poem in Prose" in his preface to the book, he too

refs to the great "Pattern" of Homer's comic epic, now "entirely lost," and makes the same analogy between the two modes of ancient epic and comic versus tragic dramatic forms (3). Adams's account, however, adds to the analogy the clear subordination of drama to epic by making it directly derivative; and Adams extends his claims for epic over drama—and therefore, implicitly, for the book in which he appears, as defined by its preface—as he rises to the rapturous conclusion of his remarks. Adams asserts the great inferiority, in particular, of Sophocles' "Imitation" of Homer's treatment of Andromache, singles out the epic poet's descriptive creation of "Scenery" for special praise, and then simply turns himself over to the language of the poem he so loves, rapping out "a hundred *Greek* Verses, and with such a Voice, Emphasis and Action, that he almost frighten'd the Women" (199).

For the moment, Adams's speech serves to relegate dramatic forms to the place of inferior imitation of epic ones, as Fielding's prefatory chapter to this book had seemed to domesticate satire by banishing its more problematic applications from the realm of literature and assimilating its others to a genre of mythic "history." But drama and satire, the characteristic medium and mode of Fielding's earlier career, reappear as powerful and unruly forces within the narrative of *Joseph Andrews* as soon as Adams, Joseph, and Fanny have left the Wilsons' house. Before they leave, they and we spend a long night with Wilson as he relates to Adams the story of his life. Within the proto-novelistic form of the spiritual autobiography, this interpolated tale contains and flattens satiric materials—Wilson's life as a beau, his acquaintance with the hypocritical Free-thinkers and Deists, his rejection of women, which he compares to Juvenal's (citing Juvenal's *Sixth Satire*, a poem that Fielding had translated earlier in his life)—and it includes comments on the stage, where Wilson had tried to make a living. Wilson's blending of forms somehow renders all of them inert.[12] In the aftermath of the travelers' visit to the Wilsons, however, in their encounter with the Roasting-Squire and his men, the forms of drama and satire will again be represented within the novel's narrative, and represented not as neatly contained or subordinated by epic models, but in confused conflict with them.

The man referred to by critics as the "Roasting-Squire" bursts into the action of *Joseph Andrews* in book 3, chapter 6, and dominates the few chapters that follow. In the two scenes primarily centered on him Fielding carefully stages a generic conflict, a tension between forms created by the language he chooses to describe those scenes, as well as a physical conflict between the forces of the Squire and of Adams, Joseph, and Fanny. At the same time, he bodies forth in the Squire the negative dimensions of conventional masculine identity that Joseph may be created to evade. When the Roasting-Squire first appears he not only invades a peaceful natural scene of rest for the three main characters, galloping into their idyll with his followers in a hunt, but he disrupts and dispels a kind of alternative space within the novel constructed carefully out of echoes from Milton's *Paradise Lost*. While the clearly signaled allusions to Milton in the first two chapters of book 3 both referred us to the hell of *Paradise Lost*'s book I, Fielding's description of the meadow in which Adams, Fanny, and Joseph take a respite from their travels quietly echoes Milton's description of Eden in book IV, making the meadow a specifically Edenic scene.[13]

Fielding describes Fanny and Joseph's "dalliance" in this retreat in terms close to that of Adam and Eve's: the word "dalliance" itself recalls Milton's first description of Adam and Eve in Eden (*PL*, IV.338), and the word "Rivulet" with which he describes the stream that edges the meadow will be used later in *Paradise Lost* to denote the stream by which Adam and Eve sit (IV.336 and IX.420). Fielding had echoed the same passage in book IV earlier, in his reference to Joseph's "wanton Ringlets." Here he emphasizes the absence of witnesses to Fanny and Joseph's dalliance, as to that of the first couple. But the force of the allusion resides not only in the investment of the scene with Edenic overtones, but in the very act of invoking Milton's Christian epic, suggesting an alternative tradition both to Richardson's precedent and to the satiric and dramatic forms Fielding himself had earlier employed. The most extended echo of *Paradise Lost* in this passage comes in the description of the spot itself, "one of the beautifullest Spots of Ground in the Universe":

It was a kind of natural Amphitheatre, formed by the winding of a small Rivulet, which was planted with thick Woods, and the Trees rose gradually above each other by the natural Ascent of the Ground they stood on; which Ascent, as they hid with their Boughs, they seemed to have been disposed by the Design of the most skillful Planter. The Soil was spread with a Verdure which no Paint could imitate. (232)

Fielding recalls Milton's description of the ascending trees above Eden, and repeats his word "verdurous" (*PL*, IV. 143) in praising the scene, but he most closely echoes Milton's reference to Eden as a "woody Theatre."

> and over head up grew
> Insuperable highth of loftiest shade,
> Cedar, and Pine, and Fir, and branching Palm,
> A Silvan Scene, and as the ranks ascend
> Shade above shade, a woody Theatre
> Of stateliest view.   (IV. 137–42)

In calling his own beautiful spot of ground a "natural Amphitheatre" Fielding at once, through the echo, introduces Milton's Christian epic as an alternative space of literary tradition within his novel and suggests an identification of Edenic retreat with an escape from drama, or at least a naturalizing of drama's forum. The verdure of the scene is beyond what "Paint could imitate" in a stage set; if we recall Adams's comparison of dramatic and epic scenery—"did ever Painter imagine a Scene like that in the 13th and 14th Iliads?"— we might identify what lies "beyond what Paint could imitate" here as both epic and natural landscape. And the "Dalliance" in which Fanny and Joseph indulge once they discover that Adams has fallen asleep is one, Fielding tells us, which, "tho' consistent with the purest Innocence and Decency, neither he would have attempted, nor she permitted before any Witness" (236). Milton tells us that Adam's and Eve's innocent sensuality also was absolutely nontheatrical, dependent, like Joseph's and Fanny's, on its freedom from witnesses. They did not want for

> youthful dalliance as beseems
> Fair couple, linkt in happy nuptial League,
> Alone as they. About them frisking play'd
> All Beasts of th' Earth, since wild, and of all chase
> In Wood or Wilderness   (IV. 338–42)

But into the peaceable kingdom of innocent sexual pleasure and Miltonic allusion comes bursting the Roasting-Squire's hunt in relentless pursuit of a hare, and that hare is immediately associated with one version of feminine weakness, described as a "silly Creature," "spent and weak," and "fainting almost at every Step," while the Roasting-Squire provides a version of violent masculinity that implicates both satire and the drama. Before this invasion, Joseph had been discoursing on Charity while lingering in the natural amphitheatre they have found, and as he muses on the honor to be won by acts of charity he asserts: "I defy the wisest Man in the World to turn a true good Action into Ridicule. I defy him to do it. He who should endeavour it, would be laughed at himself, instead of making others laugh" (234). With the arrival of the Roasting-Squire, however, Joseph's rhetorical claims are quickly contradicted. The Squire is "a great Lover of Humour," Fielding tells us, or "not to mince the matter . . . a great *Hunter of Men*"; and when his hunting dogs literalize this phrase by turning their attack from the hare to Adams, the Squire is thrown into "a violent Fit of Laughter" by Joseph's loyalty and courage in defending his friend. This Squire, who is called "manly" and "authoritative" and who is repeatedly referred to as the "master"—"the Master of the Pack," "the Master of this House," and "Master of his own Fortune" (238, 244, 245)—is identified with satire at greater length when Fielding describes his character in the chapter that follows this one.

What distinguished him chiefly, was a strange Delight which he took in every thing which is ridiculous, odious, and absurd in his own Species; so that he never chose a Companion without one or more of these Ingredients . . . if he ever found a Man who either had not or endeavoured to conceal these Imperfections, he took great pleasure in inventing Methods of forcing him into Absurdities, which were not natural to him, or in drawing forth and exposing those that were; for which purpose he was always provided with a Set of Fellows whom we have before called Curs . . . Their Business was to hunt out and display every thing that had any Savour of the above mentioned Qualities . . . But if they failed in their Search, they were to turn even Virtue and Wisdom themselves into Ridicule for the Diversion of their Master and Feeder. (245)

The word "ridiculous" identifies what the Roasting-Squire takes a strange delight in seeking out with what Fielding says the legitimate object of his own humor will be in his preface to this novel; but the Squire shows the satiric impulse used irresponsibly and even violently, creating imperfections where it cannot find them, and contradicting Joseph's assurance that laughter is necessarily moral in its choice of objects.[14] Joseph's idealization of laughter's force is exploded before the chapter is over, and so is Fielding's confidence, in the first chapter of this book, that satire can always be separated from libel. The Squire uses the economic and social power of his masculine position as "Master" to turn laughter against innocent objects—and, specifically, against a series of feminized figures—first the hare, who is described in just the terms Watt associates with the new feminine ideal epitomized by Pamela;[15] then Adams, who is ridiculed as feminine in his role of cleric; and, finally and most seriously, Fanny, who is threatened with the violence of rape. In the episode that follows that of the man-hunt, Adams is a guest at the Squire's table, and the practical jokes played on him make the Squire's home a kind of dark House of Satire, a space in which the possibility that satiric aggression is continuous with crude physical abuse can be explored within this novel whose preface seems to commit itself to the practice of satire.

But in the first entrance of the Roasting-Squire into the idyllic scene of book 3, chapter 6, he and his followers represent not only the intrusion of satiric forces into a harmonious Eden but the fall of the natural amphitheatre into the realm of witnessed and conventional drama. The dogs that attack Adams bear names from a hunting song in Thomas D'Urfey's play, *The Marriage-hater Matched*;[16] and the two of the Squire's followers we see the most of are a poet and a player, who argue at length about the theater while Fanny is being carried off to face possible rape (259–64). Significantly, Joseph beats the dogs off Adams with a cudgel that conjures and then effaces scenes from Fielding's own satiric drama. The narrator begins to describe what was intended to be engraved on the cudgel—the first night of a play by Lord Hervey, and Mr. Cock the auctioneer in his pulpit—but then says the workman "was forced to leave all out for want of room" (239–40). As we saw in Chapter 1, Hervey and Cock both had been objects of Fielding's satire in his plays, specifically as figures of ambiguous gender. Here, Joseph seems to contain and control the possibility of his own implication in their kind of satiric dramatic role when he wields the cudgel against the Squire's dogs. (Fielding asks us to imagine the possibility of a cudgel inscribed with scenes of the dimension and movement and even sound of something on stage—and then collapses them, rejecting them as unsupported by the kind of "room" to be found on a cudgel.) In pausing to give the history of Joseph's cudgel Fielding comically recalls Homer's description of the shield of Achilles in the *Iliad*, combating the invasion of the natural amphitheater by the forces of dramatic satire with the conventions of epic, even as rendered mere mock-epic.

In the chapter following the battle between Joseph and the

Squire's dogs, we are shown the crude forms the Squire and his followers employ to expose the Ridiculous in which they delight. In a chapter entitled "A Scene of Roasting," the Squire's men play a series of practical jokes on Adams, culminating in one which reintroduces the background context of Milton's *Paradise Lost,* this time not to project an Edenic state that satire destroys but to provide a damning account of the origins of satire by placing it within the larger frame of Christian epic. Within that frame, as constructed by the particular passage Fielding echoes here, satire is the form belonging to the rebelling angels. After Adams has been invited to take the woman's part in a dance with the lame dancing-master (for, the dancing-master says, "his Cassock would serve for Petticoats"), the captain plays a more violent joke upon Adams by pinning what's called at different points both a "Devil" and a "Serpent"—kinds of firecrackers—to Adams's cassock. When he lights it, Adams, we are told, "believing he had been blown up in reality, started from his Chair, and jumped about the Room, to the infinite Joy of the Beholders, who declared he was the best Dancer in the Universe. As soon as the Devil had done tormenting him, and he had a little recovered his Confusion, he returned to the Table" (247).

On the surface of the passage, the terms "Devil" and "Serpent" that Fielding uses for the firecracker might evoke the fallen angels in a trivial and general way, while Adams's name echoes that of the innocent original man who is corrupted by their evil. Fielding's description of Adams's torment, however, more specifically recalls Milton's account of the fallen angels' attack upon the ranks of the faithful on the second day of the War in Heaven. This is the day on which they first employ their new and distinctly fallen invention of firearms.[17] The faithful angels are baffled by the engines discharged at them, and wonder what to do:

> if on they rush'd repulse
> Repeated, and indecent overthrow
> Doubl'd, would render them yet more despis'd,
> And to thir foes a laughter

Indeed, Satan is already laughing, calling to his mates "in derision":

> O Friends, why come not on these Victors proud?
> Erewhile they fierce were coming, and when wee,
> To entertain them fair with open Front

And Breast, (what could we more?) propounded terms
Of composition, straight they chang'd thir minds,
Flew off, and into strange vagaries fell,
As they would dance, yet for a dance they seem'd
Somewhat extravagant and wild, perhaps
For joy of offer'd peace   (VI.600–617)

Satan's speech provides the source for the Squire's men's wit-
ticism that the devil-tormented Adams must be "the best Dancer in
the Universe." It also typifies a way of speaking that seems to be
another of the fallen angels' inventions on this second day of the War
in Heaven. Throughout the passage, they speak in "scoffing" or
"ambiguous words," and their word-play consistently has to do
with ambiguous terms that seem to refer to verbal negotiations for
peace and really refer to the violent "argument" of artillery.[18]
Through this allusion Fielding not only associates the Roasting-
Squire and his followers with the fallen angels but invokes a context
in which satire may be suspected of passing off forms of physical
violence under the claims of purely verbal negotiation.

The distinction that Fielding has made in the introductory
chapter to book 3 anticipates this idea, with its striking and severe
image for particular satire or what he calls libel: "for the former [gen-
eral satire] privately corrects the Fault for the Benefit of the Person,
like a Parent; the latter publickly exposes the Person himself, as an
Example to others, like an Executioner." Fielding explains his distinction between forms of verbal aggression—one analogous to parental correction, the other to fatal violence—in terms not only of
their different objects, particular or general, but of their different forums, private or public. Fielding's association of illegitimate forms
of satire with witnessed public exposure may help explain the way
drama and satire appear together as the two literary provinces of the
Roasting-Squire's abuses of authority. Of course, earlier in his career, Fielding had joined drama and satire in practice in his highly
successful topical plays, which he termed "dramatic satires." But in
Joseph Andrews, the Roasting-Squire and his men present a very diminished and unflattering picture of theatrical means: the dancing-
master "mimics" Adams from a distance, and the Squire's servants
construct a throne for the final practical joke played against Adams
out of stools, a tub, and a blanket, like a stage-set's tacky and perilous
imitation of grandeur.

Fielding tells us in the first chapter of book 3 that it would be a mistake to think that his satirically conceived lawyer "endeavours to mimick some little obscure Fellow" in particular, and in 3.7 he works to separate his act of recounting the practical jokes against Adams from the Squire's followers' engineering of them.[19] But the intent to expose the ridiculous that he declares in his preface to the novel remains dangerously close to their preoccupations, and they enact within the novel those applications of laughter that the preface warns us would express "very diabolical Natures." In a general way, Fielding associates the Squire's delight in and encouragement of "every thing which is ridiculous, odious, and absurd in his own Species" with the devil.[20] (For example, when Adams discovers that the Squire's men have also stolen his half guinea he exclaims, "Sure the Devil must have taken it from me" [254]). More particularly, he uses the echoes of *Paradise Lost* in 3.7 to frame the Squire's misapplication of satire with Milton's story about the fallen angels' invention of both gunpowder's violence and ambiguous, antagonistic word-play on the second day of the War in Heaven. At the same time, the echoes of Milton serve to suggest a tradition alternative to those of drama and satire so severely questioned in this episode.[21]

Fielding's use of *Paradise Lost*, however, does not imply that Milton can provide an easy escape from the problematics of genre, gender, and social behavior that occupy *Joseph Andrews*. The echoes of book IV of *Paradise Lost* in the novel—in the descriptions of Joseph's hair and of the "natural Amphitheatre"—invoke the Eden described there and, with it, a kind of Edenic space of epic tradition within Fielding's mixed mode. But in the passage in book IV of *Paradise Lost* that Fielding twice recalls, the fall already shadows Eden, and it shadows it specifically through the presence of an unsuspected witness—the devil-intruder whom we have followed into the garden—in what should be a "woody Theatre" without audience. When Adam and Eve indulge in a "youthful dalliance as beseems / Fair couple, linkt in happy nuptial League, / Alone as they," they are not alone: Satan looks on. The conversion of experience into dramatic spectacle describes, specifically, the fallen nature of erotic life in this novel, as we have seen in the characters of Beau Didapper and Lady Booby. And when Fielding gently conjures the pocket of Eden within the world of *Joseph Andrews* as the travelers stop in their beautiful meadow, he then quickly reminds us that their social world is a fallen one; a figure of corrupt social and economic power soon intrudes into the scene and transforms it into one of violence and public humiliation. Fielding's other echoes, significantly, are of Milton's hell and of the War in Heaven which led to it. The inversion of genders in Fielding's allusion to Eve's "wanton Ringlets" reminded us of the distance between Joseph's world and Adam and Eve's, and also of the distance between Richardson and Fielding's world and Milton's. But Fielding's use of echoes of *Paradise Lost* is not entirely nostalgic: in his complex evocation of Milton's War in Heaven, Fielding reminds us of the generic problems and limitations of Christian epic itself as well as of satire.

Fielding chooses to echo a scene from *Paradise Lost* in which the epic form which he introduces as an alternative tradition to satiric drama itself seems questionably viable, teetering, unintentionally, on the brink of mock-epic. With his own flair for burlesque and mock-epic bathos, Fielding could not have missed the odd tonalities of the book in *Paradise Lost* in which we are asked to imagine, for example, that when the artillery hit the faithful angels, "angel on archangel rolled." As Samuel Johnson was to comment, "the confusion of spirit and matter which pervades the whole narration of the war in heaven fills it with incongruity."[22] Fielding had expressed his interest in just this confusion when he capitalized upon its burlesque possibilities in *The Author's Farce* and in *Tom Thumb*, where ghosts are threatened by swords, and he would again in "Journey from This World to the Next" (where, for example, a question arises as to whether there is enough room in the coach traveling to the afterlife to accommodate the spirits of all the recently dead). At times in Fielding's plays, as we have seen, a burlesque confusion between matter and spirit coincides with the burlesque of gender confusion, as Fielding draws upon an uneasy but profound alignment of sexual and ontological oppositions; when we reencounter the male-female, matter-spirit association in our study of *Amelia*, we will find Fielding invoking that alignment in quite another mood. In *Paradise Lost*, the confusion of matter and spirit not only pervades the episode of the War in Heaven but, as Dr. Johnson observes, troubles Milton's project of translating the epic into Christian terms throughout. Though critics have emphasized Fielding's difference from Richardson in his knowledge of classical languages and traditions, the epic that Fielding engages in the most extended and complex way in *Joseph Andrews* is the great epic written in English and shaped by modern faith, with all the contradictions and promise of such a project.

Fielding's use of *Paradise Lost* in the scenes of *Joseph Andrews* involving the Roasting-Squire shows him meditating upon the possibilities and problems in the various literary traditions feeding into his new form, the novel. These generic concerns are complexly intertwined with the issues of gender and sexuality that his novel's opening ploy foregrounded. Within the epic tradition, Milton's poem provides a model for a work that attempts to redefine the heroic, and that places both a male *and* a female hero at its center. At the same time, within a response to the immediate precedent of Richardson's *Pamela*, Milton's poem appears as a representative for the eighteenth century of a view of sexuality very different from Richardson's. Though Richardson at times uses allusions to Milton for his own purposes, within *Joseph Andrews* echoes of *Paradise Lost* recall the mutual sensuality of love in Milton's Eden, the attachments to earthly and erotic bonds that his spiritual drama includes, in the face of Richardson's intense focus on the ideal of the "decarnalised woman" and on female chastity as the locus of sexuality.[23] Finally, the extended recollections of *Paradise Lost* that surround the figure of the Roasting-Squire offer a dark perspective on the "masculine" exercise of satire in which the Roasting-Squire so delights. That dark perspective on satire helps us understand some of what was at stake in imagining a new kind of hero in Joseph, one that might initially, at least, have something in common with "those soft Italian warblers" Fielding had rejected in his plays.

Through Joseph's implication in feminine roles Fielding also develops a less purely critical argument: Joseph's feminized identity becomes the means by which Fielding attempts to imagine some positive response to the fall from Eden, which "brought Death into the World, and all our Woe." As we shall find in Chapter 4, Joseph's compromised gender identity functions in the elegiac and sentimental operations of the novel, as well as in its reflections on its own satiric vein.

FOUR

"The Exact Picture of His Mother"

Misrecognitions, Mortal Loss, and Joseph's Promise of Reunion

> "O Sir," cried *Joseph*, "all this is very true, and very fine; and I could hear you all day, if I was not so grieved at Heart as now I am."
>
> —Fielding, *Joseph Andrews*

Joseph's cry, interrupting Adams's long exposition of the comforts of philosophy and Christian submission, at once acknowledges the integrity of Adams's arguments and asserts their irrelevance to the feeling they claim to address—Joseph's present grief at Fanny's abduction by the servants of the Roasting-Squire. The two men have been left together at the inn, tied "back to back" to a bedpost by Fanny's abductors, and the dialogue between them that constitutes book 3, chapter 11, of *Joseph Andrews* might be said to bring back to back separate human "truths" of reason and of feeling—to place them in a forced conjunction, but looking off in diverse directions rather than confronting each other face to face. The scene provides an emblem for a quality that a number of critics have admired in Fielding's fiction: his willingness to sustain "unresolved dualities" or to "wrestle central contradictions . . . only to a standoff";[1] Joseph's exclamation, with its twinned acceptance and rejection of offered principles, seems to me the characterizing cry of *Joseph Andrews*.

Henry Knight Miller gives one pair of names to the "unresolved dualities" in Fielding's work when he cites Joseph's exclamation as evidence of Fielding's willingness to value "feminine" feeling as well as "masculine" reason, adapting the gender terms that have always been used to contrast Fielding's "masculine" sensibility with Richardson's "feminine" sentimentalism to describe a tension he sees within Fielding's work itself. Miller observes this tension specifically as it appears in Fielding's treatment of diverse responses to the prospect of loss: noting what he calls an "elegiac undertone" in Fielding's comedies, Miller argues that Fielding gives "equal weight" or value to Joseph's resistance to Adams's stoic philosophy and to Heartfree's "manly firmness of behavior" at parting with his children for what seems the last time (*Jonathan Wild*, 4.5). He thus calls our attention to the recurrent threat of final partings in Fielding's comic novels, and he employs the terms of gender to characterize alternative responses to that threat, responses that he feels Fielding, at different moments, honors equally.[2]

Miller employs these terms, however, in an admittedly impressionistic way, placing them always in quotation marks and assuming that Fielding's implicit definitions of "feminine" and "masculine" values rely upon those of the eighteenth century as a whole. Miller implicates Joseph in the "feminine" through his citation of Joseph's cry, but he does not suggest that this moment characterizes Joseph more generally or partakes of any larger problematics of gender within the novel. As we have seen, from the first chapters of *Joseph Andrews*, Fielding actively places Joseph in feminine roles; and he uses allusion, description, and narrative event to sustain and extend Joseph's identification with the female, developing an increasingly complicated, contextual meaning for this identification in the course of the novel. Beginning as a means to parody Richardson, Fielding's construction of a compromised gender identity for his title character becomes not just a device of comedy but a vehicle for an imaginative negotiation between opposite allegiances traditionally systematized by gender. The prospect of mortal loss appears repeatedly in *Joseph Andrews* as a kind of crisis, or moment of reckoning, for the conflicting loyalties that Fielding customarily holds in suspension together; and the two terms of gender provide the novel with its most abiding structure of double response to the conflicting claims voiced in Joseph's cry.

In Chapter 3 I argued that Joseph's ambiguous gender becomes a means for Fielding to express his own vexed and partial acceptance of the legacies of different literary genres, including the traditionally masculine mode of satire. To accept the validity of satiric method is to accept its assumptions about the proper sources and nature of personal identity: satiric critique exposes divergences from what it assumes as identity's proper constancy, integrity, and autonomy, its rightful independence from affectation or borrowing from other selves. As distant as the scene of loss, elegy, and consolation seems from the scene of satiric ridicule, it too demands the acceptance or rejection of particular assumptions about the nature of individual identity. An expectation that the self is crucially located in and defined by time, by personal feeling, by a sense of identification with and attachment to others, calls for one form of mourning and of comfort; a heroic or stoic view of the self as, at best, abstracted from these features of mortal experience demands quite another. Joseph's characteristic manner of possessing and defining a sense of self ill-suits him to embrace the account of loss and the offer of consolation voiced by Adams in this scene. *Joseph Andrews* suggests a deep, though often obscure connection between the absoluteness with which Joseph claims attachment to his female lover, his own implication in feminine roles, his recurrent association with death, and the alternative form of consolation he eventually gives voice to himself.

In its direct and indirect responses to *Pamela*, *Joseph Andrews* also suggests surprising connections between familiar critical issues of novelistic representation in Fielding's and Richardson's work—third-person versus epistolary form, external versus internal characterization—and the "elegiac undertone" in Fielding's comedies, that bass note of threatened loss sounded in Joseph's expression of grief. Fielding's first novel renders up its own deep and complicated inscription of the costs of the literary and philosophical position it opposes to Richardson's; in it, Fielding comes to different terms with the meaning of substitute, affected, or borrowed gender identity from those accepted by his plays.

What Joseph opposes to his recognition that Adams's arguments are "very true, and very fine" is the "now" of his grief, that present tense of personal feeling that Richardson had represented to famous effect in *Pamela*'s epistolary form. In *Shamela*, Fielding had debunked the epistolary novel's armchair imitation of speaking "to the moment": "—Odsbobs! I hear him just coming in at the door. You see I write in the present tense, as Parson Williams says. Well, he is in bed between us, we both shamming a sleep" (313). In the more complicated project of *Joseph Andrews*, Fielding again includes mockery of *Pamela*'s form. The comedy of Slipslop's confused verbal pretensions seems aimed partly at the surprising literacy of another maid, that little scribbler, Pamela. More obviously, early in the novel, when the parody of *Pamela* most shapes it, Joseph writes his sister Pamela several letters about Lady Booby's attacks on his chastity. Joseph's letters are comic remembrances of Pamela's because they are so much shorter and cruder than hers, mixing high rhetoric and unschooled practical language without the self-consciousness about literary form that Fielding mocks in Shamela's lines above. Joseph's letters are also comic because they are redundant: by the time he sits down to write Pamela about the events that have occurred, we have already received a much fuller account of them from a third-person narrator, so that within this novel the first-person epistolary form actually looks belated, undramatic, somehow even secondhand. While *Shamela* provides only a parodic reduction of Richardson's form of narration, the narrator of *Joseph Andrews* represents an alternative to the counterfeit first-person moment of the epistolary form.

Yet, although Fielding explodes as a sham Richardson's particular means of producing a present tense of personal feeling, in the scene following Fanny's abduction he allows Joseph to voice the insistence of that point of view even alongside an alternative one that attempts to quiet or replace it. Suggestively, as Joseph's response to Adams's arguments moves beyond his recognition of their value to the nonetheless unanswered matter of present feeling, his expression of this insistent second clause of experience falls into the markedly iambic rhythms of drama or of poetry: "if I was not so grieved at Heart as now I am." Joseph's exclamation not only raises the problem of the interior, what's "at Heart," of the sufferer, within a novel consistently described by critics as treating character externally; it also implies the question of what form the expression of spontaneous feeling may take, within a novel that toys repeatedly with the conventionality of verbal expression. As Joseph's and Adams's dia-

logue lapses into silence at the close of the chapter, the one's grief
and the other's "comfort" unable to find common ground, Joseph
will again give voice to spontaneous feeling in the formal rhythms
of verse, "bursting out":

> *Yes, I will bear my Sorrows like a Man,*
> *But I must also feel them as a Man.*
> *I cannot but remember such things were,*
> *And were most dear to me—*

Adams does not recognize Macduff's words from *Macbeth*,[3] and Joseph explains that they are "some Lines he had gotten by heart out
of a Play" (267). Joseph's common phrase, "by heart," renders familiar his experience of formal, indeed memorized, language as personal and immediate, not solving this puzzle but giving it the cast
of the everyday.

The lines Joseph finds to express his grief are at once appropriate and inappropriate to his own situation. The occasion of Macduff's lament, echoed by Joseph, is the news of mortal loss, the death
of his wife and children, while Joseph's loss is of a more uncertain
nature: the Roasting-Squire's abduction of Fanny most directly
threatens Fanny with the enforced loss of her virginity, not her life.[4]
Joseph's quotation of Macduff's lines out of context and his treatment of the consequences of Fanny's abduction throughout the discussion conflate rape with death, implicitly associating mortality
with woman's special vulnerability to sexual coercion, or with the
particular irreversibility of her virginity's loss within a code of female chastity. At the same time, Macduff's response to his loss considers what it is to receive sorrows "like a Man"—he insists that
there is room both for "bearing" and for "feeling" within masculine
grief.[5] As this chapter closes, then, it quietly introduces the terms of
gender into its staging of problems of loss, of reason and feeling,
and of conflicting forms of expression and narration. It is Joseph,
through his quotation of Shakespeare, who frames these problems
within a more expansive definition of the masculine, a definition
that allows for a double response "as a Man."

Joseph's own fitness, however, as a masculine hero has been
thrown into question at the very beginning of the chapter by the narrator, who comments upon that "Heart" that would remain untouched by Joseph's sorrow and adds: "His own, poor Youth, was
of a softer Composition; and at those Words, *O my dear* Fanny! *O*

my Love! shall I never, never see thee more? his Eyes overflowed with Tears, which would have become any but a Hero" (264). The narrator's criticism balances carefully here—it might fall either against Joseph or against the idea of a hero. As we saw in Chapter 2, however, the question of Joseph's fitness as a male hero was raised much earlier, and much more devastatingly, by the joke that initially generated the novel's plot. On the other hand, before we reach the narrator's comment in 3.11, Fielding has provided some skeptical commentary on the very notion of the masculine hero. In the scene in which we first meet Fanny, Adams's crabstick falls unregarded on the head of Fanny's attacker only because, as Fielding explains, Nature had

taken a provident Care . . . to make this part of the Head three times as thick as those of ordinary Men, who are designed to exercise Talents which are vulgarly called rational, and for whom, as Brains are necessary, she is obliged to leave some room for them in the Cavity of the Skull: whereas, those Ingredients being entirely useless to Persons of the heroic Calling, she hath an Opportunity of thickening the Bone . . . and indeed, in some who are predestined to the Command of Armies and Empires, she is supposed sometimes to make that Part perfectly solid. (137–38)

Fielding follows up his identification of this thick-skulled rapist with "Persons of the heroic Calling" with a reference to the "impenetrable" heads of "some modern Heroes, of the lower Class," who can use their heads "like the Battering-Ram of the Ancients, for a Weapon of Offence." As in *Jonathan Wild*, he equates lower-class criminals with public military and political leaders; as in the *Champion* essays on vanity, male coxcombs, and the present "Wooden Age," he suggests that a man's reliance on force—whether a public official's reliance on institutional authority or a poor man's reliance on physical strength—turns him into a kind of solidified puppet, which might as well have been made of straw, brass, or wood, as of guts and skin.[6] In this scene, the aggression of the lignified hero poses a specifically sexual threat to a woman. Perhaps, then, in the next episode in which Fanny is threatened with rape— the scene of her abduction—if Joseph's tears, "which would have become any but a Hero," reflect some limitation in his character, they at least distinguish him from one ironically conceived kind of hero, the "impenetrable" ravishers that surround Fanny. The question of what kind of puppet or wooden effigy Joseph would make was raised several times in the first book of the novel, and linked to the question of his masculinity: Joseph fails in the fields as a human scarecrow because of the sweetness of his voice, and the description of this failure associates him with the Italian castrato singers (21–22); pages later, Slipslop is clearly misrepresenting Joseph on both counts when, after he has rebuffed her advances, she tells Lady Booby that he is "horribly *indicted* to Wenching" and "as ugly a Scarecrow as I ever *upheld*" (35).

Even as he deflates the notions of feminine virtue and feminine feeling that Richardson had exploited in *Pamela*, Fielding interrogates traditional notions of the masculine hero in *Joseph Andrews*, suggesting that heroic roles may only aggrandize destructive aggression and may be as void of individual and spontaneous life as public effigies. Fielding renegotiates the conventional idea of a literary hero—seen under pressure in Joseph's cry and in the narrator's comment upon his tears, as well as in the ironic labeling of Fanny's ravisher—largely through the terms of gender. If Joseph's feminized heroism at times implicitly, glancingly, complicates Fielding's rejection of Richardson's first-person epistolary form, it also comes to express a wistfulness, or an element of regret, in his choice of "external" over "internal" methods of characterization. More immediately, within the novel's dialogue and plot, Joseph is allowed to speak for a response to threatened loss that is linked to female values, yet not deprecated.

The scene of apparent loss and of offered consolation that prompts Joseph's cry recurs later in the novel, though this time with Adams in the position of the bereaved and Joseph the comforter. Adams has in fact been delivering another speech to Joseph about submission to Providence in response to Joseph's fears for Fanny's safety when "one came hastily in and acquainted Mr. *Adams* that his youngest Son was drowned." Joseph attempts to comfort the parson, who begins to "deplore his Loss with the bitterest Agony," with arguments from his own discourses—which Adams himself now finds irrelevant to the matter of present personal grief. But when Adams's lament becomes most pained, with a question that closely echoes Joseph's after Fanny's abduction—"'My poor *Jacky*, shall I never see thee more?'"—Joseph answers with what seems a spontaneous affirmation, words of consolation not repeated from Adams's lectures: "'Yes, surely,' says *Joseph*, 'and in a better Place, you will meet again never to part more'" (308–9). The promise of a lasting reunion offered here by Joseph provides a very different form of comfort than does the imperative for acceptance of final partings presented by Adams earlier. In this scene, Joseph must present his own response to the claims of present feeling rather than simply reject Adams's response; and, though the interests have turned from comic to elegiac at this moment in the novel, Joseph's compromised gender position, at first apparently only a source of the ridiculous, remains crucial to recognizing and understanding the alternative he offers. It is here to have become a more substantial resource. But how?

The news soon arrives, in the person of Adams's son himself, that the report of his drowning was premature. After a joyful reunion, the parson turns back to Joseph and resumes his lecture on the sin of carnal attachments and on a man's duty not to "set his Heart on any Person or Thing in this World, but that whenever it shall be required or taken from him in any manner by Divine Providence, he may be able, peaceably, quietly, and contentedly to resign it" (308). Joseph finally loses his patience, protesting the contradiction between Adams's words and conduct, and when Adams insists on a difference between paternal and conjugal love, Joseph refuses to wish to restrain his love for Fanny:

"Well, sir," cries *Joseph*, "and if I love a Mistress as well as you your Child, surely her Loss would grieve me equally." "Yes, but such Love is Foolishness, and wrong in itself, and ought to be conquered," answered *Adams*, "it savours too much of the Flesh." "Sure, Sir," says *Joseph*, "it is not sinful to love my Wife, no not even to doat on her to Distraction!" "Indeed but it is," says *Adams*. "Every Man ought to love his Wife, no doubt; we are commanded so to do; but we ought to love her with Moderation and Discretion."—"I am afraid I shall be guilty of some Sin, in spight of all my Endeavours," says *Joseph*; "for I shall love without any Moderation, I am sure." (310)

Joseph earlier faced the same spiritual conflict between his love for Fanny and his sense of a duty higher than mortal attachments when he was counseled by Barnabas in the expectation of his own death. Joseph admits to Barnabas (whose name, ironically, means "the son of consolation," underlining the importance of this issue in the novel)[7] that "there was one thing which he knew not whether he should call a Sin," and "that was the Regret of parting with a young Woman, whom he loved as tenderly as he did his Heartstrings"—

Barnabas bad him be assured, "that any Repining at the Divine Will, was one of the greatest Sins he could commit; that he ought to forget all carnal Affections, and think of better things." *Joseph* said, "that neither in this World nor the next, he could forget his *Fanny*, and that the Thought, however grievous, of parting from her for ever, was not half so tormenting, as the Fear of what she would suffer when she knew his Misfortune." *Barnabas* said, "that such Fears argued a Diffidence and Despondence very criminal; that he must divest himself of all human Passion, and fix his Heart above." (59)

Although in the context of the domestic novel Joseph's absolute devotion to Fanny may seem far from "very criminal" or "one of the greatest Sins he could commit," we might recall that, within Milton's account of the fall, it is just this error that leads Adam into catastrophic transgression of God's will. What Joseph confesses to Barnabas, and later to Adams, is what the Adam of *Paradise Lost* confesses to Raphael before the fall (VIII. 521–94), and the cause that Milton assigns for Adam's participation in the fall when it comes (IX. 896–999). When Eve offers the forbidden fruit to Adam, having eaten of it herself, he knowingly chooses his attachment to her over obedience to God and deathless life. Adam makes the wrong choice, and Milton explains his choice as the result of his too absolute attachment to Eve: his unwillingness to break the "Bond of Nature" that draws him to a female self is what involves him first in death. Yet this passage in Milton's narrative of the fall evokes confusedly mixed emotions in most readers: the reader may share the fallen Eve's tender emotion at the testimony of Adam's love, his "choice to incur / Divine displeasure for her sake, or Death" (IX. 990–93), though Milton passes scathing judgment on it in the lines that follow. At least one eighteenth-century reader took Adam's description of his admiration for Eve as something to be emulated, overlooking Raphael's response to it with "contracted brow" (VIII. 560); the editor of *The Royal Female Magazine* concludes his introduction to the journal by expressing the "ardent devotion to [women's] real interest" that has overbalanced his fears in undertaking the project, quoting Adam's words to Raphael (VIII. 547–59) as his own proud declaration of respect.[8]

Fielding draws out the ambivalence of Milton's simultaneous poignant evocation of Adam's passion for Eve and devastating moral commentary on it when he gives the already fallen Joseph a similar spiritual conflict, but he more clearly sides with the claims of mortal attachments. He discredits both of the spiritual advisers who exhort Joseph to struggle against such an earthly claim: Barnabas's answers to Joseph's appeals for spiritual guidance are hasty, formulaic, and vague, and his real interests lie in the company and punch waiting for him downstairs (58–60); Adams's own behavior, which contradicts his earnest rhetoric, is presented more sympathetically than his words. Nonetheless, like Milton, Fielding suggests that his hero's relationship to death has something to do with his committed connection to female identity.

We discover at the end of the novel that the fates and identities of Joseph and the woman "whom he loved as tenderly as he did his Heartstrings" are historically more closely linked than they or we had known: their past literalizes in an odd way the identification created between them by their love, for in a brief interval they occupy the same space in the Andrews cradle, and then Joseph takes over Fanny's place in the Andrews family. As we noted in Chapter 2, the gypsies seem to have left Joseph in Fanny's place because of his closeness to death: Mrs. Andrews describes how she returned to the cradle and found "instead of my own Girl that I had put into the Cradle, who was as fine a fat thriving Child as you shall see in a Summer's Day, a poor sickly Boy, that did not seem to have an Hour to live" (337). Suckled and soon loved by Mrs. Andrews, Joseph returns to life, but even as a strong and brawny twenty-one-year-old, Joseph is repeatedly seen in postures of apparent death. We will consider a particularly interesting example of this pattern later, but it appears most insistently in the episodes following Joseph's beating by the highwaymen. In chapters 12 through 14 of book 1, Joseph is referred to eight or nine times by different characters as a "dead man": the postilion who stops the coach for him says "he was certain there was a *dead* Man lying in the Ditch, for he heard him groan" (52); Joseph himself says he is "almost dead with the Cold" (53); Betty imagines "by his being so bloody, that he must be a dead Man" and calls him "a poor naked Man, who hath been robbed and murdered" (55–56); Mrs. Tow-wouse worries about the expense of his funeral (61); and even the doctor says that "his Case is that of a dead Man" (63).

Timotheus, the keeper of the inn where Joseph has taken shelter just before his beating, prepares us for this emphasis "with an excellent Observation on the Certainty of Death, which his Wife said was indeed very true" (50). Fielding has attached the *memento mori* provided by Timotheus more specifically to Joseph when he supplies him in book 1, chapter 2, with an admittedly imaginary genealogy. Introducing Joseph to us, Fielding confesses that he has not been able to trace Joseph's genealogy farther than his great-grandfather, and so offers in place of ancestors an epitaph, "which an ingenious Friend of ours hath communicated."

> Stay Traveller, for underneath this Pew
> Lies fast asleep that merry Man Andrew;
> When the last Day's great Sun shall gild the Skies,
> Then he shall from his Tomb get up and rise.
> Be merry while thou can'st: for surely thou
> Shall shortly be as sad as he is now.   (20)

Fielding goes on to discount the epitaph as evidence of Joseph's ancestry ("*Andrew* here is writ without an *s*, and is besides a Christian Name"), but nonetheless retains this peculiar gesture of imagining Joseph's origins in a generalized figure of the mortality of man.[9]

In Chapter 1, we observed the ghostly existence to which Fielding consigned women in several of his plays as he attempted to resolve the contradictions in his notions of female identity.[10] Already in his plays, Fielding began to suggest the costs of a geography of gender that renders women ghostly, disembodied, and men mere puppets of materiality. He pointedly asserts in *Joseph Andrews* that his title character is no scarecrow or lignified puppet of heroism. Indeed, as he continually implicates Joseph in feminine roles, he also repeatedly (at least playfully) associates Joseph with the feminine realm of ghostly presence or voice: his groans are those of a "dead man." The epitaph that Fielding entertains briefly as a clue to Joseph's identity speaks of the universal inevitability of death—but it also speaks crudely, darkly, of the day of judgment and the final raising of the dead. Curiously, the sickly little boy that Gammar Andrews finds in Fanny's cradle, apparently so near death, comes to represent to her a hope for the restoration of her own child: "A Neighbour of mine happening to come in at the same time, and hearing the Case, advised me to take care of this poor Child, and G-- would perhaps one day restore me my own" (337). As a grown man, Joseph will console Adams for the mortal loss of his son with the promise of a lasting reunion between them in the next life; as an infant, he served as a token to Mrs. Andrews of the hope for a reunion with her daughter in this one. The recurrent fear of mortal loss in the novel and the hope for reunion represented by Joseph reflect on

some of the most basic characteristics of Fielding's novelistic methods and on the way readers have understood his difference from
Richardson.

The hope for a reunion after death heard in Joseph's voice within this
novel will reappear at several points in Fielding's other works: Fielding makes it Allworthy's comfort for the loss of his wife in *Tom
Jones*, extends it as "the sweetest, most endearing, and ravishing"
hope in his own discourse on consolation ("Of the Remedy of Affliction for the Loss of our Friends"),[11] and imagines its attainment
in the narrator's reunion with his little daughter upon entering Elysium in "Journey From This World to the Next." In this last work,
the narrator's account links the fantasy of an absolute and lasting reunion with the fantasy of an intuitive recognition of others: "I saw
infinite Numbers of Spirits, every one of whom I knew, and was
known by them: (for Spirits here know one another by Intuition)."[12]
Presented here as fantasies about the next world, the fantasies of
complete reunion and of transparent identity, instantaneous and ef-
fortless mutual recognition, nonetheless take their peculiarly poignant power and importance within Fielding's corpus from the way
his fictions typically render *this* world. Whether defending or dis-
paraging the characteristic qualities of his fiction, Fielding's readers
have agreed that his characters seem separate, present to us only "externally," their inner lives opaque to the reader and to each other,
their encounters full of misunderstandings and misrecognitions and
an obscure or only shorthand sense of individual identity.

As noted in the introduction to this book, readers have defined
this quality of Fielding's fictional world largely through contrasts
with the "interiority" achieved in Richardson's. They have generally
understood it as a deliberate choice reflecting designs or beliefs different from Richardson's, though some have emphasized its creative
limitations and others its existential veracity. Ian Watt concedes that
Fielding's treatment of character is shaped by his deliberate designs
but describes those designs as ones of comedy and plotting that have
limiting consequences for what can be done with character. "Fielding's avoidance of the subjective dimension, then, is quite inten-
tional," but "it denies him a convincing and continuous access to the
inner life of his characters." If Fielding suffers from a self-denial of
access to his characters' selves, those characters, Watt observes, blun-
der helplessly within a fictional world kept in motion by their lack

of access to each other. "The structure of *Tom Jones* as a whole depends on the lack of any effective communication between the characters"; it requires accidental misunderstandings, bad characters that deliberately mislead, and good characters that are both misled and unable to make themselves properly understood; the purposes of its plot "would be impossible if the characters could share each other's minds and take their fates into their own hands."[13] Though Watt maintains a decorous appearance of fairness in his respective treatments of Richardson and Fielding, granting to each what belongs to each, he here conveys an impatience with what he sees as Fielding's absorption in elaborate plotting and a rather avuncular, chiding implication that perhaps Fielding's characters *should* get on with it and "take their fates into their own hands."

But the situation that keeps them from doing so, their inability to "share each other's minds," seems to David Marshall exactly Fielding's point in his response to Richardson and in his treatment of character: "Arguing against Richardson's fictions of immediacy and transparency, . . . Fielding maintains that the only knowledge we can have of characters in novels and characters in the world is the knowledge we can construe from the outside."[14] J. Paul Hunter observes that Fielding is "intrigued by the inherent ambiguities of action," concerned with the problem "of knowing how to construe accurately,"[15] and Ronald Paulson connects the elaborate plotting observed by Watt to Fielding's interest in the problem of judging action and character: "Through the ironic complexity of *Tom Jones* Fielding also says that motive too is so difficult to assign that only much later, by surprise, by accident, can we see behavior as good or evil. . . . the reader as well as the character never knows all he needs to know in a given situation."[16] Marshall cites Fielding's "Of The Knowledge of the Characters of Men" as Fielding's expression, outside his fiction, of just how difficult it is to construe character from the "vizors" of outside appearance—just how likely it is that it will be "only much later, by surprise, by accident," that we will be able to recognize the true nature of an action or a person. If ever. The afterlife that Fielding imagines as the scene of a "melting" union of souls[17] and of an intuitive and universal recognition of others might be described as a mythological provision for that "much later" moment when all could come clear; the interests of the elegiac Fielding that Henry Knight Miller discovers are related to the features of the more familiar Fielding of critical discourse, and they reveal that

Fielding's difference from Richardson is not without thought or wishful ambivalence.

Within the particular fictional world described as Fielding's by Watt, Marshall, Hunter, and Paulson, an elegiac strain may represent not only mourning for the absence of the dead but some element of mourning for the absence of the living to each other—an absence otherwise accommodated as the comedy of Adams's absentmind-edness, for example, or as slapstick confusions—an absence treated largely satirically rather than sentimentally. Yet it is as if Joseph's and Adams's question—"Shall I never, never see thee more?"—took the occasion of a threatened mortal loss to express some sense of pri-vation, an uncertainty as to whether people ever really do see each other. Joseph's consolation to Adams must express some wish about this life as well as about the next.

In their journey on the road from London to the Booby estate, Adams and Joseph move through a world apparently rigged for mis-recognitions of every sort. When Adams runs to rescue a woman struggling against a violent ravisher, not only does he not recognize until much later that that woman is his parishioner Fanny, nor she that he is Parson Adams, but she for a time misidentifies her deliverer as a potential ravisher himself; though they eventually identify each other, they are then taken by the group of fellows that comes on the scene as themselves the criminals, the ravisher their victim (137–42). When Slipslop encounters Fanny on the road, whether out of class snobbery or sexual jealousy she pointedly denies any recognition of her (155–58). In the most extended motif of misrecognition, Adams encounters a series of hypocrites, posted along his route for clearly satiric purposes, and enacts with each a little mistaken drama, an emotional recognition scene with an apparent "brother" in his be-liefs. As if his journey might be a quest to discover such soul-mates, with tears in his eyes Adams tells the falsely courageous Patriot, the falsely charitable Parson Trulliber, the false promiser, and the Rom-ish priest that he has found a brother in each, and that he "would have walked many a Mile to have communed with you," or "have taken a Pilgrimage to the holy Land to have beheld you" (131–32, 161–68, 172–75, 252–54).

Among these satiric scenes of hypocrisy's refusal of recogni-tion or its staging of false recognitions, the one possible sentimental scene of true recognition and reunion between blood relatives on this journey remains narrowly averted. The reunion between Joseph and his father which will restore him to his true identity and provide the resolution of the novel's plot occurs first just two-thirds of the way through the novel—but passes unrealized. Joseph, Adams, and Fanny's visit to the Wilsons constitutes a strangely failed recognition scene. Though Wilson tells not only the long story of his own life in London but the story of his lost son, down to that identifying mark by which he "should know him amongst ten thousand," Joseph, while present at Wilson's fireside account, might as well be absent, for during its final hours he remains "buried" in sleep (226). When Adams misunderstands Wilson's reference to his loss of his eldest son as a mortal loss, and begins to console him that death is "common to all," Wilson hastens to explain that Joseph was lost when stolen by gypsies and complains that this uncertain loss has proven even harder to accept than death (224). Joseph's "burial" in sleep extends his effective absence from his father by preventing recognition, serving, like his abduction by the gypsies, as a kind of provisional, living equivalent of death, and mixing tragedy with comedy in the small chance by which a destined encounter is missed.

Though both this first, unrealized reunion and the eventual successful restaging of it take place between Joseph and his father, the identifying mark which would have allowed Joseph to recognize himself in Wilson's account had he stayed awake, and which does prove his identity in the end, links him specifically to his mother rather than to his father. Remembering the little boy that was taken from him so many years before, Wilson cries, "Poor Child! he had the sweetest Look, the exact Picture of his Mother"; and, imagining the possibility of a reunion with him in the future, he tells Adams that "he should know him amongst ten thousand, for he had a Mark on his left Breast, of a Strawberry, which his Mother had given him by longing for that Fruit" (225). Wilson's recollection of a family resemblance between mother and son so strong as to be "exact" heightens the strangeness of Joseph's presence there among his family, unknown, and makes us wonder about the status of that resemblance: Has it passed with age? How is the difference in sex accommodated by an *exact* resemblance between mother and son?

Any sense in which Joseph remains an "exact Picture" of his mother has become complicated enough not to serve, anyway, as a cue to recognition, but his link to her survives as the clue to his true history. The external mark he bears that will make him known memorializes a "longing" she felt when she bore him within—*pre partum*—before the first of familial partings. He carries this mark on his left breast, over that heart that the narrator makes a vexed subject in the chapter on Joseph's grief; the mark brings together the internal and the external; it is outward yet hidden, physical yet a sign of someone's inner longing. Wilson's story of its origin fancifully plays upon the strange confusion of inner and outer, and of self and self, in the biological facts of pregnancy and birth. It harks back to a moment in the history of each identity when attachments are palpable, and when physical process provides not an allegory of the absence of one person to another, as in death, but a hyperbolic emblem of continuity between selves.

Wilson's story of the birthmark's origin also draws on a long medical tradition about the cause of birthmarks and deformities which was the subject of great popular controversy from the 1720's to the 1760's. This tradition explained any extraordinary feature with which a child was born as the "sad Effect of the Mother's irregular Fancy and Imagination," or, as in Joseph's case, the physical trace of some longing she conceived while she carried him. Cravings for particular fruits were most commonly cited as examples of the phenomenon.[18] The celebrity of Mary Tofts in 1726 for allegedly giving birth to seventeen rabbits, having craved them throughout her pregnancy, sensationalized the medical issue (Fielding used the Tofts case for satiric material in his epilogue to *The Author's Farce* in 1730); a dispute in print between James Augustus Blondel and Daniel Turner in the late 1720's and early 1730's gave the controversy new currency; and G. S. Rousseau observes that "throughout the 1740's cases of extraordinary childbirth of every sort continued to interest the English public."[19] The effects commonly attributed to a pregnant mother's cravings are suggestive for our reading of *Joseph Andrews*: Rousseau reports that, according to Nicholas Culpepper's *Directory for Midwives* (first published in 1651), "even a single instance of bizarre desire would produce 'Hermaphrodites, Dwarfs or Gyants,' and this idea was repeated again and again in medical works of the period."[20] Could Wilson's reference to his wife's desire for strawberries not only explain the identifying mark on Joseph's breast but, within this popularized medical tradition, quietly offer a folk-etiology for the compromised gender that marks his identity again and again?

The pseudo-medical concerns of the "doctrine of imagination" speak for a fascinating constellation of cultural anxieties: explanations for marked and even monstrous births provide a locus of morbid suspicion of woman's imagination and desire. They express a fear of that spiritual "interiority" with which she is credited and of the formative influence she is said to exert—here turned to deformation—as well as a horror of her literal powers of conception—here turned vengeful, or in the service of her own spontaneous desires. In the fantasy set forth by this doctrine, the intervention of a woman's own illicit desire in reshaping the fetus she and a man have together produced leads to the creation of a hermaphrodite, whose double sex reflects, perhaps, its mother's double and transgressive power to "conceive," as if on her own.

But Joseph's ambiguous gender identity, sometimes drawing him into ridiculous positions, sometimes advancing him as a new kind of hero, never seems to partake of the horror often attached to hermaphroditism;[21] and Wilson's mention of the imprint of his wife's longing on his son seems casual and unalarmed, even affectionate. Fielding seems to have been aware of the controversy over the influence of a mother's imagination and desire on a fetus—he also alludes to the relation between a pregnant woman's longings and her child's nature in *Jonathan Wild*[22]—but he makes the power of Mrs. Wilson's desire neither threatening nor damaging: her desire only marks her child, otherwise lost, as her own. Joseph is marked by female imagination and desire, but not as one of Culpepper's "monsters." Fielding even naturalizes the trace magically left by Mrs. Wilson's longing when he names the strawberry as the specific fruit she desires, for "strawberry" is a common slang word for a nevus, a birthmark or a mole.[23] He grafts the highly charged, sensationalized material of this pseudo-medical dispute onto the stable and idealizing conventions of romance: the mark left on Joseph by his mother's desire becomes the conventional token or distinguishing sign required by the standard recognition scene in romance, and it leads to the reunion for which they all wish. A female capacity for continuity with other selves—embodied literally in pregnancy and rendered horrific in Fielding's time by the "doctrine of imagination's" account of monstrous births—extends a special promise within the world described by *Joseph Andrews*.

When Fielding, at the end of his own life, came to write of what he foresaw would be his final parting from his children, he expressed the power of his resistance to that parting by describing his feelings as those of a mother rather than a father. He opens his *Journal of a Voyage to Lisbon* with the entry:

On this day, the most melancholy sun I had ever beheld arose, and found me awake at my house at Fordhook. By the light of this sun, I was, in my own opinion, last to behold and take leave of some of those creatures on whom I doated with a mother-like fondness, guided by nature and passion, and uncured and unhardened by all the doctrine of that philosophical school where I had learnt to bear pains and to despise death.

In this situation, as I could not conquer nature, I submitted entirely to her, and she made as great a fool of me as she had ever done of any woman whatsoever: under pretence of giving me leave to enjoy, she drew me in to suffer the company of my little ones, during eight hours; and I doubt not whether, in that time, I did not undergo more than in all my distemper.[24]

In describing his feelings, Fielding makes explicit the association that Miller observes of "nature and passion" with women and of stoic philosophy's "reason" with men,[25] and he openly owns the feminine attachment to worldly things heard in Joseph's cry of protest against Adams's urging "to despise death." He gives these abstract associations specific content, describing his feelings not just as womanly but as "mother-like," and opening the journal that will, self-consciously, record his journey toward death with a scene of wrenching parting not just with any worldly things but with loved ones. Joseph's consolation to Adams, his promise of a lasting reunion in the afterlife, might here answer to the initial emphasis of Fielding's anticipation of his own death. Fielding tells us that he suffered not only at the moment of farewell but for the final eight hours he spent in "the company of my little ones," for he was drawn in by nature—a female personification—to linger with them; and he presents the period of this parting almost as the grueling labor of parturition which he elsewhere pities as women's fate:[26] "I doubt not whether, in that time, I did not undergo more than in all my distemper." This passage from Fielding's account of his own life might interpret, within the sentimental and the elegiac moods of *Joseph Andrews*, that birthmark which identifies Joseph and which links him to his mother as the sign of his implication in "feminine" feelings such as grief, his mother-like resistance to final partings, his advocacy of hope for reunion rather than resignation to absence in a world characterized not only by violence and death but by separations and mistakings.

Even the title of this novel is a testimony to its world's mistakings. As Homer Obed Brown notes, the title of *Joseph Andrews* memorializes the error about Joseph's identity that is only cleared up in the novel's concluding scenes.[27] Our title character should be called, we eventually learn, Joseph Wilson, except that to name the book that way would undo its process of revelation—and besides, the novel never seems to become very concerned about establishing that the character we had thought of as Joseph Andrews is really Joseph Wilson. It never forms the whole name for us, just as it never articulates the revision of Fanny Goodwill to Fanny Andrews that its revelations imply. After all, the former Joseph Andrews and the new-christened Fanny Andrews will share one name through the marriage with which the story ends. If Joseph were to take Fanny's family name in marriage, he could keep the name he'd always thought was his: what was his original childhood name in error might be given back to him in fact through his adult union with Fanny (and the novel's title could stand). But that would be for a man to take his wife's name in marriage, and the interpolated tale of Horatio and Leonora has reminded us earlier in the novel of the long-standing legal and social convention that the woman take the man's name when they are wed. Horatio proposes to Leonora by declaring that "there is something belonging to you which is a Bar to my Happiness, and which unless you will part with, I must be miserable. . . . —It is your Name, Madam. It is by parting with that, by your Condescension to be for ever mine, which . . . will render me the happiest of Mankind" (104–5).

Horatio's way of framing his proposal is peculiar, but it serves to remind us that social conventions, shaping identity differently for men and for women, even determine how one possesses that most basic marker of continuous personal identity, one's own name. The circumstances of the novel's plot resolution arrange that if (influenced by the title of the novel, and by its silence about new names) we are to imagine Joseph, like a man, retaining always one name, we must imagine him, like a woman, taking on his spouse's name in marriage. The legal practice of name-changes expresses, more generally, the greater tenuousness of woman's possession of her own identity ("It is your Name, Madam. It is by parting with that, by your Condescension to be for ever mine").[28] Clothing can function, like a name, as a public sign of personal identity, and the way Joseph bears his clothing has the same fluid and relational quality that the way he bears his name shares with conventional feminine identity. Before book I has ended, Joseph has lost his clothing twice—stripped of his livery by the authority of his employer, Lady Booby, in 1.10, and stripped "entirely naked" by the brute force of the high-waymen in 1.12—and has donned a series of loaned garments: a frock and breeches borrowed from one of his fellow servants (47); the greatcoat of the generous postilion (53); the shirt provided by Betty from her sweetheart, the hostler (57); and the shirt provided by Mrs. Tow-wouse from her husband's wardrobe when she thinks Joseph a gentleman (68). At the end of the novel, he will be married in one of Mr. Booby's suits—which, we are told, "exactly fitted him" (342). The "something borrowed" in Joseph's wedding regalia might be at once his name and his entire apparel.

But then Joseph has grown to maturity, without knowing it, as himself "something borrowed," dependent for his place in the Andrews family on Mrs. Andrews's willingness to take up, as her own, a merely substitute child. She explains how Joseph became Joseph "Andrews":

A Neighbour of mine happening to come in at the same time, and hearing the Case, advised me to take care of this poor Child, and G-- would perhaps one day restore me my own. Upon which I took the Child up, and suckled it to be sure, all the World as if it had been born of my own natural Body. And as true as I am alive, in a little time I loved the Boy all to nothing as if it had been my own Girl. (337)

The connection between mother and child represented by the child's intimate relation to its mother's "own natural Body" here appears not as something inherent, essential, truly natural, but as something that depends on an act of hypothetical faith, on an acceptance of a substitution as the token of future restoration. The substitution only becomes "as if" an original bond.[29] Gammar Andrews did not feel confident that her husband would embrace the same substitution ("seeing you did not suspect any thing of the matter, [I] thought I might e'en as well keep it to myself, for fear you should not love him as well as I did"), and her fears are borne out by Gaffar Andrews's wariness when she and the Pedlar have told their tales: " 'Well,' says Gaffar *Andrews*, who was a comical sly old Fellow, and very likely desired to have no more Children than he could keep, 'you have proved, I think, very plainly that this Boy doth not belong to us; but how are you certain that the Girl is ours?' " (337–38).

The Andrews' two attitudes toward the child's "belonging" might roughly correspond to Hélène Cixous's feminine and mas-culine realms of the Gift and of the Proper: Gammar Andrews shows a feminine willingness to make "vertiginous crossings" with the Other, while her husband expresses (in a folksy key) a typically masculine obsession with classification, systematization, and property.[30] Parson Adams and his wife, however, provide an interesting complication to the scheme. Repeatedly, Adams is characterized by his willingness to regard all his parishioners as his children (he says of Fanny and Joseph, for example, "these two poor young People are my Parishioners, and I look on them and love them as my Children" [196; see also 172, 277]), while it is Mrs. Adams who insists on a more literal and legalistic definition of family.[31] Adams's pastoral role might be said to feminize him in this respect (the Roasting-Squire's men certainly regard his clerical office as a mitigation of gender, proposing that his cassock serves as "petticoats" and refusing to fight with a man in a "gown"), but Fielding's emphasis on Adams's willingness, like that of Gammar Andrews, to accept a substitute or second self as his own makes the point that the quality Fielding is interested in here, expressed largely through the terms of gender, does not inhere only in biology.

Fielding's plays concentrate on exposing acquired or borrowed identities as merely that—including, prominently, affectations of gender. What one might expect to be the most inborn element of identity—gender—is repeatedly shown up in Fielding's plays as conventional, unstable, merely theatrical, or put on. *Shamela* discloses, through parody, the self-serving dramatizations and mediated, mechanical desires that underlie Pamela's feminine claims to spontaneous personal expression and identity.[32] So does *Joseph Andrews.* But *Joseph Andrews* also draws a limit to the legitimacy of satire's practice of exposure, which Fielding expresses this way in his Preface: "What could exceed the Absurdity of an Author, who should write *the Comedy of* Nero, *with the merry Incident of ripping up his Mother's Belly*; or what would give a greater Shock to Humanity, than an Attempt to expose the Miseries of Poverty and Distress to Ridicule?" (7). In Joseph, marked by his own connection to a mother's belly—by his hidden identification with another self, and a self of the other gender—Fielding imagines a character predicated on the borrowing of identities—from Pamela, from Fanny, from his mother—who yet achieves a kind of autonomous stature. In Joseph, Fielding calls the satirist's bluff: that there might ever be a simply natural and unconstructed self, belonging only to its self. Giving up the implied alternative to satire's exposure of false fronts—that clothing, for instance, might ever "properly" belong to and express inner identity—Fielding attempts to create a male character whose circumstances are initially borrowed from another book, whose name (that signifier of patrilineal descent) is borrowed from his adoptive mother or from his wife, whose clothes are borrowed from anyone generous enough to lend. How we recognize Joseph—if we do—must not depend, then, on the public authority or outward distinction of the scarecrow's clothing or the heroic puppet's wooden staff. As Joseph is initially associated with the castrato singers, even the natural "private parts" of his male sex must be acquired or achieved through a gradual and complex rhetorical process, as we saw in Chapter 2. The narrative of Joseph and Adams's travels places an insistent emphasis on the financial question of borrowing (on matters of exchange, debt, loans, and gifts),[33] and the two men that must converge on Adams's parish at the end of the story to reconstruct Joseph's history have either lent or given the travelers money at critical moments. Even words, Fielding's methods of narration imply, are not invented by or innate to one's self, but borrowed—though perhaps in some way made one's own.

Alongside Pamela's method of "writing to the moment" (as if simply, without mediation, from the heart), Fielding offers a third-person narrative that bodies forth its own ambivalences through complicated echoes of other, absent texts. Joseph speaks a playwright's lines, learned "by heart," to express the "now" of his personal grief, and is recognized most fully, perhaps, when overheard from another room, as when Fanny hears him singing and then is reunited with him in the flesh. At times we too must recognize Joseph's voice as heard from another room. Sometimes in this novel that neighboring room is Milton's *Paradise Lost*; sometimes it is the satiric works of Fielding's own earlier career; sometimes, of course, it is Richardson's *Pamela*. These background texts allow Fielding to meditate upon the question of how spontaneous feeling may be framed within the space of convention—and of how a character like Joseph, beginning as a parodic revision, might develop some autonomy. Gender and sexual desire, the "natural masques" of his early satiric work, at once the most personal marks of identity and suspect as purely constructed, remain focuses in *Joseph Andrews* for the study of these questions. Gender here, however, must function both as the ground for violent satiric attack and as the hinge for imaginative reconciliation of opposites.

PART III

'TOM JONES' AND 'THE JACOBITE'S JOURNAL'

When we turn to *Amelia*, we will observe how the marking of Amelia's face in the destruction and artificial reconstruction of her nose transforms her face into a kind of accidental mask. The emphasis on Amelia's nose both in the novel and in its reception makes her most distinguishing feature an ambiguously gendered one, and one that is at once a social construction and part of her own body. But this does not make Booth (or sympathetic readers) love her the less. Indeed, Fielding presents the strange continuity between Amelia's original, undamaged nose, the mask she wears after her accident, and the reconstructed nose that emerges from under that mask, as the very basis of Amelia and Booth's binding romantic love.

In a clever reading of the scene in which Square is revealed crouching in the tight triangle of Molly's attic closet while Tom stands upright in the room's center, Eleanor N. Hutchens allegorizes the scene's spatial relationships to conclude that "good nature" in *Tom Jones* "is an image with no shape but its own and no earthly measure encloses it. . . . [Allworthy] walks solitary and free. . . . Human goodness stands forth spontaneous, natural, and organic, while human badness crouches in the shelter of a rule."[1] Hutchens's emphasis on humanity's proper spontaneity, autonomy, and "organic" naturalness suggests that one of the "rules" from which it must stand forth freely is the rule of history; but the hero and heroine of *Tom Jones* do not do that. Rather, Fielding asks us to see how they specifically spring forth from the convergence of conflicting and dynamic historical forces, as if alive in the play between separate geometries rather than because free of "earthly measure." It is historical forces that construct their very positions as man and as woman, and that create the particular form of heterosexuality that gives shape to their love.

Peter J. Carlton provides a politically sophisticated turn on Hutchens's approach to *Tom Jones*, arguing that the positive characters' particular form of goodness is not "natural" but actively "natural*ized*" by Fielding with specific ideological intent; and Carlton's analysis of Tom's and Sophia's characters locates them, persuasively and very instructively, within the historical movement from Restoration to Whig ideology in this period.[2] A direct confrontation between the old Stuart order and the presiding Whig government obtrudes directly into the novel's plot, of course, when Tom encounters soldiers on their way to fight against the 1745 Jacobite rebellion and decides to volunteer and join the King's army himself. In doing so, he avows his allegiance to the government that Fielding himself defends against the Jacobite cause in *The Jacobite's Journal* and elsewhere. Although Tom is soon separated from the soldiers and never does reach the scene of battle, a number of critics have argued that the larger conflicts expressed in the historical event of the 1745 rebellion are broadly present in *Tom Jones*.[3] In particular, observing that Tom's pursuit of the troops and of their glorious cause is gradually replaced by a pursuit of Sophia and of love, critics have suggested that the passage of the novel's plot between the Jacobite rebellion and Sophia and Tom's romance marks significant connections between political and domestic ideology: they have observed, for instance, that Squire Western's support of the Jacobite cause accords neatly with his "patriarchalist" understanding of his own absolute authority over his daughter.[4]

Indeed, the circumstances that first prevent Tom from marching toward battle—the chaotic nature of the army company he joins,[5] a fellow-member's attack first on Sophia's reputation and then on Jones's head, the reluctance of his companion, Partridge, to go to war, especially when he discovers that he and Tom are on opposite sides—all suggest that the struggle between Jacobitism and the government needs to be carried out as much on ideological as on military grounds. When the King's soldiers can hardly be distinguished from their Jacobite opponents (plot events suggest), perhaps this conflict needs to be worked through on the level of belief.

In any number of *Tom Jones*'s scenes, Fielding does seem to encourage us to look for connections between the beliefs about national government at stake in the Jacobite revolt and beliefs about other parts of experience, such as domestic concerns: when the Jacobite Western engages in violent arguments with his Whig sister, the subject of their disagreement slides easily between the rule of the nation and of Sophia; Sophia, running from her tyrannical father, is mistaken by an innkeeper and his wife for Jenny Cameron, the Pretender's mistress, on the run from the King's forces.[6] These scenes, however, frequently associate the connections they assert between political and domestic ideology with a sense of confusion, misrecognition, or contradictions in belief; and it is more difficult to systematize the novel's treatment of Jacobitism and matters of domestic rule than critics have acknowledged. While Western, for example, asserts not only the King's absolute right to obedience but also that of a husband and a father, the other main Jacobite character in the novel, Partridge, submits to the inverted rule of "petticoat government" from beginning to end. Carlton's analysis suggests at once the depth at which the conflict between Jacobite and Whig ideologies may be seen to shape *Tom Jones*, and the complexity with which that conflict is played out there. He argues that *Tom Jones*'s engagement with this conflict extends beyond the specific episodes involving the rebellion, or even involving debates about domestic government, to the construction of Tom's character in general: he delineates the alternatives of a "Cavalier" heroism associated with the Restoration court and a "Christian" heroism associated with the Whig ethos, and demonstrates how Fielding draws on both in imagining Tom.

Although Carlton does not frame his analysis specifically in terms of gender, his account of the different versions of heroism contending for authority in 1745 suggests that one of the matters at stake in the Jacobite rebellion was the definition of proper masculine (and feminine) roles. Indeed, the Whig pamphlets we will examine in Chapter 5 and Fielding's own *Jacobite's Journal* illustrate how explicitly propagandists at the time insisted that the rebellion posed a challenge not only to the presiding national government, but to the prevailing system of gender roles. Even as these overtly political writings thus confirm the connections between political and domestic government discerned by critics of *Tom Jones*, they require us to complicate our sense of those connections, both because they present a different set of claims about the connections than the ones that critics, arguing from homology, have expected, and because they make those claims so directly and polemically, not seeking to conceal the political interests attached to their accounts of male and female "nature."

Rather than warning that male Jacobites' patriarchalist beliefs about kingship encourage them to rule tyrannically over women at home, Whig polemics of the 1740's repeatedly insist that Jacobite men (such as Partridge) are dominated by their wives and subject to a "petticoat government" that expresses not only their own inadequate masculinity but also the transgressive energies released in women by the Jacobite cause. These works frequently pair portraits of weak-willed, effeminate, and ineffectual Jacobite men, from Bonnie Prince Charlie down, with portraits of passionate, willful, and fiercely aggressive Jacobite women. In describing the Amazonian women who, they claim, are the real force behind the Jacobite cause, Whig writers invoke the notions of female nature that Watt and others have suggested were an innovation of the mid-eighteenth century, complaining that Jacobite women grotesquely depart from woman's proper character as timid, compassionate, and delicately chaste. Published in the same decade as Richardson's and Fielding's first novels, these works of propaganda lend support to the claims of literary historians such as Watt and Armstrong that this period saw the development of new assumptions about female character, associated with the interests of the middle class and to be advanced by the emerging genre of the novel. These works explicitly intertwine the assertion of assumptions about womanhood, however, with polemics about the proper nature of manhood, requiring us to bring together our literary histories centered on "heroism" and our literary histories centered on the domestic feminine ideal, and to see each within a changing system of interrelated gender roles. Because these works present their claims about proper male and female character on the occasion of a specific political and military conflict, they also allow us to see that one ideology of gender need not silently or invisibly replace another, but that they may appear in active and explicit contestation with each other. For English Whigs, the Jacobite rebellion, beginning in the "backward" regions of Scotland and seeking to restore the old line of Stuart kings, threatened the return not only of a retrograde political regime but of an old economic and social order as well; in depicting the consequences of such a return, anti-Jacobite propaganda highlights the matter of gender, warning that a reversion to older notions of masculine and feminine identity would dramatically diminish male control.

Fielding's descriptions of both Tom and Sophia draw on the terms of gender identity in which the debate about Jacobitism was thus often explicitly cast. As Carlton suggests, however, at length about Tom and in passing about Sophia, Fielding does not locate his leading characters entirely within either the new or the old models of gendered identity, but instead pointedly combines the two in each. Carlton sees Fielding's decision to combine Restoration and Whig "heroisms" within Tom not as any mitigation of his Whig agenda in writing *Tom Jones*, but as a strategic response to the active contention between the two ideologies in the 1745 rebellion, and to the awareness of historicity created by one order's explicit struggle to replace the other. In the conclusions to both his essays on *Tom Jones* he argues that, through the creation of Tom's character, Fielding seeks primarily to efface the process of historical conflict and change, symbolically denying the "discontinuity which 1688 introduced into the political order," "negating history," and therefore " 'naturaliz[ing]' the political status quo."[7] In Chapter 6 I argue that Fielding neither conceals the conflicts created for his main characters by the coexistence, within them, of competing, "residual" and newly dominant models of gendered identity, nor consistently works to "naturalize" the terms of their individual identities as man and woman. At times Fielding in fact underlines the specifically "adoptive" or constructed nature of both Tom's and Sophia's gendered identities, though he does not thereby renounce the ideological potential of his fictional creations. Indeed, in the pages of *Tom Jones* Fielding directly addresses the question of whether a thoroughgoing illusion of unconstructed reality needs to be achieved for political spectacle or literary performance to exert ideological force.

Although Fielding expresses his allegiance in *Tom Jones* to the Whig cause, he does not there present us with a closed world and clearly defined characters, statically modeled in terms of Whig ideals (or in terms of Restoration ideals cleanly subordinated to Whig ones). Instead, he represents a world in a chaotic state of ideological contention, where confusions about personal identity and about political causes occur largely because what was politically orthodox—or properly masculine or feminine—yesterday is not so today. In such a world, individual character must be seen as inevitably constructed or marked, like Amelia's face, by the accidents of history, rather than as spontaneous, natural, or free; Fielding acknowledges as much, but counters in both *The Jacobite's Journal* and *Tom Jones* by presenting a negative model of what it would mean to be marked by the transmission of beliefs that remained unchangingly intact. In Chapter 7 we will examine Fielding's sustained attack in *The Jacobite's Journal* on schoolmasters and university teachers, whom he accuses of instructing their students in the Jacobite creed and inducting them, through passionate floggings on the ass, into sexualized relations of knowledge and power. *The Jacobite's Journal* locates Jacobite ideology in the transmission not only of knowledge but of belief, identity, and sexual feeling from man to man; and it stigmatizes that transmission as potentially homoerotic, or more generally as unnatural, as a force that leaves individuals permanently "marked" by specific historical acts of instruction and violent discipline. In *Amelia* Fielding will develop the suggestion, which he makes in passing in *The Jacobite's Journal*, that it is only the fully domestic woman and the feminine care and instruction she offers her children that can provide a solution to this problematic.

The Jacobite's Journal thus gestures toward the "companionate marriage" that was emerging in eighteenth-century England as an ideal of heterosexual union,[8] and toward proper "feminine" and "masculine" roles, as possible repositories of natural identity and experience, existing outside historical circumstances and rooted most securely in the timeless female sphere of domestic life. *Tom Jones* and *Amelia*, too, draw on this faith. They also, however, repeatedly figure the private "feminine" sphere and personal experiences of gendered identity and heterosexual desire as historically marked themselves, as the sites of historical conflict, contradiction, and change.

Male Pretenders and Female Rebels

Whig Responses to the '45

The anonymous author of *The Female Rebels*, published in 1747, only renders more explicit, and narrates more elaborately, a common implication in anti-Jacobite polemics of the period: that support for Prince Charles, "the Young Pretender," is synonymous with the dissolution of proper gender roles, and that Jacobite sentiment threatens not only the rule of King George over England but of every Englishman over his wife. This author devotes his entire pamphlet to the most eminent among "the Number of Female *Jacobites*, which discover themselves in this Kingdom" and under whose "Petticoat Patronage," he asserts, the 1745 rebellion was fought. Indeed, he interprets the content of that rebellion as centered, finally, in the competing claims of the two sexes rather than in competing claims to the English crown. He warns his male readers that the Jacobite movement may be "a Plot of that ambitious crafty Sex, to deprive Mankind of their Dominion over the Ladies . . . a traiterous Conspiracy of our leige Subjects, the Women, against their sovereign Lord Man," for:

How else can we account for that Number of Petticoats, that have appeared encased in Armour under the Banner of the Chevalier *Charles*? Women, (I had almost said Men) who, regardless of Danger, and forgetting the natural Softness of their Sex, appeared openly without *Head-Pieces*, amidst all the Horror and Confusion of undistinguishing Bullets, and uncomplaisant Swords and Bayonets. . . . Must it not be some Motive stronger than Regard to the Rights of the abdicated House of *Stewart*, that could work this Miracle, to prevail on Women to forget the natural Timidity of their Sex, their Love of Ease, the Danger of their Lives; nay, what is more to Women, the Danger of their Beauty? . . . Yet all this they suffered, all this they risked. Could it be upon any meaner Motive, than to recover the long contested Empire of the Males, and to fix us for ever in their Chains, in spite of our Beards and boasted Wisdom![1]

On the one hand, the author regards it as a miracle that women have overcome the natural softness and timidity of their sex as well as their preoccupation with beauty and ease to venture into battle; on the other hand, he refers familiarly to women as "that ambitious crafty Sex," eager "to fix us for ever in their Chains." His interpretation of Jacobitism as feminist revolution draws upon two popular but conflicting notions of female nature: in the main body of his pamphlet, while he generally denounces the behavior of "Highland Amazons" as unnatural and unfeminine, when he details their actions, he employs terms that evoke a traditional view of women as by nature more irrational, passionate, jealous, zealous, unruly, and malicious than men.[2] Like the passage in Fielding's "The Masquerade" warning men that their "Empire" over women "shortly will be ended"—for "Breeches our brawny Thighs shall grace / (Another *Amazonian* Race)"—or like the many scenes of "petticoat government" in Fielding's plays, this pamphlet's vision of women's attack upon "the long contested Empire of the Males" at once asserts that women are naturally subordinate, the timid "leige Subjects" of "their sovereign Lord Man," and that they are perpetually inclined to rebellion.

The treatments of "petticoat government" from Fielding's early career, so often connected with his satire of Robert Walpole's administration, repeatedly suggest that it is the *new* shape of society—the destruction of a traditional social order by the antiheroic forces of bureaucracy, fashion, and commercial exchange, the eclipsing of the king by his ministry, and so on—that has allowed the hierarchy of gender to be overturned. When the author of *The Female Rebels*, the Fielding of *The Jacobite's Journal*, and other Whig polemicists[3] sound the alarm that Jacobitism threatens not only Hanoverian rule but proper relations between the sexes, they instead locate the threat to male domination in the older social and economic order of the Scottish highlands, with its resistance to bourgeois culture, its aristocratic and military traditions, and its reactionary support of the ousted Stuart lineage.[4] The female warriors who, according to these writers, defied male rule and feminine roles, bullying their husbands into support for the cause, raising hundreds of clansmen, and engaging in battle themselves, did so in fervent support of the absolute authority and right to rule of the Stuart king, "father" of his people.[5]

Although the connection between Jacobite and feminist sentiments may thus initially seem obscure or even paradoxical, a fixation on female Jacobitism takes any number of forms in contemporary accounts of the '45. Other than Prebble's book on Culloden, modern histories of the rebellion place little stress on women's participation,[6] but Whig news items about the rebellion, prints depicting its battles or main characters, and retrospective accounts from the period all frequently place women in the foreground on the Jacobite side. For example, the print "*Tandem Triumphans. The Victory Obtain'd over the Rebels, at Culloden*" (1746; Fig. 10) prominently features four female Jacobites in battle, one of them exposing the masculine jack-boots beneath her skirt, beside a male Jacobite in a short kilt who kneels and begs for mercy from the Duke's forces.[7] An "Extract of a Letter from a Lady at Preston," reprinted in several London newspapers, focuses on the Jacobite ladies accompanying the Young Pretender in his retreat;[8] and three book-length accounts written shortly after the rebellion's suppression dwell to varying extents on women's zealous championing of the Prince's cause.[9] While some of these polemics against the rebellion make their point about Jacobitism and gender by insisting upon, and sometimes elaborately mythologizing, the participation of particular women in the Jacobite cause, others, such as Fielding's *The Jacobite's Journal*, give a generalized picture of the necessary connection between support for the Stuart line and male capitulation to female mastery.

Fielding heads the first twelve numbers of the journal with a woodcut that pictures "John Trott-Plaid," the ironically conceived Jacobite persona of the journal, mounted upon an ass with his wife behind him; she appears open-mouthed, apparently hollering belligerently, wearing riding boots and holding a naked sword aloft (Fig. 11). In the second number of the journal, Trott-Plaid explains that he has learned to submit to his wife's will, for she is "a most masculine Spirit" and "is not more zealous in the Cause of Jacobitism than in that of her Sex, of whose Privileges she is most strenuously tenacious, constantly asserting that Women are, in every Consideration, equal to Men"; and he promises that, as the ladies "form so considerable (perhaps the most formidable) Branch of our

Party, so will a very considerable Part of this Paper be allotted to their Use."[10]

When Fielding makes the politics and domestic relations of a Jacobite character part of the plot of *Tom Jones*, he again suggests a connection between advocacy of the Stuart cause and cowering submission to female will: the Jacobite Partridge is henpecked and literally browbeaten by his first wife; intimidated by the learning of his female student, Jenny Jones; deathly afraid of old women, whom he feels sure are powerful "witches"; and—apparently hopelessly dedicated to female domination—last seen as the novel concludes on the brink of marriage to the "masculine" Molly Seagrim. As the treatments of Trott-Plaid and Partridge illustrate, Whig writers often complemented their descriptions of Jacobite Amazons with characterizations of Jacobite men as weak, superstitious, or easily swayed. In calling into question the masculinity of Jacobite men, Whig writers had to contend, however, with pro-Jacobite propaganda and popular practices that associated the Stuart cause with patriarchal authority and a traditional masculinity lost under Hanoverian rule.[11] They did so by insisting on a different definition of masculinity, which they claimed only their own cause could protect. The proper nature of masculinity is thus often in sharp dispute in the exchanges between Whig and Jacobite polemicists after the '45. The propagandists on both sides frequently translate the conflict between Stuart and Hanoverian ideology into a one-on-one confrontation between the figures of Prince Charles and the Duke of Cumberland, who led George's forces against him; and both sides invoke the superior masculinity of their leaders as substantial proof of the truer hero and his truer cause.[12]

In the spring of 1746, a succession of anti-Jacobite prints appeared with titles such as "The True Contrast—The Royal British Hero—The Fright'ned Italian Bravo" and "The agreable Contrast between the *British Hero*, and the Italian Fugitive" (Figs. 12 and 13). The titles of the prints and their captions emphasize Charles's association with the supposedly effeminate country of his exile; and the latter print, for example, shows Charles seated in a passive and meditative posture, while the castigating female figure of Britain towers above him to one side and the Duke of Cumberland stands erect on the other, vaunting his victory, the straight line of his sword appearing between his legs in marked contrast to the broken anchor of hope lying at the Prince's feet. While other Whig illustrators exploited the idea that Prince Charles's masculinity was compromised by his youth, his supposed physical beauty, or his reputation as a lady's man,[13] one Jacobite printmaker responded sharply to the Whig prints with his own version of the contrast, not only reversing its force but developing in more elaborate and ludicrous detail the phallic comparison suggested by the imagery of sword and broken anchor. Contentiously titled "THE AGREABLE CONTRAST. Shews that a Greyhound is more agreeable than an Elephant, & a Genteel personage More agreeably Pleasing than a Clumsey one, a Country Lass is better than a town trollop and that Flora was better pleas'd than Fanny," his print presents the Young Pretender next to a totemic animal, a greyhound, and attended by Flora MacDonald, who exclaims, "Oh! the Agreeable Creature W[ha]t a Long tail he has," while the Duke of Cumberland appears in a butcher's apron beside an elephant and a woman who rejects him, crying, "Let no body Like Me be Deceiv'd W[i]th such a pittifull tail" (Fig. 14).[14] This judgment of the two princes' relative claims, advanced through a crude comparison of the length of their "tails," is supported as well by a distinction between the kind of woman who accompanies each: "a Country Lass is better than a town trollop."

The rival claims of the two princes, juxtaposed so directly in these prints and elsewhere, obviously represent the larger contest between their causes for authority and authenticity: as the verse beneath the Whig "True Contrast" exhorts, "*Britons*, behold presented to your View, / *In Contrast*, the *Mock Hero*, and the *true*!" The terms habitually used by the anti-Jacobite press to refer to Prince Charles— "the Young Pretender," "the Mock-Prince," and so on—resonate with a kind of ontological as well as political doubt, and at times the suspicion of impersonation and pretense that surrounds him calls into question his authenticity not only as a prince and a hero but as a man. Whig narrators and illustrators took up with particular enthusiasm the stories of both Prince Charles and the Jacobite chief, Lord Lovat, donning female disguises as they attempted to elude pursuit (Figs. 15 and 16),[15] linking the political "Pretender" with the highly charged threats of masquerade and gender impersonation. It is the supposed cross-dressing of a female Jacobite, however, that was most elaborately imagined and energetically reported in the Whig press: although little or no evidence can be found of her historical existence, the woman whom Fielding calls "the famous *Jenny Cameron*" in *The Jacobite's Journal* (98, 173), and for whom Sophia is mistaken in *Tom Jones*, became the locus of frequent and quite extravagant Whig speculation, sometimes appearing as "Colonel Cameron," leading men into battle, sometimes referred to as the Prince's mistress and as a woman of shocking and indiscriminate sexual appetites, but repeatedly and most memorably portrayed as a highly successful male impersonator both in and out of war.[16]

Whig writers repeatedly invoke the authenticity of feminine "softness," "timidity," "modesty," and "compassion" as the guarantee of their own cause's "truth," and they point to the supposed abandonment of these qualities by "the female rebels" as the most egregious proof that the Jacobite cause defies both tradition and nature. This revolution, they warn, threatens to overthrow not only the present king of England, but the timeless categories of "mock" and "true"—and, most particularly, the basic, age-old categories of man and woman. In framing these warnings, however, they must acknowledge and address the relative recentness of their political order's accession to power; the complex entanglement of their own political philosophy, as it was framed in defenses of the Glorious Revolution, with the terms of feminist argument; and the persistent presence and power of older ideas about male and female nature associated with the Jacobite cause. As we shall see, the wider force of Locke's attack on patriarchalist political philosophy—its implications for questions of sexual roles and of male rule—was a subject of open debate among eighteenth-century Englishmen, and remains ambiguous. After considering the connections between philosophies of kingship and of domestic government, we will turn to a closer study of *The Female Rebels* and of one of the pamphlets focused on the figure of Jenny Cameron, *A Brief Account of the Life and Family of Miss Jenny Cameron* (1746). Both of these pamphlets denounce the Jacobite cause as a threat to the present system of gender roles, but they differ in the extent to which they rely on a rhetoric of the "natural" in defending that system. *A Brief Account*, in fact, explicitly rejects the idea that the feminine attributes it recommends are founded in any sense in nature. Both pamphlets finally urge their case in terms of the superior powers of governance afforded to men by a Whig interpretation of masculine and feminine roles; *The Female Rebels*, in particular, underlines the class interests at stake in the advancement of this interpretation.

The titillating narratives and scandalized rhetoric of works such as *The Female Rebels* do not resolve the apparent contradictions in the

Figure 10. "Tandem Triumphans. The Victory Obtain'd over the Rebels, at Culloden, by the Duke of Cumberland," 1746. Figure #7 in the print (the lady to the left wearing jack-boots) and Figure #8 are identified in the legend as Ladies Ogilvy and Murry. They cry out, begging for "Mercy. Mercy." Courtesy of the British Museum.

THE JACOBITE's JOURNAL.

By JOHN TROTT-PLAID, *Esq;*

SATURDAY, DECEMBER 6, 1747.　　　NUMB. I.

—— *Ridiculum acri*
Fortius & melius.—　　　Hor.

IF ever there was a Time when a Daily or Weekly Writer might venture to appear without any Apology to the Public, I think it is the present; I believe, imagine it Presumption in any Author to enter the Lists against those Works of his Cotemporaries, which are now known by the Name of News-papers, since his Talents must be very indifferent, indeed, if he is not capable of shining among a Set of such dark Planets.

I do not therefore scruple to declare, that I conceive myself to be much better qualified for the Task of instructing and entertaining my Countrymen than any of these Writers; who, by their Productions, have vilified and degraded the Office of Censor as well as that of Historian; both which have formerly exercised the Pens of Men of true Learning and Genius; nay, they have even furnished one Argument to the Enemies of the Liberty of the Press (if there be any such); for the Baseness and Badness of the Manufacture hath been always held a good Reason for restraining it.

And as it seems to require no Apology to appear as a Writer, so neither can I persuade myself it requires any, at this Season, to appear as a Jacobite. A Title which I assume in the most public manner in Taverns, in Coffee-Houses, and in the Streets; may surely, without any Impropriety, be assumed in Print.

To say the Truth, our Party hath been very unfairly accused of having formerly concealed themselves from deep political Principles; whereas those who know us thoroughly, must know we have not any such Principles among us: For we scorn to regulate our Conduct by the low Documents of Art and Science, like the Whigs; we are governed by those higher and nobler Truths which Nature dictates alike to all Men, and to all Ages; for which Reason very low Clowns, and young Children, are as good and hearty Jacobites as the wisest among us: For it may be said of our Party as it is of Poets;

JACOBITA NASCITUR, NON FIT.

In Reality, the Party hath so long chose to lay dormant, and have hitherto disavowed their Principles, from one or more of the following Reasons:

First, many have been afraid to reveal their Opinions, not from the Apprehension of Danger to their Persons, or of any Persecution on that Account; for I scorn to lay more to the Charge of the Whigs than is honestly their Due; but they have suspected that it might be some Objection to them in their Pursuit of Court-Favours, or Preferment, that they were desirous of removing the present King and his Family, and of placing another on the Throne in their stead. Moreover, they conceived, and that without the Help of any deep Politics, that Outcries against Ministers, on Pretence of their attempting to undermine the Liberty of the Subject, would not come with so proper a Weight from Men who profess the Tenets of indefeasible, hereditary Right, arbitrary Power, and prostrate Non-Resistance. Again, they apprehended that Republicans, who are an artful kind of People, might decline any Union with Men who wanted to exchange a limited for an absolute Monarch. And lastly, that the Dissenters would be extremely timorous on account of their Religion, and would rather chuse to tolerate a Church which tolerates them, than to run the Venture of being extirpated by the Popish-Christian Methods of Fire and Faggot.

2dly, There are others, and those perhaps not a few, who, tho' they have been very staunch Jacobites in their Hearts, have yet been ashamed of owning themselves so in all Companies; for though, when amongst one another, and while the Glass goes merrily round, they freely drink the Healths and talk the Language of the Party, according to the old Observation, *Defundit incaerus,* &c. yet in the Presence of wicked Whigs, who look grave at the King over the Water, the Royal Exchange, the three W's, (a great Health) and other such witty Jests; a modest Man may be put out of Countenance, should he discover himself; for Men of Wit generally blush when their Jest is not laughed at. Besides, he may thus be drawn into Argument, and may be put on the Defence of those Doctrines by Reason, which are far above the Reach of it: For it may be truly said of Jacobitism (what a modern Writer, with as much Malice as Falshood, says of Christianity) *that it is* NOT FOUNDED ON ARGUMENT.

3dly, Much the largest Part of our Body have declined the public Profession of our Principles, because they have really not known what they were. We are not such severe Task-masters as to require of the whole Party, that they should search to the Bottom of the Matter. In all Mysteries, such as Jacobitism is, Faith is sufficient, without the least Knowledge: And whoever wears a Plaid Waistcoat, roars at Horse Races and Hunting-Matches, and drinks proper Healths in Bumpers, is a good and worthy Jacobite; tho' he should not be able to assign any Reason for his Actions, nor even to tell what he would be at.

Now from these Motives it hath proceeded, that so large a Body of Jacobites should have been (like

Figure 11. Frontispiece of the first twelve numbers of *The Jacobite's Journal*, 1747 (attributed to Hogarth). The ass eats a copy of the *London Evening Post*, and Trott-Plaid's wife wears boots with spurs and carries a sword and a copy of Harrington. Courtesy of the Beinecke Rare Book and Manuscript Library, Yale University.

Figure 12. "The True Contrast—The Royal British Hero—The Fright'ned Italian Bravo," 1749. The small banners to the upper right above Charles read "Popery and Slavery, Monkish Legends, The Bloody Inquisition, Arbitrary Power, No Faith with Hereticks." The poem at the base of the print begins, "Britons, *behold presented to your View, / In Contrast, the Mock Hero, and the true!*" Courtesy of the British Museum.

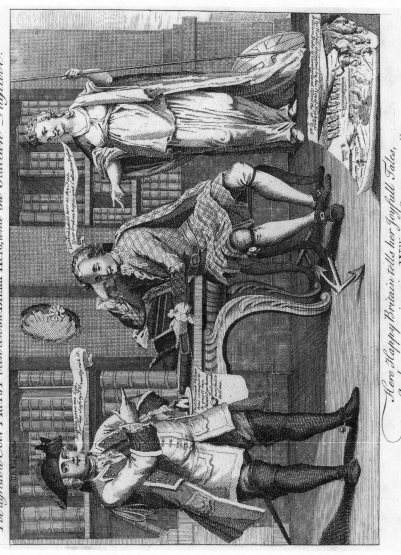

The agreable CONTRAST between the Britiſh Hero, and the Italian Fugitive.

Here Happy Britain tells her Joyfull Tales,
And may again ſince Williams Arms prevails.

Figure 13. "The agreable Contrast between the *British Hero*, and the Italian *Fugitive*," 1746. The figure of Liberty tells Charles, "Vain *Fool* behold here at thy Feet, / Your broken hopes and Cullodens Defeat." The print curling at Charles's feet depicts "The Rebels defeated by his Royal Highneſs . . .." Courtesy of the Print Collection, Lewis Walpole Library, Yale University.

Figure 14. "THE AGREABLE CONTRAST. Shews that a Greyhound is more agreeable than an Elephant, & a Genteel personage More agreeably Pleasing than a Clumsey one, a Country Lass is better than a town trollop and that Flora was better pleas'd than Fanny," 1746. Flora cries out, "Oh! the Agreeable Creature W[ha]t a Long tail he has," while Fanny complains, "Let no body Like Me be Deceiv'd W[i]th such a pittifull tail." Courtesy of the British Museum.

THE AGREABLE CONTRAST.

Shews that a Greyhound is more agreable than an Elephant, & a Genteel personage
More agreeably Pleasing than a Clumsey one, a country Lass is better y.n a town trollop
and that Flora was better pleas'd than Fanny, to be[ca]d of the author in Bromley Street.

Figure 15. Prince Charles disguised as Betty Burke, Flora MacDonald's maid. Courtesy of the Mansell Collection, London.

Figure 16. "Lord Lovat a Spinning," 1746. Courtesy of the Print Collection, Lewis Walpole Library, Yale University.

Lord Lovat a Spinning.

Sold at Nº 39 Holborn Hill.

According to Act of Parliamt 1746.

Figure 17. "Scotch Female Gallantry," 1746. The poem at the base of the print tells the tale of how "Charley" set the "Scottish Nymphs on Flame," but it concludes: "But while these foolish Females take / And to their Bosoms clasp the Snake / Let English Nymphs the Pest beware / For Poison lurks in Secret there // No base-born Wretch Let William stand / The Pride and Darling of our Land / William on Earth the young Nassau / Born to defend the World below." Courtesy of the Print Collection, Lewis Walpole Library, Yale University.

connections they claim between Jacobite political philosophy and the inversion of gender roles. A revealing moment occurs early in *The Jacobite's Journal*. When John Trott-Plaid introduces his wife Peggy to us and informs us that "she is not more zealous in the Cause of Jacobitism than in that of her Sex . . . constantly asserting that Women are, in every Consideration, equal to Men," he confides that these tenets caused "much domestic Disquiet in the early Days of our Matrimony" and that he has "often quoted Texts of Scripture, which I thought had commanded some little Obedience to Husbands." To no avail: "she gave very little Attention to them, tho' she preached up the Obedience and Non-Resistance of Subjects on the same Authority" (100). The political views around which Fielding constructs the character of Peggy are reactionary—she accepts a principle of absolute kingly authority and necessary obedience that her country had rejected, with the Glorious Revolution, more than fifty years earlier—while the views on relations between the sexes that he ascribes to her are radical, based upon an equality of the sexes still centuries away from acceptance in England, and challenging the assumed authority of husbands and fathers. Moreover, the absolute inseparability of beliefs about national and about familial government stands as the first premise in theorizations of Peggy's own position on monarchy: Sir Robert Filmer, in his defense of Stuart claims and the divine right of kings, had founded his argument upon an identity between monarchical and paternal power, locating the source of both in the same scriptural texts.

Filmer derives the absolute authority of all kings over their subjects from the power granted by God to Adam as the original ruler, arguing that "God ordained Adam to rule over his wife, and her desires were to be subject to his; and as hers, so shall all theirs that should come of her. Here we have the original grant of government, and the fountain of all power placed in the Father of mankind."[17] When Locke justified England's rejection of Stuart claims and the events of the Glorious Revolution, he therefore centered his arguments in an attack on Filmer's account of the "patriarchal" origins of political power, advancing in its place a contractual theory of the origins of government and insisting upon a fundamental distinction between political and familial power. One might sooner have expected that Peggy, who rejects her husband's arguments from scripture that she owes him obedience, would be an adherent of Locke's political theories—and therefore a supporter of the Revolution settlement and the Hanoverian succession—than that she would zealously take up the cause of the Stuart kings, defended theoretically in terms of Eve's subjection to Adam.

Indeed, at the end of the seventeenth and the beginning of the eighteenth century, the Glorious Revolution and its justification by Locke were themselves seen by some as throwing into question traditional male authority. Locke's contemporaries sensed that his theories of government, depending as they did on the premise that men are born not to subjection but in freedom and equality, might have implications for the status of women as well. Women who embraced Locke's political theories and longed for recognition of their own rights asked whether "arbitrary dominion" could still be granted to the heads of families when it had been denied to heads of state; men who opposed Locke's doctrines and the political order he defended made the same demand for logical consistency, arguing that such doctrines must be false, as they entailed the obviously unacceptable conclusion that women and children were born free and equal as well.[18]

Because patriarchal theories of monarchy depended so explicitly on an identification between paternal and political power, arguments about the proper nature of the state and about the proper nature of family and sexual relations were often quite directly linked in this period. Thus it is not surprising that in *Tom Jones,* when Squire Western and his sister argue, they frequently move seamlessly from disagreements about family government and women's place to scornful denunciations of each other's support for Jacobitism or the Hanoverian court. The Whig Mrs. Western uses Lockean rhetoric when she insists upon the rights of women (320–22, 845–47);[19] Western identifies the Hanover government he so despises with conspiracies of women and a dispensation that places women "above the Law" (337, 805–6, 880–81). The picture of *Tom Jones*'s treatment of relations between domestic and political ideology grows more complicated, however, when we recall the figure of Partridge, and how neatly he fits into the paradigm of Jacobite emasculation presented in other works of Whig propaganda; *or* when we observe how sharply the figure of the Whig Mrs. Western, described not only as feminist but as "commanding" and Amazonian (846), departs from the frequent Whig insinuations that Amazonian aggression characterizes women who support the Jacobite cause. Within a single work, the Jacobite husband and father is cast doubly as a male tyrant and as the victim of female domination; and it seems that the specter of female self-assertion, of female demands for equality and social change, may appear as a feared attendant in the train of either Jacobite or Whig political claims.

According to some modern historians of family life and of political theory, it was in fact the political philosophy articulated by Locke, and certainly not that of Filmer, which eventually led to a revolution in relations between the sexes.[20] As Melissa A. Butler has shown, however, Locke himself remained evasive about the implications of his theory for the rights of women,[21] and other contract theorists were less ambiguous in the sharp distinction they drew between the natural freedom of men and the natural subjection of women. Though seventeenth- and eighteenth-century women might seize upon Locke's ideas as arguments for their own rights, male contract theorists such as James Tyrrell dismissed the suggestion that the theory logically must be extended to women and children, asserting, "There never was any Government where all the Promiscuous Rabble of Women and Children had votes, as being not capable of it."[22] Butler generalizes that Filmer's adversaries "wished to destroy the patriarchal base of monarchy, and sever the connection between patriarchalism and divine-right politics, yet they were unable to reject less comprehensive forms of patriarchalism as basic principles of government and society. . . . They attacked the theological-historical justifications for political patriarchy, but basically supported the institutional arrangements promoted by patriarchy where women were concerned."[23] Perhaps, then, what Butler identifies as an inconsistency or contradiction within Whig ideology in this period—an attempt to maintain patriarchal authority over women in the family while discrediting it as the basis for political power—helps explain what seems contradictory or at least puzzling in Whig depictions of Jacobitism: the insistence that support for patriarchal absolutism in national government was necessarily associated with a relinquishing of male authority at home. Anxious to deflect the suggestion that their own position logically or ultimately would entail a change in the structure of relations between the sexes, Whig ideologues declared the Jacobite uprising a feminist cause.

The fervency and repetition of Whig assertions that Jacobitism involved the abandonment of proper feminine roles can be only partially accounted for, however, as a tactic of preemptive name-calling on the very ground of Whig vulnerability. If on one level these claims do seem to function as a form of aggressive denial, they function quite differently on another. For these claims at times seem to express a genuine intuition that Whig ideology was developing ways of containing women within a very powerful system of male-female roles which the older "patriarchal" model of the Jacobites *did* defy in allowing women certain kinds of fuller equivalence. Whig theorists and practitioners who, as Butler describes it, wanted to explode patriarchy as the justification for state government but preserve patriarchy at home did not simply, if inconsistently, preserve the powers of husbands and fathers—they transformed them. The very fact of severing those powers from the powers of monarchy, while it weakened their authority in some ways—while it cut them off from a thoroughgoing system of beliefs about history and society—greatly amplified them in others. When, in 1707, the patriarchalist Henry Gandy invoked the identity between monarchical and paternal power to argue against the Glorious Revolution, he asserted that, as Providence had created civil authority out of natural, paternal government, "the whole diffusive body of the Governed were to be (in this respect . . .) reputed in the state of *Wives*, or of *Children*, or *Minors*."[24] The identification between monarchical and paternal authority provided a powerful justification for a man ruling absolutely, like a king, within his family; but it also required that his own position within the state be conceived through analogy to his wife's (and children's) at home. Locke and his allies insisted that man was not born to subjection but in freedom; in effect, they were involved in the invention of the modern notion of the free individual. But if wives were excluded from this invention, if they were still, by nature, the subjects of God-given authority, that subjection might seem to separate their existence at an even deeper level than before—now, almost ontologically—from that of their husbands.

Furthermore, Locke's brilliant and vastly consequential argumentative stroke of breaking the necessary correspondence or homology—indeed, the unity—assumed by the patriarchalists between state and family allowed a newly sharp articulation of different realms of experience and authority: the public or political world and the home. If the home (and the social world generally) could now be understood as unrelated in some basic way to the world of political power, women might be seen as inhabiting a sphere more separate from men's than ever; and broad economic and social changes in this period made this part of Locke's response to Filmer not only a possible but a compellingly descriptive reformulation.[25] In his *Jacobite's Journal*, Fielding suggests that one of the most egregious things about Jacobite women is their failure to recognize an absolute demarcation between their realm of interest and experience and the political realm belonging to men. Writing in his ironically conceived Jacobite persona, he pretends to approve of this quality in Jacobite women, and inquires,

> do the poor-spirited Wretches [Whig women], in private Conversation, ever shew that Attachment to their Party which so nobly distinguishes the Petticoats on our Side? May you not often pass a whole Day in the Company of a Whig-Lady without knowing her political Principles, unless indeed that her Silence on that Head declares her not to be of our Party? Whereas, with our Women, it is hardly possible to sit an Hour, without incurring a Premunire in Times of Whig-Government. The very Scandal at their Tea-Tables is political. (99)

The "political Principles" of a "Whig-Lady" appear only negatively: only by "her Silence on that Head," by the absence of any manifestation of political opinion. A Whig lady herself would not think to attach "Whig" to her self-description, though her very failure to identify herself by political allegiance sets her against the Jacobite women whom Fielding later calls, oxymoronically, "Jack-Women"—women who act like "jacks" or boys in their political enthusiasms (124).[26] While the patriarchalists conceived of a man's relations to his wife and children as political ones, of the same type as those obtaining in the national-political sphere, the new Whig conception of a wife allowed her no experience of political relations at all: unqualified for participation in national politics, she was the inhabitant of a domestic sphere cut loose from affairs of the state, and the relations of power that obtained there.

The author of *The Female Rebels*, too, emphasizes that women's sphere is properly quite separate from that of the state. Opening his long satiric treatment of female Jacobites, he comments, "I apprehend it can be no Insult upon the profound Parts of the *British* Ladies, to suppose that they are very bad Judges in political Matters. It can be no Affront to feminine Judgment to alledge, that the Arcana of Government, the several Windings, Springs, and Wheels of the political Machine, are many Degrees removed from their Sphere of Knowledge" (6). According to this author, woman's proper "Sphere of Knowledge" encompasses, at its most trivial, matters of beauty and of ease, and at its most profound, not only domestic relationships and concerns but all human emotional ties. In this context, the engagement of the female rebels in both political argument and military action becomes a "Miracle," a freakish and unnatural event (7–8). Yet the author of *The Female Rebels* presents his portraits of female Jacobites as readily recognizable incarnations of a familiar problem or an unfortunate type, rather than as innovators in an unheard-of vein. In fact, in the course of his narrative, he refers to the women's passion, rebelliousness, and fierce spirit in the pursuit of their political cause as peculiarly female, sometimes likening them to "Furies" or condemning the "barbarity" of "Female Rage and Revenge" (e.g., 7). At these points in his pamphlet, he seems to locate the female rebels not within the realm of the unnatural but within an older view of women's "nature"—the traditional view of woman as unruly, contentious, and passionate which the ideal of the "new woman" described by Watt and Armstrong was at that moment in the process of replacing.[27]

The Female Rebels does not pursue its polemical aim, then, simply by denying that any version of male and female roles has ever preceded its own. Rather, it presents two contending versions of both male and female nature, suggesting that a Jacobite triumph would restore an older view of gender as well as of government, and warning its readers of the grave consequences of that restoration for the possibilities of male control. The pamphlet directly treats the problem of the discontinuities introduced into English political history by the Revolution of 1688; and it uses antifeminist rhetoric to promote arguments from reason over those from tradition or heredity. It suggests that a clear division of male and female spheres is a more effective method of male control than any assertion of patriarchal absolute authority. Finally, in the course of its narrative, as it moves from a satiric to a seminovelistic mode, it enacts the possibility that novelistic forms may be more powerful tools of discipline than either the literal lash of physical punishment or the figurative "lash" of satire.

The author of *The Female Rebels* complicates the apparently simple values of loyalty and inheritance invoked by the Stuart cause by laying great weight upon the fact that women form part of a bloodline as well, and that they may be the recipients of inherited loyalties and principles as easily as men. Indeed, in the account of Jacobitism provided by *The Female Rebels*, devotion to inherited principles is most fully the property of women, whereas men balance the value of tradition and inheritance with a rational sense of the common good. The author explains that the ancestors of the Duchess of Perth, for example, demonstrated great loyalty to the English kings during the Civil War and at the Restoration, and he does homage to the Duchess's noble blood and to her forebears' loyal acts, but he describes her support for the '45 rebellion as a distinctively female perversion of this historical inheritance. He retroactively interprets support for the Stuarts by the Duchess's seventeenth-century male ancestors in the post-1688 terms of limited monarchy and the contractual relations between a king and his people, expressing confidence that they fought for the Stuart kings on the basis of Lockean rather than absolutist or patriarchalist principles (27–28). The author thus maps the obscure difference between support for the Stuarts in 1660 and continued adherence to them in 1745 onto the difference between the sexes, remarking that the later, female support for their cause lacks the crucial masculine characteristic of "rational Loyalty," and is characterized instead by "blind Affection" and delusion. He simultaneously bows to the traditional value of "noble Blood" and suggests the instability of that value, as blood is always in danger of being "tainted" when it is passed on to women (28).

Throughout his pamphlet, this author stresses the innate "irrationality" of women (5, 27, 48), as does Fielding in discussing women's support for the rebellion in *The Jacobite's Journal*. Both authors thus work to discredit Jacobitism by associating it with women's unreasoning zeal. More profoundly, they thus counter the claim exerted by Stuart kings as the representatives of traditional masculinity and patriarchal authority with a claim that proper distinctions between men and women can be preserved only by their own cause. Authority based solely on tradition and birth, these authors suggest, cannot be kept out of the reach of women, who share their families' loyalties and blood, and so leads to rebellion both in the state and at home. They propose another model of authority, explaining women's exclusion from the rights of the subject in Lockean society on the basis of their lack of reason. They thus place a bar between the sexes that women (they assure us) can never overcome.

The striking progression of female characters described in *The Female Rebels* points to the particular class interests at stake in this political-philosophical argument about authority, kingship, and gender. The progression also suggests how much the concerns of this pamphlet have in common with some of the earliest canonical English novels, produced in the same decade. The first two rebels the author depicts, the Duchess of Perth and Lady Ogilvy, become dangerous and repellent villains as they seize the powers of their aristocratic husbands, summoning hundreds of clansmen and marching with them into war, while the third woman he portrays, "Miss Flora M'Donald," though she has served the rebel cause by assisting Bonnie Prince Charlie, emerges as a positive alternative to the titled women who precede her. This final portrait offers resolution to what quickly comes to seem a repetitious pattern of inverted authority in the long satiric accounts of the Duchess and Lady Ogilvy: although identified, like them, with nonrational qualities, Flora MacDonald represents a version of those qualities that does not threaten the order of masculine, rational control. Indeed, the author describes Flora's feminine qualities of the heart as sustaining a realm of experience that is separate from the entirely rational world of politics, and a needed supplement to it. If the aristocratic women who come before her in the pamphlet exemplify older ideas of women as unruly, fierce, and passionate, Flora steps forward in the pamphlet's closing section as a perfect embodiment of the new middle-class feminine ideal described by Watt and Armstrong: she manifests "Softness" of both "Temper and Constitution," tenderness, delicacy, meekness, chastity, and compassion (53–60).

Significantly, the Duchess and Lady Ogilvy exert their destructive powers within an older aristocratic version of the "family" as a widely inclusive political, economic, and military unit; as they are the wives of Scottish clan leaders, their family position merges easily with an authoritative public one that eventually takes them into battle. Flora, on the other hand, though descended from a once-powerful clan, is primarily defined by her position within the much smaller unit of a nuclear family consisting of herself, her mother, and her late father. The little information we are given about Flora's family portrays it as focused intensively upon providing Flora with a thorough "Female Education" (59–60). This final section, then, shifts the pamphlet's mood from satiric invective, with its negative method of proscribing female behavior, to a sentimental, seminovelistic one, in which the proper sphere of women's experience is depicted positively, and is located in the nuclear family, in a nonaristocratic class, and in the process of feminine education. The story of Flora serves to demonstrate that, placed under these special conditions, woman can achieve her "natural" character, from which the Duchess and Lady Ogilvy have grotesquely diverged (53).

The story of Flora moves beyond the episodes that precede it to make explicit the lineaments not only of a new female role but also of a new male one in sharp contrast with the characters of the Jacobite men it has depicted. The pamphlet's portraits of aristocratic female Jacobites as embodiments of the old "unruly" type of womanhood are matched with portraits of "Cavalier" manhood in the female rebels' husbands and in Prince Charles. While the aristocratic female Jacobites described in the pamphlet are treated with horror, their husbands, and even Prince Charles himself, are generally presented as rather charming, if ineffective. As good "Cavalier" gentlemen, the Duke of Perth and Lord Ogilvy both express great interest in pursuing women (18, 42), are witty and engaging conversationalists, and even possess great "Sweetness of Temper" (18, 47). Their relatively harmless dalliance in the female world of "Toilet and Tea-Table" (18–19), however, seems implicitly to feminize them, and to unleash tyrannical masculine powers in their wives, who first rebel against the supposed order of authority in the home and then join a national rebellion. Both Ogilvy and Perth give themselves "wholly up to [their wives'] Management" (21, 45), and their continued participation in the '45 rebellion is forced upon them by their wives' fierce, unrelenting zeal: the Duke of Perth wants to turn back to Scotland rather than marching into England, "but the Old Proverb must be verified, a Man cannot thrive unless his Wife let him; for her Grace bullied him out of his Reason" (33a). The likelihood of "petticoat government" is the import, significantly, of a specifically *old* proverb. The pamphlet calls the true "masculinity" of the old Cavalier type into question; most damagingly, it suggests that such masculinity provokes dangerous, destabilizing responses in women.

This suggestion is part of a general Whig strategy of portraying Jacobite men, and Charles in particular, as vulnerable precisely because of their erotic charisma. Both Jacobite and anti-Jacobite portraits of Charles emphasize his attractions for women; but, while Jacobite writings and prints point to this as evidence of his incontrovertible masculinity, anti-Jacobite depictions of him sometimes play on the suggestion that it represents a feminine aspect of his own character. In the print "Scotch Female Gallantry" (Fig. 17), for example, Charles appears in the center of a group of admiring women;

the mild delicacy of the face the artist has given him, and the visual echoes he creates between the waving lines of the women's figures and those of Charles's own slender body and feathered cap, work to imply that Charles shares the feminine characteristics of the women who encircle him. These women themselves are referred to with the masculine term of "gallantry." The representatives of Whig masculinity evoked at the pamphlet's close are invulnerable to this kind of reversal of roles.

The pamphlet openly admits, however, that the alternative male role it describes is not entirely attractive, and it underlines the function of Flora's special brand of femininity to secure the acceptability of the new order it supports. While Lady Ogilvy's and the Duchess of Perth's support for Jacobitism involved their abandonment of female nature, Flora's contribution to the cause only occurred because she "carried those social and endearing [female] Virtues of Mercy and Compassion to an unreasonable Height" (53–54). When Flora assists Charles in his escape after the rebellion's failure, we might regret the object of her compassion, the author comments, but would we have wanted her "to be divested of Humanity? To be deprived of Heaven's darling Attribute Mercy?" He replies:

Nothing that's feminine surely would: A surly plodding Statesman, may be possessed of such adamantive Hearts . . . They may judge of Men and their Actions, by the dull Rules of Philosophy, and puzzling Politicks, and divest themselves of all Passions peculiar to them as Men, act only by the selfish Notions of the Cabinet, and be deaf to the loudest Cries of Nature; but Woman, while she remains Woman, and possesses the genuine Characteristicks of her sex, must still be under a Temptation to act as Miss *M'Donald* has done. (54–55)

The lofty "reason" that has been opposed earlier in the pamphlet to the female rebels' dangerous passions here appears to have devolved into purely pedantic and bureaucratic systems of thought, from which we are grateful to be rescued by woman's passionate "Humanity," even when carried to "an unreasonable Height" (54). The private values associated with women in this passage—mercy, social feeling, "humanity," and impulsiveness—provide a necessary supplement *not* to the masculine public order represented by Prince Charles and the male Jacobites we have met earlier in the pamphlet, but to the new masculine public order of a government centered in "the Cabinet" and in the figure of the "surly plodding Statesman"—

the new order, that is, of the highly "reasonable," legalistic, and increasingly bureaucratic government of post-1688 England, which has been favorably opposed throughout the pamphlet to the retrograde order of the Scottish military and aristocratic chiefdoms. In this passage, however, the representative of the new order seems markedly less attractive than the good-natured and debonair, if henpecked, male Jacobites that have preceded him; he is absorbed in the intricacies of an elaborately technical political system, and he lacks all "heart." What secures the superiority of the new order of government and of gender relations is the role women are assigned by it: it provides them with the responsibility of presiding over a sphere that is to contain certain social and emotional values now explicitly excluded from the realm of government.

This conception of women's special role at once serves to keep the volatility of those values out of the debate about government (while still nominally preserving them), and to keep women out of the realm of real power struggles, within their newly defined sphere apart. It promises to respond to the threat of female rebellion in a way the charming Duke of Perth, Lord Ogilvy, and Prince Charles could not. Ultimately, even the destabilizing attractions of these men can be safely contained and preserved by such a conception: in the last section of *The Female Rebels*, we are allowed to sympathize with Flora MacDonald's feminine desire to assist the dashing hero of the Jacobite cause because she takes him under her protection only after the rebellion has utterly failed, after the Whig middle-class ethos within which Flora is defined has decisively triumphed. The author makes it clear that Flora responds to Charles not as the representative of a political cause (not as the rightful heir of England's throne), but as one of "the Distressed."

Significantly, the most memorable event within the "Flora" section of *The Female Rebels* involves Charles's dressing as Flora's waiting-maid to avoid capture:[28] in this final section of the pamphlet, it is the male prince who has passed into a feminine realm of fantasy and feeling rather than a woman who intrudes into the masculine one of politics, war, and power. As the pamphlet's closing section replaces its earlier satiric mode with a sentimental narrative one, Charles reappears not only in female dress but within the new and feminized discourse of novelistic fiction; he also symbolically enacts the displacement of traditional class distinctions by other systems of value, as he, the Prince, temporarily takes on the role of a servant.

In the final section of this pamphlet, Charles has become a fugitive rather than a military leader, and he is well on his way to becoming a mere character within the genre of historical romance.

The author of *The Female Rebels* does not discuss the most famous among the Amazonian rebels of 1745: Jenny Cameron, for whom Sophia Western is mistaken on her journey to London. The popular mythology surrounding Jenny Cameron was exploited and extended in a number of prints, news items, and pamphlets on the rebellion, including one entitled *A Brief Account of the Life and Family of Miss Jenny Cameron, the Reputed Mistress of the Pretender's Eldest Son. Containing Many very singular Incidents* (1746). This pamphlet, like *The Female Rebels*, vilifies the Jacobite cause by associating it with the overturning of proper gender roles, although it emphasizes the specifically sexual transgressions of Jacobite women in a way *The Female Rebels* does not. The story of Jenny Cameron, as told by this pamphlet, stresses the importance of a proper feminine education even more heavily than *The Female Rebels*; and it too links the problem of female rebellion to an outdated model of masculinity that provokes usurpation by women. This pamphlet is very clear, however, that it is important to educate women in the role of "the new woman" precisely because that role has no particular foundation in nature.

Only a short final episode of *A Brief Account* deals directly with the '45 Jacobite rebellion, as a middle-aged Jenny is shown leading the men of her clan to attend Prince Charles, but its narration of this female rebel's many earlier transgressions of gender roles and sexual norms works to undermine Jacobite claims to insure order through a masculinity at once traditional and charismatic. In the episodic series of wild adventures presented by *A Brief Account*, Jenny proves herself the very antitype of the delicate, timid, compassionate, and chaste female character evoked at the end of *The Female Rebels*. Instead, she fulfills to excess the older ideas of female nature described by Natalie Zemon Davis: she is violently unruly, strong-bodied and stronger-willed, endowed with a "piercing wit," and "abundantly amorous" (17, 26). In defiance of the new ideal of the "decarnalised woman," Jenny not only experiences sexual desire, but experiences it almost indiscriminately, "picking up the Women of the Town" when dressed as a man, becoming pregnant by her great-aunt's footman when confined to the house and then by a father-confessor when confined to a nunnery, eloping from the nunnery with an Irish officer, flirting with an Italian count when again in male dress, and ultimately discovered in bed with her own brother.

Jenny's enthusiastic adoption of male dress at several points in her story provides an outward expression of what the narrator calls her "masculine" disposition (17). When she and the maid in her aunt's house take to sallying out every night in male apparel, Jenny feels impatient during the day "till Night came, that she might get rid of her Petticoats, and assume the Breeches, which suited her Temper much better than her own Dress: Then she gave a Loose to the natural Fire of her Spirits, and acted the Cavalier to a Miracle" (24). But if it is primarily Jenny's relentless sexual appetites that seem to define her disposition as masculine, the narrator of *A Brief Account* declares quite explicitly that women are in no way less inclined to sexual passion by nature. Only early and comprehensive discipline trains women to control their desires and so distinguishes them from men; and Jenny's easy and eager adoption of male clothing expresses, in the context of this pamphlet, more about the general interchangeability of sexual identity than about Jenny's own egregious constitution. The seventeenth-century type of the "Cavalier"—a masculine type defined by daring, wit, and sexual exploits—remains particularly open, the author suggests, to appropriation by female transgressors.

When Jenny becomes pregnant by her great-aunt's footman at the age of sixteen, her father dies of shock, her mother refuses to see her, and her biographer pauses to lament Jenny's singular lack of "that Reservedness of Behaviour, that quick Sense of Shame, and that Delicacy of Thought, which is so much the Ornament of the Fair-Sex." He blames not Jenny but her parents for this lack, observing that she was never given "an Opportunity to acquire" these feminine ornaments. He comments:

That Modesty we so much admire in the Ladies, that Chastity of Behaviour which they assume in the Company of Men, we are not to suppose flow from any innate Principles: No, Nature understands no such Distinctions; it is wholly the Result of Education and an early Habit. Let Miss and Master's Education be the same, and their Behaviour will be similar, even when they are grown to adult Years. (29)

Jenny acts as she does not because she is a monster but because she has been "left in a pure State of Nature" (30); her parents have failed to impose the specialized "Education" and "early Habit" that would distinguish her from her male peers.

Throughout, the author of *A Brief Account* stresses the necessity of "inculcating" principles of modesty and "Delicacy of Thought" at the earliest possible moment in a girl's life. If her family attempts to impose them, he suggests, after a girl has already grown and become conscious of her own natural inclinations, she may always be aware of only *playing* at female character when she does fulfill the imposed role; like Jenny, she may feel as though in female drag when dressed in petticoats. Jenny's parents not only neglected to instill in her feminine "Principles," but they failed to impose a physical regime that would lead her to experience her body as delicate, weak, and naturally suited to the restrictions of female behavior and dress.

> She was by no means delicately or tenderly brought up; that being an Error which Parents never fall into in that Country: There was no Care taken of her Complexion, or her Shape, no Regimen of Diet observed to keep her lean; but in every Thing Nature left to take its Course, in as wild a Manner as the Animal Creation: She grew very soon to be a lusty robust Girl, and began now to be too big to be allowed any longer to romp with the Boys; and tho' she was yet but turned of eleven, she . . . was discovered in the Haggard one Evening attempting a Game of Romps with a Boy some Years elder than herself: This convinced her Parents that there was no manly Exercise in which Miss could not bear a Hand. (17–18)

A physical discipline of diet, corsets, and skin care, and the internalized notions of female beauty that would have accompanied it, might have formed Jenny as something other than a "lusty robust Girl," capable of any "manly Exercise," including sexual experimentation. Once her body has been left to develop naturally, however, the explicit and external physical discipline of corporal punishment proves entirely ineffective in re-forming her.

When Jenny is "put under the Tuition" of her father's aunt, and this aunt decides to administer "some moderate Correction" of the ungovernable Jenny with a birch, Jenny first laughs, then "fell foul with her Fists at the old Lady," and finally "held her down, beating her all the while with a Birch-Rod which the old Lady intended for another Use" (20–21). Even when her great-aunt has righted Jenny's inversion of the order of discipline and taken her revenge by having

Jenny flogged every day for a fortnight, she only drives Jenny into more devious forms of subversion and usurped institutional authority. It is at this point in her life that Jenny learns the power of affecting that feminine character which it is too late to persuade her she naturally possesses (21–22). In the period immediately following these events, Jenny both becomes "a Coquet" and first experiments with passing for a man: she thus launches, at the same time, her careers as a kind of female impersonator and as a male one (22–25). When Jenny is next forced by her family to join a convent, she extends her powers of affectation to encompass "the Character of a Devotee," quickly discovering that the convent's codified, explicit forms of authority and discipline merely offer new opportunities for masquerade, and enthusiastically entering into its pervasive, diffuse eroticism, which links women to women as well as women to men.

Soon after Jenny has eloped from the nunnery with a colonel, she replaces her nun's habit with "a Habit and Equipage fitting for a young Gentleman," so that she can travel with the Colonel on his military campaign in Flanders. "In that Dress," we are told, Jenny "quite ravished the Colonel, who grew every Day more fond of her"; and she herself takes great pleasure in "this kind of perpetual Masquerade" (51–52). Though the reasons for Jenny's disguise are supposedly pragmatic, the results seem to be erotically gratifying to both Jenny and the Colonel, layering their heterosexual relations with the homoeroticism of attraction between a man and a male impersonator. The little we learn about the Colonel presents us with the conventional outlines of the dashing "Cavalier"—he is an army officer, a man of "condition" (47), and a sexual adventurer—but the notion of masculinity embodied in that type is here drawn into question by the logic of homoeroticized relations among military "men." Earlier in the pamphlet, when Jenny dressed in male clothing not to pursue an affair with a man but to "pick up the Women of the Town" (24), the author already suggested something unstable about the masculinity of the Cavalier type by repeatedly referring to Jenny and the maid who accompanies her on her sexual masquerades as "Maiden Cavaliers" and "She-Cavaliers" (24–25).

In the final episode of *A Brief Account*, when Jenny appears at the Pretender's camp at the head of two hundred and fifty clansmen, wearing a sea-green riding habit and a velvet cape and carrying a naked sword in her hand, she rides directly up to the Prince and an-

nounces to him that he himself is responsible for her remarkable behavior: "for she found that so glorious a Cause had raised in her
Breast every manly Thought, and quite extinguished the Woman"
(60–61). Like *The Female Rebels*, *A Brief Account* acknowledges a certain attractiveness in Prince Charles, "the young Chevalier" (61), as
a figure, but at the same time emphasizes that it is the very nature of
the masculine figure Charles cuts to incite destabilizing responses in
women. Although the author of *A Brief Account* does not provide
any explicit depiction of an alternative "Whig" masculinity, he implies that the seventeenth-century image of the Cavalier, associated
with support for Charles I during the Civil War and with the culture
of the Restoration Stuart court, constitutes a highly theatricalized
masculinity that only invites female usurpation. Thus he suggests
that the apparently rigorous strictures of the Catholic religion and
the apparently virile promiscuity of Cavalier culture, both identified
with the Jacobite cause, prove equally vulnerable to subversion, re-
sulting equally in gender confusion, inversions of authority, and
sexual desire that cannot be contained within the bounds of normative heterosexuality.[29]

In *The Jacobite's Journal*, Fielding develops the insinuations in
A Brief Account that Jacobite masculinity may be associated not only
with heterosexual promiscuity but with various forms of homoeroticism; and the *Journal* grounds this problem of sexuality specifically in questions about proper *male* education and discipline. As we
shall see in Chapter 7, Fielding's most scandalized treatments of male
Jacobitism concentrate on the relation between Jacobite tutors and
their pupils, whose subjection to corporal punishment teaches them
not only to submit absolutely to authority but also to look for pleasure in a kind of homoeroticized pain. The Whig cause thus attaches
itself both to a newly sharp delineation between male and female
roles and to a redefined and newly adamant account of heterosexuality as the proper nexus of emotional relations. While never described as a Jacobite, the figure of Roger Thwackum appears as the
representative of a homoeroticized and pathologically absolute notion of authority within the heterosexual world of *Tom Jones*.

In the pages of *Tom Jones*, Fielding, like the author of *A Brief
Account*, suggests the greater effectiveness of a discipline that is discursive and internalized rather than coercive and explicitly hierarchical; at the same time, he too refrains from insisting that the in-

ternalized rigors of modern gender roles, and of normative sexuality, are based upon nature's dictates alone. Indeed, the plot of *Tom Jones* and Fielding's rhetoric there call attention to the specifically "adoptive" or constructed nature both of gender roles and of sexuality.

'Tom Jones,'
Jacobitism, and Gender

History and Fiction at the Ghosting Hour

> Why is an Author obliged to be a more disinterested
> Patriot than any other? And why is he, whose
> Livelihood is in his Pen, a greater Monster in using
> it to serve himself, than he who uses his Tongue to
> the same Purpose?
>
> —Fielding, *The Jacobite's Journal*, no. 17

Supremely voluble as it is, there are moments at which *Tom Jones* becomes reticent. In this way it is like its own heroine. For example, when Fielding explains that Sophia was not in fact so much offended with the freedoms Jones has taken with another woman as with the freedoms she thinks he has taken (though he has not) with her own name and character, he describes two opposite morals that might be drawn from this, and then comments: "Now perhaps the Reflections which we should be here inclined to draw, would alike contradict both these Conclusions, and would shew that these Incidents contribute only to confirm the great, useful and uncommon Doctrine, which it is the Purpose of this whole Work to inculcate, and which we must not fill up our Pages by frequently repeating" (652). Teasingly, Fielding refrains from naming "the great, useful

and uncommon Doctrine" that his whole work is meant to inculcate; he indicates its content only negatively, by withholding his assent from *both* the moralizing conclusions he has just described.

We might recall this moment later in the novel when Allworthy cites Sophia's reticence as proof of her properly feminine character. Her reticence is structured like Fielding's: Allworthy reports
that he "once, to try her only, desired her Opinion on a Point which
was controverted between Mr. *Thwackum* and Mr. *Square*," and that
she confirmed his good opinion of her by refusing to take either side.
Sophia presents her refusal modestly (or coyly?), explaining it in
terms of her own incapacity, and Allworthy interprets it as evidence
of her "highest Deference to the Understandings of Men" (882–83).
The male narrator, on the other hand, hints at the inadequacy of the
choices before him, suggesting that his own reflections perhaps
would "contradict" both. Fielding has left no question in the course
of *Tom Jones* that the two moral systems advanced by Thwackum
and Square offer as unacceptable a pair of choices as the two moral
conclusions that he himself has refused to choose between, and Sophia's judgments of people and of situations have consistently
proved sound; so that we might interpret her withholding of assent
from both men's views as confirmation of the higher wisdom inherent in a "Sophia," rather than as humble deference to the superior
learning of men.

The wisdom of *Tom Jones* itself is characterized by the
"neither-nor" quality that this scene attributes to its heroine; its novelistic narrative provides Fielding with a form depending crucially
on "suspense," both as an experience of a plot's unfolding and as a
particular stance toward the paired choices of the public political and
intellectual world. Within this form, however, "woman" does not
simply occupy a position outside the terms of public controversy.
She functions, more profoundly, as a promised final recompense for
the ambiguities and uncertainties present in the working out of those
terms. The private value of her name (as Sophia so strongly feels)
must be protected, just as the high truth of Fielding's novel's "uncommon Doctrine" must not be degraded by being reduced to a position within one historical conflict. At the same time, Fielding acknowledges that the purely private status of Sophia's "Name and
Character" is only an appealing fiction. If his novel's characters can
seem to come to life for us, centuries after the novel's composition,
it is not because they exist outside a history that would place them

upon a static, determining grid of opposed terms; it is, rather, because they are so much inside a history that is always multiple and in motion, in a state of ongoing material conflict and struggle over the meaning of terms.

In Fielding's overtly polemical writings on the Jacobite Rebellion, when he clearly writes not as a "disinterested Patriot" but in the service of the Pelham ministry (as in *The Jacobite's Journal*, *The History of the Present Rebellion in Scotland*, and *The True Patriot*), he insists on the righteousness of the government cause, praises the bravery of the Duke of Cumberland, and exhorts his readers to join in armed loyal associations against the rebellion.[1] Within these writings themselves, however, as we will see, tonal uncertainties and ambiguities in the use of a persona trouble his polemic. In *Tom Jones*, Fielding greatly heightens and highlights a sense that the two sides of the conflict, even in the situation of armed struggle, cannot be clearly distinguished: he there depicts the King's army as unruly, inchoate, and divided, populated with men who either don't care what they fight for or who might be identified with the enemy (such as the enlisted man named "Tom French," the officer who actually is French, or the villainous Northerton, whose name echoes the common phrase, "the rebellion in the North").[2] The novel throws the Whig view of government and society into question in a number of ways—by its satirical rendering of the Whig Mrs. Western, for instance, or by its cynical treatment of "prudence," "system," and financial self-interest,[3] evoking some of the same reservations about Whig bureaucracy voiced at the close of the progovernment *Female Rebels*. Significantly, critics have even disagreed as to whether the novel's hero should be identified with the young leader of the Jacobite cause or with that of the government.[4]

Given this picture of the confused and fluid nature of public political conflict, perhaps it is not surprising that Fielding at times pins his hopes for the enduring meaning and power of his novel not on the record it provides of war and governance, but on the testimony it offers to a private relationship of love. Invoking the "bright Love of Fame" to inspire his work, he specifies, "Not thee I call, who over swelling Tides of Blood and Tears, dost bear the Heroe on to Glory, while Sighs of Millions waft his spreading Sails." Rather, he asks that the Love of literary Fame

Foretel me that some tender Maid, whose Grandmother is yet unborn, hereafter, when, under the fictitious Name of *Sophia*, she reads the real Worth

which once existed in my *Charlotte*, shall, from her sympathetic Breast, send
forth the heaving Sigh. Do thou teach me not only to foresee, but to enjoy,
nay, even to feed on future Praise. Comfort me by a solemn Assurance, that
when the little Parlour in which I sit at this Instant, shall be reduced to a
worse furnished Box, I shall be read, with Honour, by those who never
knew nor saw me, and whom I shall neither know nor see. (683)

Fielding here invokes his own heterosexual relationship to describe
what he hopes will save his novel from "that dreadful Hole" of sor-
did ephemerality into which he fears his periodical essays have
quickly disappeared (*Jacobite's Journal*, 425); and he locates his present motivation and reward, even sustenance, in a fantasy about the
timeless revivability of female worth.

 Fielding's novel has indeed outlived any popular experience of
his periodical essays. Its ability to do so depends upon an evolution
of subject matter that its own plot enacts when Tom's progression
toward battle with the rebels is gradually transformed into a pursuit
of Sophia—that is, of female virtue, of heterosexual union, and of
personal happiness. The novel thus promises that its story will still
speak to us long after the '45 Rebellion has been forgotten; that it can
unite people from disparate centuries (and particularly women) in
transparently shared feelings of sympathetic identification; that we
do not need to be "marked" by any particular Jacobite *or* Whig instructor to feel its power. The novel thus also seems to come into
accord with Nancy Armstrong's model of domestic fiction—a form
which, she says, refers to "the private regions of the self," establishing "a specialized domain of culture where apolitical truths" can be
told and unfolding "the operations of human desire as if they were
independent of political history." And yet the direct inclusion of this
process of deflection within the plot's own movement seems to distinguish *Tom Jones* from Armstrong's paradigmatic novel, as this one
fails to perform, in silence, "the operations of division and self-
containment" between politics and private life which she describes.
It relies upon this division, and yet it does not respect a prohibition
against referring to "the use of words that created and still maintains
these primary divisions within the culture."[5]

 Rather, this novel actively shows us the interconnections between historically specific political purposes and this experience of
private pursuits; and it acknowledges the historicity of experiences
of gender and sexuality. It implicitly suggests that Tom's search for
Sophia and his commitment to protecting her may themselves func-

tion as an effective ideological response to a generalized "Jacobite" threat of political unrest, which it frames as present even within the King's army, as epitomized by Northerton, who aggressively abuses a woman's good name and honor, and who is later discovered in a violent attack upon a woman's body. When Fielding pauses in the progress of his novel's plot to comment on the nature of his own writing—when he fantasizes about the particular form in which its vindication and reward might come—he emphasizes a version of authority central to the Whig rather than the Jacobite political philosophy: an authority that will be realized through individual acts of private (and especially female) experience to be consummated in a promised future, rather than an authority grounded in the past of patrilineal descent. He does not deny that the form of authority he claims is associated with a particular political allegiance, but instead recommends that form for its superior power. Even as *Tom Jones* turns away from the public events of the 1745 rebellion and concentrates increasingly on the concerns of the private "feminine" sphere, it repeatedly figures personal experiences of gendered identity and heterosexual desire as historically marked themselves.

Fielding creates a strange and ambivalent emblem of such when he invents a fanciful plot device to explain how Tom communicates with Sophia during her confinement. Knowing Sophia's special appetite for the eggs enclosed in female fowl, Black George uses a pullet's belly as the vehicle in which he transmits Tom's letter to Sophia. When Sophia begins to "dissect the Fowl," she discovers that within it are not only eggs but written words. Fielding asks,

at what Price shall we esteem a Bird which so totally contradicts all the Laws of Animal Œconomy, as to contain a Letter in its Belly? *Ovid* tells us of a Flower into which *Hyacinthus* was metamorphosed, that bears Letters on its Leaves, which *Virgil* recommended as a Miracle to the Royal Society of his Day; but no Age nor Nation hath ever recorded a Bird with a Letter in its Maw. (842–43)

In his discussions of "the ridiculous" both in the preface to *Joseph Andrews* and in *The Jacobite's Journal*, Fielding invokes the "mother's belly" as the very image of an honored natural space that should not be violently assailed by ridicule, with its aggressive drive to dissect affected from authentic or natural identity; within the plot of *Joseph Andrews*, I have argued, a mother's belly comes to represent the lost possibility of complete, unmediated connection between separate selves, and of a kind of marking of one self by another that is purely natural, fusing biology with imagination and desire. Here, Fielding stages the unlikely intrusion of the written word into a female bird's belly, alongside the eggs of her offspring, and he then confronts his heroine with this conjunction, showing her discovery that Tom's highly rhetorical declaration of heterosexual love has been inscribed and inserted into the biological cavity of female reproduction.

The tone of this passage is odd and is complicated by Fielding's comparison of the letter Sophia finds in the pullet with another instance of verbal markings upon nature—Apollo's commemoration of his love for Hyacinthus in the flower he inscribed with the letters of his lamentation.[6] Fielding develops his comparison of Tom's and Apollo's inscriptions by pretending to locate them, to absurd effect, within various social institutions (of economics, of literary tradition, of science, and specifically the Royal Society).[7] These institutions, like Hyacinthus and Apollo's erotic bond, are constituted between men, and they are clearly social constructions, so that the references to them heighten a sense of the special egregiousness of imagining the female belly as a site for temporary and artificial inscription. Fielding's willful conflation of two different meanings of "Œconomy," telescoping questions of "price" with those of biological law, introduces the tension between social or artificial and natural phenomena that will dominate the passage; and the letter from Tom that follows confronts us with the conventionality of expressions of romantic love ("Pardon me this Presumption, and pardon me a greater still, if I ask you whether my Advice, my Assistance, my Presence, my Absence, my Death or my Tortures can bring you any Relief?"). Tom's declarations of love (like Joseph's protestations of virtue or of grief) are absurdly formal and inflated, but the context of the novel as a whole asks us to take them as effectively sincere. The vehicle of those declarations in this episode is highly contingent itself, and it specifically draws into question one symbol of natural sentiment and human connection.

Recall that in Fielding's first published work, *The Masquerade*, in a passage immediately following the discussion centered on affectation and unstable gender roles, the poet sees what he takes to be a man in a hideous mask, and asks how it could possibly come into the man's "Gizard / T'invent so horrible a Vizard?" He is shocked to learn from the muse that the monstrous but natural mask the man wears came not into his "Gizard" but into "his Mother's Belly":

"you must know, that horrid Phyz is / (*Puris naturalibus*) his Visage."
He is shocked because he assumes that the mother's belly is the site
of a pure and recognizably "natural" creation, which should be
easily distinguished both from artifice and from the fluidity of identity (and specifically of gender roles) characterizing the world of the
masquerade. He thus gestures toward the space of biological reproduction as one source of secure identity for the self. *Tom Jones* leaves
that space empty—or as much filled with words as any other—locating its title character in a network of specifically adoptive relations, and indicating that the features of private identity (including
one's gender), historical in nature, are as much characterized by confusion, multiple reference, and fluidity as the features of this novel's
political world.

The construction of Tom's gender, or the ongoing process of his
adoption of particular features and forms of masculinity, begins at
the moment of his literal adoption by Allworthy. Found sleeping in
Allworthy's bed, the infant Tom is initially described by the narrator
in terms that leave his sex undetermined.[8] Until Tom has been accepted into the Allworthy family and given a social identity as part
of that family, he has no gender, even if his little body (presumably)
has a manifest biological sex: the narrator, Mrs. Wilkins, and Allworthy all refer to Tom as "it" and with ungendered terms ("the
Child," "the Creature," "the little Wretch") until Allworthy announces in the morning that he intends "to breed *him* up as his own"
(39–44; emphasis mine). Before this declaration, Wilkins for one
sees the child only as "a kind of noxious Animal" (44) rather than
recognizably either a human "boy" or a human "girl"; but after it,
the child takes on not only a grammatical gender—the same as its
adoptive father's—but that adoptive father's first name. This, however, does not summarily settle the matter of the boy's gender: it initiates, rather, a sustained and complicated process by which Tom's
own version of masculinity must be negotiated and defined.[9] As several critics have noted, the description of Tom's appearance, unlike
that of Captain Blifil's, carefully balances conventionally "masculine" with "feminine" attractions rather than identifying him with
a masculinity defined narrowly by strength, coarseness, and bulk
(510, 65–66).[10]

Sophia, on the other hand, is the Westerns' own biological
child. She is never presented in the novel as an infant "it" to be dis-

covered and adopted, but is introduced to the reader first as the eighteen-year-old "Heroine of this Work, a Lady with whom we ourselves are greatly in Love" (149). Indeed, when Fielding pauses on the brink of introducing Sophia and begins a new book, he opens the book's introductory chapter with a remark that seems to root his novel's characters specifically in "Nature": "As Truth distinguishes our Writings, from those idle Romances which are filled with Monsters, the Productions, not of Nature, but of distempered Brains" (150). However, the comments that follow quickly problematize the category of nature, just as, in the very first chapter of the novel, Fielding's elaboration on the promise that its "provision" will be "no other than HUMAN NATURE" (32) soon estranges that familiar category, making it seem at once grotesque and inaccessible in any "raw" state.[11] Here, Fielding says there could be no more proper occasion for "inserting those ornamental Parts of our Work" ("sundry Similies, Descriptions, and other kind of poetical Embellishments") than that of introducing "the Heroine of this Heroic, Historical, Prosaic Poem"(151–52); and when he explains why he cannot simply present the character of Sophia to us but must "prepare the Mind of the Reader for her Reception," he locates her identity not among the productions of nature but in the effects of theatrical and political spectacle.

Both playwrights and playhouse managers, Fielding observes, exploit the extent to which our experience of character depends upon highly conventionalized effects of spectacle: we recognize that an actor represents a hero if drums and trumpets herald his approach, a lover if soft music conducts him or her onto the stage, or a king if he is "ushered on the Stage by a large Troop of half a dozen Scene-shifters." Developing the last example to demonstrate how necessary these attendants are to the theatrical magic of a king's "Appearance," Fielding begins to suggest how public identity is structured by role-playing and spectacle outside the theater as well; he refers to an actor playing Pyrrhus simply as "King *Pyrrhus*" and so conflates the historical king, a role in a play, and the actor who plays it. In the paragraph that follows he explicitly extends his observation to actual politicians such as the Lord Mayor, who "contracts a good deal of that Reverence which attends him through the Year, by the several Pageants which precede his Pomp." His comments on the illusion of personal authority created by "much preceding State" suggestively prefigure the insights of a Stephen Orgel or a Louis

Montrose, but this train of thought seems to have taken him far afield from the private virtue and beauty of the heroine he is about to introduce. "When I have seen a Man strutting in a Procession," he remarks, "after others whose Business was only to walk before him, I have conceived a higher Notion of his Dignity, than I have felt on seeing him in a common Situation." In the last turn of this prefatory chapter, Fielding settles on "the Custom of sending on a Basket-woman, who is to precede the Pomp at a Coronation, and to strew the Stage with Flowers" as the example of "preceding State" best suited to his present purpose (153).

This example sets a more flatteringly feminine scene for his heroine's entrance than the images Fielding has conjured of pompous strutting, military drumrolls, and stately processions. Even it, however, brackets the notion of nature by asking us to imagine flowers that have been strewn deliberately and on a political occasion; and the sustained discussion of how heroes, kings, and lord mayors create their public roles provides an oddly masculine and politicized model of identity for our first view of the novel's heroine. The following chapter quietly extends this suggestion of a connection between the creation of political authority and the private character of women by likening Sophia to famous beauties associated with the post-1688 court or with the Whig party: "the Gallery of Beauties at *Hampton-Court. . . . each bright* Churchill *of the Galaxy . . .* all the Toasts of the *Kit-cat. . . .* the Picture of Lady *Ranelagh*" (155–56).[12] While Fielding's discussion of pomp suggests that the appearance of Sophia's distinctly feminine character may in some sense be theatrically constructed too, these references to beauties raise the question of whether that feminine character may itself contribute to the dignifying pomp or authority of a particular government. In *The Jacobite's Journal*, we might recall, Fielding alludes to the superior beauty and femininity of Whig women as proof of the justice of his political cause (e.g., 98–99, 101). With the example of the basket-woman strewing flowers at a coronation, Fielding reminds us that apparently nonpolitical figures may be used to authorize claims to political power: He comments that "The Antients would certainly have invoked the Goddess *Flora* for this Purpose, and it would have been no Difficulty for the Priests or Politicians to have persuaded the People of the real Presence of the Deity, though a plain Mortal had personated her, and performed her Office." The politician's exploitation of theatrical effects in this case passes into an actual illusion about who or what is present, at once drawing upon and shaping the people's most basic beliefs and experience.

If Fielding here meditates on what we might describe as "ideological" methods of preserving power, he does not, however, treat those methods as typically operating through simple or total illusion, mystification, or the creation of "false consciousness." After all, he pauses to share his thoughts on such methods specifically because (he says) he is about to try to use them on us; and, though he will indeed invoke Flora in introducing Sophia, he assures us that "we have no such Design [as the Ancients'] of imposing on our Reader; and therefore those who object to the Heathen Theology, may, if they please, change our Goddess into the above-mentioned Basket-woman." The tone of the passage to follow, with its Flora and Zephyrus and singing birds, is layered: it is of course, on one level, self-consciously comic, a mock-epic excursion that thrives on the incongruous identification of goddesses and mere basket-women;[13] on another, it seriously serves to herald the heroine in whose difficulties we will share and in whose beauty and virtue we must trust. Dwelling on the basket-woman/Flora, Fielding sketches the possibility of a kind of layered consciousness in a viewer's or reader's reception of a spectacle or text: we are not "imposed" upon to believe in Flora's actual presence at Sophia's entrance, but her invocation influences or impresses us as "preceding Pomp" nonetheless.[14] As Fielding describes it, this layered consciousness is created by the process of historical change; we inherit the heathens' reverence for or awe of Flora, because they believed in her, though we do not.

When he compares Sophia to famous English beauties, Fielding emphasizes the even more fleetingly historical nature of their names' evocative power. "Thou may'st remember," he tells the reader, "*each bright* Churchill *of the* Galaxy, and all the Toasts of the Kit-cat. Or if their Reign was before thy Times . . .*" (155). Fielding ends this series of comparisons with an acknowledgment that some beauties' reigns were before *his* time: "She was most like the Picture of Lady *Ranelagh*; and I have heard more still to the famous Duchess of *Mazarine*." In pointing back to the "reign" of Hortense Mancini, Duchess of Mazarin, in the 1670's, Fielding also points back to a time when court beauties cast their glow upon a royal court in the possession of the Stuarts, whose ongoing claims to the throne Fielding actively opposed (and who he elsewhere insists are supported by ugly Amazons in unflattering plaid [*Jacobite's Journal*, 101]). From this last dissonant entry in the series, Fielding swerves to assert the finally private frame of reference for Sophia's character. "Most of all, she resembled one whose Image never can depart from my Breast, and whom, if thou dost remember, thou hast then, my Friend, an adequate Idea of *Sophia*." Few readers, certainly, could remember; none now can; and yet the very suggestion that we might have known and remember Fielding's first wife—the gesture toward his own life, and toward Charlotte's purely domestic and personal reign in his heart—provides one kind of powerfully affecting "preceding Pomp" to the introduction of Sophia—an invocation of the increasingly privileged notions of companionate marriage and of private female character. The Sophia we will come to know, however, is neither a purely private and ahistorical creation, nor a strictly Whig construction of feminine character, but a highly individual paragon of "femininity" as construed, simultaneously, within residual and newly dominant political cultures.[15] These cultures' conflicting accounts of gender appear in the tensions and fluidities that characterize Sophia's feminine identity as well as Tom's masculine one; and in this preface to his introduction of Sophia, Fielding prepares us to see claims to purely private character as themselves one form of public "preceding State."

In creating his heroine in *Tom Jones*, Fielding engages directly with the alternative possibilities for female character set up by Whig pamphlets such as *The Female Rebels* or *A Brief Account*, where the physical and moral "delicacy" or "softness," timidity, chastity, and compassion of a properly female "nature" are opposed to the passion, strength, and willful courage of women associated with Jacobitism or, more generally, with an old economic and political order. Although he frequently invokes the terms used to describe these opposed versions of female character, however, Fielding fails to locate Sophia clearly on either side of the opposition they sustain. While the Duchess of Perth, Lady Ogilvy, and Jenny Cameron do not hesitate to ride along with the men of Charles's army and even into battle, Sophia only reluctantly accompanies her father on the hunt, and Fielding is careful to note that the sport "was of too rough and masculine a Nature to suit with her Disposition" (199). While the Duchess and Lady Ogilvy also insist on seizing the metaphorical reins of family government, ruling over their husbands, Sophia assures Mrs.

Fitzpatrick that she would rather give up her own understanding than see any defects in her husband's (595). Fielding emphasizes Sophia's "Innocence," "Modesty," and "Gentleness" (157, 559), and of course there is no question about her unshakeable chastity. On the other hand, Fielding is also at times careful to distinguish Sophia's profile from that of "the new woman" which Watt first described and which we found advanced in the closing pages of the Whig *Female Rebels*. Flora MacDonald's most paradigmatically feminine virtues are described there as those of irrational feeling, but Sophia, we are told, exercises an especially "strong" capacity for reason from an early age (199). Fielding may have Richardson's heroines particularly in mind when he makes a point of informing us that Sophia does not faint when startled by the unexpected appearance of a man (559); that she is incapable of exploiting the appearance of physical weakness or illness (897); that, when threatened with marriage to a villain, she is able to escape on her own two legs (351); and that, "with all the Gentleness which a Woman can have, [she] had all the Spirit which she ought to have" (559).

Repeatedly, Fielding asserts Sophia's possession of this last quality, "Spirit" (167, 559, 579, 797, 903)—a quality that is particularly associated with female Jacobites both in Fielding's own *Jacobite's Journal* (e.g., 98–99) and in such pamphlets as *The Female Rebels* and *A Brief Account*. He dwells most upon this quality and on the element of "natural Courage" in Sophia when she runs away from her father's house to avoid marriage to Blifil, having answered Honour's fears for their safety with the blustering promise that "I will defend you; for I will take a Pistol with me" (351). The situation is reminiscent of Shakespearean comedy, and we might almost expect Sophia, like *As You Like It*'s Rosalind or *Two Gentlemen*'s Julia, to don male clothing as she sets out on her dangerous journey with her waiting-maid.[16] Even without actual male masquerade, Sophia's venture away from home is also reminiscent of the adventures of Jenny Cameron and other daring female rebels, and as Sophia stealthily unlocks the door of her father's house and sallies out, Fielding offers this distinction between her strengths and the negative terms in which the female rebels are often described:

Notwithstanding the many pretty Arts, which Ladies sometimes practice, to display their Fears on every little Occasion, (almost as many as the other Sex uses to conceal theirs) certainly there is a Degree of Courage, which not only becomes a Woman, but is often necessary to enable her to discharge her Duty. It is, indeed, the Idea of Fierceness, and not of Bravery, which destroys the Female Character. . . . perhaps, many a Woman who shrieks at a Mouse, or a Rat, may be capable of poisoning a Husband; or, what is worse, of driving him to poison himself. (559)

The first and last moments in this paragraph express doubts about the authenticity of the "new woman's" timidity and delicacy and serve to differentiate Fielding's heroine from that model of female character, while the middle of the paragraph carefully distinguishes between Sophia's admirable quality of "courage" or "bravery" and the "fierceness" that appears in *The Female Rebels* or *The Jacobite's Journal* as the mark of Jacobite women's unfeminine monstrosity. It is following this paragraph that Fielding asserts Sophia's simultaneous "Gentleness" and "Spirit," and a short way into Sophia's journey, Fielding reiterates the fact that she possesses "some little Degree of natural Courage" (579). The context of this later assertion suggests, however, that the subtle verbal distinctions employed by Fielding to define Sophia in the passage above cannot be relied upon to steer her character steadily on a "neither-nor" middle course between new and old ideas of female nature. For, though Sophia may be "brave" without being "fierce" like the female rebels, as far as the innkeeper on the road to London is concerned, she looks and acts like one of them. This innkeeper first embarrasses Sophia with a practical joke—he pretends to fall as he helps her off her horse so that she lands in a sexually suggestive posture on top of him—placing her literally, though involuntarily, in the position of the passionate and unruly "woman on top" (574).[17] Then he decides that she and Honour, riding about the countryside without even a footman, "are certainly some of the Rebel Ladies, who, they say, travel with the young Chevalier" (576–77).

Sophia is not Jenny Cameron, but the innkeeper's misrecognition of her serves not only to demonstrate his confident stupidity but also to activate some sense in which she might be. Carlton indicates as much, commenting, "Evidently Fielding wishes to portray Sophia as a union of politically significant opposites: Whig heroine on the one hand, 'Jenny Cameron' and her Jacobite father's daughter on the other." He reads Sophia's character in the same way he reads Tom's, for he argues that "Tom represents the best aspects of both, Whig liberty and Jacobite vitalism."[18] Carlton's argument very usefully suggests, then, that Tom and Sophia cannot be located within a single period's paradigms of ideal male and female character, but instead combine elements of paradigms from the two political cultures at issue in the Jacobite revolt. Since Carlton sees Fielding's political purpose in *Tom Jones* as that of defending and "naturalizing" the Whig order of government, however, he goes on to suggest that, if Fielding includes elements of the Stuart ethos in his idealized main characters, it is only to incorporate and clearly to "subordinate" them within an overall Whig scheme.[19] The interpretations of character and the readings of individual scenes that this notion of subordination produces sometimes seem tellingly strained, as when he comments that Sophia speaks in one scene "like a good Lockean."[20] Fielding is not himself, in any straightforward way, a "good Lockean" in *Tom Jones*; he does not there present a finally stable or unconflicted case for the principles of political society formulated by Locke.[21] In constructing the political significance of his characters—and, specifically, in assigning them "politically significant" traits from one or another paradigm of masculine or feminine character—Fielding shows, in fact, a particular interest in creating scenes of sustained conflict between these opposed traits, rather than in cleanly reconciling them in a character who can embody "the best aspects of both."

Fielding sets the two most striking of these scenes at what he describes as the ghosting hour. Sophia's most urgent experience of prolonged internal conflict consists of the struggle within her between filial obedience and romantic love—or, we might say, between the old model of arranged marriage and the new one of companionate marriage[22]—but it is when she has decided this conflict in favor of love and acts on that decision by leaving her father's house, that Fielding brings to the fore a complication or conflict in her character as viewed from the outside: the paradox of Sophia's "Gentleness" coexisting with her "Spirit" or "Courage." These contrasting if not contradictory virtues draw on opposed models of female nature—the passively virtuous "new woman" and the unruly old one—and, significantly, as he prepares to explain their coexistence in Sophia to us, Fielding locates Sophia's manifestation of spirit this way in time:

Twelve Times did the iron Register of Time beat on the sonorous Bell-metal, summoning the Ghosts to rise, and walk their nightly Round.—In plainer Language, it was Twelve o'Clock, and all the Family, as we have said, lay buried in Drink and Sleep, except only Mrs. *Western*, who was deeply engaged in reading a political Pamphlet, and except our Heroine, who now softly stole down Stairs, and having unbarred and unlocked one of the House Doors, sallied forth. (559)

Sophia's successful execution of an act more consonant with the female rebels' independence and daring than with Pamela's fainting virtue takes place, Fielding tells us, at the juncture between days, at a time when the spirits of things past might seem to rise and walk among us.[23] Most of the family lies "buried" in a kind of drugged sleep; the two women who wake both revive possibilities for female action largely suppressed by the notions of feminine nature increasingly dominant in Whig culture. These ghostly revivals, however, are enmeshed in contradictions: Mrs. Western's active interest in politics harks back to a period when women were not so absolutely disqualified from local political action,[24] but the pamphlets she reads, we assume, are Whig ones; Sophia's willfulness in escaping from her father's house evokes older notions of the unruly woman, but she escapes to protect her access to the newly central ideal of romantic marriage. These crisscrossing conjunctures of different historical models for feminine action and nature will lead initially (we have learned in the preceding pages) to "Confusion," and to a confusion that Fielding renders specifically as a dissonant volley of voices mingling feminine with masculine identity:

The Squire himself now sallied forth, and began to roar forth the Name of *Sophia* as loudly, and in as hoarse a Voice, as whileome did *Hercules* that of *Hylas*: And as the Poet tells us, that the whole Shore ecchoed back the Name of that beautiful Youth; so did the House, the Garden, and all the Neighboring Fields, resound nothing but the Name of *Sophia*, in the hoarse Voices of the Men, and in the shrill Pipes of the Women; while Echo seemed so pleased to repeat the beloved Sound, that if there is really such a Person, I believe *Ovid* hath belied her Sex.

Nothing reigned for a long time but Confusion. (556)

A frantic reiteration of Sophia's name cannot locate her in this scene—she has temporarily disappeared—and it only raises questions about her relation to male and to female characters in the traditional narratives in whose confused echoes she is meant to appear.

A near-babel of voices also erupts within that episode in which Tom appears most pressingly caught between conflicting versions of masculinity. As Carlton points out, "when Northerton affronts Jones's honor, the Cavalier code demands a duel. But Christianity forbids it," so that Tom's "Cavalier" and "Christian" heroisms are here brought into direct contradiction. Carlton sees this as a contradiction that Fielding is eager to "mute," or to seem to resolve: "Fielding's solution to this dilemma is to have Tom anguish over it for awhile, consult with a good Christian officer who nonetheless advises him to fight, finally decide to issue the challenge—and then to conclude the episode with a comically terrified sentinel, and Northerton vanished. The author has it both ways here: Tom is a Cavalier hero by intent and a Christian hero by the event."[25] This summary rendering of the episode, however, discounts Fielding's pointed emphasis on the disorientation and confusion that surrounds the conflict in the masculine roles it stages. The episode begins with Northerton's injury to Tom, which unleashes such a multitude of garbled voices that Fielding says he would need forty pens writing at once to recount them (the broken words of the French officer who no longer speaks French *or* English; the medical kibitzing of the crowd; the landlady's blithering iteration of her first husband's maxims; the surgeon's incomprehensibly technical pronouncements on Tom's wounds, to which the Lieutenant responds that he cannot "understand a Syllable" [377–82]); the episode concludes with the general uproar following Northerton's supposedly supernatural escape. In between, the nature of the conflict between Cavalier and Christian codes is less straightforward than Carlton allows, and the action that emerges from it, as from Sophia's experience of conflict, must unfold at the ghosting hour.

Though military notions of masculine honor demand a duel, and Christianity forbids it, it is paradoxically Tom's Christian convictions that determine him to seek out the duel that very night: he tells the Lieutenant that he is concerned at any delay in presenting his challenge to Northerton, for he is "really a Christian" and cannot willingly "cherish Malice in his Breast, in Opposition to the Command of him who hath expressly forbid it" (383). If he therefore determines to act in a way characteristic of old notions of masculinity, it is partly on the basis of motives to be located within a new model of masculine identity, that of the "Christian hero."[26] This complicated crossing of old and new paradigms of gendered behavior, like Sophia's, results in action that occurs at the turning point between one day and another; in this case the ghosts who are summoned by the midnight hour become the hero and his antagonist themselves. When "the Clock had now struck Twelve," Tom issues forth from his room, and with his coat covered with blood, his face white, a bandage around his head, and a sword and candle in his hands, he exhibits a "tremendous Figure" which Fielding says is more frightening than that of "the bloody *Banquo*."

"When the Centinel first saw our Heroe approach, his Hair began gently to lift up his Grenadier Cap," and he later swears that he has seen Tom appear as a ghost, "vomiting Fire out of his Mouth and Nostrils" and carrying Northerton off in a clap of thunder (387–89). Northerton himself might seem spectral in this scene, having disappeared without a trace from a guarded room. As the real explanation for Northerton's disappearance emerges in the following chapter, we find that, though it does not involve his actual ghostliness, it does reveal a ghostly admixture in him of past and present masculine roles: this "Cavalier hero *manqué*"[27] is not only reluctant to face either a duel or an honorable trial, but has relied on Whiggish bribery to achieve his escape rather than on a Cavalier conquest of the landlady's heart, as Fielding first leads us to believe (391–92). If there is any kind of supernatural force at work in this episode—and Fielding informs us in the pages that follow that ghosts are "the only supernatural Agents which can in any Manner be allowed to us Moderns" (399)—it is one that arises from the operations of history—that is, from a historical process that haunts the present with the lingering traces of past conceptions and social forms. As Fielding asks in *The Jacobite's Journal*, "what is our Idea of a Ghost, but that it is the Shadow only, or Appearance of something which hath once existed, but at present is no more" (381).

"Tho' [Partridge] was Coward enough in all Respects, yet his chief Fear was that of Ghosts" (443). This is unfortunate for Partridge, because he exists in the novel within a kind of perpetual ghosting hour—with himself as chief ghost of the kind I have been describing. "I thought you had been long since dead," Allworthy tells him when they meet again at the novel's close (935–36); Partridge himself says repeatedly, "*non sum qualis eram* [I am not what I was]" (829, 935, 515). He appears successively in the guise of schoolmaster, barber, and surgeon, presenting himself in this last capacity "with so different an Air and Aspect . . . that he could scarce be known to be the same Person" (423). When Tom stumbles over how to formulate such a strangely composite identity ("'Mr. *Barber,* or Mr. *Surgeon,* or Mr. *Barber-Surgeon,*' said *Jones*"), Partridge responds that the separation of barbers and surgeons in 1745 into two distinct corporations was a cruel blow "to me who unite both in my own Person" (424, 424n). But Partridge's very name encodes, from the first, a ghostly contradiction created within his identity by national political change.

When Allworthy tells Partridge that he thought he had been "long since dead," we might fancy that he has momentarily confused the fictional Partridge with the historical John Partridge, who had indeed died thirty years before the main action of *Tom Jones.* The identity of names is in some ways apt: our Partridge is a part-time doctor and avid interpreter of omens, while the earlier Partridge was a doctor, astrologer, and almanac-maker. The life of the historical Partridge itself might be said to anticipate the fictional Partridge's revival from presumed death—John Partridge achieved his most enduring fame for the dogged persistence with which he survived the social fact of his own death. Jonathan Swift granted this minor figure his measure of immortality by beginning a parody of Partridge's almanacs with a prediction of Partridge's imminent demise. In due time Swift issued a report that the prediction had been accomplished, followed by a broadside "Elegy on the Death of Mr. Partridge"; this literary joke took on the status of social reality when the company of stationers struck the dead Partridge from their rolls; and Partridge advertised in vain that he was "not only now alive, but was also alive upon the 29th of March in question."[28]

If Swift thus created an involuntarily spectral existence for the original Partridge at the crossroads of history and fiction, the historical reference within the name "Partridge" in *Tom Jones* gives him the specific kind of ghostly status, arising from a contradiction between past and present models of identity, that we have found in Fielding's scenes of historical juncture. Both the historical and the fictional Partridges support rebellions against England's reigning government; however, since the Glorious Revolution has occurred between the rebellions they support, this likeness only marks a sharp conflict between the Partridges' politics, with the earlier one a zealous opponent to the Catholic succession and the later a Jacobite. This conflict points, in turn, to one between the writers who satirize the two Partridges: the Tory Swift ridicules the Protestant alarmism of John Partridge, while the Whig Fielding portrays his Partridge's Jacobitism as superstitious and absurd.

Earlier in his writing career, however, Fielding had so identified with Swift and his Tory literary friends that he had signed some of his own satires "Scriblerus Secundus," and his politics, like theirs, had been those of Opposition. Despite Fielding's dramatic change in avowed political allegiance, Swift remained a kind of alter ego for him to the end, embodying for Fielding the Augustan ideal of corrective satire.[29] As is evident in *Joseph Andrews*, *The Jacobite's Journal*, and elsewhere, Fielding's relation to satire became increasingly ambivalent and vexed, in ways closely interconnected with his divided and unstable political allegiances. The disjunctive frames of historical reference within which we may simultaneously place the identity of "Partridge," and the contradictions that arise from them, thus speak of Fielding's own ghosting hour: not only did he live through the passage between one political era and another, but those eras met within him, old ideological forms persisting alongside the new, his "character" as much the ground of crisscrossing, conflicting models of identity, of literary method, and of political value, as those of Tom and Sophia. Indeed, the character of Fielding can sometimes seem as difficult to locate as that of his strangely fluid creation, the Jacobite Partridge—like himself "a Fellow of great Oddity and Humour"—"Mr. *Barber*, or Mr. *Surgeon*, or Mr. *Barber-Surgeon*," or perhaps something different altogether.

The multiplicity, the final incoherence, of the "rules" or "geometries" that locate Fielding in history does not mean, however, that his works are without ideological force. *Tom Jones* in particular, massive in size and in the audience it has always commanded, at once draws upon and advances the increasingly dominant Whig ideology of its time, giving substance to the new fictions of an idealized female "nature" and of a separate feminine sphere that the terms of the debate surrounding the Jacobite rebellion demonstrate to have had such important and immediate political stakes. It is not chance that the prominent Whig politicians Lyttelton and Pitt actively "puffed" *Tom Jones* even before it was published and helped insure its sensational success.[30] At the same time, Fielding's novel, like his basket-woman scattering flowers, does not simply "impose" upon us: it acknowledges and questions, even as it employs and exploits, the construction of specific versions of masculine and feminine identity, and of heterosexuality as we know it.

The plot of *Tom Jones* allegorizes, for instance, the way in which Whig ideology seeks to guarantee its new financial institutions through the notion of a private female sphere and a purely personal experience of romantic love. In the transition that so shapes the apparent balance between political and personal events within *Tom Jones*, when Tom abandons his plan to rejoin the King's army and devotes himself entirely to pursuing Sophia, it is because he has been given a new specific objective in finding her: a beggar has presented Tom with a little gilt pocket-book containing Sophia's name and a bank-bill for £100, which Tom determines he must return to Sophia intact (631–35). In a sense, Tom's pursuit of Sophia is thus intertwined, narratively, with a mission that Fielding and other Whig writers argued was as essential to England's defeat of the rebellion as armed resistance—that is, the protection of the value of England's public credit.[31] Fielding concluded his *History of the Present Rebellion in Scotland* with an homage to those Englishmen who had responded to this part of the Jacobite threat: "witness that ever-memorable Association in Defence of public Credit . . . which hath totally defeated one of the most wicked and basest Designs to blow up the whole Nation, which was ever devised by Man."[32] Significantly, in *Tom Jones*, the Jacobite Partridge urges Tom to break into the bank-bill and use part of it for himself, returning it with a diminished value to its owner, but Tom is outraged at this suggestion (675–78); when he eventually finds Sophia in London and presents her with her bank-bill, he announces proudly, "I hope, Madam, you will find it of the same Value, as when it was lost" (731).

Tom's protection of the value of Sophia's bank-bill is implicitly connected by Fielding with his respect for the privacy properly afforded that female name inscribed in the pocket-book containing the bill. Shortly after Tom receives the pocket-book and bank-bill, Fielding explains, "so delicate was he with regard to *Sophia*, that he never willingly mentioned her Name in the Presence of many People." In fact, it is the Jacobite Partridge who has been so shamelessly eager to talk about Sophia in public, leading to the false impression that Tom has taken "Freedoms" with her "Name and Character" (651). Whereas the phallus served as the symbolic guarantor of money as well as of "value" more generally in the earlier satires of the castrato, the protection of a woman's private name and the pursuit of romantic union with that woman here become the vehicles with which the credit of bank-bills is insured.[33] Throughout *Tom Jones*, Fielding creates a slippage between the political villainy of Jacobitism and the sexual villainy of aggressors against women's private reputation and person: Tom's intent to fight the rebels is rerouted into the necessary defense first of Sophia's name and later of Mrs. Waters's body against Northerton's aggressions; when Partridge interprets a puppet-master's flag as that of the Jacobite army, he turns out to be mistaken, but the puppet-master's real villainy soon emerges in the form of his desire to rob and rape Sophia. The properly private character of woman's experience is underlined once more in the novel's closing pages, when we are told that Sophia "was now in private become a Bride too," and that she "had earnestly desired her Father, that no others of the Company, who were that Day to dine with him, should be acquainted with her Marriage" (978–79).

A confidence in the private nature of her union with Tom allows Sophia to get through the day of her wedding "pretty well," but when her father blurts out a toast to the bride at supper, "there was not a Person present made wiser by this Discovery." The marriage between Tom and Sophia has been a public secret, held in common by all present, and Fielding laughingly underscores not only the "privacy" of it, but the status of that privacy as shared social fiction. Throughout *Tom Jones* Fielding suggests a general connection between the creation of fiction and governance (as in his powerful, if playful analogies between authors, fathers, and kings); and in the *Hamlet* episode, for instance, he hints that the power of specifically naturalistic representation may belong to Whig government and culture in particular. The Jacobite Partridge proves incapable of comprehending the status of Garrick's naturalistic acting, though he feels its sway, and he appropriately chooses the *King* as the most powerful actor on stage simply for his conventionally commanding presence (852–57): what Partridge seems to lack that the Whig characters share is the knowledge of what it means to appreciate naturalistic illusion without being taken in. Fielding fills *Tom Jones*'s final chapters with a flurry of actions of narration within his story, and the narrative skills of individual characters actively create the resolution of the novel's plot.

Tom, in particular, employs narration quite self-consciously in

an attempt not to report or to clarify the past but to control the present: hoping to reconcile Mr. Nightingale to his son's plan to marry
Nancy, Tom does not try to persuade him directly, but rather tells
him about the marriage as something already accomplished, after
first allowing Mr. Nightingale to believe for some time that the two
of them are referring to the same intended wife, though he knows
that they are not (772–77). Tom thus exploits two narrative techniques with great potential for persuasion: a deliberate ambiguity of
reference, which allows a listener to bring his or her own convictions
to an account (even as that account pulls the listener in another direction), and proleptic narration, which designates the wished-for
future a present reality. Mr. Nightingale's brother suggests the
power of discursive methods of control in general, as contrasted
with Nightingale's own methods of coercion or threatened disin-
heritance, when he says of his daughter: "I have brought her up to
have no Inclinations contrary to my own. By suffering her to do
whatever she pleases, I have enured her to a Habit of being pleased
to do whatever I like" (780). The author of *Jenny Cameron* would
agree that a child brought up to have no inclinations contrary to her
parents', or society's, is likelier to conform to their wishes than one
whipped into the mere appearance of obedience. And the movement
between literary modes within *The Female Rebels* suggests that novelistic narrative may be a particularly effective way to inure a child
"to a Habit of being pleased to do" whatever the powers-that-be
may like.

   Tom's persuasion, at least initially, however, fails; and Uncle
Nightingale's daughter surprises him by running off with a man of
whom he does not approve. In *Tom Jones*, Fielding at once observes
and boldly exploits the potential within novelistic narrative for new
methods of "governance"—but he also expresses an interest in the
possibilities of resistance to these methods, and in the unevenness
with which they exert themselves in a world where competing beliefs and models of experience are always meeting, even within the
individual soul. Just as Sophia and Tom venture out to take action at
the ghosting hour, if an individual man's voice rises up to us from
the pages of *Tom Jones*, it does so not despite history but from it, and
of it, in all its complexity, its contradictions, in all the living ways
that it continues to be incomplete.

"The Same Birchen Argument"

Flogging, Satire, and the Jacobite's Ass

As Fielding's political position dramatically changes between the writing of *Pasquin* and that of *Tom Jones*, as he alters the stance of his writings from a nostalgic attack on new governmental forms to aggressive support for them, he shifts the nature of the connections he claims between sexual and political orders, and he also re-imagines his relation to the classical and "Augustan" literary mode of satire, earlier construed as an exercise of masculine potency and rigor. In *Joseph Andrews*, where Fielding defends satire, he already expresses a doubt that satiric attack can be clearly separated from the unscrupulous exercise of social power or the infliction of physical pain. Fielding's obsessive concern in *The Jacobite's Journal* with the dark, corrupting powers of corporal punishment further shadows the old ideal of the satiric "lash" of correction. The schoolmaster's rod, which had earlier served Fielding as a positive image of satire's instructive power, becomes an emblem in the *Journal* of suspect forms of education and discipline, forms which advance the narrow purposes of political indoctrination and which involve teacher and student in relations of homoerotic domination. Repeatedly asserting that these "unnatural" relations characterize the community of Jacobite believers, Fielding claims both the heterosexual norm and the power of nonsatiric narrative forms for the Whig government he defends.

At the same time, Fielding never frees himself from implication in the practice of satire or in the male bonds of classical education and erudition; and he suggests ways in which the heterosexual relations that form the very basis of his plot in *Tom Jones* might be termed unnatural themselves. The contradictions among Fielding's claims about this network of connections between literary, educational, sexual, and political matters appear, in *Tom Jones*, as strains within the classical allusions he employs. They appear more pervasively as problems of tone and of persona in the essays of *The Jacobite's Journal*.

Fielding introduces the episode that will lead to Tom's expulsion from Paradise Hall with two symmetrically misapplied quotations from the *Aeneid*. In the first of these, as the schoolmaster Thwackum and his pious follower Blifil appear in the same grove where Tom has just unexpectedly encountered Molly, Fielding compares the chance convergence of these characters to the coincidence that brings Dido and Aeneas, fatefully, into a single cave. He jokes about his own extension of the coincidence to include four rather than two characters by compounding his reference to Virgil's lovers:

No sooner had our Heroe retired with his *Dido*, but

> *Speluncam* Blifil, *Dux et Divinus eandem*
> *Deveniunt.*———

the Parson and the young Squire, who were taking a serious Walk, arrived at the Stile which leads into the Grove, and the latter caught a View of the Lovers, just as they were sinking out of Sight. (258)

Tom and Molly, sinking out of sight to act on their mutual desire, are here likened to the Trojan hero and "his Dido," but it is the schoolmaster and his male pupil, about to intervene in that erotic scene and to prevent its continuance, who actually take the place of the lovers in Virgil's lines about their arrival at the cave; Fielding adapts *Aeneid* IV.165–66, "Speluncam Dido dux et Troianus eandem / Deveniunt [Dido and the Trojan leader arrived at the same grotto]," to describe Blifil and Thwackum's appearance. In what sense are these two men, linked by their past pedagogical relation, equivalent to a male and a female lover? Why do they seem to compete with Molly and Tom for Dido and Aeneas's place within Fielding's allusion?

Two pages later, when Fielding compares Tom and Molly's "dalliance" with the "rutting" of any other male and female animals, he again quotes Virgil to odd effect. As Thwackum approaches Molly and Tom's hiding-place, muttering with indignation, Fielding explains that all female animals expect to be protected from such intrusions upon "the sacred Rites" of copulation,

For at the Celebration of these Rites, the female Priestess cries out with her in *Virgil* (who was then probably hard at work on such Celebration)

> —*Procul, O procul este, profani;*
> *Proclamat Vates, totoque absistite Luco.*

> —Far hence be Souls prophane,
> The Sibyl cry'd, and from the Grove abstain.
> DRYDEN. (259–60)

In fact, in the lines Fielding quotes from *Aeneid* VI, the Sibyl is not engaged in such erotic "Celebration," but warning Aeneas's soldiers not to follow as she and Aeneas enter the underworld on his visit to his dead father. If Fielding's first quotation of Virgil transfers the description of an erotic relation between man and woman to an apparently nonerotic one between two men, his next quotation transfers lines that lead toward an intense confrontation of man and man (father and son) to a decidedly heterosexual encounter.

The allusion to Virgil's priestess and the language of "sacred Rites" and "*Samean* Mysteries," interwoven with the narrator's comparison of Tom and Molly's sexual activity to the rutting of stags and hinds, ironically places that human heterosexual encounter at once among the highest rites of civilization and with pure, animalistic impulse. When Fielding refers in this passage to the feminine "Nicety or Skittishness, with which Nature hath bedecked all Females, or hath, at least, instructed them to put it on," he raises a question about how much of the character of heterosexual exchange is determined by nature and how much by learned convention. At the same time, the two Virgilian allusions in this episode ambiguously locate Tom's sexual activity within the crossings created by the quotations' original and new contexts—crossings between nonsexual and sexual relations, relations between men and between man and woman. On a further level, with the very fact of these allusions—the legacy of Fielding's own boyhood classical education—his (and the reader's) past pedagogical relations twice intrude into, and mediate, the description of Tom and Molly's "rutting," just as Tom's male tutor intervenes, muttering loudly, in the heterosexual scene.

Blifil and Thwackum's later misrepresentation of this scene and of the events immediately preceding it will lead Tom's adoptive father to banish him. Within the episode, when Thwackum asserts his authority over Tom, he does so in terms resonant with current debate about both political and educational philosophy. After Thwackum discovers that it is his own former pupil engaged with a woman in the bushes, he demands that Tom tell him who the woman is. When Tom refuses, Thwackum "commands" him to tell him immediately, saying,

I would not have you imagine, young Man, that your Age, tho' it hath somewhat abridged the Purpose of Tuition, hath totally taken away the Authority of the Master. The Relation of the Master and Scholar is indelible, as, indeed, all other Relations are: For they all derive their Original from Heaven. I would have you think yourself, therefore, as much obliged to obey me now, as when I taught you your first Rudiments. (260)

Among Fielding's many negative insinuations about Thwackum's character, he never includes any suggestion that Thwackum (like Western) is a vocal or active believer in the Jacobite cause; but he here has Thwackum give voice to an absolutist view of relations of authority very close to the one expressed by Filmer and other supporters of Stuart claims, and adamantly opposed by Locke. Crucial to the debate between patriarchal and contract theories of government was a dispute about how to interpret the phenomenon of children's dependence upon their parents and their subjection to adult authority: Filmer argued on the basis of it for the natural necessity of permanent relations of absolute authority, while Locke contended that it should be seen as a temporary condition, as children await their accession to reason and to the natural freedom to which they are born.[1] Thwackum sides clearly with Filmer in this debate about the permanence or "indelibility" of children's relations to authority, and he avows his agreement with Filmer, too, that all relations of authority "derive their Original from Heaven" rather than from Lockean social contracts.[2]

Furthermore, Tom's response to Thwackum's speech on authority might remind us of a specific connection between schoolmasters and Jacobite belief drawn repeatedly by Fielding in *The Jacobite's Journal*. When Thwackum says he would have Tom think himself "as much obliged to obey me now, as when I taught you your first Rudiments," Tom retorts, "I believe you would . . . but that will not happen, unless you had the same Birchen Argument to convince me." While Thwackum insists that his own authority partakes of the nature of divinity, Tom suggests that, in practice, it relies so heavily upon physical punishment that it instead takes on the inanimate nature of the instruments of its enforcement, its very arguments becoming "Birchen" and mechanical. A number of the essays and letters from fictional correspondents in *The Jacobite's Journal* focus on the suggestion that Jacobitism persists in England only because Jacobite schoolmasters take advantage of their pedagogical power to propagate its perverse doctrines, "for Absurdities of this monstrous Kind can only be imbibed when the Mind is young and tender, and susceptible of any Impression" (260; see 246–49, 256–61, 268–71, 299–300). Other letters and essays spell out the particular method by which Jacobite instructors impress their beliefs upon "young and tender" minds—and bodies. When one of Fielding's fictional correspondents sums up the force of an earlier editorial by saying that the persistence of Jacobitism "is an Argument a Posteriore of the vicious Education of our Youth," Fielding places this statement immediately following another letter that gives a special meaning to the idea of "an Argument a Posteriore": a schoolmaster named "Roger Strap" has also written to the journal, expressing his general conviction that "the first Principle . . . of good Education is Scourging" and his specific belief that scourging should be confined "to that Part which Nature seems to have intended, and to have well supplied for this Purpose."[3] Strap reports proudly that "I have whipt more *Latin* and *Greek* into the Lads under my Care, than most of my Cotemporaries of the same Profession. . . . Indeed none, however circumspect, hath escaped from me untouch'd, and most of them bear my Mark about them to this Day" (269–70). Like Roger Strap's, Roger Thwackum's devotion to flogging is so central to his pedagogical practice as to appear in the name Fielding has given him; and Tom's response to Thwackum's assertion of continuing authority suggests that its "indelible" nature may be reduced to the permanent "Mark" he has left on his pupils' posteriors.

In the fight that ensues in this scene between Tom and Thwackum, the two men in fact both mark each other, since the schoolmaster now finds himself "roughly handled by one who had formerly been only passive in all Conflicts between them" (261). The water from a nearby stream with which Tom eventually washes himself "could not remove the black and blue Marks which *Thwackum* had imprinted on both his Face and Breast" (265); and days later, when Blifil and Thwackum represent Tom's actions in a damning light, Thwackum is able to produce the corroborating "Record upon his Breast, where the Handwriting of Mr. *Jones* remained very legible in black and blue" (308). Although Thwackum and Blifil's intervention into Tom's dalliance with Molly has led him to mark and be marked by another man, the whole episode began with Tom's impulse to make a mark that would record his indelible relation with a *woman*: meditating on his love for Sophia, he exclaims, "The chastest Constancy will I ever preserve to thy Image. . . . *Sophia, Sophia* alone shall be mine. What Raptures are in that Name! I will engrave it on every Tree" (256). Indeed, Tom jumps up, penknife in hand, ready to carve Sophia's name on the trees—but (as the narrator relates "with Sorrow") the appearance of Molly in the flesh quickly displaces the compelling presence of Sophia's image; at the episode's close, when Western discovers a mark left by Tom's heterosexual relations, it appears in the form not of a woman's name engraved in bark, but of a woman's bodily impress in the ferns where she has lain with Tom (267). The modulation between two kinds of markings—the one verbal and ideal, the other purely corporal—expresses the same tense, ambiguous definition of heterosexual exchange produced by Fielding's ironic conjunction of "sacred Rites" and animals' "rutting" to describe Tom and Molly's dalliance. Thwackum's outraged attack on Tom, however, has interrupted the oscillation between these alternative forms of heterosexual inscription and easily rechanneled them into a mutual, violent exchange of markings between men.

In the early days of Tom and Thwackum's relationship—when Thwackum's "Meditations" were constantly "full of Birch," when the whippings he inflicted on Tom "possibly fell little short of the Torture with which Confessions are in some Countries extorted from Criminals," and when the lack of a rod was "the only thing which could have kept *Thwackum* any long Time from chastising poor Jones" (132, 122, 133)—the schoolmaster's disciplinary practice of flogging contained within it passionate impulses toward both the boy and a woman. Eager to win Bridget's hand in marriage and convinced that she must hate the boy her brother has adopted, Thwackum considered every Lash he gave [Tom] as a Compliment paid to his Mistress; so that he could with the utmost Propriety repeat this old flogging Line, "*Castigo te non quod odio habeam, sed quod* AMEM; I chastize thee not out of Hatred, but out of Love." And this indeed he often had in his Mouth, or rather, according to the old Phrase, never more properly applied, at his Fingers Ends. (137–38)

Fielding applies both the "old flogging Line" and the "old Phrase" in this passage with such extreme "Propriety" that unexpected senses emerge. Whipping Tom as a means toward sexual union, Thwackum "chastizes" him out of "Love" of a different and more specifically directed kind than the saying ordinarily suggests—the desiring love of a suitor, rather than the selfless love of a teacher; the clause preceding informs us that the love that motivates his lashings is for his "Mistress," rather than for the boy himself, as we would otherwise assume. This layering of expected and unexpected references within the "old flogging Line" works to conflate Thwackum's pedagogical relations with a boy and heterosexual desire. In explaining Thwackum's "Love" for Bridget, however, Fielding has already suggested several layers of desired object within the heterosexual relation itself.

Just as Captain Blifil, Bridget's first suitor, had quickly become "greatly enamoured" not of her but "of Mr. *Allworthy*'s House and Gardens, and of his Lands, Tenements and Hereditaments; of all which the Captain was so passionately fond, that he would most probably have contracted Marriage with them, had he been obliged to have taken the Witch of *Endor* into the Bargain" (67), when Thwackum and Square choose Mrs. Blifil as "the Object to which they both aspired," it is because they

had from their first Arrival at Mr. *Allworthy*'s House, taken so great an Affection, the one to his Virtue, the other to his Religion, that they had meditated the closest Alliance with him. . . . in reality Bosom Friends, and intimate Acquaintance, have a kind of natural Propensity to particular Females at the House of a Friend; *viz.* to his Grand-mother, Mother, Sister, Daughter, Aunt, Niece or Cousin, when they are rich. (136–37)

Sexuality, friendship, and greed—desire for a woman, for a man, and for property—circulate freely within the "Love" that leads Thwackum to lash Tom; when this circulation introduces a reference to heterosexual erotic desire within the old formulation about flogging and nonerotic, teacherly love, it also releases a possible reference to the workings of homoerotic energy (as the object of that love recedes from Tom, to Bridget, to Allworthy, and back to Tom?) within Thwackum's passionate floggings of his male charge.[4] Thwackum's rival, Square, desires the Allworthy family's estates but is also "a jolly Fellow, or a Widow's Man" (137), and he later pursues the penniless Molly out of lust. While Thwackum, on the other hand, "was not only strictly chaste in his own Person, but a great Enemy to the opposite Vice in all others" (258), the combination of his first and last names hints that physical punishment may itself constitute his characteristic sexual vice: his full name (like Roger Strap's) conjoins a slang term for either the penis or the act of coition with a reference to the flogging of boys.[5]

A passing allusion in Fielding's description of the aftermath of Tom and Thwackum's battle suggests his view of this "roger" that asserts itself in "thwacking" boys. When the rest of Western's company comes into the grove, Blifil lies breathless on the ground, Jones stands covered with blood, and "in a third Place stood the said *Thwackum*, like King *Porus*, sullenly submitting to the Conqueror" (263). As Frederick W. Hilles has pointed out, when Fielding likens Thwackum to Porus, he evokes not only the historical figure of the Indian king, described by Plutarch and Arrian, but a specific incarnation of that king on the contemporary stage: the part of Porus in Lumpugnani's opera, *Alexander in India*, performed in London in 1746, was taken by the famous castrato Monticello, who had also performed female roles.[6] Linking the tyrannical schoolmaster to Porus/Monticello, Fielding implies that Thwackum's conflation of the disciplinary rod of punishment and his own sexual organ, as well as the "homosocial" nature of his eroticized pedagogy, render him the equivalent of a glorified castrato in the role of a king. In doing so, Fielding suggests a strikingly different relation between the rod of instructional discipline and the "sting-less" penis of the castrato singer than he had fifteen years earlier in the epilogue to *The Intriguing Chambermaid*. There, we might recall, the degeneracy of London taste and morals appeared in the audience's choice of "soft Italian warblers" over satiric drama; and when Fielding opposed the entertainment offered by castrated singers to satire's moral "sting," he reinforced the link between satire and a specifically phallic power by likening both to the "rod" of schoolmasters' corrective discipline.[7] With irony, he commended the ladies' choice:

> Wisely from those rude places you abstain,
> Where satire gives the wounded hearer pain.
> 'Tis hard to pay them who our faults reveal,
> As boys are forced to buy the rods they feel.
> No, let 'em starve, who dare to lash the age,
> And, as you've left the pulpit, leave the stage.

Not only daring to lash the age but reveling in his use of the rod, which he quotes Solomon to defend (132), Thwackum might seem to present an alternative to the questionable masculinity and moral influence of castrato performers. Instead, Fielding implies that the perversity of his investment in flogging for its own sake draws his own sexuality and gender, like theirs, into question.

Furthermore, although Thwackum is never defined as a satirist, just as he never appears specifically as a Jacobite, his fixation on flogging as a means of instruction dramatizes the same problem of distinguishing between verbal and physical aggression that Fielding had associated with phallic satire in the Roasting-Squire episode of *Joseph Andrews*. In the passage in which Fielding applies the "old flogging Line" to unexpected effect, he also literalizes another "old Phrase" to bring out its grimly comic relevance: "And this [line], indeed, [Thwackum] often had in his Mouth, or rather, according to the old Phrase, never more properly applied, at his Fingers Ends." For Thwackum, flogging fuses not only with erotic but with discursive intercourse; in the following scene, when Tom says he will not tell Thwackum how he has spent the money for which he sold his horse, Thwackum exclaims, " 'you will not! then I will have it out of your Br---h;' that being the Place to which he always applied for Information, on every doubtful Occasion" (142). Recurring repeatedly in *The Jacobite's Journal* to the subjects of a patriarchal political authority that verges on tyranny, verbal aggression that merges with physical abuse, and pedagogical authority that becomes a vehicle for homoerotic violence, Fielding there draws in more detail the connections he claims between these subjects, which he thus loosely links in the character of Thwackum.

Locke begins his *Two Treatises on Government* with the observation that Filmer's *Patriarcha* "would perswade all Men, that they are Slaves and ought to be so,"[8] and Fielding and other Whig writers frequently assert the perversity of Jacobite beliefs by equating them

with the willing acceptance of a relation of "slavery" to one's monarch.[9] A number of issues of *The Jacobite's Journal* develop Fielding's
claim that only early indoctrination by Jacobite teachers could lead
men into such a perverse doctrine; and the *Journal* draws on Locke's
educational as well as political philosophy to suggest that this indoctrination takes place not only through the content of their teach-
ings but through the methods of their instruction.[10] While the six-
teenth century and much of the seventeenth century have been called
"the great age of the whip," characterized by an "extraordinary obsession with flogging," Locke's educational treatise of 1693 gave
voice to a widespread sentiment of the later seventeenth century
when it questioned the value of corporal punishment. Locke describes flogging as not only unnecessary and ineffective, but at odds
with the preparation of English boys to take their place as free subjects in civil society: flogging is unsuitable "to be used in the education of those who would have wise, good and ingenuous men,"
for "such a sort of slavish discipline makes a slavish temper."[11] Like
the opening episode of *Roderick Random* (1748), in which Roderick
and his friends revenge themselves on their schoolmaster by tormenting him with his own birch, or like the scene in *Jenny Cameron*
in which Jenny seizes the rod from her great-aunt and beats her with
it, *The Jacobite's Journal* and *Tom Jones* occasionally suggest the danger that the structure of physical discipline may be inverted, and violence used by social subordinates against their betters.[12] The *Journal*
dwells most insistently, however, upon the danger that physical
forms of discipline may create "a slavish temper" in boys that they
will never outgrow, forging a physical bond between master and
student which is easily eroticized, and which readies students to accept a Jacobite doctrine of man's natural enslavement.

Fielding places one of several letters in *The Jacobite's Journal*
about Jacobites' "vicious Education of our Youth" next to the letter
from "Roger Strap" about scourging knowledge into boys' posteriors (268–71); and when he laments the nation's apparent wish for
enslavement to the Stuarts, he frequently describes it as a perverse
enthrallment to the boyhood thrills of corporal punishment. Comparing Jacobite sympathizers to the Jewish people, he says that "no
sooner was the Rod taken from their Backs, than (like the *Jews* after
every Deliverance) they began again to long for its Stripes" (286).[13]
Later, complaining that even "a hungry Ass" has more sense than a

Jacobite, he asks what beast of burden is so silly that, after "a happy Exchange of Masters," he "would yet languish after his former Yoke and Whip . . . ?" (391). Late seventeenth-century treatments of corporal punishment had evoked the possibility that flogging might encourage not only "a slavish temper" but an addiction to masochistic pleasures of the flesh: in Shadwell's *The Virtuoso* of 1678, the elderly Snarl asks his mistress to produce "the Instruments of our pleasure"—birch rods—and then explains, "I was so us'd to't at *Westminster*-School I cou'd never leave it off since. . . . Do not spare thy pains. I love castigation mightily."[14] According to Fielding, nations are subject to a specifically political version of Snarl's masochism ("No Nation ever endured [Slavery] long, without being enamoured of its Charms" [410]), which may itself be erotically charged (English Jacobites think of the tyrant who enslaved them as "our Idol, our Darling, and our Delight" [409–12]).

Fielding's account matches the masochism of the flogged pupil or the enslaved nation with the eroticized sadism of a Roger Thwackum or a Roger Strap. Suspicion of schoolmasters' own motives for flogging had also been anticipated by late-seventeenth-century discussions. The author of an anonymous pamphlet of 1669 had argued that schools become houses of prostitution, wherein boys' "secret parts . . . must be the anvil exposed to the immodest and filthy blows of the smiter," and he asked, "who can think that if the punishment were not suffered on those parts, that it were like to be so much?"[15] This last question, raised implicitly by *The Jacobite's Journal* when Roger Strap recommends the buttocks as the only proper place to beat a boy (270), is also diffusely present throughout the *Journal* in its obsessive and various play upon the word "ass."

Fielding decorates the *Journal's* first twelve numbers with a woodcut representing an ass being ridden by a man and woman (see Fig. 11), and, in the essays that follow, he frequently employs crude, punning references to the beast of this frontispiece and the Jacobite "ass" who rides upon it.[16] As we have noted, at one point, he compares a Jacobite with an ass in order to describe his longing for "the Lash" (391); at another, ironically insisting that his "Emblematical Frontispiece" was intended "to do Honour to the Jacobite Party," he proposes "that by the Body of the Ass we intend to figure the whole Body of Jacobitical Doctrine," and then defends the dignity of "Asses" in terms of the great respect afforded them in classical civilization (173–76). Later, he develops an elaborate comparison be-

tween the effeminacy and childishness of Jacobite enthusiasm for
horse racing and the Roman Caligula's excessive affection both for
a male jockey and for his horse. This comparison culminates in a
double play on the word "ass": in this case, Jacobite men are not only
identified with "*that* Ass which we exhibited so many Weeks in his
Plaid, at the Head of this Paper," but also ridiculed as "bare-ars'd"
(in Highland dress), at once unmanly because "*unbreeched*" and
apparently open to the anal sexuality associated with Caligula (369–
75).[17] All these essays imagine anal eroticism as necessarily sado-
masochistic; and some specifically link the anal sexuality they diffusely attach to Jacobitism with a loss of phallic identity. Shortly
after Roger Strap boasts that most of his students "bear my Mark
about them to this Day" (269), Fielding reports that the "Mark in
the Flesh" which Jacobites have imposed upon themselves is actually
the mark of circumcision, a marking of the penis that he blurs with
castration and associates with Jacobites' "strange desire of being enslaved" (283–86; 333–35).

The "rod" of childhood corporal punishment is thus negatively portrayed in the *Journal* as both a figure for and an actual material instrument of Jacobite ideology; and the conventional image
of satire's "lash," invoked approvingly by Fielding in his earlier
writings, becomes suspect as well in these essays, at times subject to
the same associations with sadism, castration, and anal sexuality as
literal lashing. In the first issue of the *Journal* John Trott-Plaid explains that his newspaper will allow him to appear "in my *Scotch*
Plaid all over the Kingdom at one and the same time," and that

In this Dress I intend to abuse the ***, and the ***, and the ***. I intend to
lash not only the M---stry, but EVERY MAN who *hath* any P--ce or P-ns--n
from the G-v-rnm-nt, . . . let his R-nk be never so *high*, his F-rt-n- never
so *great*, or his Ch-r-ct-r never so *good*. For this Purpose I have provided
myself with a vast Quantity of *Italian* Letter, and Astericks of all Sorts: And
as for all the Words which I *embowel*, or rather *emvowel*, I will never so man-
gle them, but they shall be all as well known as if they retained every Vowel
in them. (96)

Fielding had in fact made his name in the 1720's and 1730's by "lashing" the ministry of Robert Walpole in his plays and periodical essays. Here, of course, the intention to lash Pelham's ministry is declared within Fielding's ironic persona as Trott-Plaid, and is clearly
discredited in the passage by the accompanying promise to lash the

minister's allies no matter how good their rank, fortune, and character. Furthermore, while Fielding had earlier opposed the moral, manly endeavor of satiric correction to the emasculated decadence of Italian operatic entertainment, Trott-Plaid here introduces his satiric intentions with a picture of himself in the Highland dress that Fielding elsewhere treats as unmanly; and he expands on those intentions by saying he has provided himself with "a vast Quantity of *Italian* Letter"—highlighting the origin of italic type in the land of the castrati—and then playing with the idea that he will be "emboweling" words when he follows satiric convention by omitting their vowels.

If these associations of a degraded form of satiric expression with an "unbreeched" dress, with Italian decadence, and with the bowels seem glancing and slight, Fielding returns to them much later in the *Journal* when he again suggests the difficulty of separating corrective satire from undiscriminating "abuse." In number 31, he considers a short poem decrying both Walpole's and Pelham's ministries; and he there refers to the "emboweled" words of the poem as "castrated Words" and to the poem as a whole as "Ordure" (325–28).[18] This anxiety about the indistinguishability of satire and abuse, and the suggestion that verbal aggression may disrupt rather than enforce gender divisions, are most fancifully played out two issues later in a mock trial for false advertisement of the author of a prominstry poem.

In the *Journal's* "Court of Criticism," Thomas Scandal, Esq., and Mrs. Grace register complaints that they expected to find "Satire against an honourable Gentleman" in Edward Moore's *Trial of Selim the Persian,* but did not. After Scandal proves unable to answer the Prisoner's Council's question about the difference between satire and abuse, Mrs. Grace testifies that she too was disappointed in the poem's contents.

PRISONER'S COUNCIL. So you expected Abuse too, Madam?
MRS. GRACE. I cannot help saying, I did.
PRISONER'S COUNCIL. I am sorry a Lady should have such a Taste.
MRS. GRACE. Sir, I am a true *Englishman,* (here was a great Laugh) *Englishwoman,* I mean; and I shall always relish Satire against any of the present Copulation of Ministers. (Here was another great Laugh, but the Lady afterwards explained her Meaning to be Coalition.) (345–46)

In his Opposition plays and essays, Fielding called upon satire as the only proper corrective for a government and culture so degraded as to have confused the roles of hero and housewife; writing in 1748 in defense of the ministry, he suggests that it is, rather, the public's own unthinking appetite for satire/abuse that garbles the distinction between "Englishman" and "Englishwoman." His satiric treatments of Lord Hervey, in particular, like Pope's and Pulteney's, had stigmatized the bonds among men within Walpole's newly bureaucratic system of government by suggesting that they might be homoerotic as well as political.[19] Such an implication appears here in the verbal slippage between a "Coalition" and a "Copulation" of ministers, but that slippage occurs in the mouth of Mrs. Grace and is intended to express her own eroticized, transgressive "relish" of satiric abuse rather than anything suspect about the ministerial coalition itself. In *The Jacobite's Journal* and in *Tom Jones*, Fielding relocates the stigma of male homoeroticism which he had earlier attached to the contingent and constantly shifting relations of ministers, placemen, and pensioners, now announcing its dangerous presence instead within the rigidly hierarchized relations of authoritarian tutor and student or absolutist monarch and subject—relations he associates with the reactionary Jacobite cause against which he has come to defend the new institutions of Walpole's and Pelham's ministries.

Fielding does not abandon satiric methods of persuasion as the aims of that persuasion change over time; but those methods come to seem implicated in the forms of authority and aggression he now elaborately derides. Fielding's use of satire in *The Jacobite's Journal* is therefore highly vexed, often proceeding in conflicted or contradictory ways.

Fielding constructs the persona of Trott-Plaid in his *Journal* in order to satirize perverse Jacobite attempts to satirize the ministry—but his control over the force of this layered satiric irony is from the first uncertain. This uncertainty appears in the original response to his *Journal*: apparently, some of his contemporaries mistook the *Journal*'s irony and referred to it as an Opposition paper.[20] But it also appears within the *Journal*'s pages both in the inconsistency with which Fielding handles the satiric vehicle of Trott-Plaid and in his eventual avowed abandonment of that vehicle. From early on, Fielding attempts to control the response to his irony by including references to readers' suspicions that he must not be "a Jacobite in Earnest"

(116, 162–63, 172–73), but before long he decides to throw over his persona altogether. He begins number 17 of the *Journal* by referring to his earlier abandonment of the *Journal*'s frontispiece, and announcing:

When the Ass disappeared from this Paper, it might be reasonably concluded that the Jacobite would not stay long behind.

   In plain Fact, I am weary of personating a Character for which I have so solemn a Contempt; nor do I believe that the elder *Brutus* was more uneasy under that Idiot Appearance which he assumed for the Sake of his Country, than I have been in the Masque of Jacobitism, which I have so long worn for the same amiable and honest Purpose; in order, if possible, to laugh Men out of their Follies. (210–11)

Even this unusual gesture of clarification and Fielding's resolution to speak "in a plainer Language" (212), however, are quickly compromised. While Fielding sustained the fiction of his persona, he could not seem to remain completely within it, but when he decides to give it over, he cannot seem to step entirely out of it either: "Here then I shall pull off the Masque," he declares, "and openly avow that I *John Trott-Plaid*, Esq; notwithstanding my Name, do, from my Heart, abhor and despise all the Principles of a Jacobite" (211). The oddity of Fielding retaining the manifestly Jacobite title of his ironic persona while removing the "masque" of that persona—as if there may be a mask under the mask?—gives his explicit rejection of Jacobite principles the same equivocal status as his earlier declarations of allegiance to them; and he only makes matters worse in what follows by providing a number of different and sometimes contradictory reasons for his turning away from "ridicule" and "irony."

   Fielding says first that "tho' Irony is capable of furnishing the most exquisite Ridicule; yet . . . there is no kind of Humour so liable to be mistaken"; next, "that there is no Species of Wit or Humour so little adapted to the Palat of the present Age," which hungers only for violent verbal abuse; then that Jacobitism is "too low and contemptible" for ridicule; and finally "that the Matter is past a Joke," for the consequences of Jacobitism "are of a very serious Nature," so that "it is high time to speak in a plainer Language than that of Irony" (211–12). Thus, he begins by explaining the abandonment of his satiric persona in terms of his audience's inadequacies and ends by explaining it in terms of its inherent unfitness for the subject at hand. He dwells most on this final explanation, which he says is his "strongest Motive" for the change, and he supports it with an expanded version of the same image he'd used in his preface to *Joseph Andrews* to argue that satiric "ridicule" is sometimes wildly inappropriate: "To consider such Attempts as these in a ludicrous Light, would be as absurd as the Conceit of a Fellow in *Bartholomew-Fair*, who exhibited the comical Humours of *Nero* ripping up his Mother's Belly; and surely a Man who endeavours to rip up the Bowels of his Country, is altogether as improper an Object of Ridicule" (213).

Although Fielding asserts the absolute difference between satire and libel in *Joseph Andrews*, in this issue of the *Journal* he explains his decision to abandon satiric methods by pointing to the destructive prevalence of libelous speech, which he associates with the insidious influence of that bad version of the moral instructor, the Jacobite tutor. How could he remain within his satiric mask, Fielding asks, "when conceal'd Popish Traytors are crept into the Seminaries of Learning, and endeavour to taint the Minds of our Youth; and when the most bare-faced Libels are every Week spread all over the Nation, in order to spirit up the Vulgar to rise and cut the Throats of their Betters"? (212). Here, Fielding links the false instruction offered by "Popish Traytors" and the false verbal corrective of "barefaced Libels" to warn that these forms of social discipline and order may be seized by insurrectionary forces and used to encourage "the Vulgar to rise and cut the Throats of their Betters." Later, when he discusses the actual beating of a nobleman, the Duke of Bedford, by a Jacobite mob, he again connects the mob's usurpation of the disciplinary powers of flogging with its usurpation of the force of satiric correction, moving quickly from the physical insult suffered by the Duke to the "Libels cramm'd with Lies" propagated about the incident, "array'd in all the Wit of *Grub-street* and *Billingsgate*" (307).[21] *The Jacobite's Journal* dwells often upon the terrible dangers of "Detraction," "that poisonous Arrow, drawn out of the Devil's Quiver . . . against which no Virtue is a Defence, no Innocence a Security" (308), expanding upon the doubts expressed in *Joseph Andrews* about whether ridicule might be used against good men and about the difficulty of distinguishing satire from abuse. Obsessed with the possibility that verbal aggression, like corporal punishment, may be used to provoke rebellion rather than to maintain order, the *Journal* seeks forms of noncritical (including sentimental) discourse with which social categories may be enforced; and it begins to imagine forms of discipline associated with the protection of that "Mother's Belly" before which ridicule must fall silent.

In the final issue of *The Jacobite's Journal*, explaining why he brought the *Journal* into being and why he now discontinues it, Fielding still describes the method of persuasion he has employed within it in terms of ridicule: "As it seemed necessary to apply some Remedy, in order to stop the Progress of this dangerous, epidemical Madness [Jacobitism] at so critical a Season; so none seemed more proper, or likely to be more effectual than Ridicule" (424). He expresses the hope that his paper may have at least "palliated the Distemper," but then says that few Jacobites could have read it because it was either barred from public houses or discarded immediately upon arriving: "where it hath found Admission, it hath been often condemned, on its first Arrival, to that dreadful Hole, which common News-papers have sometimes had the good Fortune to escape for a whole Week together" (425). Coley glosses "that dreadful Hole" into which Fielding fears his writings have disappeared: "That is, in the privy, with the other 'relics of the bum'" (425 n. 2). However curative his "ridicule" was meant to be, Fielding finally imagines it destined to mingle with ordure, perhaps indistinguishable from mere malicious abuse and somehow involved in the negative images of anality that he associates with Jacobite discourse and discipline.

In fact, in the course of *The Jacobite's Journal*, Fielding increasingly emphasizes his desire to offer more than ridicule in its pages. He insists that his "Court of Criticism" has been created to provide commendation as well as censure (118–19, 188), and eventually formulates the importance of this endeavor:

That Court of Criticism in which we preside is so far from being a Court of Damnation only, that one main End of its Institution is to correct a malevolent Spirit, which at present too generally prevails, and which seems to go about *seeking what it may find Fault with*.

The Part, indeed, of the Critical Office in which we are most delighted, is that which consists in giving Praise and Recommendation to Merit; and this we shall extend to every new Scheme and Invention whatever, that anywise tends to public Utility. (250)

Significantly, the charitable scheme recommended in the letter that follows ("a Fund for maintaining the Widows and Children of inferior and distress'd Clergymen") was inspired by this experience of the letter writer:

some time ago I went with a Friend of mine to visit the Widow of an Officer. . . . She has two Children . . . and I think a fonder Mother, and more
dutiful or lovely Children, I never saw. When we came in, the little Boy was
reading to his Mamma, and Miss was working; and, as I found afterwards,
they had no other Instructor. I was so charmed with the obliging Behaviour
of this Lady, and the Pains that the little ones took to imitate their Mamma,
that I could not help saying that she was quite happy in having such Children. (251)

Shortly before introducing the subject of perverse relations between
male tutors and students which will occupy a number of the *Journal*'s
issues, Fielding thus presents a scenario of an exclusively *maternal*
instruction; and he positions that scenario to suggest that it represents a crucial escape from the "malevolent Spirit" of censure—as
from a tutor's sadistic lashings—into a discourse of praise and charity. In his last novel, *Amelia*, Fielding will develop the implications
of this scenario at length. Tonal uncertainties, however, as we shall
see, will plague that endeavor, as Fielding's wonted mask of irony
seems to meld with his avowedly sincere face of sentiment.

Even in *The Jacobite's Journal*, having explicitly pulled off the
mask of his ironic persona, having rejected ridicule as inappropriate
for truly serious subjects (such as Jacobitism or violence to a mother's belly), Fielding retains an ambiguous relation to satire and to
sentiment. The imaginary correspondent who offers the charitable
scheme begins his letter with these doubts about "Squire Trott-
Plaid," the editor to whom he writes:

To penetrate into the Heart of so comical, so odd, and so unaccountable an
Animal as you seem to be, is beyond all human Art, and a Task too hard for
the D---l himself. . . . if you are that generous, candid, and well-disposed
Creature that you profess yourself to be, I do not doubt but the Sequel will
meet with your Approbation. But if, on the Contrary, you are a sad Dog in
the Shape of Goodness, both myself and my Scheme will be the Object of
your Ridicule and Contempt. (250–51)

Fielding "professes" his desire to sponsor praise, generosity, and a
charitable scheme epitomized by a mother's loving instruction of her
children;[22] in *Joseph Andrews*, he had fantasized about a recognition
of identity entirely determined by a mother's crucial and lasting
mark upon her son. He himself, however, had received the classical
education that very few eighteenth-century women might offer their
children, and, as he attests in *Tom Jones*, he himself had been marked
by early flogging, having long ago "sacrificed" his blood "to thee

[O Learning], at thy birchen Altar, with true *Spartan* Devotion"
(687).

The villain Northerton, too, attests to the sacrifice he has made
at learning's birchen altar: "D--n *Homo* with all my Heart," he exclaims when the conversation turns to classical texts, "I have the
Marks of him in my A-- yet" (372). The classical education Northerton has received at school has apparently marked him without informing him; it seems to have been all material means of enforcement and no content. Politically, Northerton seems ambiguous: although he marches in the King's army, his name evokes the territory
conquered by the rebels; he expresses contempt for the Protestant
clergy whose cause (the Whigs insisted) his army was to defend
(373); and he repeatedly is seen committing verbal or physical violence against women, whose names and whose bodies the Whigs
claimed only they could properly protect. Within the plot of *Tom
Jones*, Northerton seems to represent the inadequacy of military
force alone as a response to the Jacobite threat: his attack on Jones
precipitates the diversion of the plot from direct engagement with
the Jacobite revolt to matters of crucial ideological importance to the
Whig cause. In *Tom Jones*, with its deeply interfused domestic and
political plots, Fielding attempts to create a new force of instruction
and discipline—something other than "the same Birchen Argument" of satire and forcible indoctrination which he represents as
perverse and unstable both in the *Journal* and in his novels.

PART IV

'AMELIA'

EIGHT

"If This Was Real"

Female Heroism in 'Amelia'

"I dreamt," said he, "this Night that we were in the
most miserable Situation imaginable. Indeed in the
Situation we were Yesterday Morning, or rather
worse, that I was laid in a Prison for Debt, and that
you wanted a Morsel of Bread to feed the Mouths
of your hungry Children. At length (for nothing
you know is quicker than the Transition in Dreams)
Dr. *Harrison* methought came to me, with
Chearfulness and Joy in his Countenance. The
Prison Doors immediately flew open; and Dr.
Harrison introduced you, gayly tho' not richly
dressed. That you gently chid me for staying so
long; all on a sudden appear'd a Coach with four
Horses to it, in which was a Maid Servant with our
two Children. We both immediately went into the
Coach, and taking our Leave of the Doctor, set
out towards your Country House: for yours I
dreamt it was.—I only ask you now if this was real,
and the Transition almost as sudden, could you
support it?—"
         —Fielding, *Amelia*

Each epoch not only dreams the next, but also, in
dreaming, strives toward the moment of waking. It
bears its end in itself and unfolds it—as Hegel
already saw—with ruse.
        —Walter Benjamin, "Paris, Capital of the
                Nineteenth Century"

Booth has not, in fact, dreamed the scene he describes to Amelia. Rather, he has reason to believe that some version of that scene will truly come to pass; what he describes to Amelia as a past dream is an anticipated future, which he wants to make sure Amelia can "support" if it is to become "real." Amelia has indeed shown herself, throughout the novel, eminently able to support the role sketched for her in this scene: this "most worthy, generous, and noble of all human Beings," blessed with "Sweetness, Softness, Innocence, Modesty," and with "every Perfection in Human Nature"—at once "heavenly Angel" and "best" and "beloved Wife," a "great Mistress" of "Cookery" and an "excellent Example" for "all Mothers"—surely will make the transition with grace to presiding over the country house which Booth emphasizes belongs first to her alone (89, 71, 101, 435, 488, 167).

Of course, when Booth says he dreamed that they set out toward "your Country House: for yours I dreamt it was," it is because the plot resolution that releases Booth and Amelia from their prolonged spiral downwards makes their deliverance come in the form of an inheritance from Amelia's family rather than from Booth's; but the events of this plot resolution are so unprepared-for by what precedes them—the recovery of Amelia's inheritance intervenes so abruptly in what seems a nearly hopeless, ever-worsening financial situation[1]—that these events themselves have the status almost of a dream (of wish elevated to fictional plot), with their dream-logic depending on the extent to which Amelia, rather than Booth, deserves this outcome. What prepares us for the happy ending of *Amelia* in the rest of this dark novel is its sustained portrait of Amelia as domestic heroine, and in 1751 this portrait was itself a kind of proleptic cultural dream, a vivid projection of a role that was not to become central to the lived, dominant ideology of England for some time to come.[2] The world of fiction, like that of dreams, suffers more rapid transitions in outlook than the larger social world of which it is a part. This very feature allows it to help bring about the more gradual and uneven transitions of what's "real."

In reading *Tom Jones*, I have sought to describe Tom's masculine identity and Sophia's feminine one in terms of competing notions of gender that meet and conflict in each of their characters, as powerful new ideas about men's and women's natures emerge in the mid-eighteenth century but do not immediately displace the old; and I have used the scenes of internalized historical conflict that Fielding locates at the "ghosting hour" as emblems of his interest in the ghostly persistence of past beliefs and allegiances within the present. Fielding's interest in the incoherencies in personal belief and social institutions created by the process of historical change appears in his last novel as well, but there the emphasis seems to have moved forward—to the conjunctures between present and future dominant ideologies as well as those between past and present. Alongside our guiding image of ghosts, then, we here add that of dreams. As Atkinson comments earlier in the novel when he dreams of something that he *fears* may come to pass: "Dreams have sometimes fallen out to be true" (379).

Booth seems to have something to fear as well as to hope for from the dream made real by this novel. I have treated Tom and Sophia as equally caught and brought into life and action by the conflicting codes of gender that meet within each of them; but the changing landscape of gender that Booth and Amelia inhabit affects the man and his wife in quite different ways. While Amelia seems to be dramatically enabled and given coherence, definition, and purpose as a character by the change in female roles between her mother's generation and her own, Booth is rendered passive, uncertain, and dependent by the mixture of new and old expectations about masculine behavior that surround him. In two episodes of *Tom Jones*, Tom confronts a contradiction between "Cavalier" and "Christian" codes of male heroism when he finds himself expected to engage in duels. The vexed social issue of dueling is much more pervasive in Booth's story, confronting him over and over again, and presenting him, as a professional military man, with a challenge more central to his identity. The temporary breakdown of discourse that accompanies Tom's experience of conflict—the unleashing of a confused and incoherent babel of voices—becomes, in *Amelia*, a generalized failure of communication, as the contradiction between a man's need to defend his "honour" and the Christian prohibition against shedding blood leads to sustained secrecy and concealment within the Booths' marriage.

The explicit controversy over dueling, debated at several points in the novel, represents a kind of fault line along which the larger, underlying forces of contrary social systems become visible; and the incongruence of these social systems repeatedly leads Booth into confusion both about how to behave himself and about how to understand others' actions and motivations. Most damagingly,

Booth's preservation of old notions of upper-class masculine identity seems to place him at an economic impasse: the time-honored
gentlemanly choice of a military career does not offer Booth a viable
form of support, but he finds it unthinkable to look for other means
to support his family in trade or manual labor. This economic impasse results in Booth's physical confinement for much of *Amelia*.[3]
When Booth does venture abroad, he repeatedly encounters ethical
and interpretive impasses that leave him stymied about how to act
or how to explain others' actions to himself. Booth has as much difficulty making good on his narrative as on his financial accounts; and
Fielding allows us to see at several points that it is Booth's assumptions about class identity or about gender that blind him to certain
obvious explanations of events. At other points, Booth's adoption
of emerging social values alongside old ones confuses and disrupts
his rendering of experience, leading him to offer not only incomplete but inconsistent or insufficiently integrated narratives.

In this way, however, he is not so different from the narrator
of *Amelia* himself, who frequently offers incompatible descriptions
of characters or accounts of events in succession, seeming to hold
himself responsible for local coherence but not for a sustained and
total vision of the novelistic world he describes. After discussing
Booth's problems of action and of self-definition in the first section
below, I will turn to his difficulties of narration, investigating the
ideological premises that seem to limit Booth's powers of explanation. Fielding emphasizes the role of Booth's education and classical
reading in constructing his ways of seeing the world; but he also emphasizes that those ways of seeing are not rigidly limited or rigor-
ously self-consistent. Indeed, the space of *Amelia* itself, as well as the
space of Booth's identity and views, seems able to sustain directly
competing models of experience and value; and the same major
ideological elements (Christianity, or a classical education) may even
support very different social structures at different times.

In the third section of this chapter, we will turn from Booth
back to Amelia, who, unlike Booth, seems to have moved forward
into full possession of an emerging social identity. The post of domestic "angel," which we often think of as really materializing in
the Victorian era and only beginning to take shape at the end of the
eighteenth century, is apparently already available to Amelia as an
active and coherent role. Until the discovery of her usurped inheritance occurs, Amelia has no more means than Booth to sustain her

little family economically, but from quite early in their story, she is given a sphere of honorable activity and self-definition in the labor of caring for their home and children. The story of the Booths' courtship underscores Amelia's own mother's lack of involvement in rearing her daughters: Booth and Amelia take refuge in the home of Amelia's "nurse," or foster mother, when they elope from under Mrs. Harris's unsympathetic eye. This foster mother has breast-fed Amelia and raised her (107); she provides her with a beloved adoptive brother; and she reappears in the novel's final scene, preparing their homecoming dinner at Amelia's estate and then sitting at the table with them like a member of the family (531). Though the narrator makes no explicit comment on the change of expectations, there is never any question but that Amelia will nurse and raise her own children, and the maternal role sketched for her as moral influence and teacher could not be shifted to a hired nurse.

An idealized maternal role was also being projected in nonfictional tracts on child rearing and education published in the mideighteenth century, such as the one entitled *On the Management and Education of Children* (1754), which we will consider alongside *Amelia* in this chapter's closing section. These tracts, however, assume that the idea of a mother's direct involvement with her children will be seen as a novelty by well-off English readers; Lawrence Stone locates "the cult of maternal breast-feeding" among the upper classes later in the century.[4] Amelia's function as housekeeper and mother, on the other hand, provides the present economic as well as moral anchor of the Booth household: while Sophia's name served symbolically as the guarantor of financial value, Amelia is made the actual safekeeper of whatever money her family has (433–36, 450, 489), and it is her identity that ultimately accomplishes their financial salvation. The conflict between this idealized version of the domestic woman, with her function as guarantor of values, and older but still prevailing notions of female nature has not, however, disappeared in *Amelia*. Rather, this conflict appears most palpably in the relation between Amelia and her various "doubles" in the novel—particularly Mrs. Atkinson and Blear-Eyed Moll—and more subtly in problems of tone that haunt Fielding's treatment of those doubles, and sometimes of Amelia herself.

Amelia is repeatedly referred to as a "heroine" (for example, 84, 103, 163), and Booth and others extol her female heroism as nobler than the traditional heroism of generals or kings (67). At one point, the narrator asserts directly that the trials of maternal effort and feeling provide "juster" material for heroic tragedy than those of masculine military struggle (359). When Amelia herself listens to Mrs. Bennet/Atkinson's tale of familial loss and suffering, she expresses a sense that the events of that tale—the death of a mother, a husband, and a child, as well as sexual betrayal—are as tragic as any could be (237, 270, 304). The episodes in *Amelia* involving Mrs. Atkinson, however, are characteristically dotted with strangely banal details, which seem to introduce a burlesque element into the melodrama of her life: her mother dies by falling in a well, clutching an empty teakettle as she tumbles (270); her husband's "dear, dear Corpse" appears inexplicably to have been stolen from her house by ruffians, who "threaten to deny it burial" (237); when she herself seems to have been killed by Atkinson in the grip of a dream, it emerges that what looked like blood all over her body is only cherry brandy (378).

Though the story of Mrs. Atkinson's mother's death greatly affects Amelia's "tender Heart," the gratuitous inclusion of the teakettle within its tragic outlines makes it teeter perilously (as C. J. Rawson comments) on the edge of comedy,[5] and we might recognize the source of this comic effect from Fielding's own earlier parodies and burlesques: there, he repeatedly exploited the comic incongruity of introducing references to the lowly sphere of domestic objects and concerns into moments of conventional high drama. The false alarm about the theft of Mr. Bennet's corpse involves a related incongruity, although in this instance it is a conventional feature of classical epic and drama that seems bizarre when introduced into ordinary domestic life; Mrs. Bennet's passing fear that her husband's body is in the possession of enemies who will deny it proper burial is more founded in the classical works she is fond of reading (*The Iliad* or *Antigone*) than in the common dangers of English life. The cherry brandy incident extends this pattern, and clarifies one of its important features. The burlesque deflation that occurs in the incident depends not only on the substitution of mere household brandy for tragic blood but on Atkinson's discovery that the man with whom he thought he was struggling as he acted on his dream is actually a woman, and his wife. When Atkinson, dreaming that Colonel James threatens Amelia, catches his wife by the throat and cries, "D--n you, put up your Sword this Instant, and leave the Room, or by Heaven I'll drive mine to your Heart's Blood" (377), he suffers a dream version of the theatrical illusion presented to Fielding's audiences in 1730 when the actress Miss Jones appeared on the stage in the guise of the "great" Tom Thumb. The conflation of an imposing military figure and a mere woman, like the conjunction of momentous events and objects from the feminine domestic sphere, may convert the heroic or tragic into the mock-heroic; so that these apparently arbitrary and perverse details of Mrs. Atkinson's story, with the tonal questions they raise, speak to the novel's very premise as a serious work centered on female heroism.

Atkinson's confusion of his sleeping wife with a sword- and phallus-brandishing Colonel James may be a very silly error, mistaking one thing for its opposite; on another level, it may also be a significant and expressive error, suggesting that Atkinson unconsciously feels threatened (and emasculated) by his wife's classical "learning," by her more elevated class background, and by her rather fierce and domineering temper.[6] This suggestion within the cherry-brandy dream scene (supported by other scenes in the novel) connects it to another recurrent source of humor in Fielding's burlesque and satiric drama: the comic inversion represented by "petticoat government." In 1730, the crowds that came to show after show of *Tom Thumb* laughed not only at its cross-dressed hero but at its portraits of an overbearing queen and henpecked king. Twenty years later, Fielding presented his public with a different kind of work: in *Amelia*, he offers a female hero to us with a straight face, a serious face, even a teary-eyed, sentimental one. As Rawson has observed, however, burlesque possibilities lurk within the novel's treatment not only of Mrs. Atkinson but of Amelia herself: in Booth's speech on Amelia's fortitude after the breaking of her nose, for example, the praise of her sometimes reads like "a serious or tragic reembodiment of the earlier comic manner. . . . not like a primary example of the grand manner, but as though mock-heroic were being retranslated into a secondary seriousness."[7]

In fact, we might adopt this striking formulation of a general impression of *Amelia*'s tone and apply it more literal-mindedly to moments of specific "re-translation" from Fielding's (or others') mock-heroic works back into an apparently serious mode. Suggestively, for instance, Miss Mathews quotes from Buckingham's burlesque of tragic drama, *The Rehearsal*, to describe what she feels as the real tragedy of her own fate (99); and Fielding lifts the plot device that leads to *Amelia*'s resolution—a recognition of identity and recovery of inheritance that depend on the protagonist's desperate visit to a pawnbroker—from one of his own spoofs on serious drama, *The Author's Farce*, where this device contributes to the general absurdity of the denouement's mixture of low life and a high manner. Contemplating the elements of plot and character shared by *Amelia* with some of Fielding's early comic works, we might arrive at this puzzling reformulation of Marx's famous comment on French history: that if all great literary-historical facts and personages might be said to occur in Fielding's corpus, as it were, twice, we would want to add—the second time as tragedy, the first as farce.

Indeed, the particular means by which Fielding most memorably translated serious works into the farcical extravaganzas of his early career almost seem to anticipate the particular nature of the "re-translation" that would occur in serious literary forms in the 1740's and 1750's, not only in Fielding's own work but in that of his literary culture generally. For when Fielding was to create "a serious or tragic reembodiment of the earlier comic mode" later in his career, he would place the emotional and aesthetic claims of tragedy and heroism in a different body—a female body—rather than in a simply resuscitated body of the conventional male hero who had ruled the late-seventeeth- and early-eighteenth-century stage. The comic figure of a female Tom Thumb was to prove a significant kind of pivot point in literary history, looking forward (if obliquely) to the reign of the Pamelas and the Amelias of the new novel form— and to the culture that form expressed, and helped bring into being. In 1730, Fielding could exploit the egregiousness of a hero played by a woman as a source of ridicule, relying on his audience's identification with the older dominant ideology associated with the "Scriblerian" mode, even as the increasing influence of new social institutions and ideas (Walpole's bureaucratized government, the Bank of England and the stock market, a greater emphasis on fashion and on commodity exchange) put that ideology into threat—and made the axis of gender seem an especially compelling one, for laughter and for fear. Just twenty years later, the prevailing literary forums in which Fielding might write were strikingly different; and he found himself more interested in creating a serious portrait of the new kind of female "hero" who was to become more and more central in the century to follow, than in exposing the decline of traditional male heroism by embodying it in a woman.

The personal and cultural transformation that this literary contrast marks was not simple, however, or complete: just as the craze for "she-tragedies" in the first decades of the century expresses an early interest in the serious possibilities of female heroism, the elements of incredulity, ridicule, and resistance in the reception of *Amelia* demonstrate a continuing readiness to see powerful female figures as necessarily either silly or threatening. Significantly, the ridicule of *Amelia* focused particularly on the breaking of Amelia's nose. Booth makes Amelia's damaged nose the symbol of her singular and distinctly feminine heroism, but unsympathetic readers pounced on the ambiguities of this feature as an identifying one for a female hero, playing upon the comic association of the nose with male sexuality,[8] or pretending to mistake Fielding's account of the accident's outcome, so that Amelia might be left as much without a nose as Blear-Eyed Moll, whose disfigurement reflects the consequences of her unbounded sexuality rather than of suffering virtue.[9] Thus the very mark of a new ideal of exemplary female selflessness and strength could easily collapse back into a sign either of woman's absurdly inadequate impersonation of male identity or of her own threatening qualities of unruliness and passion within an older model of female nature. These dangers are connected and coincide, for example, in the figure of the Jacobite Amazon that we studied in relation to *Tom Jones*; the Whig lady, inhabiting only the private sphere of domesticity and feeling, emerges as a proper alternative to her in *The Jacobite's Journal* and at the end of *The Female Rebels*.

In rendering this last role substantial in *Amelia*, Fielding still had to negotiate the issue of "petticoat government"—or a suspicion that the new outlines of the domestic heroine might conceal the old substance of the "unnaturally" overbearing wife we encountered so often in his plays. Unlike his earlier, satiric works, *Amelia* implies a defense of admittedly constructed or historically "accidental" roles—as Fielding's response to criticisms of the novel defended the dignity of Amelia's explicitly reconstructed nose—and it identifies the new domestic heroine as the worthy safekeeper of her family's financial and moral value. To grant this heroine such authority was not, however, entirely to reject or replace older forms of authority, associated with classical learning and with other male preserves. In the final section of this chapter, we will explore the extent to which Amelia's new female authority must be sponsored by aspects of existing masculine authority, which proves more resilient than it might seem. Both *On the Management and Education of Children* and, more complexly, Fielding's *Amelia* demonstrate that the multiple and often inconsistent elements of a prevailing ideology do not always compete or contend with each other for dominance, but may form expedient (though often unstable) alliances, enlisting partial versions of each other for mutual support. The effect of direct contradiction between ideological materials—such as that insisted upon in *On the Management* between certain aspects of classical texts and its own Christian and domestic ideals—is brought into being actively, at moments of crisis, and for polemical ends; and it may lead to mutual adaptation and partial circumscriptions of authority, rather than to a struggle for exclusive control.

Despite Fielding's suggestion that Amelia's autonomous agency is limited in various ways by her dependence on traditional male authority, the fear remains that she may break loose from that dependence and take on a separate and even punishing authority of her own. Doubts and ambivalences shadow her, therefore, in odd uncertainties of tone; and they reassert themselves with a vengeance in Fielding's last work, *Journal of a Voyage to Lisbon*, which we will examine briefly in the epilogue below. In the account of his own journey toward death, Fielding himself takes Booth's place as an upper-class male protagonist rendered ineffectual and peripheral by time's passage. The redemptive possibilities of an Amelia are forgotten in the final chapter of his career, as Fielding elaborates the portrait of a domestic "fury" he encounters on his journey, a vengeful messenger both of historical transience and of the approaching end of an individual life.

Martin C. Battestin suggests that, in some ways, the fictional *Amelia* itself tells the story of Fielding's own life: he notes the long tradition of identifying Booth with the novel's author, and he adds that some features of Booth's identity—the story of his courtship, his military office, his failed attempt at farming, his weakness for gambling, and his confinement for debt—seem to draw on the life of the author's father as well.[10] In its autobiographical references, then, Fielding's portrait of Booth constructs him in some quite specific ways as an amalgam of the present and of the recent past, of personal experience and of a receding paternal experience of manhood.[11] This character, with his divided location in two generations, repeatedly appears as an unworthy or inadequate partner for Amelia, whom Battestin describes simply as an "idealized portrait" of Fielding's first wife.[12] Booth himself recognizes, and feels enervated by, his un-worthiness of his wife.[13] "O my *Amelia*," he cries out on one occa-sion, "how much you are my Superior in every Perfection! How wise, how great, how noble are your Sentiments! Why can I not im-itate what I so much admire?" (162); on another, he exclaims, "Upon my Soul, I am not worthy of you.—I am a Fool, and yet you cannot blame me—" (382; see also 235, 250, 421, 498).

When Booth confesses his inferiority in both scenes, he refers nominally to the greater fortitude, faith, and constancy shown by Amelia, but the reader knows that something remains unspoken in each of these conversations, and that the source of these conceal-ments itself suggests the deeper nature of Booth's "unworthiness." In both cases, concealment on one side or the other is made necessary by aspects of Booth's implication in the old "Cavalier" masculinity observed by Carlton. In the first, Booth has actually been tormented by an awareness of his "gallantry" in Newgate with Miss Mathews, though when Amelia concludes that he must be agonizing over his family's future, he responds as though she is right; in the second, it is Amelia who conceals Colonel James's designs on her from Booth, but she must do so only because she fears that Booth would have to duel with James to preserve his "honour" if he knew. In the dream narrative with which we began, Booth imagines his own inadequacy as a kind of tardiness: "you gently chid me for staying so long—." We might interpret this comment as a reference to the elements of backwardness in Booth's character—his vexed preservation of no-tions incompatible both with the real nature of his marriage and with his present circumstances.

For much of *Amelia*, Booth seems suspended in a kind of gap between prevailing past and future masculine roles. He responds with aggression, as if reflexively, to demands to defend his mascu-line honor; he reacts with tears of gratitude or sympathy, as if re-flexively, to sentimental situations; and he apparently lacks any dom-inant code of behavior and belief with which to organize his identity or to mediate between these contradictory claims upon it. As a "hu-mor" character intent on applying the dueling code in its most rigid form who can also be found dressed in a woman's bed-gown, ten-derly nursing his sister (128), or arguing for the dignity of the Chris-tian religion (508–10), Colonel Bath provides a caricature version of one of the central contradictions in Booth's identity (and the close proximity of their names reinforces the link between their identities). Bath seems both comically outlandish and doomed from the start, and we are informed in passing at the end of the novel that he has indeed been killed in a duel "by a Gentleman who told the Colonel he differed from him in Opinion" (531). Though Booth's version of military honor is less extreme than Bath's, it also quickly comes to seem unviable as a guide for behavior or for interpreting social relations; yet it is not until the novel's closing pages that Booth seizes upon Christianity as an alternative source of identity, explanation, and value.

Suggestively, we are told very little about the particulars of Booth's life before the time he courts Amelia, his background and education, or the identity he inherits from his family, whereas we do learn a certain amount about Amelia's family and upbringing.[14] The most specific reference in the novel to Booth's family and past occurs when he encounters a "great Author" as a fellow inmate at the bailiff's. The narrator explains Booth's readiness to enter into a learned discussion with this author:

Booth, as the Reader may be pleased to remember, was a pretty good Master of the Classics: For his Father, tho' he designed his Son for the Army, did not think it necessary to breed him up a Block-head. He did not perhaps imagine that a competent Share of *Latin* and *Greek* would make his Son either a Pedant or a Coward. He considered likewise, probably, that the Life of a Soldier is in general a Life of Idleness, and might think that the spare Hours of an Officer in Country Quarters would be as well employed with a Book, as in sauntering about the Streets, loitering in a Coffee House, sotting in a Tavern, or in laying Schemes to debauch and ruin a Set of harmless ignorant Country Girls. (324)

Booth's father is conjured here as a largely hypothetical entity; and the reasons assigned to this shadowy figure for providing his son with a classical education suggest that any past ideal of the gentleman officer either has fallen into self-parodic decline or was fraught with contradictions all along. Only the most decayed remnants of the outlines of the "Cavalier" hero appear in the brief sketch of a soldier's life offered here;[15] the substance of the classical education given to Booth seems to represent a kind of stay against this emptying-out of the officer's role. While Booth's personal knowledge of both Latin and Greek authors gives him dignity in his exchange with the professional author which follows, however, the superiority demonstrated by Booth to this author (who, it soon emerges, knows neither Greek

nor Latin, though he has been soliciting subscriptions for his translation of the *Metamorphoses*) appears to be an entirely inconsequential
or impractical kind of superiority in the present world. The author
treats the world of letters as a mere "Market," where some literary
"goods" now sell better than others, and where one needs no more
qualification than impudence to make a bid for the bookseller's
wages. Booth may be more learned than the "great Author," but he
is equally in prison for debt, and he is actually less well prepared than
the author to try to convert his literacy into some kind of living.

Booth is not guilty of laying schemes to debauch "ignorant
Country Girls," but during his first visit to prison for debt, he does
engage in an adulterous affair. George Sherburn suggests that this
affair should be seen in the context of an upper-class masculine code
of gallantry which Booth merely fulfills by responding to Miss
Mathews's inviting hints: "no man of his station (except Sir Charles
Grandison)," he comments, "could have refused the overtures of
Miss Mathews in Newgate."[16] Booth is not Sir Charles Grandison,
and his sexual intrigue early in the novel may signal the element of
Cavalier gallantry in his character; but he shares more with Grandison than he might seem to, for he is also serious enough about the
ideal of marital friendship and fidelity to be tormented by his sexual
betrayal of Amelia. Even in the course of the intrigue, "his Virtue"
at times "alarmed and roused him, and brought the Image of poor
injured *Amelia* to haunt and torment him" (154–55). When he leaves
Newgate and returns home to his family, Booth settles into a melancholy so deep that he is "scarce animated," like "a dull lifeless
Lump of Clay" (161), as if paralyzed and drained by the conflict between the masculine codes of Cavalier gallantry and of virtue.

As we remarked earlier, Booth also repeatedly finds himself
either paralyzed or isolated by a conflict between Christian ideas and
the Cavalier or military code of masculine honor that requires a
man's willingness to duel (135, 210–13, 363, 376, 397, 437). This
conflict reaches the level of articulated debate at several points in
Amelia (364–67, 503–5); and the debates within the novel echo a
lively controversy about dueling in the English press, recurring
throughout the early and middle eighteenth century and flaring up
especially in 1750, the year before *Amelia*'s publication.[17] Booth at
one point attempts to end a dispute on the topic among his friends
by concluding flatly that the contradiction involved is absolute: it is
impossible, he says, "to reconcile accepting a Challenge with the

Christian Religion, or refusing it with the modern Notion of Honour." But he adds a comment in favor of complying with the demands of honor when forced to choose between its claims and religion's: "'you must allow it, Doctor,' said he, 'to be a very hard Injunction for a Man to become infamous; and more especially for a Soldier, who is to lose his Bread into the Bargain'" (366–67). Nonetheless, in practice Booth is generally more inclined to avoid duels than to engage in them. On several occasions, Amelia protects Booth from any awareness of the conflicting demands upon him by simply concealing threats to his honor; when Amelia's protection of him fails, Booth takes part in dueling only reluctantly.

Significantly, in the first such situation, Booth's caricature-double, Colonel Bath, relieves him of the conflict by taking the demands of Booth's honor upon himself and fighting a duel with Monsieur Bagillard, who has plotted to seduce Amelia. Since Bagillard recovers from the wounds he receives in this duel, Bath congratulates Booth on the opportunity he therefore has to fight a duel with Bagillard himself, but Booth responds by speaking for that Christian side of the dilemma which Bath neglects: "I answered, I could not think of any such Thing: For that when I imagined he was on his Death-bed, I had heartily and sincerely forgiven him" (135). Somewhat later in the novel, Bath provokes Booth into a duel with himself. Booth exclaims after they have done sparring, with "great Concern and even Horror in his Countenance," "'Why, my dear Colonel, . . . would you force me to this?'" (210). "Forced" into dueling against his will by the older notions of masculine honor Bath represents, Booth finds he has slipped into a kind of time warp while "at the Lists" with Bath: he arrives home much later than planned, and then waits quietly, in oblivious expectation of dinner, which Amelia has served hours before (212).

If Booth thus appears an ambivalent, if reasonably competent, duelist, he is, we are assured, an unequivocally good soldier. When Harrison asks a nobleman he knows to exert his interest in Booth's favor, he says that Booth has "very extraordinary Merit" and behaved "with distinguish'd Bravery" at the siege of Gibraltar. He demonstrates this, however, by quickly adding that Booth "was dangerously wounded at two several Times in the Service of his Country" (457); and the fact of Booth's two injuries is the most specific information we receive about his military service as Booth himself recounts it to Miss Mathews. Booth's valor and military merit are evoked by him not through descriptions of aggressive actions or conquests, but through these references to his willing suffering of injuries. Both times Booth is injured his life is preserved not by his own actions but by the practical skill as well as bravery of his "servant," Atkinson, who carries Booth to safety on each occasion (113–14, 115–16). From the little we learn, Booth's character in war seems as marked by passivity as it is elsewhere, but not because of any simply personal inadequacy. The treatment of Booth's actual military activities is shadowed or constrained by the possibility that, when rendered concrete and active, Booth's identity as a military captain will not mesh easily with his identity as a man of sentiment, empathy, and tenderness.

At some points, characters in *Amelia* are careful to distinguish between the suspect violence of man-to-man combat over matters of "honour" and the legitimate violence of national conflict in defense of religion, country, or friend (364). At others, however, the much-discussed conflict between Christianity and dueling comes to seem only a localized version of a deeper conflict between Christianity and military aggression. The narrator conveys a disaffection from the heroes of war as well as of personal honor when he declares that he finds the sight of a mother weeping over her children more properly tragic than he would that of "all the Heroes who have ever infested the Earth, hanged all together in a String" (359). Characters within the novel themselves seem to register an ambiguity in the nature of Booth's military identity when they misrecognize it as one involving criminal violence: the keeper at Newgate takes Booth for a highwayman, interpreting his title of "captain" as an homage to his daring on the road (95–97); more devastatingly, on her deathbed, Booth's own sister mistakes him for "a Highwayman who had a little before robbed her," at once terrified by his presence and calling constantly for the brother whom she so loves (79). Nancy's delirious confusion points to some real doubleness in Booth's character, with its different components of sentimental private feeling and a public heroism that sometimes seems potentially indistinguishable from villainy.

The bailiff at the sponging-house where Booth is next imprisoned points to another possible ambiguity in Booth's military identity when he insists on likening Booth's employment to his own. "I am the King's Officer, as well as you," he asserts, "and I will spend Guinea for Guinea as long as you please" (353). To Booth's extreme aggravation, the bailiff thus links Booth's gentlemanly standing as captain not to criminality but to a government function that is socially disrespectable, unheroic, ignoble. Most pointedly, he draws into question Booth's assumption of a superiority based on class: he reminds Booth, jeeringly, that his own money is worth no less than Booth's; he asks what it means to be at once a gentleman and a debtor who can't raise bail; and he eventually concludes about Booth, "a Gentleman, indeed! Ay, ay, *Newgate* is the properest Place for such Gentry" (352–53). Indeed, the only prospect for financial viability Booth ever gains—the only suggestion of a properer place for him than prison—is his hope for a post in the West Indies, where he might escape from the desperate confinement of debt but only by moving far from the English society in which he seems no longer a workable participant (191, 197, 369). In the West Indies, Booth might perform the upper-class labor of colonial rule, which was to become a much more central function for England's male upper classes in the century to follow, as its empire grew; but within Booth's own story, such a post fails to materialize. The most urgent, constant, and disabling contradiction within Booth's military role is that between its class standing, by tradition and in the abstract, and the actual financial means it offers to Booth and his family.

Booth is not alone within the binding straits of this contradiction. When he arranges, for example, to meet some fellow officers at a tavern, they must meet at one within the verge of the Court:

for of five Officers that were to meet there, three besides *Booth* were confined to that Air, which hath been always found extremely wholesome to a *broken* military Constitution. And here if the good Reader will pardon the Pun, he will scarce be offended at the Observation; since how is it possible that without running in Debt, any Persons should maintain the Dress and Appearance of a Gentleman, whose Income is not half so good as that of a Porter? (187)

While the other conflicts or contradictions I have described within Booth's identity may be said, figuratively, to constrain his freedom of action, this one quite literally constrains his freedom of physical movement, often keeping him confined within the home which one would expect to be his wife's own characteristic domain.

The lower-class Atkinson, on the other hand, is not disabled by this contradiction, and proves himself much more capable than Booth of making a viable means of support out of a military career.

Booth assumes a condescending attitude toward Atkinson early in the novel, generally referring to him as his "servant" rather than by his proper name, and explaining that he himself has arranged for him to be made a serjeant (115). But as the novel goes on, Booth's own dependence on Atkinson's practical abilities becomes more and more evident and general: not only does Atkinson save Booth's life twice in battle, but he saves him from drowning in a storm at sea (111–13); he comes to his aid in the skirmish with the bailiff described above, providing an "Example" of bold aggression which Booth can only "imitate" (353–54); and he ultimately offers him financial assistance on several occasions, trying to save his gentleman-master from imprisonment for debt with the money he has saved from his wages (123, 191, 200, 333). While Booth is a half-pay officer in search of a regiment, when he reencounters Atkinson, the serjeant is actively employed on duty in London (and rescues *both* Booth and his little son from an abusive sentinel in the first moments of their reunion [181]). Apparently, military service offers a feasible form of employment for a working-class man, who labors at it as at any other job, but survives only as a "broken" vestige of a past social "constitution" for the gentleman,[18] who fruitlessly seeks to maintain his dignity within its frame.

Both Atkinson, as a lower-class man, and Amelia, as a woman, should be subordinate to Booth within a traditional social order, but Amelia as well as Atkinson apparently moves about and acts more freely than her husband. When Amelia visits Booth during his final stay in the sponging-house, her pleasure in seeing him is eventually shattered by the thought that, "tho' she had the Liberty of leaving that House when she pleased, she could not take her beloved Husband with her" (499). Amelia's greater sense of freedom, as well as her greater fortitude and faith, seems to depend partially upon her claimed freedom from implication in class identity: at a number of points in the novel Amelia insists that "all Stations of Life were equal to her," that she feels herself a "Partaker of one common Nature" with "the Wife of the honest Labourer," and that her own hands "are as able to work" as those "which have been more inured to it" (146, 527, 436; see also 162).[19] Though the narrator apparently accepts the well-born man's felt need to "maintain the Dress and Appearance of a Gentleman" (187), Amelia is shown resolutely (even, finally, cheerfully) pawning both jewelry and clothing until she has "no other Cloaths but what I have now on my Back. . . . not even a clean

Shift in the World" (435, 473–75, 478, 487). Booth is supported, both emotionally and practically, by his wife's willingness to sacrifice; but her proposal that she must work to earn money to save them from ruin seems to challenge Booth's deepest sense of his own identity, touching him "to the Quick." Booth's frantic reaction to this suggestion strangely confuses the prospects of debt and of cuckoldry as equally overwhelming threats to his masculine honor and control (346).

This suggestion thus seems to evoke not only the economic contradictions of Booth's class identity but also the contradictory conceptual frameworks within which he experiences, and seeks to explain, his own emotions. In *Joseph Andrews* and *Tom Jones*, as we have seen, Fielding explores what it means to misrecognize others' identities or motivations, or even the nature of one's own. He does so in *Amelia* as well, but there he repeatedly suggests that misrecognition is not followed in any simple way by a revelation that undoes earlier mistaken impressions. The conversation in which Amelia offers to support their family through her labor illustrates the kind of sustained dissonances that often exist within Booth's interpretive framework—and which also characterize the narrator's own ways of proceeding.

After Booth has indulged in a disastrous night of compulsive gambling, he confesses to Amelia that he has lost his money playing cards, but withholds the news that he has also lost fifty pounds that he borrowed in the frenzy of play. He is at first comforted by Amelia's assurance that they "will contrive some Method to repair such a Loss," but when, after a little further dialogue, she enters into a longer and more concrete discussion of how they must put themselves "into some mean Way of Livelihood," avowing her own willingness to perform manual labor, Booth reacts extraordinarily, turning pale, gnashing his teeth, and crying out "Damnation! this is too much to bear" (435–36). Called upon by the terrified Amelia to explain his reaction, Booth seizes upon Amelia's passing remark in the course of this discussion that she believes Booth's dependence on James's friendship "is all vain" and formulates his sense of frantic desperation in terms of sexual jealousy, with his overwrought language drawing on the script of *Othello*.[20] Quickly the discussion of their financial woes and Amelia's plan to right them becomes a heated exchange about Booth's "Honour," with Booth angrily suggesting that Amelia, "from a weak Tenderness for my Person," is willing to "go privately about to betray, to undermine the most invaluable Treasure of my Soul" (437). Although their argument thus unfolds, and is eventually resolved, in terms of Booth's (justified) fear that James may attempt to cuckold him, the narrator closes this chapter with the remark that Amelia thus "generously forgave a Passion, of which the sagacious Reader is better acquainted with the real Cause, than was that unhappy Lady"—apparently, that is, the concealed fact of the real depth of the Booths' financial troubles, or the true extent to which Booth falls short as his family's material provider.

When Amelia begins to talk of a "mean Way of Livelihood" and of working with her hands, Booth has no vocabulary to express how deeply this challenges his upper-class masculine "Honour." If, however, he therefore seizes upon the established language of male sexual jealousy to express something other than itself, the narrator encourages us to believe that Booth nonetheless does experience that jealousy as he and Amelia argue: he observes that Booth has "some of *Othello*'s Blood in him," just before telling us that jealousy is not the *real* cause of his sudden, wild agitation. This scene, therefore, exemplifies a further aspect of conflict and difficulty for Booth in *Amelia*: both his own emotional responses and his interpretations of others' behavior are frequently garbled by his overlaying of disjunctive scripts and situations. Sometimes, as here, Booth is not unaware of the "real" content of the situation, even as he experiences it in terms adopted from another context. At other times, he seems more simply, if somewhat willfully, oblivious to the actual nature of the events around him. Repeatedly, a gap opens between Booth's model for interpreting and narrating social relations and the nature of those relations as represented, ultimately, by this novel. At a number of points, Booth's interpretation of events is shaped by his expectation that class identity sharply limits the possibilities of human action and emotion; characteristically, he also assumes that the most significant bonds take place between men, whether in male friendships or within hierarchical institutions, rather than in relations between men and women.[21]

Assumptions about class and assumptions about the relative importance of homosocial and heterosexual bonds both influence Booth's understanding of Atkinson, whose actions and motivations he consistently either overlooks or mistakes. When Booth tells Miss

Mathews about the anonymous letter Amelia received, summoning her to attend her husband in his illness at Gibraltar, he explains that its author remains unknown "to this Day," for he has considered and ruled out all likely and even unlikely candidates. His story contains various clues that Atkinson in fact authored the letter, but Booth does not even register the possibility that his "servant" is capable of taking such initiative and communicating with Amelia; Miss Mathews briefly raises that possibility, but only by imagining that Atkinson might have been acting on specific instructions from his mistress, which idea she quickly rejects (117–18). Later, when Booth is imprisoned for debt and provides his friends with an account of what he owes, debt by debt, Atkinson deducts 100 pounds from the total to express his willingness to contribute that sum; but Booth "did not apprehend the generous Meaning of the Serjeant," and instead "answered, he was mistaken; that he had computed his Debts, and they amounted to upwards of four hundred Pounds" (333). Booth fails to apprehend Atkinson's meaning because he is readier to believe that his former servant is capable of making errors in addition than that he is capable of making such a gesture of freely willed generosity (or of backing it up with cash). But Booth's most sustained and serious misreading of Atkinson results from his confident assumption that Atkinson's loyalty to the Booth family grows first out of his attachment to his "master" and military superior, Booth himself, rather than out of devotion to his foster sister and secret love object, Amelia.

Booth acknowledges that he "can hardly account for" the extreme fidelity Atkinson shows toward himself (115), but he never swerves from his supposition that it must evidence a "heroic Affection in a poor Fellow towards his Master" (111; also 107–8, 112, 118, 123). We, of course, eventually learn of Atkinson's devotion to Amelia, and when Colonel James asks Atkinson point-blank, "is your Attachment to Mr. *Booth*, or to his Lady?" Atkinson responds unequivocally: "Certainly, Sir, . . . I must love my Lady best. Not but I have a great Affection for the Lieutenant too, because I know my Lady hath the same; and, indeed, he hath been always very good to me, as far as was in his Power" (341). This information makes better sense of some of the incidents Booth has earlier described, but Booth himself has determinedly missed this explanation of those events. For example, when Booth sends Atkinson back to retrieve the casket Amelia has prepared for him when he leaves for Gibraltar,

Atkinson returns in tears from Amelia's house, and Booth comments, "I never could account for those Tears, any otherwise than by placing them to the Account of that Distress in which he left me at that time" (108). At another point, Fielding contrives this complicated coinciding of events to show us the nature and extent of Booth's misapprehension: Atkinson is made a serjeant on the same day the news arrives that Amelia has safely passed through childbirth. Although Booth himself is very happy about his family news, he assumes that Atkinson can only be happy about his own military promotion, which he owes to Booth ("I shall never forget the extravagant Joy his Halbert gave him" [115]). Atkinson's actions and feelings, Booth presumes, can only be understood in the context of attachments between men within the hierarchical social institutions of class and of the military. It does not occur to him that Atkinson might enter into the relations of romantic love, heterosexual desire, or domestic felicity that have so shaped Booth's own life.

As Booth's more-than-social-equal, Colonel James does not elicit Booth's condescending assumptions about class and identity, but his behavior too is interpreted by Booth within the expectation that bonds between men are primary and determining. At several points in the novel, this expectation is identified as a specifically old and possibly outdated one. For example, when he tells Amelia about James's offer to take care of her if Booth is sent abroad, Booth interprets James's willingness to be not only "a Father" to their children but "a Husband" to Amelia as a sign of his moving devotion to Booth himself, and Harrison comments that James thus "gives Credit to the old Stories of Friendship" (370–72). Earlier, Mrs. Atkinson has expressed doubt that such "old Stories" should be given any credit in the present: she says that she has read "of *Pylades* and *Orestes*, *Damon* and *Pythias*, and other great Friends of old," but that she can only make sense of James's extravagant "Portraiture of Friendship" as a cover for (illicit) heterosexual desire (336–37). Mrs. Atkinson's examples point to a specific literary past in which the old stories of idealized male friendship might be found—that of classical drama and epic; and the emphasis on male-male relationships in those forms contrasts sharply with the premise of *Amelia* itself, and of the English novel more generally, that the most important and central narratives (whatever Booth may assume) have to do with heterosexual love.

This organizing premise is sometimes voiced explicitly within

Amelia.[22] In Dr. Harrison's letter to Colonel James, read aloud by "the Bucks" at the Hay-market, he announces: "Domestic Happiness is the End of almost all our Pursuits, and the common Reward of all our Pains. When Men find themselves for ever barred from this delightful Fruition, they are lost to all Industry, and grow careless of all their worldly Affairs. They thus become bad Subjects, bad Relations, bad Friends and bad Men" (414–15). At this moment anyway, Harrison justifies the centrality of (heterosexual) domestic relationships not by privileging them in religious terms but by insisting on their crucial role in maintaining civil society: they, rather than the male hierarchies of the army, of class relations, or of politics, keep men industrious, attentive to their "worldly Affairs," and responsible to their government. At a number of points, Booth fails to recognize the various kinds of centrality granted by the novel he inhabits to domestic love, and also to the adulterous desire that appears as the dark double of that love.

In the first instance of this pattern, Booth himself tells Miss Mathews how he has misrecognized certain relationships. By his own account his confusion is linked to matters of literary genre and education. While Amelia and Booth were staying in Montpelier, Booth relates, he became friends with Monsieur Bagillard, "a *Frenchman* of great Wit and Vivacity" as well as learning.

Indeed I spent so much of my Time with him, that *Amelia* (I know not whether I ought to mention it) grew uneasy at our Familiarity, and complained of my being too little with her, from my violent Fondness for my new Acquaintance; for our Conversation turning chiefly upon Books, and principally *Latin* ones (for we read several of the Classics together) she could have but little Entertainment by being with us. (125)

In this case, classical literature provides not only models for "violent Fondness" between men which compete with the prevailing model of married love, but also the specialized subject matter of a modern male friendship, creating an arena of shared interest for well-bred men that specifically excludes wives. At this point in his tale, Booth describes Amelia as jealous of his friendship with Bagillard and threatened by it: "When my Wife had once taken it into her Head that she was deprived of my Company by Mr. *Bagillard*, it was impossible to change her Opinion" (125). Soon, however, he reveals what he later discovered, when Bath and Bagillard engaged in a duel: that Bagillard was actually more interested in sharing Booth's wife than in sharing his classical learning, and that Amelia only pretended to feel excluded by the men's learned discussions in order to spare her husband from knowledge of Bagillard's designs. The classical education with which Booth's father was careful to endow him contributes to his misreading of Bagillard's motives both by teaching him to give credit to "old Stories" of idealized male friendship and by encouraging him to believe in the importance of a special masculine and upper-class arena of interest.

The story Booth tells in Newgate that includes this episode is one of several long narratives presented by one character to another within *Amelia* rather than by the novel's omniscient narrator to his readers. Booth is of course not omniscient; however, as his narrative is retrospective, he has gained some knowledge about the events he relates (as about Bagillard's concealed motives) that he did not possess as those events occurred. And yet the way that Booth handles that knowledge in presenting his narrative is peculiar. When Booth tells Miss Mathews about his strained relations with Amelia over Monsieur Bagillard, he first describes the situation as though he still believes that Amelia objected to his "violent Fondness" for Bagillard only because it led him to spend so much time with a companion in pursuits she could not share: he asserts her responses and motives flatly, and then revises them *a posteriori* when he gets to the point in the story when he himself learned something different. Thus, his story as it unfolds is about something different—about the intense bond between two men, the excitement of shared classical learning, and women's jealous exclusion from these pleasures—from what it is about when it concludes.

Although Booth now knows what the story of this episode proved finally to be "about," he temporarily recreates the framework within which he first understood Bagillard's and Amelia's actions as he tells the story. That general framework, as we have seen, continues to be essential to Booth's understanding of social relations and events, even if Booth can describe to Miss Mathews one rebuke to its explanatory powers that occurred before the novel's opening scenes. This "framework," or set of basic ideological tenets, is not easily falsified or abandoned: it guides Booth's interpretations of people and events in terms of the broad social structures of class relations and gender; and Booth apparently need not find all of his experience consistent with it—whether in reality or in illusion—for him to maintain it. The few details included in the Bagillard episode suggest, further, how literary experience—both the content of literary works and their specific functions within education and adult society—can enter into that ideological framing of experience which the disjunctions in Booth's account serve to register.

The reader of *Amelia* becomes accustomed to such disjunctions in her experience of the novel generally. The narrator of the novel, standing outside the events of the plot and not limited, as individual characters are, by a particular position within that plot, is not subject to the kind of misrecognitions (and occasional belated enlightenments) that Booth suffers. Yet he nonetheless repeatedly takes us through a disorienting process of shifting perspectives, offering one account of a character or event only to withdraw it and replace it with an unexpected alternative. Often the incompatibility of his successive accounts (like Booth's of Bagillard) seems to mark the uneasy coexistence of much larger structures of belief (and their associated literary forms) that are potentially in conflict; so that these instabilities of plot and character may also make us aware of the ideological assumptions involved in one act or another of narrative explanation. Far from exploiting the illusions of "transparent narration," as John Bender contends,[23] the narrator of *Amelia* often makes his readers uncomfortably aware of the willfulness of his explanations through the very unsteadiness with which he sustains them.

The example of multiple and inconsistent acts of narration that Andrew Elfenbein traces is instructive: the reader struggles, unsuccessfully, to attain a confident and coherent picture of Mrs. James's character because the narrator repeatedly provides, in retrospect, contradictory explanations of her behavior. She behaves coldly toward her old friend Amelia because she has been transformed into "a fine Lady," concerned only with "Form and Show," by her marriage to the high-ranking James (181, 208); she then responds with warmth and some sympathy to Amelia's misfortunes because, the narrator now reveals, every fine lady "hath some real Character at the Bottom," and Mrs. James was "at the Bottom a very good-natured Woman," despite her airs (343); yet she ultimately proves willing to cooperate in her husband's sexual designs on Amelia and even (we learn after the fact) eager, herself, to engage in adultery with Booth (494).[24] We can imagine each of these portraits of Mrs. James as at home in some literary genre: the simple portrait of Mrs. James as a personification of female triviality and vanity, and the somewhat more complex portrait of her as given over to the pursuit of pleasure and selfish power, would both slip comfortably into the misogynist galleries of female types found in satiric poetry or drama (Pope's "Epistle to a Lady," or any number of Fielding's own plays); the second account of Mrs. James, which reaches to describe some "natural" aspect of her personal character, "at the Bottom," beneath the outlines of her satiric type, aspires to a treatment of individual subjectivity more characteristic of the emerging novel form. What is confusing here is that these approaches to character—with their conflicting premises about human identity and about female identity in particular—exist together, turned on a single character within one work, without any indication of ultimate priority of truthfulness to mediate among them.

On the other hand, when the narrator provides different impressions, in succession, of a single event, authority adheres to the later version as a belated revelation of the event's *real* contents. Nonetheless, our initial, partial understanding of the event is not without consequence. For example, when the narrator tells us about the episode at the masquerade, he allows us to receive it, as we read, as *one* kind of familiar story—a story about (among other things) the famous instability of female character, for, in the dangerous setting of the masquerade, Amelia suddenly appears in the role of "a mere Woman of this World," willing to have "very fervent Love" made to her if she can turn it to her advantage (411).[25] This story is startling (even incredible) in the context of what precedes it, but only later does the narrator transform the episode, retroactively, into another kind of story, as we learn of Mrs. Atkinson's secret replacement of Amelia in the party attending the masquerade. We find, then, that Amelia's character should indeed be set apart from such old stories of female nature, though Mrs. Atkinson's may perhaps be left within them in her place. Thus, if traditional ideas about female triviality, changeability, or passion are soundly rejected by *Amelia*'s main plot, their force is felt in the novel not only in its margins, in secondary characters and subplots, but in the provisional spaces of the plot's unfolding, in impressions that may be temporarily entertained if not later confirmed. The specific kind of suspense created by such deferred and nontotalizing acts of explanation—a suspense about the meaning or nature of what has already happened, rather than about what will happen next—allows for one kind of dynamic ideological suspense in *Amelia*, as the narrator sustains, side by side or one after another, several conflicting general views of social relations or of the final sources of authority and meaning.

A number of readers have commented on the quality of "ambivalence" in Fielding's works—an ambivalence that I would want to define as a state of political as well as personal or psychological conflict.[26] In describing the ambivalences of *Amelia*, Martin C. Battestin focuses on its double and conflicted engagement with what he calls "the new psychology" and religious skepticism epitomized by David Hume and with the tradition of Christian humanism. He comments that in this case, the authority of a "last word" on the meaning of earlier events in a novel is clearly not totalizing or absolute: Booth's conversion at the end of *Amelia* suggests that "the message of the book is *meant* to be the reaffirmation of the Christian humanist tradition," but the frame of reference invoked, retroactively, by this conversion does not undo our experience of the narrative itself as more thoroughly rooted in the skepticism associated with Hume.[27] Battestin thus sees the larger conflicts embodied in *Amelia* as finally unresolved by the working-out of the novel's plot, as do I. He formulates the conflict he describes as essentially an intellectual one, however, whereas I have been seeking to trace connections between problems of narration or of Booth's interpretations of events and the changing material social structures of class and gender. Further, Battestin assumes that Booth, in embracing a real faith in Christianity at the end of this novel, turns to an old system of belief from his flirtation with a new religious skepticism and psychology of the passions; I have made the apparently more peculiar assumption that, with his conversion, Booth moves forward to a *new* social position, into which his wife has already proleptically advanced.

When Booth converts belatedly to unconflicted belief in Christianity (Dr. Harrison is surprised to learn that Booth did not hold this belief before [511]), he identifies himself with a position that has been treated earlier in the novel as specifically feminine. At one point, for instance, Harrison responds to Bath's insistence that a man must challenge whoever arrests him to a duel by asking him what a man should do if he is arrested by a woman—or by a clergyman such as himself. "Women and the Clergy are upon the same Footing," Bath declares. "The long-robed Gentry are exempted from the Laws of Honour" (364; and see 367). Booth does not become a clergyman when he accepts Barrow's arguments "in Proof of the Christian Religion," but he does thereby take up the faith that has animated his wife's identity all along, and also moves away from the specifically masculine "Honour" that has provided a tense alternative locus of conviction for him up to this point. Neither this code of honour nor the Christian faith can be described simply as "new" or "old" systems of belief. The very date on the novel marks the considerable age of Christianity *per se* when *Amelia* appears; but the particular existence of Christianity as a special province for women—as a system of beliefs associated with the domestic sphere, and set against a public world that is increasingly secularized and defined by economic exchange—is decidedly new. Thus the old tenets and texts of Christianity serve a new function within an emerging social configuration. Significantly, Booth is not converted by rereading the scriptures while in prison but by reading, for the first time, the sermons of Isaac Barrow, a leader of the modern Latitudinarian movement, whose works Booth's wife has been reading for some time (256).[28]

Conversely, although Booth's beliefs before his conversion may draw on a "new psychology" articulated by Hume (as Battestin argues), Booth melds psychological theory with a reiteration of old claims about the unbridgeable divisions between classes (450–51); and his dilemmas of *action* for much of the novel have less to do with the influence of radical new intellectual views than with his commitment to certain lived beliefs about masculinity and about upper-class identity that seem to have become outdated, untenable, in Booth's changing world. In one of the key passages quoted by Battestin, Booth's skepticism is described not with reference to Hume or any other mid-eighteenth-century writer, but with allusion to Claudian's *In Rufinum* (30).[29] This is not to say that Booth's non-Christian beliefs before his conversion should be identified in any direct way with the intellectual content of classical writings, but that they might be usefully located in the traditional social practices of upper-class English male life, including a classical education. New and old materials meld in continually varying combinations as the demands of ideology change; the dominant authority of Christianity and the prestige of classical literature both persist in English society in some uneasy balance, from the Renaissance onwards, despite important changes in the nature of that society; aspects of each system of belief come into question, or are suddenly given new prominence and force, as those old systems are adapted to serve new social ends and purposes. Amelia's (and others') assertions that Christianity supports the dignity of labor and disallows the claims of class distinction seem to adumbrate the new alliance between Protestant religion and a middle-class ethic that has been so frequently noticed in later eighteenth- and nineteenth-century Britain (304–5, 377, 527). Booth, on the other hand, finds the upper-class badge of his classical learning to be without value in the modern "market-place" of literature, though classical literature retains enough superficial prestige for the "great author" to be soliciting subscriptions for his translation of Ovid (324–30).

One way to describe Booth's conversion in the concluding chapters of *Amelia* would be as a change in his reading habits. At the beginning of the novel, he is "a good classical Scholar" but "not deeply learned in religious Matters" (31), and his interest in classical literature, as we have seen, figures in the novel at several points. At the end of the novel, Booth has put down his reading in Latin and Greek to study the sermons of an English theologian, and declares himself forever changed by them (510–11). When he says that he shall be a "better Man for them as long as I live," we might ask whether he means specifically that he shall be a "Man" who is more like a woman—for another way to describe Booth's conversion (I have been suggesting) would be as a change in the construction of his gender. In taking up the " 'Series of Sermons, which are contained in that Book,' (meaning Dr. *Barrow*'s Works, which then lay on the Table before him)," Booth takes up his wife's most valued reading material (256), and turns away from the classical reading which both he and Harrison have treated as a distinctively masculine province. In granting Christianity a final authority in his life, Booth also turns away from the masculine military code of honor which has repeatedly been presented in specific conflict with Christian belief.

Earlier, the prestige of the classical world has been actively protected from the questions raised by the novel about "modern" masculine "Honour": when Bath and Harrison argue about dueling, and Bath invokes "Mr. *Pope's Homer*" and "*Dryden's Virgil*" to demonstrate that ancient heroes were constantly engaged in duels, Harrison corrects him (after underlining that *he* reads classical epics in their original languages, rather than as they are transmitted by his English contemporaries): " 'But are you sure, Colonel,' cries the Doctor, 'that you have not made a small Mistake? For I am apt to believe, both Mr. *Pope* and Mr. *Dryden* (tho' I cannot say I ever read a Word of either of them) speak of Wars between Nations, and not of private Duels: For of the latter, I do not remember one single Instance in all the *Greek* or *Roman* Story'" (366).[30] In the final pages of the novel, the figure of the male hero in classical epic is no longer protected from implication in the novel's indictment of dueling, or from its suggestion that models of masculine greatness may be in conflict with Christian ideas. When Amelia tells Harrison about the challenge that James has sent to Booth, and expresses concern that Booth's honor "be preserved as well as his Life," Harrison reiterates his condemnation of duels but now directly contradicts his earlier statement by derisively referring to the characters of Paris and Menelaus in the *Iliad* as "Duellists." Harrison's comments in this final conversation about dueling, like the means of Booth's conversion, mark a striking diminishment of classical literature's authority as a source for masculine roles. These comments, however, neatly dramatize the way that women's faults may be invoked as a cover to preserve male dignity and integrity when history demands that masculine roles be sharply redefined.

Suddenly, it is Amelia who speaks for the necessity of observing a masculine code of honor; Harrison complains that that code has been chiefly "upheld by the Nonsense of Women"; and classical literature is now advanced as an authority on women's failings, if not on male heroism:

"Indeed, Child," cries the Doctor, "I know you are a good Woman; and yet I must observe to you, that this very Desire of feeding the Passion of female Vanity with the Heroism of her Man, old *Homer* seems to make the Characteristic of a bad and loose Woman. He introduces *Helen* upbraiding her Gallant with having quitted the Fight, and left the Victory to *Menelaus*, and seeming to be sorry that she had left her Husband, only because he was the better Duellist of the two; but in how different a Light doth he represent the tender and chaste Love of *Andromache* to her worthy *Hector*! She dissuades him from exposing himself to Danger, even in a just Cause. This is indeed a Weakness; but it is an amiable one, and becoming the true feminine Character; but a Woman, who out of heroic Vanity (for so it is) would hazard not only the Life, but the Soul too of her Husband in a Duel, is a Monster, and ought to be painted in no other Character but that of a Fury." (504)

The "old *Homer*" Harrison briefly offers Amelia in this passage is a newly novelistic one: he is defined, for the moment, as the narrator of Hector and Andromache's love, and as an early source for the mid-eighteenth-century contrast between natural and unnatural womanhood which we saw developed at length in *The Female Rebels*. Here, as there, the monstrous "Fury" of fierce, unnatural womanhood provokes men into battle and becomes an excuse for the long-standing existence of masculine roles that now must be discredited; like Flora MacDonald, the tender and chaste Andromache, with her amiable weakness, emerges as a properly feminine alternative in the course of the passage.

Thus, Harrison implicitly defines Booth's conversion as his escape from the demands placed upon him by a false version of femininity, rather than as an abandonment of traditional masculine ideals for ones sponsored by women. Suddenly, the true source of conflict for men becomes the coexistence of two sharply opposed versions of female nature rather than a doubleness or contradiction within masculine roles. The authority of classical epic, long the privileged source for traditional male heroism, is now invoked in support of an "amiable" feminine "Weakness"—and of the new male character, which defines itself in relation to that weakness. As Benjamin suggests, each epoch, in dreaming the next, unfolds its own end "with ruse"—that is, with a backward motion that wraps the new in the familiar authority of the distant past.[31] In Booth's "dream," his wife, apparently dramatically empowered by the new world of *Amelia*, is brought to him and "introduced" by Dr. Harrison, the classicist, the male divine, the symbolic father-figure and representative of England's honored past.[32]

Such a "ruse" is inevitably unstable, a complex and passing negotiation of a particular moment. In the final section to follow, we will examine the almost comically clumsy attempts of a 1754 manual on child rearing to encompass, at once, the traditional authority of a classical education and the new authority of the mother as a specially privileged educator for her own children. If both this manual, *On the Management and Education of Children*, and *Amelia* itself create (at moments) a precarious alliance between these two kinds of authority, the nature of that alliance suggests (finally) that the powers of each are radically circumscribed. Like *Tom Jones* and *The Jacobite's Journal*, *On the Management and Education of Children* suggests that the emphasis on attachments between men in the subject matter of classical epic and in the institution of classical education has become potentially scandalous in mid-eighteenth-century England; when the picture of the "amiably feminine weakness" of Andromache has become central to "old Homer's" continuing relevance, he has become old indeed.[33] At the same time, when the domestic heroine must be sponsored by various forms of masculine authority, the real possibilities of her agency and power must, in the end, be questioned. The nature of masculine authority is changing within the span of *Amelia* (and its time), as Booth's paralyzing experience of conflict and uncertainties of identity suggest. The fact of that authority, however, is not.

"Juliana-Susannah Seymour," the female letter writer whose epistles compose *On the Management and Education of Children*,[34] is concerned that the prestige afforded classical literature may lend force to ideas in direct conflict with the morality and religion that children must be taught. "It is much better," she warns her niece, that "[your sons] should be ignorant of some Part of the most elegant Writings in the World, than that by reading them they should have their Minds poison'd by infamous Opinions, which they will be naturally taught to hold in some Reverence, because of the Respect they have been ordered to pay on other Occasions to the Names of those Writers in whose Works they stand" (226). Her solution to this alarming situation provides one strikingly literal emblem of the ideological effect I have been describing, by which old cultural materials are constantly being reshaped and reproportioned to meet present needs.

'tis shameful that there are none of these Books to be had without the bad Passages; but as that is the Case, and as blotting them out would only be giving the Children more Curiosity and Eagerness to read them, I would advise that they never see the Books at all, at least while they are Children; but that their Lessons be chosen out of the innocent and virtuous Parts of the Writings, and put down in their Tutors Hand-writing on Paper separately as they are wanted. It will be easy for him to devise some Reason for this, nay, it may have great Use; they may be employed to copy them out on other Papers, and at the same time be imprinting the Lessons in their Memory, and learning themselves to write. (230–31)

Since the selectivity with which classical writings are to be honored and transmitted should not be immediately visible as a willful blotting-out of unacceptable content, a new transcript of classical texts must be made in the instructor's own accredited hand; children may then be safely set to copying this transcript, simultaneously internalizing the messages the tutor chooses to pass on ("imprinting the Lessons in their Memory"), training themselves in the practical skills of literacy, and physically reproducing this literally partial version of classical culture.

"Mrs. Seymour" explains that this expurgation is necessary because, although Greek and Roman texts include "the noblest Lessons of Morality," they also offer "Stories of the Heathen Gods" which are of course not in accord with Christian belief (224–25). "The early Notions Children are thus made to receive of Gods," she speculates, may lie at "the Root of Infidelity, and that Disrespect for Religion which is so universal" (228). She thus expresses a general fear that classical education may promote irreligious thoughts; but she speaks with greatest horror of the specific sexual acts it might provoke. "Is it possible," she asks, "that *Horace*, whose Sentiments of Honour and Virtue I have so often admired, can be the Patron also of Lewdness and Debauchery; and even speak, without Offence, of Crimes that are too unnatural to be mentioned" (225). Later, she again refers to homosexuality as the unnameable crime (33 n. 3), and as a crime that may be irreversibly damaging even to see named or discussed by ancient authors.

And if Drunkenness, and Crimes too bad to name, are in the same Manner as this Gentleman says they are, spoken of with Unconcern and Freedom by the Poets, as practised by themselves openly, and without Disguise or Blushing; the Effect must naturally be an accustoming the Mind in its Infant State, when it is most susceptible of Impressions, to look upon them without Horror: And this is laying the most dangerous Foundations that can be laid for the Practice of them in the Course of their Lives. I tremble while I write this to you, my Dear. (230)

In one way, "Mrs. Seymour's" authority to speak about the value of classical literature appears drastically limited by her repeated admission that she has never read any of it in the original herself (198, 205, 222, 231); as a woman, she did not receive the classical education which she includes among the subjects of her advice, and she must rely on the report of the man in charge of her great-nephews' education as the basis of her remarks. In another way, however, this feminine lack of knowledge serves here as the precise source of her special authority to judge and reject part of the works' contents: having never read them, she can speak as an independent voice about the odiousness of their contents (as reported to her), for she has never been touched by their insidious influence to accept the "unnatural" as natural. Simply to have read these dangerous works might render one suspect as the passive receiver of such corrupt "Impressions," and to have read them in an all-male social context (most devastatingly, in the single-sex world of a boys' school) is to appear too vulnerable to a blurring of literary content and personal practice.

Earlier in *On the Management*, "Mrs. Seymour" has expressed horror at "the debauched Principles" which are "propagate[d] so strongly and universally at Schools," and has recommended absolutely against sending boys to school rather than raising them at home (196–97). In her letter "Concerning the Classick Authors," she says she now understands the reason for "the debauch'd Principles and abandoned Lives of Youth in great Schools," having received "this Account of the Books which they are taught there" (226–27). Homosexuality, the unspeakable extreme of the debauchery encouraged by these books, constitutes a frightening and criminal horizon to the homosocial world of studies away from the family. This horizon becomes the subject of explicit and insistent concern about boys' schools for the first time in the course of the eighteenth century;[35] we have seen how Fielding, in *The Jacobite's Journal*, repeatedly invokes the threat of homoerotic bonds between tutors and pupils to discredit the Jacobite cause. Like Fielding, "Mrs. Seymour" also rejects flogging and other forms of authoritarian discipline because they produce "a broken Spirit, a mean, contemptible, and fearful Creature," unfitted for life as a free English citizen (119–21, 133–34). She offers herself, and mothers like her, as the proper alternative to this male and authoritarian world, repeatedly emphasizing the crucial importance of children's rearing within the nuclear family and the special powers of the mother to "form their Minds" without distorting them (8, 125, 168, 199, 233–34).

As we enter the world of *Amelia* through the dark passageway of Newgate, one of the figures conjured briefly but vividly before us in the prison's swirling, dreamlike procession of social ills is that of the homosexual. Immediately after the crowd has rushed enthusiastically to see a man stripped and whipped, "another Bustle" announces the disciplinary abuse that Blear-Eyed Moll and her companions are heaping upon a man "committed for certain odious unmanlike Practices, not fit to be named" (33).[36] This little scenario quickly melts away, like the others, when the authorities intervene, to be replaced by the image of a young girl holding her father's head on her lap as he dies. But the scenario of the homosexual's punishment provides a powerful initiatory emblem for the narrative of *Amelia*, which never again refers to the possibility of specifically sexual relations between men but which broods endlessly on the tension between homosocial and heterosexual bonds.

As we have seen, Booth is presented repeatedly as misinterpreting the events around him because of his investment in male-male friendship and in exclusively masculine institutions (classical education, the army, master-servant loyalty). The system of male relationships within which he defines himself consistently turns out to be either illusory or corrupt; and the conflict between Booth's hopes for male relationships and his role as husband and father only gets worse as the novel goes on. By the time that Booth gives away fifty pounds to a "great Man" who promises to help him find a post—the fifty pounds that Amelia has raised by pawning the last of her own clothes and her children's trinkets—the conflict has become excruciating to witness. Booth is not sure that he should turn over their money in this way but he is "ashamed to confess his wavering Resolution" in front of "his old Friend the Lieutenant" (475–76), and so he submits to the Lieutenant's arguments that "the great Man must be touched; for that he never did any Thing without touching" (475). The Lieutenant's term for bribery, which the narrator underlines when he condemns "this abominable Practice of touching" (477), plays upon some possibility of an erotic valence within such corrupt financial and political relations.[37] Booth's search for favor from the capricious men who might find him a military position can at times seem like a search for erotic attention: when Mrs. Ellison praises Booth's military service to the Noble Lord and hints that the Lord should help him find a post, "*Booth* blushed, and was as silent as a young Virgin at the hearing her own praises" (193). Booth's bashful blushing and his "touching," like his classical learning, prove as ineffective practically as they are made to seem suspect in other ways. In the world of *Amelia*, it is only the domestic scene centered on Amelia herself that can save Booth and his family either economically or spiritually.

Amelia enacts the role of the attentive mother sketched in outline in *On the Management and Education of Children*; what is only crudely conceived and polemically recommended there is rendered subtle and individual and concrete by Fielding.[38] While Amelia's mother has turned over her maternal responsibilities to the lower-class foster mother whom we meet early in the novel, Amelia is seen almost constantly in the company of her children, and declares herself most pleased when with them and her husband. The mixture of indistinctness and particularity with which Fielding treats these children bespeaks the transition that is in progress during the eighteenth century in how children are imagined:[39] the Booths' children are not really individualized in the way we might expect, for example, in a Victorian novel (they don't have consistent individual names, although the older boy is occasionally called "Billy" after his father, and their number seems to fluctuate without explanation between three and two), and yet their importance to Amelia is crucial to the definition of her character. If their importance remains, for the most part, rather abstract, Fielding does offer us several carefully realized and affecting vignettes of Amelia conversing with her children; and he is unusually scrupulous about explaining who cares for the children when Amelia must leave them temporarily, as if to acknowledge the particular unceasingness of such a responsibility.[40] Amelia's concrete practices of attending to her children become crucial, in fact, to the happy resolution of the novel's plot.

Midway through the novel, Dr. Harrison wavers in his resolution after having Booth arrested for debt only because "the wretched Condition of his Wife and Family began to affect his Mind"; and then it is the actual sight of Amelia and her children crying together that sways him to go and release her husband (358–59). At the end of the novel, in a more complicated chain of plot circumstances, Harrison's visit to Booth at the bailiff's, his discussion with Robinson there, and therefore the discovery of the forged will, the recovery of Amelia's estate, and the novel's miraculously happy ending all depend upon Amelia's decision to stop in at her own lodgings on the way from the bailiff's to Harrison's house "to pay a momentary Visit to her Children." There she in fact finds the doctor and tells him the news of Booth's imprisonment, whereas "had she call'd at the Doctor's House, she would have heard nothing of him" (501). Thus the general suggestion created by the plot's resolution—that it is appropriate that Amelia prove the source of her family's financial salvation—is confirmed when we "observ[e] minutely the several Incidents which tend to the Catastrophe or Completion of the whole, and the minute Causes whence those Incidents are produced," as Fielding instructs us to do in the novel's opening pages (17). Those minute circumstances attach the family's abrupt elevation of fortune not only to Amelia's identity in general, but to her interpretation of her duties as a mother in particular. And the large consequences that follow, contingently, from these slight circumstances are supported by Amelia's role throughout the novel as the moral instructor of her children—a role upon which the happiness of society itself may depend, according to the authors of both *On the Management and Education of Children* and *An Essay on the Government of Children*.[41] Nonetheless, these nonfictional works, like *Amelia*, draw the autonomy of this maternal power sharply into question.

When Fielding first shows us Amelia's methods of teaching her children, he says that she provides an "excellent Example" to all mothers, for she "never let a Day pass, without instructing her Children in some Lesson of Religion and Morality" (167). Somewhat later, Dr. Harrison tests the results of Amelia's efforts by quizzing her son about whether he would forgive the Doctor were he to have his father arrested again. When the child cries out, "Yes . . . I would forgive you; because a Christian must forgive every Body; but I should hate you as long as I live," Harrison is delighted, and apparently so with both parts of the answer, acknowledging but also approving the manifest contradictions within the child's response. When he asks Booth and Amelia "which of them was their Son's Instructor in his Religion," Booth answers "that he must confess *Amelia* had all the Merit of that Kind," but Harrison is convinced that there is something of value in the boy's response that must come more from Booth's outlook than from Amelia's. "'I should have rather thought he had learnt of his Father,' cries the Doctor, 'for he seems a good Soldier-like Christian, and professes to hate his Enemies with a very good Grace'" (360). The child insists that he has heard Amelia "say the same thing a thousand Times"; apparently, the "lessons" Amelia offers to her children convey something to them that might be more identified with their military father than with her Christian self.

Later, when Amelia tries to offer a "Lesson of Religion and Morality" to her husband rather than to her children, she falls back not only on "a Sentiment of Dr. *Harrison's*" in her attempt to persuade Booth, but on a Sentiment "which he told me was in some *Latin* Book"—that is, from the realm of classical literature so strongly identified with men. Booth rejects her argument, and she only sighs that she has often wished "to hear you converse with Dr.

Harrison on this Subject; for I am sure he would convince you, though I can't, that there are really such Things as Religion and Virtue." The narrator confides that Amelia has sometimes feared that her husband "was little better than an Atheist," but that when she has raised religion in their discussions, Booth "immediately turned the Discourse to some other Subject; for tho' he had in other Points a great Opinion of his Wife's capacity; yet as a Divine or a Philosopher he did not hold her in a very respectable Light, nor did he lay any great Stress on her Sentiments in such Matters" (451). However deep Amelia's personal authority as a living paragon of Christian virtue, her active, persuasive power over others is radically circumscribed and ultimately dependent on the authority of men, whose characteristic values of military or classical virtue strangely mix and meld with the Christian wisdom Amelia herself is allowed to purvey.

The author of the letters collected in *On the Management and Education of Children* draws on the special authority of a mother to speak about rearing children ("a Woman can best advise a Woman in Things which herself has experienced" [6]). But if she is to advise her readers on the value and dangers of a classical education, for example, she must depend upon the word of a man, "this Gentleman," who not only supplies her with information about the content of classical literature but also places the stamp of his more accredited approval upon her suggestions ("I am pleased extremely that so good a Judge of what I proposed, in regard to the instructing your Sons in the learned Languages, approved of it . . . and I shall have the better Opinion of my own Thoughts as long as I live, for finding them countenanced by such a Person" [223]). Thus *On the Management* divides the sources of its authority between a mother and a learned gentleman, who claim very different forms of knowledge but who here agreeably countenance each other's opinions. This division of authority is crucial in *Amelia* as well; the figure of Mrs. Atkinson, with all the tonal difficulties that surround her, demonstrates the unacceptable results of combining certain forms of traditionally male authority with female ones.[42] The particular *relation* between the two sources of authority in *On the Management* is, however, something other than it might seem. While "this Gentleman" might appear a kind of convenient projection of "Mrs. Seymour's," invoked to give the weight of masculine approval to her own opinions, in fact he is more like a representative of the book's real author, actually one John Hill, a male acquaintance and sometime friend of Fielding, who thus reemerges beside the female persona he has created in order to claim the special authority of maternal experience for his book.[43] Despite the redundancy of feminine identity heaped up within "Juliana-Susannah Seymour's" first name, she is quite literally a mere construct of a man's imagination, advanced to serve his own aims. One might argue that in this way she provides a fitting prefigurement of those maternal lives, both fictional and real, to be given an increasingly central and honored place in English culture in the century to follow.

Amelia also is of course the creation of a man's imagination, however compelling an embodiment she may provide of female strength and virtue. The circular nature of her supposed influence over men is dramatized at points within the novel, as well as in her relation to her author. In the final sentence of the novel, she voluntarily declares that if she is "the best of Wives" it is because Booth has "made her the happiest of Women" (533). Earlier, Harrison seems to formulate, directly, the idea that women can control men through their moral influence (an idea at the center, for instance, of *Pamela*), only to assert playfully, and a little spitefully, that they can do so only by behaving in the ways that men want them to, anyway. He tells Amelia:

"as unreasonable as the Power of controuling Men's Thoughts is represented, I will shew you how you shall controul mine whenever you desire it."

"How, pray!" cries *Amelia*. "I should greatly esteem that Power."

"Why, whenever you act like a wise Woman," cries the Doctor, "you will force me to think you so; and whenever you are pleased to act as you do now, I shall be obliged, whether I will or no, to think as I do now." (372)

Harrison has in fact raised Amelia, and so shouldn't be surprised to find qualities in her he approves. When he describes his education of Amelia, however, his wording is suggestive: "as she grew up, she discovered so many good Qualities, that she wanted not the Remembrance of her Father's Merit to recommend her. I do her no more than Justice, when I say, she is one of the best Creatures I ever knew . . . I may call her *an* Israelite *indeed, in whom there is no Guile*" (387). Harrison claims that Amelia revealed or "discovered" good qualities from within rather than simply assimilating the qualities that he inculcated in her; and he comments that her merit eventually stood on its own, rather than depending on the remembrance of her father's. In the last sentence of his description, he describes Amelia in the words that Jesus used to describe Nathanael, thus identifying her with one of the original male disciples of Christ.

If this cross-gender allusion seems quite unthreatening in itself, there are a number of ways in which the character Amelia may slip the moorings of her safely "feminine" identity, as constructed for masculine ends, and raise at least the possibility of real female moral power. The sense expressed by her first readers that there might be something grotesque about Amelia indicates that, despite the severe "domestication" of her female heroism, she nonetheless raises the threat of reversed roles. The author of *On the Management* was himself, in fact, one of Amelia's severest critics, unconvinced that she embodied a female ideal in a convincing and attractive way.[44] Although Mrs. Atkinson, on one level, seems to divert anxiety about female appropriation of male authority away from the central character of Amelia, the emphasis on her and Amelia's physical interchangeability (237, 421) also repeatedly reminds us that (though she is safely ignorant of classical learning) Amelia, too, may make her husband's "Understanding" at times look inferior (408). Finally, the scenario in which Moll and her companions discipline the homosexual raises very early in the novel the possibility that female authority, within the newly empowered structure of heterosexuality,[45] may allow women to punish men for their traditional homosocial as well as criminal homosexual ties to each other.

When Dr. Harrison reveals the news of Amelia's inheritance to her, he does it by reading it out of a newspaper, which he jokingly compares to classical literature by referring to comments provided "in the Delphin Edition of this News Paper" (529). A new age has come, in which the newspaper, with its daily, vernacular view of the world, will displace the traditional authority of masculine learning. But that learning has already been reshaped by its appearance in Delphin editions—editions of the classics issued on a specific political occasion[46]—as old learning is made new by its continually varying appropriations in a changing world. In *Amelia*, Fielding moves forward energetically, though with deep ambivalence, into that new world, and frames his affirmation of it in terms of his "love" for its heroine, beautiful despite (because of) the marks of accident and of history upon her. In *The Journal of a Voyage to Lisbon*, he recoils in horror at a powerful female figure who heralds the passing of an era, and of his own life.

Epilogue

Death, Witches, and Bitches in 'The Journal of a Voyage to Lisbon'

The male protagonist of *Amelia*, Captain Booth, is paralyzed in a number of senses by the changing definition of masculine roles: He is unable to support his family and is therefore confined to his home to escape arrest for debt; he feels the conflicting demands of the codes of masculine honor and of Christianity, and so responds to calls to duel with uncertainty and confusion; he fulfills the expectations of a Cavalier sexual license by sleeping with Miss Mathews in prison, but then is rendered almost inanimate by a sense of guilty betrayal of the wife he so loves. The male protagonist of Fielding's last work, the author himself, also experiences a bitter sense of helplessness in the face of historical change—change that he associates with a nearly fantastic empowering of women, and with the debilitation and marginalization of men. In *The Journal of a Voyage to Lisbon*, the paralysis suffered by the central male figure, marooned and humiliated by the movements of time, is literal as well as figurative, as Fielding traces his own progressive bodily decay in a halting journey across the ocean and toward death.[1]

The threat that provisional social beliefs—systems of order that hold for a circumscribed realm but not for the whole world, or for all time—may be no more than arbitrary, may be manipulated or tyrannically imposed, or may collapse suddenly, hangs over Fielding's final journey from beginning to end. As he has throughout his career, Fielding renders the implications of this threat most vividly in the terms of gender. He returns in *The Journal* to the images for socially constructed male and female identity that we have seen from his plays and *Champion* essays onward: the image of man as a lifeless effigy and of woman as a haunting ghost. The situation in which Fielding contemplates these matters in the final months of his life provides a perfect figure for the constructed, circumscribed, and precarious nature of social orders that only claim to be universal ones, and he exploits the situation's resonance to the fullest. For the social and political order within which he spends his final months is literally ungrounded: he has set out to sea in the small, separate world of a ship ruled by an imperious and tyrannical captain.

The sphere of the captain's authority is sharply bounded, of course,[2] but within that sphere his authority is absolute. In all forms of travel, Fielding says,

the passenger becomes bound in allegiance to his conveyer. This allegiance is indeed only temporary and local, but the most absolute during its continuance, of any known in Great Britain. . . . [The traveler's subjection] consists of a perfect resignation both of body and soul to the disposal of another; after which resignation, during a certain time, [the conveyer's] subject retains no more power over his own will, than an Asiatic slave, or an English wife, by the laws of both countries, and by the customs of one of them. (49)

While they are his passengers, the commander of a ship can control the motions of all his "subjects" as much as any puppet-master does those of his puppets (87), and the very circumscription of his power by both time and place seems to encourage his absolute exercise of it. "Every commander of a vessel here seems to think himself entirely free from all those rules of decency and civility, which direct and restrain the conduct of the members of a society on shore; and each, claiming absolute dominion in his little wooden world, rules by his own laws and his own discretion" (65). Transported away from society on shore within this "little wooden world," feminized (like an English wife) by his subjection to strictly "temporary and local" forms of power, Fielding repeatedly complains that class structures do not obtain in this new dominion, or are even inverted by its own structures of dependence (71, 83, 129). Gravely ill, he seems to experience this dissolution of the class structures he had relied upon on shore in close association with the dissolution of his own physical powers; and the *Journal* intertwines the disintegration of a social system with that of a bodily system in the final voyage it describes.

In his first entry in the *Journal*, Fielding comments that the necessary resignation of a passenger's own will to his conveyer makes him little different from the goods or luggage that might accompany him on board. Indeed, "as the goods to be conveyed are usually the larger, so they are to be chiefly considered in the conveyance; the owner being indeed little more than an appendage to his trunk, or box, or bale, or at best a small part of his own baggage" (49). Later in the *Journal*, this fanciful description of the passenger as an extension of his trunk or box comes to refer more particularly, and painfully, to the loss of physical motion and control wrought by Fielding's illness:

> though I am a great lover of the sea, I now fancied there was more pleasure in breathing the fresh air of the land; but, how to get thither was the question: for, being really that dead luggage, which I considered all passengers to be in the beginning of this narrative, and incapable of any bodily motion without external impulse, it was in vain to leave the ship, or to determine to do it, without the assistance of others. (68–69)

The image of a man's limbs moved by external impulse might remind us of the "potentate *alias* puppet" controlled by the hidden puppet-master in *Jonathan Wild*, or of the puppet-man who dances to a woman's will in *The Covent Garden Tragedy* (I. vii)—images of political corruption or of the domestic disorder of "petticoat government"—but here the image darkly conveys the limitations and disorders of a more general condition: that of mortality. For Fielding, the helplessness of the gentleman within a captain's "little wooden world," like the helplessness of his will within an inert physical form, heralds the approach of death.

Though the melancholy autobiographical drama of the *Journal* feels a long way from *Tom Thumb*'s literary and political burlesque, the threat of "petticoat government" we saw King Arthur bluster against there returns in one of the most extended episodes of Fielding's final work. The inn at Ryde at which the travelers stop, waiting for a favorable wind, becomes the last version of Fielding's many sketches of domestic dominions ruled by petticoat: Mrs. Francis, the innkeeper, entirely controls her husband and the house (78–79).[3] And, as the author of "An Epistle to John James Heidegger" imagined that "Silver Tickets may as well be Pewter" where a castrato

could take the man's place and a woman the castrato's, value becomes wholly indeterminate under Mrs. Francis's rule.

> If her bills were remonstrated against, she was offended with the tacit cen-
> sure of her fair-dealing; if they were not, she seemed to regard it as a tacit
> sarcasm on her folly, which might have set down larger prices with the same
> success. On this latter hint she did indeed improve; for she daily raised some
> of her articles. A penny-worth of fire was to-day rated at a shilling, to-
> morrow at eighteen-pence; and if she drest us two dishes for two shillings
> on the Saturday, we paid half a crown for the cookery of one on the Sunday;
> and wherever she was paid she never left the room without lamenting the
> small amount of her bill. (80–81)

In *Tom Jones*, the honor afforded Sophia's private name serves to
guarantee the value of a bank-bill; in *Amelia*, the worth of the domestic heroine makes her the safekeeper of her family's paltry, and
then providentially expanded, wealth. In *The Journal*, the possibility
that money may have no ground in real, measurable value comes to
be associated again with the transgressions of a female figure, the
keeper of a commercial rather than a private household, whose demands for money escalate wildly until whatever she receives "was
almost as entirely clear profit as the blessing of a wreck itself" (77).[4]

Mrs. Francis proves an even more tyrannical local governor
than the ship captain (90); the power she exerts in defiance of gender
hierarchies finally encompasses even the power that he claims in defiance of Fielding's superior class. The ultimate image in the *Journal*
of a morbid helplessness, of both political and physical decay, is not
Fielding's confinement within the captain's "little wooden world,"
but their shared impotence when that ship stays windbound for
weeks—which the captain interprets as the effect of Mrs. Francis's
malignant powers.

> In truth, he talked of nothing else, and seemed not only to be satisfied in
> general of his being bewitched, but actually to have fixed, with good cer-
> tainty, on the person of the witch, whom, had he lived in the days of Sir
> Matthew Hale, he would have infallibly indicted, and very possibly have
> hanged for the detestable sin of witchcraft; but that law, and the whole doc-
> trine that supported it, are now out of fashion; and witches, as a learned
> divine once chose to express himself, are put down by act of parliament.
> This witch, in the captain's opinion, was no other than Mrs. Francis of
> Ryde, who, as he insinuated, out of anger to me, for not spending more
> money in her house than she could produce any thing to exchange for, or
> any pretence to charge for, had laid this spell on his ship. (117)

Earlier, Fielding had identified Mrs. Francis with the wind (79). Here, his report of the captain's suspicion that she can exert an unseen power through the wind must expand to contain a long aside about the changing laws on witchcraft. This aside reminds us that beliefs and social forms, even laws, come and go "out of fashion," as constructed and contingent as the little ship that can't choose when to get under way. Perhaps it is the capriciousness of laws themselves, subject to the winds of changing times, that leaves their enforcers finally helpless and inert: one can't believe that witches, if they ever existed, may be "put down by act of parliament," and laws that cannot be enforced, Fielding says elsewhere in the *Journal*, are as much "dead letter" as his body has become "dead luggage" (85).

"How could hell be better represented than by supposing the people under petticoat government?" the author of the play-within of Fielding's farce *Eurydice* had asked years before. In Mrs. Francis, Fielding found a frightening figure of woman's ghostly power as it has taken possession of *this* world, while Fielding himself moves toward another. When he and the others have returned to the ship, they "all chearfully exulted in being returned from the presence of Mrs. Francis, who, by the exact resemblance she bore to a fury, seemed to have been with no great propriety settled in paradise" (93–94). In *Joseph Andrews*, Fielding figured his hero's mysterious association with death through his various links to feminine identity; those links, rendered at first in a parodic but then in a sentimental vein, came to represent some promise of restoration as well as of loss. In *The Journal* he again associates the prospect of mortality with female identity, but there shadows forth its unwanted approach in the ugly image of Mrs. Francis, whom he describes, half comically, half horrifically, as a fury at death's door, exacting an unbounded toll.

The autobiographical *Journal* is at once a literary document and a rendering of Fielding's own experience. The letters Fielding wrote to his brother John from Portugal relate a final episode in that life, one not included within the pages of the *Journal*, but one that drives Fielding's literary thematics of gender even deeper into the substance of his life's text. Installed in a foreign city, short on funds, nearly without local acquaintance, ill of body and sometimes of mind, Fielding focused his feelings of social isolation and disempowerment, confusion, and fear on the women who surrounded him in the little household he established there. He insisted to John that his wife Mary was trying to wrest control of the household from him; that Mary and her friend Margaret Collier were conspiring to convince the English community that he was incompetent; that Margaret Collier was plotting to deprive him of his favorite male companion by ensnaring the man in marriage; that he could recover his health and exceed the highest prosperity he had ever known if only these aggressive, transgressive female house-mates could be contained.[5]

Desperately struggling to control the community's perception of himself, Fielding attempts to enlist his brother's aid from afar, begging him to send the textual evidence of testimonial letters to prove the worth of his own character and the ingratitude of "the B----," Margaret Collier, who has thus betrayed him. He asks his brother, too, to send the aid of a masculine ally: "Get me a conversible Man to be my Companion in an Evening, with as much of the Qualifications of Learning, Sense and Good humour as you can find, who will drink a moderate Glass in an Evening or will at least sit with me 'till one when I do." Like Booth, he looks for comfort and reassurance in an apparently unstable world in the old "homosocial" bonds of male learning and conviviality. Unlike Booth, he seems, at the end of his life, to have lived within the old paradigm of the depredations of the unruly "woman on top," rather than within an even partially achieved new ideal of heterosexual love. But he does dimly conjure the possibility of an Amelia-like honorable woman who might be sent by John to offset the destructive female figures who surround him: "send over [H]Jones or Mrs. Hussy," he commands. ". . . I shall be destroyed unless I can be reliev[ed] from the greatest Folly and the greatest Bitchery that ever w[er]e united in 2 Women by a 3d who hath some Degree of Hon.r and Understanding."[6]

Even his own brother—the co-inheritor of his father's dated and now worthless legacy of masculine style, the partner in his career of dispensing justice from the bench—could not rewrite the final scenes of Fielding's life from a distance. Fielding was to live those scenes as on the stage of a Fieldingesque drama: one of burlesque reversals and blustering male claims to power. If he played his final scenes within a stage set constructed by his own idiosyncratic imagination, he also played them amid the workings of a historical "machinery" capable of both tragedy and farce.

REFERENCE MATTER

Notes

Introduction

1. Fielding, *Tom Jones*, 225. Page references for further quotations from *Tom Jones*, as from other novels by Fielding, will be provided parenthetically in the text.

2. Battestin, *Henry Fielding*, 388.

3. On the sense in which, in their final novels, Richardson and Fielding "trade places," see Sitter, *Literary Loneliness*, 190–91, as well as Sabor, "*Amelia* and *Sir Charles Grandison*."

4. Battestin, *Henry Fielding*, 389, 421–23, 475.

5. See Coley; Cleary, especially 52–62; Battestin, "Fielding's Changing Politics" and *Henry Fielding*, 317–18.

6. Miller, 269; and Hunter, *Occasional Form*, 45.

7. Barbara Johnson provides a useful theoretical context for understanding this critical tendency to relocate "differences within" one text or one identity as "differences between" two texts or identities; see her *Critical Difference*.

8. Blanchard's exhaustive study of Fielding's critical reputation through 1926 traces the long-standing practice of characterizing Fielding's works through a (largely fictional) account of his life, and of contrasting his life and works with Richardson's in the terms I summarize here. See particularly 60–70, 156–69, 188, 320–21 and 408–45.

9. The latter contrast, which was given early and graphic formulation by Samuel Johnson, has been developed most influentially in this century by Ian Watt in *The Rise of the Novel*, particularly in chapter 9. Watt also emphasizes Fielding's debt to the epic, in chapter 8. Hahn briefly reviews the other critical studies that have concentrated on Fielding's use of epic form. A particularly interesting application of this approach to Fielding's novels appears in Maresca, 216–31.

The many critical essays devoted to comparing Richardson's and

Fielding's novelistic techniques include: Brooks; Kermode; Mack, "*Joseph Andrews* and *Pamela*"; Moore; and Sabor. Alter provides suggestive commentary on the relative rise and fall of Richardson's and Fielding's reputations in the history of these critical contrasts.

10. *Joseph Andrews* and *Shamela*, Houghton Mifflin edition, v. Unless otherwise noted, subsequent references to *Joseph Andrews* will be to Battestin's Wesleyan edition of the novel, rather than to this one.

11. Smallwood, 3, 6, 19–25. The traditional male critics discussed by Smallwood as promoting the idea of Fielding's "masculinity" include Henley and Cross. The feminist critics she refers to as accepting this idea as well are Janet Todd and Susan Staves (200 n. 12). In addition, Katherine M. Rogers argues for a sharp contrast between Richardson's "radical feminist" views and Fielding's "male chauvinism" (257). In her defense of Fielding against Rogers's indictment, Lenta observes a general "tendency in recent years to praise the novels of Richardson at the expense of those of Fielding on the grounds that the former are 'feminist'" (13). Eagleton suggests not only that Richardson is in some sense a "feminist," but that he should be interpreted as a kind of "honorary woman" because of his position in the middle class.

The different applications of this more generalized and figurative feminine-masculine opposition to describe Richardson's and Fielding's class positions, personal behavior, proper readerships, literary styles, and generic sources are numberless. One of my favorite formulations of the opposition appears in Robert Etheridge Moore's account of why Samuel Johnson should have preferred Fielding to Richardson: "[*Tom Jones*,] like its creator, is virile and forthright, qualities which appealed especially to Johnson. Richardson, on the other hand, is fussy and hesitant. Johnson, like Fielding, is a man, and what is more, a man's man. 'Brandy is the drink of heroes!' he exclaimed. Richardson may be called, in all seriousness, one of our great women" (172).

12. Michael McKeon observes this effect and provides one theoretical context for understanding its significance. Commenting on the way that the "birth" or the "rise" of the English novel has as much to do with its new status as a category, as a conceptualized abstraction, as with its new appearance as a set of literary practices, he argues that one value of his own "dialectical theory of genre" is that it "fully accounts for the well-known complexity of the genre at the moment that it attains its institutional and canonic identity: its capacity, that is, to comprehend not only Richardson but Fielding" (*Origins of the English Novel*, 15–21).

13. This is one of the well-known objections to Watt's indisputably, enduringly important study of "the rise of the novel": although he acknowledges Fielding as a crucial figure in the English novel's early history, the definition of the genre he offers, and his account of its development, heavily favor Richardson and relegate Fielding to something of the margins

of the novel's history—an imbalance he seeks to address and explain in his "Serious Reflections on *The Rise of the Novel.*"

McKeon discusses this problem in Watt's study, and the trade-off in attempting to explain it away (*Origins of the English Novel*, 2–4). William B. Warner has accused McKeon, in turn, of giving Fielding a place privileged over Richardson's in his own study of the novel's origins ("Realist Literary History," 77). Although McKeon stoutly refutes this charge ("A Defense of Dialectical Method," 84–86), it seems to me that there is some substance to Warner's charge, given, if nothing else, the place afforded Fielding over Richardson in the triadic progression of *The Origins of the English Novel*'s dialectical organization. More absolutely and unapologetically, Nancy Armstrong places Richardson at the very center of her account of the novel's emergence, largely dismissing Fielding as an "unsuccessful" divergence from the primary line of the novel's history (30, 38). I will discuss the more particular implications of Armstrong's exclusion of Fielding from the history of the English novel in my chapters on *Tom Jones.*

14. Phrases quoted from Moore, 172.

15. Hunter, "Fielding and the Disappearance of Heroes," 116–42; Carlton, "The Mitigated Truth," 397–409, and "*Tom Jones*," 361–73. I will discuss Carlton's articles on *Tom Jones* in my chapters on that novel. Other essays on the decline of the epic hero in eighteenth-century England appear in Folkenflik's collection.

16. See, in Scott, especially 3, 6, 24, 26–29.

17. Scott, 2; Butler, referring to the work of Scott and, more generally, to those "historical and anthropological positions that understand gender as a *relation* among socially constituted subjects in specifiable contexts," 10; Haraway, referring specifically to the work of Evelyn Fox Keller, 143.

18. See Scott, 2; Haraway's discussion of this problematic within Anglo-American feminism, 130–36; and especially Butler, 6–8. Butler argues: "Gender ought not to be conceived merely as the cultural inscription of meaning on a pregiven sex . . . gender must also designate the very apparatus of production whereby the sexes themselves are established. As a result, gender is not to culture as sex is to nature; gender is also the discursive/cultural means by which 'sexed nature' or 'a natural sex' is produced and established as 'prediscursive'" (7).

I am in general agreement with this position, though it seems to me to rely more than Scott, Haraway, and Butler acknowledge on the very depth of our assimilation of the notion of bodily "sex," which can then remain on the receding horizon of such arguments, even after being banished from their conceptual ken.

19. Scott, 42–43; Harding, 17–18, 52; Haraway, 130.

20. Although Garber notes the danger of "looking through" the figure of the transvestite, interpreting him/her as somehow "about" some-

thing else, it seems to me that she falls prey to this danger when she attempts to distinguish so clearly between what she calls "transvestite logics" and "transvestite effects"—or when, for example, she insistently underlines "elsewhere" in arguing that the transvestite may be an "index" to "a *category crisis elsewhere*" (e.g., 16–17). The challenge is to analyze how the language of gender consequentially *connects* matters of sexual difference with other urgent matters—by speaking simultaneously of other things and of itself.

21. See Butler, 16–17 and 33, as well as Haraway, 135, and Garber, 16.

22. Scott, 41.

23. The theorists I cite above all bring up the possibility that the different forms in which gender appears in social life may converge in oppositional or conflictual as well as mutually supportive ways (see Harding, 52, as well as Haraway, 142, and Scott, 25). As Butler puts it polemically, "the very complexity of the discursive map that constructs gender appears to hold out the promise of an inadvertent and generative convergence of these discursive and regulatory structures" (32).

24. See Plumb and Kramnick on these developments.

25. See Dickson on "the financial revolution" that took place in late-seventeenth- and eighteenth-century England; and McKendrick, Brewer, and Plumb on the subsequent "consumer revolution" in England.

26. A helpful discussion of the writer's changing economic and social position in the eighteenth century appears in Kernan. For one interesting discussion of the evolution, later in the century, of the position of the writer in the marketplace, see Rose.

27. In *The Family, Sex, and Marriage in England, 1500–1800*, Lawrence Stone provides the classic study both of the new predominance of the model of the companionate marriage and of the growing emphasis on the "natural" bond of maternal feeling as the eighteenth century progressed. Following Mary McIntosh's influential essay on "The Homosexual Role," published in 1968, a number of historians have elaborated on her thesis that the modern conception of the male homosexual developed in eighteenth-century England. Despite important differences in their accounts, Bray, Rousseau, and Trumbach all make the eighteenth century a period of crucial change in their histories of male homosexuality. Framing his subject in more general terms, Henry Abelove has argued that reproductive heterosexual behavior was given an unprecedented centrality in eighteenth-century England, while "nonreproductive sexual behaviors [of all kinds] come under extraordinary negative pressure" in a new way (125–30).

Thomas Laqueur makes even more sweeping claims for the importance of the eighteenth century in the history of sexuality: "sometime in the eighteenth century," he asserts, "sex as we know it was invented" (149). His work centers on the depiction of male and female sexual organs, which he argues evolved from a "one-sex" to a "two-sex" model in the course of the eighteenth century. Literary critics who draw on the histories of sexuality provided by Foucault and others include Armstrong, Nussbaum, and Straub.

28. See especially 28–32 in Smallwood.

29. The work of John Sitter, Carole Fabricant, Ellen Pollak, and Laura Brown has called attention to the importance of questions of gender to Pope's poetry in general. See Sitter, *Literary Loneliness* and "Mother, Memory, Muse"; Fabricant, "Binding and Dressing Nature's Loose Tresses" and "Pope's Portraits of Women"; Pollak, *The Poetics of Sexual Myth*; and Brown, *Alexander Pope*, especially 6–28, 76–78, 94–117.

30. See *Literary Loneliness*, chapters 3 and 4, and the influential early version of this argument, "Mother, Memory, Muse, and Poetry After Pope."

31. Noble and Dugaw have both suggested the complexity and interest of Gay's rendering of gender issues.

32. See Dugaw, 178–79, and Spacks, *John Gay*, 127.

33. It is Terry Castle, of course, who has established the wide cultural significance of the institution of the masquerade in eighteenth-century England. On transvestism in particular, at the masquerade and elsewhere, see *Masquerade and Civilization*, 1–6, 46–47, 63–64.

34. This is the primary subject of Dugaw's study.

35. I quote from a copy in Yale University's Beinecke Library of *The Masquerade*, "by Lemuel Gulliver, Poet Laureate to the King of Lilliput" (1728), dedication and 5–6. The poem is also available as reprinted in *The Female Husband and Other Writings*, ed. Claude E. Jones.

36. Butler, *Gender Trouble*, 33.

37. Castle, *Masquerade and Civilization*, 179–80.

38. McKeon's concept of "instrumental belief," developed in his study of Fielding's works, is relevant here, as are Rawson's account of Fielding's struggle to accept provisional in the place of cosmic sources of order and Hunter's view of Fielding's reconciliation with the "chains of circumstance" (McKeon, *Origins of the English Novel*, chap. 12; Rawson; Hunter, *Occasional Form*).

39. In "Contradiction and Overdetermination," Louis Althusser provides the most compelling account I have seen of why any truly "materialist" history must not simply invert Hegelian causality and look for a single force, exerting itself in various spheres; the material world, he observes, unlike "Spirit" or "Reason," is irreducibly multiform by its very nature; the various forms of the superstructure have an existence that is "largely specific and autonomous, and therefore irreducible to a pure *phenomenon*" (*For Marx*, 113).

40. Battestin briefly relates this "yarn" in "Pictures of Fielding," 1. In his discussion of Hogarth's frontispiece, Paulson summarizes Garrick's story as well as other anecdotes related to its making (*Hogarth*, 2: 342–43).

41. 1: 33, essay for November 27, 1739.

42. Alan Liu describes this tendency in New Historicism in particular ("The Power of Formalism," 730–44).

Chapter 1

1. *The Tragedy of Tragedies*, ed. Hillhouse, I.iii. For ease of reference, I at times refer to both *Tom Thumb* and its 1731 adaptation, *The Tragedy of Tragedies*, simply as *Tom Thumb*; I here quote from the text of *The Tragedy of Tragedies*, since it is the fullest and final version of Fielding's play. The exchange between Arthur, Dollalolla, and Tom is shorter in the play's original version but similar, and includes Arthur's lines about the exchange of petticoats and breeches.

2. As noted by Morrissey, "Fielding's First Political Satire," 338. For an inspired as well as intimate contemporary account of Caroline's control of George, see Lord Hervey's *Memoirs*, particularly 14, 38, 102. Historical and critical discussions of Caroline's indirect power include Quennell, *Caroline of England*, 125–28, and Mack, *The Garden and the City*, 128–30.

3. See the casting information for original productions of both *Tom Thumb* and *The Tragedy of Tragedies*, collected from playbills, advertisements in newspapers, and cast lists from first editions, in *The London Stage 1660–1800* part III, vol. 1: 1729–47. The 1730 edition of *Tom Thumb* lists Miss Jones as the hero, and she seems to have appeared in this role from the play's opening night on April 24, 1730, at the Haymarket through its long run into March 1731. When the play reopened as *The Tragedy of Tragedies* on March 24, 1731, the role of Tom Thumb seems to have been taken for a while by a young male actor, billed as "Young Verhuyck," but the role reverted to female actors such as "Miss S. Rogers, the Lilliputian Lucy," Miss Jones Jr., Miss Brett, and Mrs. Turner in subsequent productions in the early 1730's.

Princess Huncamunca was played by the comic actor Harper at Drury Lane in 1732 and 1733, and by Pearce at Goodman's Fields in 1731. Also, Glumdalca the giant-queen was played by Hall at Lincoln's Inn Fields in 1732, and Charlotte Charke played Lord Grizzle at Lincoln's Inn Fields in 1735.

A certain amount of cross-gender casting was part of the English farce tradition, and "breeches roles" for the actresses that first appeared on the English stage following the Restoration became a minor tradition within establishment drama. See Nicoll, *Eighteenth-Century Drama*, 49–50; Ackroyd, *Dressing-Up*, 90–98; Wilson, *All the King's Ladies*, 72–86; and Rogers, "The Breeches Part," 244–58. Only Rogers and Ackroyd consider "breeches roles" as more than a dramatic convention.

None of these sources, however, discuss how specific cross-gender casting choices might have been strategic and significant in productions of particular plays. I have been unable to find accounts of the original productions of *Tom Thumb* that comment on this feature—the accounts in *The Daily Advertiser* and other periodicals and in the Earl of Egmont's *Diary* are all very spare—and Gray's *Theatrical Criticism in London to 1795* confirms that theatrical criticism of production details appeared very infrequently in this decade. I believe, however, that this feature of Fielding's own productions of *Tom Thumb* at the Haymarket is significant, and I will be constructing an interpretive context for its signification from the treatment of gender reversal or impersonation in his other early writings.

4. They usually pass over it in silence. When they do note it, they seem to feel that it warrants no interpretive comment. Two recent book-length studies of Fielding's drama (by Robert Hume and Peter Lewis) do not comment on this feature of *Tom Thumb* and of Fielding's other plays. In an older commentary on *Tom Thumb*, Hillhouse's excellent and very scholarly introduction to the play, he notes the casting of Harper as Princess Huncamunca, but says nothing about the casting of Tom Thumb, though he acknowledges it in passing in his notes on the dramatis personae. In his more recent introduction to the play, Morrissey follows Hillhouse in noting the casting of male actors in female roles but gives no comment on the surprising original casting of Tom, which he reproduces in a cast list in his edition. Craik comments on the incongruity of naming one of the Princess's maids of honour "Mustacha" but not on the incongruity of casting a woman as the Princess's husband; Macey says the most on the topic but says only that "the giantess Glumdalca and the tiny Tom were frequently played by a male and a female performer, respectively, thereby undercutting what beauty or heroism might otherwise have been left in the protagonists" (413–14).

In his book on the burlesque tradition in the English theater, Clinton-Baddeley says that "the part of Tom Thumb was normally played by a child actor—not infrequently by an infant of only five years old" (58). This may have been true in productions of the play late in the century (he reproduces a portrait of a tiny "Miss Rose in the part of Tom Thumb" from 1770), but the actors listed for Tom Thumb in the first decade of the play's production seem to be young women rather than little girls: one is referred to as "Mrs. Turner," and the Miss Jones that appeared most frequently in the role seems to have been at least a teenager at the time. See Highfill, Burnim, and Langhans, *A Biographical Dictionary of Actors, Actresses, [Etc.] in London, 1660–1800*, vol. 8, 226–28.

5. This is the subject of Castle's deeply illuminating treatment of Fielding's *The Female Husband*, which I will consider at this chapter's close.

6. Garber argues, for example: "Transvestite theater recognizes that *all* of the figures onstage are impersonators. The notion that there has to be a naturalness to the sign is exactly what great theater puts in question" (see 34–40). Butler uses the term "performative" to describe gender's status as a "doing" rather than a "being," but she also draws on the more specific

sense of a theatrical performance in describing gender's status as a constructed and outward phenomenon (see especially 24–25 and 33). In the conclusion to *Gender Trouble* she explores the promise held out by the self-consciously parodic performance of gendered identity.

7. *A Proper Reply to a late Scurrilous Libel; intitled, Sedition and Defamation display'd*, published under the pseudonym of Caleb D'Anvers (1731), 6. For a brief discussion of the satire on Hervey's bisexuality in this period, see Dubro.

8. Satire of the Italian castrato singers is obsessive in this period. The castrato singers were widely abused as the cause of the degeneracy of English drama, and James Ralph (Fielding's partner in *The Champion*) considers them in this and other lights in *The Touch-Stone* (1728). Verse satires on castrati also appeared in London in this period, and we will sample two of them on the castrato singer Farinelli later in this chapter.

9. Kern comments, "Of all the individual types in polite society, the beau received the lion's share of criticism and ridicule. He was represented in almost every comedy, particularly if it had a London setting" (78–79). For a short history of the beau or fop's role in Restoration to mid-eighteenth-century drama, see Staves.

10. *Love in Several Masques*, I.ii; *The Modern Husband*, II.ii. Unless otherwise indicated, I quote throughout this chapter from the Henley edition of Fielding's plays (New York: Croscup & Sterling, 1902).

Until the Wesleyan Edition of the Works of Henry Fielding is complete, quotation from good editions of Fielding's large body of works remains a necessarily complicated and rather awkward task: I have used Wesleyan editions of Fielding's works for which they have been issued and more recent editions of Fielding's plays when they are good ones, but have used the Henley edition of works for which no more recent scholarly edition is available. (I have used first editions for some works not reprinted in Henley.) Throughout the book, parenthetical references to Fielding's plays will be given by act and scene number and references to his novels will be given by page numbers in the Wesleyan editions.

11. Castle discusses this poem, as well as the masquerade scenes in *Tom Jones* and *Amelia*, in *Masquerade and Civilization*. My general debt to her writings on the masquerade and on Fielding's *The Female Husband* can be only inadequately acknowledged in my specific citations below.

12. On masculine and feminine domains and the disruption of those distinctions, I am indebted to Guillory's "Dalila's House: *Samson Agonistes* and the Sexual Division of Labor."

13. On this subject, see *The English Hero, 1660–1800*, especially Hunter's very suggestive essay on heroes in Fielding's work. See also Edwards, chapter 1, "The Disappearance of Heroic Man"; Wilding; and Paulson, "Feminizing the Hero," in *Breaking and Remaking*, 168–92.

14. See Partridge's *Shakespeare's Bawdy*, as noted by Rothstein in

"The Framework of *Shamela.*" Rothstein's essay addresses several of the issues I am interested in here—the relation between domestic or sexual and political material in Fielding's satire, Fielding's satiric interest in figures that combine compromised sexual with compromised political categories, etc.—and it casts a brilliant, though sometimes flickering, light on these issues.

15. Pulteney, 6.

16. See Rothstein, 383–84.

17. In her first letter to her mother, who lodges (we learn in the letter's heading) in the theater district of Drury-Lane, Shamela exclaims, "O! How I long to be in the balcony of the Old House!" Her mother writes back: "Your last letter hath put me into a great hurry of spirits, for you have a very difficult part to act" (*Shamela*, in *Joseph Andrews* and *Shamela*, Houghton Mifflin edition, 309–10).

My interest in Fielding's attitude toward self-dramatization has been heightened and focused by David Marshall's discussion of the theater of personal relations in *The Figure of Theater*, to which I am generally indebted.

18. In *Miscellanies, Volume One*, 161–62.

19. See Ackroyd's *Dressing-Up*: "native traditions of farce and satire . . . provid[ed] a context in which cross-dressing was already a popular device. . . . When cross-dressing was given space within the established theatre, it was simply to provide comic diversion" (98).

Fielding's choice of the word "actor" rather than "actress" and his use of adjectives and pronouns in this passage reinforce the suggestion of possible cross-dressing in my reading of it. (Although the term "actors" may include both female and male stage-players in Fielding's time, Fielding ordinarily uses the word "actress" when speaking specifically of a female player, as he seems to be when he begins this description. Examples of usage in the *Oxford English Dictionary* seem to indicate that by the 1740's "actress" was well established as the preferred term for a female player; and when Johnson defined the terms in the 1750's he divided them clearly by gender.) The sexual imagery invoked in Fielding's contrast between the "modest backwardness" of Virtue and the "harlot" Affectation heightens our awareness of gender in his use of personifications in the passage.

20. Beginning with William Prynne in 1632, antitheatrical arguments often focused on the immorality of one sex dressing as the other on the stage, using as their text the biblical pronouncement: "The woman shall not wear that which pertaineth unto a man, neither shall a man put on a woman's garment: for all that do so are abomination unto the Lord thy God" (Deuteronomy 22.5). Of course, the meaning of such arguments changed, though they continued to be made, after the Restoration stage admitted female players and made female impersonation a choice rather than a condition of the theater. On this topic, see Loftis, chapter 2; Ackroyd, 92–94; and Barish.

Garber also discusses this aspect of antitheatrical arguments in the Renaissance (28–32), and she suggests some of the wider anxieties these arguments addressed: "Renaissance antitheatricalists, in their debates about gender, cross-dressing, and the stage, articulated deep-seated anxieties about the possibility that identity was not fixed, that there was no underlying 'self' at all" (32).

21. See cast lists for these plays in *The London Stage 1660–1800*, Part III.

22. *The Historical Register*, ed. William W. Appleton, Regents Restoration Drama Series (Lincoln: University of Nebraska Press, 1967). All references to *The Historical Register* cite this edition.

23. For a brief account of Farinelli's career in London, see the entry under his name in *A Biographical Dictionary of Actors, Actresses, [Etc.] in London, 1660–1800*, 5: 145–52; as well as Heriot, 95–110.

24. Recent research confirms that stories from this period about castrato singers actually impregnating women express fantasy or humor, not fact. See Peschel and Peschel for an account of this research. In Carson's extremely interesting study of "Commodification and the Figure of the Castrato," he disputes the conclusions of the Peschels on this matter (as well as my use of those conclusions). Some uncertainty indeed seems to have existed in the castrati's own time (as it does now) about whether they might achieve an erection; and I am persuaded by Carson's interpretation of some of the double entendres in contemporaries' treatments of the castrati as suggesting that they—at least sometimes—believed that the castrati were only infertile, not impotent. Most contemporaries must have known little about what the castrati were or were not able to do; and their genitals were of such fascination partly because they afforded an occasion for titillated speculation.

The difficulty I have encountered in referring precisely but tactfully even to the general nature of the castrato's anatomical loss suggests, I think, our culture's inclination to treat the male genitals as more unitary than they are—as constituted simply in the talismanic object of the penis. Is it the loss of the penis or the testicles or both that a man fears when he suffers "castration anxiety"?

Some male readers of an early version of this chapter (published in *The New Eighteenth Century*) have responded in an agitated, if not anxious, mood to my discussion of the figure of the castrato, convinced that I have failed to understand the crucial fact that even a castrato (unlike a woman) *has a penis*. Howard D. Weinbrot, for example, in a review of *The New Eighteenth Century*, acknowledges that "Campbell seems to know what castration denotes (p. 285, n. 15)," but then complains that "she writes and writes and writes as if it meant cutting off the penis not the testicles" (385). What Weinbrot experiences as the excess of my misguided writing manifests, in his phrase, my "phallophobia." (Suggestively, Weinbrot's other substantive criticism of my argument has to do with my failure to understand that the group of ladies conversing in II.i of *The Historical Register* are discussing the use of dildos—a possibility I will consider below.) I have attempted to phrase my references to the castrato's anatomical loss carefully, but perhaps for some readers it will always seem that my discussion unacceptably conjures the scenario of the "cutting off" of "the penis" itself. For such readers, the distinction I employ between the possession of a penis and the possession of phallic capacity and authority is unthinkable, so that my attempt to describe the castrato's situation makes (as one reader put it) "no sense." I argue at the close of this chapter that Fielding himself at times uneasily acknowledges this distinction.

25. On the arrival of the castrati in London in the early eighteenth century, see White, 142–45. On the contemporary sense that they presented the viewer with a contradiction in terms, see, for example, James Ralph, Fielding's partner in *The Champion*, who refers to them in *The Touch-Stone* (1728) as "those Performers who are neither Men nor Women" (14).

26. Kowaleski-Wallace focuses in a more sustained way than I do here on "how the castrato is an important figure for the construction of *female* sexuality" (154). She offers a discerning reading of the English translation of Charles Ancillon's *Eunuchism Display'd* (1718) and concludes that "the imagined sexual liaison of the castrato and the woman introduces the possibility of a non-phallic, female sexual pleasure which is not linked to reproduction" (158).

27. Hogarth incorporates the scene depicted in this print, with some rearrangement of its figures and the addition of three kneeling noblemen, into his "Masquerades and Operas," where it appears on the banner advertising the opera (see Fig. 4). As Paulson argues, however, it would not be uncharacteristic for Hogarth to copy the design of someone else's print (*Hogarth's Graphic Works*, 1: 294–95); and Paulson places the print depicting the three operatic singers under the category of "Prints Questionably Attributed to Hogarth." Neither it nor a closely related drawing of the male figure to the scene's left have ever been authoritatively attributed to Hogarth (see Oppé, plate 11, cat. #4, on the drawing).

Furthermore, doubt exists about Ireland's identification of this figure as Farinelli: the print appears to date from 1723, and Farinelli did not arrive in England until 1734. (Ireland also misidentifies the opera portrayed in the print as *Ptolemeo*, which was not performed until 1728). Ireland, however, was not the only one to identify the tall, awkward figure in the print with Farinelli (and his posture and general appearance match the verbal description offered in *Reflections on Theatrical Expression in Tragedy*). Paulson suggests that "the fact that the Exeter and Royal Library impressions carry Farinelli's name probably means that the print was reissued later (in the third state) and connected with him" (295). If this is true, the print-sellers relied on a certain interchangeability of castrati's bodies, substituting the name of a current star under the depiction of a quite distinctive physique (either Berenstadt's or Senesino's) from a previous decade.

In *Caricature History of the Georges*, Thomas Wright seems to have derived his figures of Cuzzoni and Farinelli from some version of this print and combined them with the sketch of "Heidegger in a Rage," also from Ireland, to create his own trio of "Cuzzoni, Farinelli, and Heidegger" (72–73).

For a summary of the various problems of identification and attribution involved in this print and its related drawing, see Paulson's and Oppé's discussions.

28. The description of Farinelli in *Reflections on Theatrical Expression in Tragedy* is quoted in Ireland (257).

29. Rothstein recognizes Fielding's allusion to Teresia Constantia Phillips in Shamela's mother's name (396).

In a review of *The New Eighteenth Century*, in which an early version of this chapter appeared, Weinbrot points out that the attribution of this poem to Con Phillips (in, for example, library catalogs) is implausible on several counts (384). If that attribution has derived only from the poem's subtitle, I tend to think that he is right: the reference to Phillips there may only indicate the fictional premise of the poem's epistolary form. I have therefore treated Phillips as the imagined speaker of the poem, leaving the issue of authorship unresolved.

30. *The Happy Courtezan*, 3 and 7. I have used a copy of this pamphlet held by Yale's Beinecke Library.

31. Fielding includes satire of the castrati in *The Author's Farce, Pasquin, Eurydice*, and *Miss Lucy in Town*, as well as in *The Historical Register*.

32. Sherburn and Aubrey Williams both explore the connections between Pope's and Fielding's courts of dullness. As in Pope's *Dunciad*, the real political court of George and Caroline, with its well-known "petticoat government," is in the background of Fielding's court of Nonsense in *The Author's Farce*.

33. *The Author's Farce*, Regents Restoration Drama edition, ed. Charles B. Woods, Act III, Air VIII. Woods notes that "rich" and "great man" might refer to John Rich, the producer of pantomime, and Robert Walpole, the "great man" of the prime ministry, but feels "in this generally non-political play the point is hard to see" (57n). I find the allusion plausible, as Fielding elsewhere links Rich and Walpole in his political satire (see *The Champion* for April 22, 1740, vol. 2, 129).

34. In *The Touch-Stone* James Ralph cites the "exorbitant Prices we pay the Performers; especially the Foreigners" as one of the four common objections to opera (13). *The Biographical Dictionary of Actors, Actresses, [etc.]* tells us that one reason Porpora's opera ultimately failed "was certainly the outrageously high prices paid to singers," and that, including gifts, Farinelli's "income for the season [in 1735] was probably close to £5000." It

comments, "The English were torn between their admiration for Farinelli and their concern over what he cost them," and quotes an essay from *Fog's Journal* in 1736 that calls Farinelli "one Public Tickler of great Eminency" (5: 148–50). The salaries paid the castrati are also satirized in a passage from Fielding's *Eurydice*, which we will be considering below.

See also Carson's discussion of this aspect of the connection between "commodification" and the figure of the castrato.

35. I have used the copy of this anonymous pamphlet held at Yale's Beinecke Library.

36. "Teresia Constantia Phillips," *Happy Courtezan*, 13.

37. The pamphlet's snide allusion to the possibility of a papal male impersonator may refer to "Pope Joan," whose secret identity as a woman discovered itself when she gave birth to a child in the middle of a papal procession. See the reference to this legend in Natalie Zemon Davis, 134.

38. See Dickson on the sense in which the development of public credit in England may be termed a veritable "revolution," with all the practical and psychological ramifications inherent in such an event.

39. Appleton glosses "dear babies" as "dolls" and reads the lines about wax "Farinellos" as "an allusion to the vogue for wax figures, which were sold at the New Exchange" (see his footnotes to these lines, 25). On this vogue, see also Reilly, 71–80, and Early, who both remark that the use of molds made it possible to issue copies of wax figures in large numbers. The First Lady's exclamation, "Oh Gemini! Who makes them?" evokes the uncanny doubling of such artistic reproductions of life.

In responding to an earlier published version of this chapter, both Trumbach and Weinbrot present their conviction that the dolls should be read as dildos as a criticism of my reading of this passage (Trumbach, "London's Sapphists," 139 n. 23; Weinbrot, 383–84). I accept the suggestion as an interesting and plausible, though unsubstantiated, addition to my account of the ladies' conversation; it seems to me to provide one more link among the complexly interconnected subjects of sexuality, consumerism, and reproduction in the passage, compounding rather than exploding the constellation of concerns I have sought to trace there.

40. The references to auctions occur in *The Temple Beau* (II.xiii), *The Coffee-House Politician* (II.iii), *The Modern Husband* (II.x), *The Universal Gallant* (I.i), *Joseph Andrews* (204), and *Amelia* (344). The new institution of the lottery seems to have held a related interest for Fielding. He wrote a whole play about the craze for lotteries at this time, exploring what kind of wealth one possesses in the promise a lottery ticket offers (*The Lottery*, 1732). See Battestin, *Henry Fielding*, 124 and 639 n. 164, on Fielding's sustained satiric interest in the lottery; and Agnew for an extended discussion of the relations between the market and the theater in this period.

41. See Cassady, 29–30. W. H. Auden and Chester Kallman recognize the auction as a distinctively eighteenth-century gathering when they

make it the scene of one episode of their libretto for Stravinsky's opera *The Rake's Progress*.

42. Ash, quoted in Cassady, 29–33.

43. On the emergence of a consumer society in England in the course of the eighteenth century, see McKendrick, Brewer, and Plumb. I have relied heavily on this important book for my understanding of the historical context for Fielding's satiric interest in commodities and shopping.

44. As noted by Dudden, 198.

45. Partridge's *Dictionary of Slang* confirms that "cock" was used to mean "penis" in slang long before 1737 (164).

46. Henley, 12: 337–39. Dugaw reports upon a fashion for male riding dress among English women in the seventeenth and eighteenth centuries; and she cites a number of men's complaints (including those in Pepys' diary, *The Spectator*, and Gay's *The Guardian*) about women's adoption of this "Hermaphroditical" dress (133).

47. For example:

> Now rarities she wants; no matter
> What price they cost—they please the better.
> Italian vines, and Spanish sheep. (325)

> However liberal your grants,
> Still what her neighbour hath she wants (327)

> For what so fulsome—if it were new t'ye,
> That no one thinks herself a beauty,
> 'Till Frenchified from head to foot,
> A mere Parisian dame throughout. (331)

48. Brown, *Alexander Pope*, 103. I am particularly indebted to Brown's explication of Pope for my reading of Fielding's use of Juvenal.

49. See ibid., 104, as well as her "Reading Race and Gender: Jonathan Swift." As early as Watt's ground-breaking *The Rise of the Novel*, critics have recognized the importance of the new exclusion of women from the means of production for the treatment of women in eighteenth-century literature. Pollak has explored this subject in depth as it appears in Swift's and Pope's works. See also McKendrick for a more general discussion of the association of women with the period's new consumerism.

50. *Champion*, February 16, 1739/40, 1: 275. Fielding did not write all the essays in *The Champion*, but it is generally agreed that he wrote at least all of the essays signed "C" or "L." This one is signed with a "C."

51. See McKendrick, Brewer, and Plumb, chapter 2, "The Commercialization of Fashion," 34–99.

52. Fielding returns repeatedly to the satiric figure of the beau not only to ridicule him for his effeminacy but also to expose the affected and

mediated nature of his sexual desire: his desire is mediated both in finding its source in imitation and in taking as its object the reputation rather than the experience of fulfillment. See, for example, Owen, the "puny lover" of *The Grub-Street Opera* ("he runs after every woman he sees; and yet, I believe, scarce knows what a woman is,—Either he has more affectation than desire, or more desire than capacity" [I.v]); and Mr. Wilson's account in *Joseph Andrews* of his days as a beau, when "the Reputation of Intriguing with [women] was all I sought" (203). See also the *Champion* essay (probably not by Fielding) on male-coxcombs (April 8, 1740, 2: 80–86).

This interest in Fielding's works in what we might call "mediated desire" differs from the influential model provided by René Girard in several important ways, though the connections to Girard's model are suggestive. The scenario of a mediated self that Fielding imagines does not involve an intense triangle of personal rivalry and emulation in desire, structured around an individual human mediator; Fielding's account diffuses the mediating force among the necessarily numberless faces of fashion, making it an external and social rather than a psychological one. Girard does address this social version of mediated desire in his discussion of the Proustian "snob," who is "the slave of the fashionable" (24), but his account of desire emphasizes the function of a particular mediator who focuses the forces of fashion and sustains the triangular structure, even if that mediator can be exchanged with another in a series of interchangeable mediators (92–94).

53. See, for example, the jokes about homosexual rape leveled against the corrupt Popish confessor in Fielding's *The Debauchees; or, the Jesuit Caught* (1732), III.xiii.

As O'Neill notes, the English association of homosexuality with Italy was long-standing and even "proverbial" (19 n. 9). Homophobia and xenophobia thus are linked that they may justify each other.

54. See Brown, *Alexander Pope*, 15–18.

55. See Haraway, 135; Garber, 16; and especially Judith Butler, 16–17 and 33, on the privileged position afforded gender in our understandings of coherent and intelligible "identity" or selfhood. Indeed, Butler asserts that "the very notion of the subject" has so far been "intelligible only through its appearance as gendered" (33).

56. *Champion*, April 26, 1740, 2: 144–45. As the essay takes the form of a letter to Capt. Vinegar signed "Morpheus," the usual means of establishing that this is Fielding's own work are not available.

57. No act and scene divisions appear in this one-act farce; the passage occurs at the end of the play.

58. Quoted in Cross, 1: 218–19.

59. Though this play was presented as the work of Capt. Bodens, it was well known that Lord Hervey and Prince Frederick had written it— which may have been why it received such harsh treatment from the audience (see Woods, "Captain B----'s Play").

Fielding was peripherally involved in the production of *The Modish Couple*, writing an epilogue for its opening at Drury Lane (Battestin, *Henry Fielding*, 125–26); and he alludes to Prince Frederick's and Lord Hervey's authorship of *The Modish Couple* in *Pasquin* when he has Harlequin tell Queen Ignorance of it, "The character you give would recommend it, / Though it had come from a less powerful hand" (V.i).

60. Later in the century, Fielding's particular image of one species engaging in absurd mimicry of another would in fact be used in a famous analogy for the absurdity of one *sex*'s mimicry of the other. Boswell quotes Johnson as commenting on female Quaker preachers: "Sir, a woman's preaching is like a dog's walking on his hinder legs. It is not done well; but you are surprized to find it done at all" (*Life of Johnson*, 327; entry for July 31, 1763).

61. In *The Poetry of Pope's* Dunciad, Sitter provides an illuminating analysis of the way "inversions," including generic and moral inversions, structure Pope's vision of Dullness, but he does not consider gender inversions there. He does, however, go on in his later work to explore the figure of the regressive son who is a votary to the Mighty Mother in the *Dunciad* and the different treatments of this figure by Pope and other midcentury poets. Sitter's insight about the centrality and ambiguity of this figure involves gender issues raised to a greater level of complexity.

62. In *Miscellanies, Volume One*, 173.

63. Fielding had used the word's slang meaning of "female genitals" to give the word a double reference elsewhere. The slang meaning is recorded in Eric Partridge's *Shakespeare's Bawdy*, as noted in Rothstein's discussion of Fielding's use of the word in *Shamela* (381–402).

64. Think of the powerful death of Little Eva. For two points of view on this costly bargain, compare Douglas and Tompkins on nineteenth-century American versions of female "sentimental power."

65. Fielding also turns to the subject of ghosts in several of his *Champion* essays. As noted in my general introduction, in one of them he in fact refers to himself as "an Author who dealt so much in Ghosts, that he is said to have spoiled the *Hay-market* Stage, by cutting it all into Trap-Doors" (November 27, 1739, 1:33 n.). Fielding's joke in *Tom Thumb* of having Grizzle vengefully kill Tom's ghost when it appears achieved wide fame. The story is that Swift claimed to have laughed but twice in his life—once at the trick of a mountebank and the other time when Lord Grizzle killed the ghost of Tom Thumb (recorded in Laetitia Pilkington's *Memoirs* and recalled by Cross, 1:87).

66. *Eurydice Hissed*, published in the Regents Restoration Drama edition with *The Historical Register for the Year 1736*.

67. This is the humorous basis of his *Eurydice*, the original farce. In Fielding's version, Eurydice does not want to return from the underworld

with Orpheus and so deliberately makes him break Pluto's condition by tricking him into looking back at her.

Note also that Splatter—the author in the frame play, who has written the play-within, in which Pillage represents himself—was another role taken by Charlotte Charke. The gender plottings of this little farce are complicated.

68. Laura Brown has shown us that Pope shares this cultural legacy and its "hauntings" in her illuminating discussion of the "strange incorporeality" of women in *To a Lady*, which culminates in the passage in which "the Ghosts of Beauty . . . haunt the places where their Honour dy'd" (*Alexander Pope*, 101–7).

69. See Partridge's *Dictionary of Slang*, 55, and the *O.E.D. Supplement*, 271. For eighteenth-century examples, see Swift's "Strephon and Chloe" of 1731 ("To see some radiant nymph appear / In all her glitt'ring birthday gear"), Smollett's *Ferdinand Count Fathom* of 1753, and his *Humphry Clinker* of 1771 ("I went in the morning to a private place, along with the house-maid, and we bathed in our birth-day soot").

70. For one brief account of the figure and face of Count Heidegger, see Cross, 1: 59–61. Fielding represents this famous masquerade-master a number of times: see the character "Count Ugly" in the puppet show within *The Author's Farce*, the masquerade scene in *Tom Jones* (XIII.vii), *The Increase of Robbers*, and *Amelia*. Heidegger was also important in London society as an associate of Handel in establishing the Italian opera on the London stage.

71. This anecdote is told in full in Nichols and Steevens, 2: 322–25; in a somewhat simplified version in Ireland, 3: 323–24; and later in Thomas Wright, 72–73. "Heidegger in a Rage" appears in Ireland (3: 323, plate 43), where it is attributed to Hogarth; and Wright roughly copies it twice.

72. August 5 and December 9, 1749, *Old England*; quoted in Battestin, "Pictures of Fielding," 7.

73. Battestin, "Pictures of Fielding," 9–13. See figures 4–6 in Battestin's essay (details from "Characters and Caricaturas," from Hogarth's frontispiece to Fielding's work, and from "Hogarth Painting the Comic Muse") for his compelling visual argument for this identification of the two faces.

74. As argued by Battestin, "Pictures of Fielding," 6.

75. This essay appears in the collected *Champion*, 2: 253–59.

76. Fielding here closely follows the satiric premise of Dialogue 10 in Lucian's *Dialogues of the Dead* (as traditionally numbered; presented as 20 in Macleod's order). In Lucian's version, however, the dead boarding Charon's boat are successfully stripped by Hermes, so that the boat arrives safely on the other side of the river; in Fielding's version, the boat sinks, and the sound of its passengers' shrieks wakes the dreamer.

77. Heidegger's sometime sponsorship of an opera company at the Haymarket made him an appropriate addressee for the epistle, but it was his association with the controversial institution of the masquerade for which he was best known.

78. "When a Man is absolutely void of Capacity, it matters not whether his Skin be stuff'd with *Guts* or Straw, or whether his Face be made of Wood or Brass" (April 22, 1740, *The Champion*, 2: 128). An essay printed a week earlier is listed in the collected *Champion's* index under "*Man*, a Sort of *Puppet*, and for what form'd" (April 15, 1740, 2: 107–11); and one of Fielding's mock-scholarly notes to his mock-ancient epic, *The Vernoniad*, cites Horace as an authority for his comparison of people to puppets (33 n. 4).

79. *Champion*, May 31, 1740, 2: 280. This essay is signed "C," indicating that it is by Fielding. Fielding claims to be paraphrasing Horace in his story of Priapus's origins.

80. Castle, "Matters Not Fit to Be Mentioned," 619.

81. See Baker on the mixture of fact and fiction within Fielding's account, as well as Castle, "Matters Not Fit to Be Mentioned."

82. In *A Narrative of Mrs. Charlotte Charke*, Charke provided the public with a lively and compelling, though often fragmentary and opaque, account of her own life (she outdoes her father in Cibberian egotism: for example, she dedicates the book to herself). This autobiography did not appear until 1755, but Fielding may have known the substance of Charke's early adventures from his acquaintance with her at the Haymarket.

83. *The Female Husband*, in *The Female Husband and Other Writings*, 38. I will give further citations of this pamphlet by page number in this edition, parenthetically in the text.

84. See Stone, 195–202; and Watt, *The Rise of the Novel*, 141–42.

85. *Champion*, December 20, 1739, 1: 115. This essay is probably not Fielding's (it is signed with the double asterisk associated with Ralph, though it bears a Latin epithet, which is more usual in Fielding's contributions), but it certainly centers on the concerns and images we have seen recurring in *Champion* essays we know to be his, suggesting that it may show his collaboration or influence. The reference to the giants of Guild-Hall later in the essay, very similar to one in *Tom Thumb*, makes me feel it's possible Fielding had a hand, at least, in this.

86. In *The Ornament of Action*, Holland presents detailed and convincing evidence that expectations created by casting choices were an important part of the audience's experience of a play performed in this period; and in "'Playhouse Flesh and Blood,'" Maus argues that an awareness of actresses' offstage lives formed part of their effect on stage in Restoration performances. Fielding clearly plays upon his audience's consciousness of another aspect of Charlotte Charke's offstage identity when he gives her

these lines in the role of Lord Place in *Pasquin*: "you'll be able to make odes. . . . I can't tell you what they are; but I know you may be qualified for the place without being a poet" (II.i). The tired satire against Colley Cibber as ode-writing poet laureate is given new bite when spoken by his own daughter on stage.

Part 2

1. Sherbo, *Studies in the Eighteenth-Century Novel*, 116; Hunter, *Occasional Form*, 98.

2. For example, Dick Taylor, Jr., acknowledges Joseph's ridiculousness early in the novel by referring to his status there as a "male Pamela" (92 and 100); and Maurice Johnson speaks of the "absurdity of a squeamish male Pamela" (49, 51, 58).

3. Schilling, 49, 56.

4. Maurice Johnson, 49.

5. Maurice Johnson argues that the novel achieves a gradual alteration of such initially "antic, labelled figures" as Joseph into "heartfelt persons drawn from human nature," as it grows from burlesque to "a 'good' comic style" (47–60). And Hunter suggests that Fielding "sends Joseph on a circuitous route to moral heroism," actually using the negative "rhetorical method" of the novel's initial presentation of Joseph to manipulate expectations and allow for the eventual positive creation of his character. See *Occasional Form*, 95–116; on Hunter's interesting theory of Fielding's construction of heroes more generally, see "Fielding and the Disappearance of Heroes," 116–42.

6. Taylor, 92, 105.

Chapter 2

1. Without exploring it at length, Hunter addresses this issue in his discussion of *Joseph Andrews*, commenting on Joseph's second letter to Pamela: "The burlesque context makes it unlikely that we will be in a mood to notice, but alongside the foolish posturing and mindless canting is a certain amount of solid sense, for beyond the absurd example-mongering and exclamatory effusions about 'fine things' is the point, repeated from chapter 1, about a single standard for both sexes" (*Occasional Form*, 100).

2. At times the convergence of class and gender structures in Pamela allows her resistance to oppression to speak for all those without social authority and power, as when she asserts the equal value of her soul; at times it works to naturalize or rationalize her different forms of powerlessness by explaining them in terms of each other. As Pamela's letters approach the event of her wedding, for example, and the gradual domestication of her spirit, they recur frequently to her fear of the "happy, yet awful moment"

of her sexual union with Mr. B. The only explanation she can find for her apprehension about her wedding night has to do with her class identity: "My heart, at times, sinks within me; I know not why, except at my own unworthiness, and because the honour done me is too high for me to support myself under, as I should do. It is an honour . . . I was not born to. . . . But I suppose all young maidens are the same, so near so great a change of condition, though they carry it off more discreetly than I" (357; and see 357–72 generally).

Pamela's train of thought overlays her own specific cause to feel "lacking," unworthy, afraid—her social and economic inferiority to her husband—onto the conventional expectation that a woman's sexual desire is necessarily adjoined to dread and awe—presumably, in the face of the phallus. The effect seems to me to be to naturalize her class inferiority as analogous to biological gender identity, and to rationalize conventional constructions of her gender as analogous to lesser possession of wealth and social position. The cliché of the "blushing bride," then, serves to bring together Pamela's positions as female and as lower-class and to conceive and accept them in terms of each other—just at that point in the novel when it makes its crucial transition toward domesticating its potentially subversive message.

3. Alter describes well the particular erotics of Lady Booby's imagination in this scene as "her eager prurient anticipation of 'submitting' herself to her own footboy, the mistress deliciously mastered by a servant" (73).

4. McKeon discusses the different social functions of female and male chastity in eighteenth-century England (*The Origins of the English Novel*, 148–49 and 156–58); and he discusses chastity in *Pamela* and *Joseph Andrews* specifically, 366–68 and 398–400.

5. Hunter suggests both possible readings of the seduction scenes, allowing at one point that Joseph's assertion of "individual rights" shows him to be more sensible and dignified than we might have thought, while remarking casually at another that in these scenes "the laughter is altogether at Joseph's expense" (*Occasional Form*, 100, 95).

6. Homer Obed Brown, 202.

7. Even Richardson's own two main characters are brought within the perimeter of Fielding's narrative in the final book of the novel and reconstituted as parodic, flat versions of themselves, peripheral now to the main thrust of the action.

8. Taylor comments on Fielding's treatment of Joseph in the "night-adventures": "He holds Joseph from participating in the hurly-burly to keep him from being ridiculous, because he wants to maintain Joseph's dignity—Joseph is definitely out of the frame of either the Pamelian burlesque or picaresque high jinks. When Joseph does come into the episode the next morning in Fanny's room where Adams is discovered slumbering peacefully, he

is . . . quite positive and dominating. . . . it is Joseph who comprehends what has actually happened and how Adams made his mistake" (107–8).

9. Both Battestin and Hunter discuss the biblical significance of Joseph's name. See *The Moral Basis of Fielding's Art* and *Occasional Form*, especially 103–5.

10. Alter, 50–51.

11. The thrust of Didapper's crude wit seems to be the incongruity of the practice he mimics at the Adamses' humble and rural door, making the object of any humor attached to its violent noise simply poverty and lack of pretensions. These are objects Fielding has specifically excluded from the force of legitimate ridicule in his preface, but objects of severe and violent ridicule from the Roasting-Squire and his men. More on this subject later.

12. I am indebted to Hunter for his discerning account of the importance of expectation (and its subversion) in Fielding's unfolding of character (see both "Fielding and the Disappearance of Heroes" and *Occasional Form*).

13. Stapleton, 182–83.

14. Hunter, too, notes the phallic allusion in the reference to Priapus in this passage, but he interprets it as a leering suggestion of Joseph's "sexual potential" and "promising future" as a "sexual object" (*Occasional Form*, 96–97). If the allusion functions on some level to make this suggestion, on the surface at least its context works to assert Joseph's failure as a sexual object.

15. As several critics have observed, this combination characterizes Tom Jones's beauty as well, though with a somewhat different emphasis. I will discuss Tom's appearance briefly in Chapter 6.

16. As in the Renaissance rhetorical convention of the *blazon*, or item-by-item enumeration of a woman's beauties. See Lanham's *Handlist of Rhetorical Terms*.

17. Remarking on Fielding's reference to Joseph's "tenderness joined with a sensibility inexpressible," Jean Hagstrum notes that "the parallel portrait of Fanny endows her with a countenance 'in which, though she was extremely bashful, a sensibility appeared almost incredible; and a sweetness, whenever she smiled, beyond either imitation or description' (II.12)" (179). Thomas E. Maresca, too, notes the shared phrasings in the two descriptions and comments that they make Fanny "the female counterpart of Joseph," though he also argues for important differences between the two characters (200–201). Hagstrum identifies the sensibility Fielding grants to both Joseph and Fanny as feminine, observing that he grants it to Tom Jones as well, and commenting: "once again, as if to avoid the implication of effeminacy that sensibility could obviously carry with it, Fielding insists that Tom also possesses a 'most masculine person and mien.' The whole of *Tom Jones* illustrates abundantly both the vigorously masculine and the delicately feminine qualities of the hero. . . . As the ingredient of delicacy became more prom-

inent in love, the drive towards forms of unisexuality also became more prominent. It may be worth considering that in the spirit of so robustly a heterosexual man as Fielding delicate sensibility loomed larger than we have hitherto realized" (179–80).

Hagstrum's brief discussion of Fielding in *Sex and Sensibility* (178–85) draws attention to aspects of Fielding's work that have not been adequately recognized; and his historical study of changing notions of sex and sensibility in this period provides an illuminating context for our study of the interest in gender in Fielding's work in particular.

18. All quotations of *Paradise Lost* will be from the Odyssey Press edition, ed. Hughes; book and line numbers for further citations from the poem will be given parenthetically in the text.

19. In their notes to this passage of *Paradise Lost*, editors John Carey and Alastair Fowler cite St. Paul's similar treatment of hair length as an expression of the hierarchic relation of the sexes (I Corinthians 11: 7, 15). But they also comment that "the elaborateness of the present passage lends some support to the theory that Milton had a special interest in hair" (*The Poems of John Milton* [New York: Longman Group of W. W. Norton, 1968], 631).

20. Watt, *Rise of the Novel*, 160–63.

21. See Eaves and Kimpel, 408–9.

22. Taylor remarks that book 2, chapter 12, "marks the point of change in the appearance of Joseph in the thought and action so that he is treated on more serious levels of meaning, and it initiates a line of action which is to carry him to a dignity and a stature and an elevation of personality far beyond the original limitations imposed by the burlesque mode" (97). See also Johnson, 53–55.

23. Faustina and Cuzzoni's rivalry was burlesqued, for example, in the struggle between Gay's Polly and Lucy in *The Beggar's Opera* (1728) and in the farcical competition of the two sopranos in the anonymous *The Contretemps; or, Rival Queans* (1727). On the satirical referents of the scene between Polly and Lucy (II.xiii), see the notes to *The Beggar's Opera*, ed. Lewis, 120–21; and Erskine-Hill in Axton and Williams, 157–58.

The burlesque struggle between Fielding's own Glumdalca and Huncamunca in *The Tragedy of Tragedies* may also glance at operatic rivalries, reduced to the level of personal insult (II.vii). Fielding's footnotes to the scene between them also confirm its parallels to the famous "Altercative Scene between Cleopatra and Octavia" in Dryden's *All for Love* (Act III). Fielding completes the same collocation of associations in *Joseph Andrews* when, just on the other side of the reunion scene at the inn, he tells us that Slipslop cast a look at Fanny as she flung herself into the chaise "not unlike that which *Cleopatra* gives *Octavia* in the Play" (159).

24. See, for example, *Eurydice* and *The Author's Farce*. I take the word "intrigues" from Wilson's description of his desire for the mere rep-

utation of sexual conquest: "Nothing now seemed to remain but an Intrigue, which I was resolved to have immediately; I mean the Reputation of it" (203). The puzzle of a castrato's sexual relations represents for Fielding the wider phenomenon of the beau's desire for the empty appearance of sexual engagement.

25. Several critics have pursued this problem of narcissism in *Joseph Andrews*—here not done justice—in more depth, and have suggested its relation to other important matters in the novel. Pointing out that Fanny's name in *Joseph Andrews* strangely repeats Fielding's satiric name for Lord Hervey in the frame materials for *Shamela*, and that Lord Hervey reappears in *Joseph Andrews* as Beau Didapper, Hunter interprets the beau's attempts to ravish Fanny as the expression of a confused kind of narcissistic desire: "as he tries to ravish Fanny, [Didapper] confronts for a moment his own self-love. . . . He sees not the Fanny we have by then come to know, but some idealized vision of himself" (*Occasional Form*, 106). Hagstrum discusses the meaning of both narcissism and incest in *Joseph Andrews* and *Tom Jones*; and my awareness of this issue in *Joseph Andrews* has been informed by a paper presented by William Jewett about the relation between the principle of "exemplarity" and the problem of narcissism in Fielding's implicit critique of Richardson (graduate course presentation at Yale University, 1984).

26. On the awakening of Pygmalion's statue, see Ovid, *Metamorphoses*, X.280–95.

Pygmalion's statue would be evoked more easily by Fanny's faint because of the network of references to people turning into statues in *Joseph Andrews*. Hunter highlights Fielding's description of Lady Booby as a "*Statue of Surprize*" (*Occasional Form*, 40) and comments, "The statue becomes an important mark on the Fielding landscape, and the rhetoric of *Joseph Andrews* often honors it, not only to avert seduction for his characters but to engineer ours" (95).

27. The question of Joseph's injury arises again when the False Promiser offers to lend the travelers a horse and a servant: "a very fierce Dispute ensued, whether *Fanny* should ride behind *Joseph*, or behind the Gentleman's Servant; *Joseph* insisting on it, that he was perfectly recovered, and was as capable of taking care of *Fanny*, as any other Person could be. But *Adams* would not agree to it, and declared he would not trust her behind him; for that he was weaker than he imagined himself to be" (174). The dispute concerns how fully recovered Joseph's leg is (Adams has mentioned Joseph's "lame Leg" the page before), but Taylor assumes it has to do with Joseph's sexual self-control. He summarizes: "Adams demands [that Fanny ride] behind the gentleman's servant, since he says that Joseph is not to be trusted, 'being weaker than he imagined himself to be'—Adams has not forgotten Joseph's fiery haste to have the marriage ceremony performed on the spot without benefit of banns" (101). I think that the passage does, in some

general way, encourage a confusion between Joseph's leg and his sexual abilities and vulnerabilities, gently extending the kind of metonymic association suggested earlier by his injury.

28. Hunter, "Fielding and the Disappearance of Heroes," 136.

Chapter 3

1. I use the term "genre" in an admittedly loose and nontechnical fashion throughout this chapter, as epic, drama, and satire do not seem to me "genres" in the same sense of the word—particularly as I am interested here in tying literary methods and moods with nonliterary attitudes and forms of behavior. A distinction between epic and drama as alternative genres is justified by the origins of the concept of genre in Plato's distinction between these two possible modes of representation; and satire has historically been treated as a distinct genre (see *Princeton Encyclopedia of Poetry and Poetics*, 307–9). The history of the concept of "genre" itself introduces all kinds of confusions into the application of the concept, however; and I often use the term here in a way close to the less specific terms "form" or "mode."

2. Maurice Johnson, 51; Alter, 117.

3. Hollander, 27.

4. Ibid.

5. Hollander traces these several functions of echo, 27–31.

6. Hollander, 75. Paulson comments, "Defoe's allusions end with God and Adam; Richardson's and Fielding's extend to Milton's Satan," and he alerts us to the seriousness of Fielding's allusions in *Tom Jones*: "The allusions to Genesis and *Paradise Lost*, though sometimes ironic, are not playful" ("The Pilgrimage and the Family," 67–69). See also Maresca, 217–21.

7. Hunter locates *Pamela*'s trust in the moral exemplum in the historical context of arguments about the superiority of example to precept and the resurgence of the *Imitatio Christi* tradition in this period. For his interesting argument on this aspect of Fielding's response to Richardson, see *Occasional Form*, 85–116.

8. Paulson, "The Pilgrimage and the Family," 73.

9. Paulson also makes this connection between imitation in *Joseph Andrews* and the Girardean model of desire, and he comments, "In *Joseph Andrews* the structure is clear in Joseph's imitation of Adams's precepts, Pamela's letters, London fashion, and romantic love clichés." He goes on to describe Joseph's escape from these forms of mediation, "aided, of course, by his *unmediated* love for Fanny Goodwill" ("The Pilgrimage and the Family," 74–75).

10. Mikhail Bakhtin provides a crucial theoretical formulation of this dynamic and material aspect of language in general and of novelistic language in particular. He comments: "language is something that is historically real, a process of heteroglot development, a process teeming with fu-

ture and former languages, with prim but moribund aristocrat-languages, with parvenu-languages and with countless pretenders to the status of language" (356–57).

11. In his note to these lines, Battestin points out a similar association of bad writing with the Miltonic realm of Chaos and Night in *The New Dunciad*, "which Pope was writing at Ralph Allen's house at the time of Fielding's visit late in 1741" (188 n. 2).

12. Hunter comments: "It is more than requirements of plot that make Adams the only intent observer of what Mr. Wilson says, while Joseph and Fanny (along with many readers) tend to doze off. Except for Adams's excessive responses, Wilson's story would be nearly unnavigable in the context of *Joseph Andrews*, for even if readers need resting places they do not expect to sleep while the conversation goes on" (*Occasional Form*, 153).

13. Without tracing specific echoes, Hunter calls this meadow "an incredibly Miltonic place" into which "postlapsarian circumstances obtrude" (*Occasional Form*, 175).

14. Fielding confided his fear about the morally ambiguous nature of laughter in a letter he sent to James Harris not long before beginning to write *Joseph Andrews*. He wonders there whether "that Laughter which entitles to the general Character of Good Humour, be not rather a Sign of an evil than a good Mind"; and he comments that no record exists of Jesus Christ ever laughing, though he "is said to have had a Countenance *constantly smiling.*" "It is perhaps difficult," he concludes, "to assign the just Bounds between these two Kinds of Laughter, which are in my Opinion the Indications of the best and the worst Disposition" (letter of September 29, 1741, quoted in Battestin, *Henry Fielding*, 313–14).

We will take up Fielding's divided relation to satiric ridicule again below, in considering his treatments of it in *Tom Jones* and *The Jacobite's Journal*. By the time he was publishing *The Covent Garden Journal*, Battestin suggests, Fielding had radically "revised his conceptions of humor and the sense of his own role as humorist," repudiating Rabelais and Aristophanes—indeed, asserting that their "Design appears to me very plainly to have been to ridicule all Sobriety, Modesty, Decency, Virtue and Religion, out of the World" (March 3, 1751/52; quoted and discussed in *Henry Fielding*, 544).

15. Watt, 160–67. Fielding draws implicit or explicit analogies between a hare and a sexually vulnerable woman at many points in *Tom Jones* (267, 305, 527–28, 550, 616, 622–23, 862, and 974).

16. Sherbo, "Fielding's Dogs," 302–3.

17. It is interesting that the Roasting-Squire's men are associated with explosives or firearms not only in their use of firecrackers in this scene with Adams, but in their obsessive concern with whether or not their opponents have firearms when they abduct Fanny (see 256–57 and 269).

18. For example, Belial replies to Satan's speech "in like gamesome mood,"

> Leader, the terms we sent were terms of weight,
> Of hard contents, and full of force urg'd home,
> Such as we might perceive amus'd them all,
> And stumbl'd many   (VI.620–24)

See also lines 558–67 and 576–78 of this book.

19. For example, in describing the final trick played on Adams by the "Ambassador" game, he reveals before the game has begun the way that the throne is constructed, dissipating any effect of dramatic surprise when Adams tumbles into the tub, but also, perhaps, avoiding a sense that his narrative plays out the trick on Adams itself (251). Also, he makes a point of asserting that he had to get the story of "this Part of our History" from a servant and that it is probably incomplete (246). He does not emphasize the fiction of information-collecting elsewhere, and the gesture here seems to me to work against owning that he has invented the practical jokes himself, or is in some sense a co-persecutor of Adams.

20. In *The Jacobite's Journal* Fielding would strengthen the connection he suggests here between irresponsible ridicule and the devil, quoting Robert South's warning that "Detraction," or verbal attack that fails to register the difference between good and evil, "is that poisonous Arrow, drawn out of the Devil's Quiver, which is always flying about and doing Execution in the Dark; against which no Virtue is a Defence, no Innocence a Security. It is a Weapon forged in Hell, and formed by that prime Artificer and Engineer, the Devil; and none but that Great God who knows all Things, and can do all Things, can protect THE BEST OF MEN against it" (308).

21. Paulson observes that in intending "to set up not an exaggerated image of what he detests" in *Joseph Andrews*, but rather "an alternative of his own," Fielding is careful to connect his new form with comedy, epic, and history, but never with satire, and that he must work especially to "dissociate himself from the particular kind of satire he had written a few years earlier in *Pasquin* and *The Historical Register* and more recently in *Shamela*" (*Satire and the Novel*, 108).

22. Samuel Johnson, "Life of Milton," 439–40.

23. Hagstrum suggests that the writers and readers of the eighteenth century "looked to the bower in Eden as a sanction and source of their dreams of marital bliss," and that the ideal of heterosexual friendship was nowhere "more powerfully and beautifully expressed than in the polemical prose and the great religious epic of Milton, who imprinted it on the consciousness of the eighteenth century" (38, 49; and see 155 on Milton's influence on Fielding's *Amelia* in particular). The ideal Milton expressed was distinguished by its emphasis both on the mutuality of such a bond and on the

centrality of sexuality to its feeling: Joseph Summers argues that "despite all the possible sources, the intensity of [Milton's] conviction that there could be no original paradise for man without sexual love seems personal and original" (99).

Chapter 4

1. Miller, 269; and Hunter, *Occasional Form*, 45. In "Tied Back to Back: The Discourse Between the Poet and Player and the Exhortations of Parson Adams in *Joseph Andrews*," Dianne Osland argues that a "moral stalemate" is created by the conjunction between chapters 11 and 12 of book 3.

2. Miller, 267–69 and 271. Battestin seems to me seriously to misrepresent the mood of *Joseph Andrews* when he overlooks its bitter and elegiac elements and emphatically declares it "the most cheerful of novels" (*Henry Fielding*, 331, 341).

3. Hunter observes that Fielding uses Shakespeare as a "touchstone for knowledge of human nature" in *Tom Jones*, and that he is "at one with his age in expressing such strong admiration" for Shakespeare, "especially in the specific area of psychological motivation and the reading of human character" (*Occasional Form*, 27). Given the special meaning of Shakespeare for Fielding, Joseph might be said to show not only good taste but an instinctive recognition of psychological depth when he chooses these lines, while Adams reveals a certain opacity both to human feeling and literary value when he rejects these lines as unfamiliar "stuff" and expresses his highest approval for Steele's *Conscious Lovers*.

4. Maurice Johnson qualifies Hunter's view, cited in note 3, by underlining this difference in contexts between Macduff's speech and Joseph's quotation of it. He argues that "Joseph wants to join Shakespeare in expressing the sublimity of terror. . . . But . . . if we compare Macduff's loss to that of Joseph, the whole structure of 'sublimity' crumbles. There is sublimity in Macduff's words in their proper context, but here the danger to Fanny is only ridiculously imagined by Joseph; she is quite unharmed after all. . . . But by associating himself with Shakespeare, Joseph dignifies himself above Adams" (68). The danger to Fanny does not seem to me so insubstantial; we will consider the nature of Joseph's terror more fully below.

5. Joseph compacts an exchange between Malcolm and Macduff into a single speech; and, though his recitation of the lines expresses some resistance to Adams's call for Christian submission, he alters the lines in several ways that assimilate them more fully into the context of Christian acceptance of Providence. He replaces Malcolm's demand that Macduff "dispute it like a man" with a promise to "bear it like a man," and he breaks off Macduff's speech before Macduff turns to question Heaven's justice: "Did Heaven look on, / And would not take their part?" (see *Macbeth*, IV.iii).

Note also that Joseph quotes from a play that not only in this passage but throughout has everything to do with a struggle to define proper manly and womanly responses.

6. From the *Champion* essay of April 22, 1740 (2: 128). See also the essays, referred to above, of December 20, 1739; April 8, 1740; and April 15, 1740 (1: 113, 2: 80–86, and 2: 107).

7. Fielding pauses over the name when he introduces him: "Mr. *Barnabas* (for that was the Clergyman's Name) came as soon as sent for" (58). On the meaning of the name, see its biblical context, Acts 4–13.

8. *The Royal Female Magazine*, p. vi. Other eighteenth-century sources quoted in Joseph Wittreich's *Feminist Milton* testify to the power of Milton's descriptions of Adam and Eve's relationship over eighteenth-century imaginations, and the influential but controversial place of *Paradise Lost* in discussions of sexuality and gender in the century that followed it.

9. At the same time, he again plays with Joseph's inadequacy as an epic hero, an inadequacy both social and literary, for Joseph's lack of proper ancestors prevents Fielding from fulfilling the epic convention of the review of the hero's genealogy.

10. See, for example, *Love in Several Masques*, *Pasquin*, and *Eurydice Hissed*.

11. "Of the Remedy of Affliction for the Loss of our Friends," *Miscellanies, Volume One*, 225. Fielding's interest in the sentimental wish for reunion in the afterlife appears in his satirical works as well. There, in a different mood, he punctures sentimental expectations by imagining death as a blessed relief from married union, and a reunion in the afterlife as a distressing surprise. See, for example, the puppet show in *The Author's Farce* and the central joke of his version of *Eurydice*.

In her discussion of *The Mysteries of Udolpho*, Terry Castle, citing Philippe Ariès's work on death, observes that the fantasy of reunion in the afterlife became much more predominant in late eighteenth- and early nineteenth-century popular belief than it had been in earlier times ("The Spectralization of the Other," 243–44). Fielding's interest in this fantasy, then, may express a much wider cultural interest in the promise of continuity between selves, and between life and death, which the fantasy offers. This cultural interest would be sustained and developed in the century following Fielding: Battestin tells us that "Dickens—who esteemed Fielding enough to name his son after him—twice recalled this scene [of reunion] from the *Journey* when comforting friends mourning the death of a child" (*Henry Fielding*, 341).

12. Book 1, chapter 8, *Miscellanies, Volume Two*, 36.

13. Watt, 273–76.

14. Marshall, *The Figure of Theater*, 236.

15. Hunter, *Occasional Form*, 69–70.

16. Paulson, *Satire and the Novel*, 147–48.

17. The word "melting" appears in Fielding's description of such a reunion in "A Journey From This World to the Next" and "Of the Remedy of Affliction for the Loss of our Friends." Entering Elysium in "A Journey From This World": "I presently met a little Daughter, whom I had lost several Years before. Good Gods! what Words can describe the Raptures, the melting passionate Tenderness, with which we kiss'd each other, continuing in our Embrace, with the most exstatic Joy, a Space, which if Time had been measured here as on Earth, could not be less than half a Year" (chapter 8, 36–37). Describing "the Hope of again meeting the beloved Person" in another world: "This is a Rapture which leaves the warmest Imagination at a Distance. *Who can conceive* (says *Sherlock*, in his Discourse on Death) *the melting Caresses of two Souls in Paradice?*" ("Of the Remedy," 225).

18. My information on this subject derives from G. S. Rousseau's suggestive essay, "Pineapples, Pregnancy, Pica, and *Peregrine Pickle*." The quoted phrase is from Blondel's *The Power of the Mother's Imagination Over the Foetus Examin'd*, published in 1729 (Rousseau, 90); and the observation that cravings for exotic fruits were cited most frequently as sources of birthmarks was made by Turner in his response to Blondel (Rousseau, 91).

19. Rousseau, 93.

20. Ibid., 84.

21. Phyllis Rackin has described the historical shift that took place in the course of the seventeenth century from "the high Renaissance image of the androgyne as a symbol of prelapsarian or mystical perfection" to "the satirical portrait of the hermaphrodite, a medical monstrosity or social misfit" (29). The role of the hermaphrodite in this medical controversy of the eighteenth century seems to be an extension of the trend she traces.

22. In leading up to "the birth of our hero" in *Jonathan Wild*, Fielding reports that, during her pregnancy with him, the great thief's mother's longings foretold her son's nature: "Another remarkable incident was, that during her whole pregnancy she constantly longed for everything she saw; nor could be satisfied with her wish unless she enjoyed it clandestinely; . . . so had she at this time a most marvellous glutinous quality attending her fingers, to which, as to birdlime, everything closely adhered that she handled" (45).

23. See *Slang and Its Analogues, Past and Present*, vol. 7. Farmer and Henley do not give a date for the first slang uses of the word, but they do cite a nineteenth-century example that suggests that the word was by then a clichéd expression for an identifying mole or birthmark:

c. 1866. Burnand and Sullivan. *Box and Cox*. Have you a STRAWBERRY MARK on your left arm? No! Then you are my long lost brother. (8)

24. Entry for Wednesday, June 26, 1754, *The Journal of a Voyage to Lisbon*, 43.

25. Fielding also gave gender to these alternative responses to part-ings and grief earlier in his life, after Charlotte's death. Writing James Har-ris, he concluded that "the present Situation" of his mind was "neither soured nor deprest; neither snarling like a Cynic nor blubbering like a Woman" (quoted in Battestin, *Henry Fielding*, 386).

26. In "Of the Remedy," he recalls the pain of his wife's labor in the context of the pain of mortal loss: "I remember the most excellent of Women, and tenderest of Mothers, when, after a painful and dangerous De-livery, she was told she had a Daughter, answering; *Good God! have I pro-duced a Creature who is to undergo what I have suffered!* Some Years afterwards, I heard the same Woman, on the Death of that very Child, then one of the loveliest Creatures ever seen, comforting herself with reflecting, that, *her Child could never know what it was to feel such a Loss as she then lamented.* In Reality, she was right in both instances" (224).

27. "Before addressing larger problems of the relationship of fiction to truth (however it is defined), one might note the curious fact that even within their own respective systems of reference the titles [*The History of the Adventures of Joseph Andrews* and *The History of Tom Jones, a Foundling*] are superficially fictional or fictitious—that is to say, they are erroneous. What the reader learns along with the protagonists at the unraveling of the nar-rative riddle is among other things the answer to a riddle not even suspected. Joseph Andrews' name is not properly Andrews and Tom's name should not be Jones. On the other hand, if the novels' titles had given the 'true' name of their protagonists, the 'story' would have been 'spoiled'. . . . In neither case does the narrator or Fielding call attention to those rather obvious facts" (Homer Obed Brown, 202).

28. Both *Pamela* and *Clarissa* also acknowledge the symbolic signif-icance of a woman's adoption of her husband's name upon marriage. That identity which Pamela has sustained and "composed" for herself against all external pressures through the act of writing she surrenders, along with her name and her pen, when she confesses herself uncertain how to sign herself after marrying Mr. B.: "He then took a Pen himself, and wrote, after *Pam-ela*, his most worthy Surname; and I under-wrote thus: 'O rejoice with me, my dear Mrs. *Jervis*, that I am enabled, by God's Graciousness, and my dear Master's Goodness, thus to write myself' " (303).

29. Homer Obed Brown's notion of the slippage of genealogical into accidental or "metonymic" causality in *Tom Jones* is relevant and illuminat-ing here.

30. See Cixous, "Castration or Decapitation?" and "The Laugh of the Medusa" on these distinctions.

31. She reminds Adams that "it behoved every Man to take the first Care of his Family; that he had a Wife and six Children, the maintaining and providing for whom would be Business enough for him without intermed-dling in other Folks Affairs" (306); and she tells Lady Booby, "he talks a pack

of Nonsense, that the whole Parish are his Children. I am sure I don't understand what he means by it; it would make some Women suspect he had gone astray: but I acquit him of that; I can read Scripture as well as he; and I never found that the Parson was obliged to provide for other Folks Children" (321–22).

32. The strangely mechanical nature of Shamela's desires is observed and effectively described by Rothstein.

33. Judith Frank's "Chance Hits the Mark: Exchange and the Gift in *Joseph Andrews*" (symposium paper, Cornell University, 1985) develops this aspect of *Joseph Andrews*'s economy much more fully. I am indebted to her for sharing her fine insights into *Joseph Andrews*.

Part 3

1. Hutchens, "O Attic Shape!" 37–44.

2. In "The Mitigated Truth: Tom Jones's Double Heroism," Carlton develops an extended reading of Tom's character; and he offers a briefer but related account of Sophia's character in "*Tom Jones* and the '45 Once Again."

3. In addition to Carlton's essays, see Battestin, "Tom Jones and 'His Egyptian Majesty'"; H. O. Brown; Cleary; L. J. Davis; Golden; Hunter, *Occasional Form*; Kearney; and Paulson, *Popular and Polite Art*.

4. Carlton makes this argument especially effectively ("*Tom Jones*," 365–68); H. O. Brown traces a similar connection (220–22).

5. Not only is the company Tom joins characterized by insubordination, unruly behavior, and cynicism about the Protestant cause, but its members' names and nationalities might seem to link them to support for the rebels rather than for the government: Northerton's name echoes the common phrase "the rebellion in the north"; another soldier is named Tom French; and one lieutenant actually is French, and has never really mastered the English language, though he leads a contingent of England's army.

6. As noted by Carlton, "*Tom Jones*," 365–69.

7. Ibid., 369; Carlton, "Mitigated Truth," 407.

8. Lawrence Stone has traced the gradual replacement of the arranged marriage with the ideal of "companionate marriage" in eighteenth-century England; and Henry Abelove offers the provocative argument that, in the course of "the long eighteenth century" in England, "sexual intercourse so-called becomes . . . discursively and phenomenologically central in ways that it had never been before," while "nonreproductive sexual behaviors come under extraordinary negative pressure" in a new way (125–30).

Chapter 5

1. *The Female Rebels*, 6–8. Page numbers for all further references to this pamphlet will be given parenthetically in the text; the pages following

36 in the pamphlet are misnumbered, repeating page numbers 33 to 36, and I will refer to them as 33a, 34a, etc.

2. Writing primarily of the fifteenth through seventeenth centuries in England and France, Natalie Zemon Davis reports that "the female sex was thought the disorderly one par excellence in early modern Europe"; that women were regarded as disobedient and subject to uncontrollable bodily passions; and that they were defined, therefore, "as the lustier sex" (124–51). Ian Watt describes the emergence of a "new sexual ideology" in the mid-eighteenth century, in which this traditional idea of female nature is replaced by a new "feminine" ideal emphasizing women's "immunity from sexual feelings," their bodily weakness, their verbal purity, and their passivity. "The conception of sex we find in Richardson," he concludes, "embodies a more complete and comprehensive separation between the male and female roles than had previously existed" (*The Rise of the Novel*, 160–64).

3. I use the term "Whig" throughout in a general and inclusive fashion, rather than to indicate precise political alignments and platforms. In the context of the Jacobite movement of the 1740's, the term often serves primarily to denote a political position opposed to Jacobitism; but I also assume that it suggests support of the 1688 revolution, of a Lockean notion of limited kingship and constitutional monarchy, and, more broadly, of the new economic order of early- and mid-eighteenth-century England.

4. I here describe not the culture, economy, and politics of the Highlands themselves in the 1740's, but the contemporary Whig view of them. See Lenman, chapter 6, for a more complex picture of Highland economy and society in this period.

5. As Carlton notes, by 1745 Charles Edward Stuart had in fact renounced the principle of absolute monarchy ("*Tom Jones*," 366), but the debate between Jacobite sympathizers and their opponents in England continued to be cast in terms of support for or rejection of this principle.

6. Lenman notes at one point that "female Jacobite supporters like Mrs. Robertson of Lude, a spitfire daughter of the House of Nairne, could be as ruthless in forcing men out as their male counterparts" (257), but he otherwise does not mention any involvement of women in the progress of the '45. The Duchess of Perth and Lady Ogilvy, for example, crucial participants in the rebellion according to the author of *The Female Rebels*, do not appear in Lenman's index.

7. Stephens, in *The Catalogue of Political and Personal Satires Preserved in the Department of Prints and Drawings in the British Museum*, identifies two of the women as Lady Murray (#8) and Lady Ogilvy (#7) but comments, "These incidents are fictitious" (entry 2788).

8. *Old England, or The Constitutional Journal* reprints the item from *The London Gazette* in no. 139, Dec. 2, 1745, as does *The History of the Rebellion in the Years 1745 and 1746*.

9. *The History of the Rebellion in the Years 1745 and 1746*, 38–39, 106, 175, 194, 228–29, 268; *The History of the Rise, Progress, and Extinction of the Rebellion*, 155–57; Ray, *A Compleat History of the Rebellion*, 22–32, 268, 290, 304.

10. Fielding, *The Jacobite's Journal*, 97–103. Further references to the journal will be by page number in the Wesleyan edition and will appear parenthetically in the text.

Trott-Plaid returns to the subject of female Jacobites in numbers 5, 6, 12, 13, 34, and 38 of his journal.

11. Monod provides a fascinating account both of the Stuart kings' deliberate efforts to represent themselves as virile sun-kings and of the popular practices (such as May-Day rites) that enacted an identification between Stuart rule, fertility, and sharply defined sexual roles (55–69, 74–80, 202–6).

12. This observation, confirmed by my study of prints and pamphlets, was first suggested to me by W. B. Coley.

13. *Old England*, for example, refers to him as "the beardless Wanderer" (no. 143, Jan. 18, 1746); and a letter in a female persona to *The Daily Gazetteer* contrasts the Prince's cowardice with the Duke's bravery, saying that she "should despise the run-away young Pretender, tho' he was beautiful as an Angel" (no. 42, Oct. 18, 1746, collected in *The Fool*, vol. 1, 300). See also the print "Scotch Female Gallantry," which centers on a feminized image of Prince Charles (Fig. 17).

There is also some play in anti-Jacobite essays on Prince Charles—and Highland men in general—wearing skirts rather than breeches (see, for example, *The Jacobite's Journal*, no. 38, 372, and the epigraph to no. 6, 121); but the association of the kilt with a masculine, severe, and warfaring culture was not easily overcome, as acknowledged in the outlawing of kilts after the rebellion.

14. This print appears on the cover of Monod's *Jacobitism and the English People*, and is discussed by him in the context of Jacobite prints and popular practices that emphasize the Stuart kings' masculinity.

15. See also "The Beautifull Simon" (BM 2792) for another print depicting Lord Lovat in female disguise.

16. Graeme describes a number of the Whig prints and publications centered on the figure of Jenny Cameron. He argues that although several historical Jean Camerons can be found in the period of the 1745 rebellion, none of them provides any basis for the Whig stories of her exploits.

17. *The Anarchy of a Limited or Mixed Monarchy*, in Filmer, 283. Filmer's *Patriarcha* provides one usefully extreme expression of the "patriarchalist" views associated with the Stuart cause; and Locke's *Two Treatises of Government*, framed as a refutation of Filmer, represents the most famous defense of the 1688 Revolution. I therefore use the writings of Locke and Filmer as reference points in my discussion of alternative political philos-

ophies, though I recognize that the views they express are not always those of all the participants on either side of this extended and complex debate.

18. Lawrence Stone quotes Lady Brute in Vanbrugh's *The Provoked Wife* (1697), as well as Mary Chudleigh (1701), Bishop Fleetwood (1705), Mary Astell (1706), and Bernard Mandeville (1724), on this connection between theories of the state and of the family (240). Mary Astell's position is a particularly complicated one, since she uses an insistence on the logical consistency between the acceptance of absolute sovereignty in the state and in the family to defend both Jacobitism and feminism; see Perry, 150–80, on Astell's negotiation of these matters.

Melissa A. Butler discusses the responses of both contractualists and anticontractualists to the connection in her essay on John Locke and feminism.

19. We might also note that Western's niece, Mrs. Fitzpatrick, who has defied first her guardians by marrying without their consent and then her husband by running away from him, and who speaks of the superiority of women's understanding, has passed the time during her lonely marriage reading Locke and Chillingworth, a religious writer whom Locke commends (597; on Locke's commendation of Chillingworth, see the Norton *Tom Jones*, 456n).

20. Stone observes that "the most direct and explicit link between political theory and family life occurs in John Locke's *Two Treatises of Government*," and he describes the "incompatibility of domestic patriarchy with the political theory of contractual obligation" as "glaring" (239–40); Melissa Butler comments, "if the 'natural freedom' of mankind was to be taken seriously, obviously the natural freedom of women and children would have to be considered." She concludes that "Locke was a part of a shifting collective consciousness which made the sexual revolution a possibility" (140, 149). See Pateman for an important dissenting view; she argues that the "sexual contract," which subordinates women, is not incidental but in fact *essential* to the formulation of the "political contract," which affirms the fraternal equality of men.

21. As Schochet, 72.

22. *Patriarcha Non Monarcha* (London, 1681), 83; quoted by Melissa Butler, 139.

23. Melissa Butler, 139 and 141. Stone gives a similar account of these contradictory aims, though he emphasizes less the extent to which women absorbed the brunt of the conflict. He calls Locke's account of marriage in terms of a voluntary contract "radical," but says that Locke "covered himself on the political front" by supplementing this account with an assertion that the basis of family relations should not, in any case, be assumed to have any direct bearing on the nature of political ones. He adds that Locke's arguments about marriage nonetheless "posed a real problem for political Whigs anxious to maintain paternal authority in the home, and they helped

to undermine the psychological, although not the legal, foundation of domestic patriarchy in England" (265–66).

24. *Jure Divino* (London, 1707), 7 and 14; quoted in Schochet, 217.

25. Schochet discusses the historic importance of this new distinction between "political and social realms" or "state and society," although he treats the change throughout as a simple and clear advance in the objective analysis of human experience rather than as an ideological development with complicated consequences of its own (see, for example, 55). Eli Zaretsky locates this new distinction within the historic development of capitalism.

26. Allworthy's praise of Sophia, which he says he can express only through the use of "Negatives," is structured in something of the same way. He commends Sophia's lack of pretense to any engagement with various realms of masculine authority (wit, wisdom, learning); and he recalls how she passed a test he devised for her, in which he asked her to give her opinion on a point argued between Thwackum and Square, by saying she could not possibly hold an opinion on either side (882–83).

27. See note 2 above on Davis and Watt, as well as Armstrong's discussion of the new feminine ideal advanced by eighteenth- and nineteenth-century domestic novels.

28. Charles's disguise as "Betty Burke" was to become a particularly popular part of mythology about the rebellion, both among Jacobite sympathizers and among their opponents. It was memorialized at the time in several prints depicting him in this disguise (see Fig. 15) and recalled seventy years later in Scott's *Waverley*. In 1748, a Scottish manufacturer even produced "Betty Burke's gowns," modeled on the dress assumed by Charles in hiding, but to be worn, of course, by female sympathizers rather than by men (Monod, 289). The "Betty Burke gown" promoted a tacit, purely allusive form of cross-dressing for would-be "female rebels" after the rebellion—its wearer was a woman dressed as a man dressed as a woman—and this form of cross-cross-dressing located the appeal and significance of Charles's cause within the aesthetic and commercial arena of feminine fashion, where it could safely circulate and be consumed.

29. Other treatments of Jenny Cameron also dwell upon the confused erotics of her encounters with both men and women as she travels about in male dress during and after the rebellion. See, for example, the history of Jenny Cameron published in *The Daily Gazetteer*, no. 49, Nov. 10, 1746 (reprinted in *The Fool*, 346–53).

Chapter 6

1. See, for example, *The History of the Present Rebellion*, 73, and *The True Patriot*, 282–83, both in *The True Patriot and Related Writings*.

2. And Peter J. Carlton identifies this member of the King's army

with the "Cavalier" code of heroism linked to the Jacobite cause his army will oppose ("The Mitigated Truth," 406).

3. My view here obviously departs from that of critics such as Martin C. Battestin and Peter J. Carlton who treat Fielding's support in *Tom Jones* for the virtue of prudent self-interest and for Whig political principles as unequivocal (see notes 20 and 21 to this chapter).

4. As Carlton notes ("*Tom Jones*," 369), Ronald Paulson and Anthony Kearney have identified Tom with the figure of Prince Charles, while Morris Golden instead links Tom with the Pretender's opponent, the Duke of Cumberland (Paulson, "The '45 and Bonnie Prince Charlie" in *Popular and Polite Art*, 204; Kearney, 74; Golden, 287–88).

5. Armstrong, *Desire and Domestic Fiction*, 9 and 21.

6. Ovid, *Metamorphoses*, X.215.

7. And Battestin notes that (at least according to Pope) the men guarding Atterbury when he was imprisoned in the Tower suspected that he really might receive intelligence enclosed within his food, and so searched the pigeons carried in to him to eat (843 n. 3). If Fielding intended any reference to this precedent within the episode, that reference would link Sophia's incarceration to that of a male political prisoner.

8. We might recall that in *Joseph Andrews*, beds appear as places where gender identity is especially fluid, where a child of one sex may be exchanged for a child of the other, or a beau mistaken for a woman and a matron for a man.

9. Early in the novel, for instance, at a moment when Tom and Sophia are particularly linked, as a surgeon operates on the arm of each, a Shakespearean allusion suggests that the exact nature of Tom's gender remains in a state of suspense. At least in this moment of empathy between Tom and his female love, he can be passingly identified with Viola, the heroine of *Twelfth Night* who only appears to be a boy; Tom, we are told, "sat like Patience on a Monument smiling at Grief" (204).

10. See Hagstrum (179), Veeder (31–34), and Carlton ("Mitigated Truth," 397).

11. He imagines it as one great body divided into many parts, to be cooked and arrayed in the widest variety of sauces and seasonings before being consumed (31–34).

12. See notes to this passage in both the Norton and the Wesleyan editions of *Tom Jones*.

13. This kind of incongruity provides the comedy of some of Fielding's burlesque drama—for example, in *Tumble-Down Dick*—as well as the humor of other mock-epic moments in his novels and essays.

14. See also Fielding's more emphatic and cynical statement of this idea in *Jonathan Wild* when he describes government as a puppet show directed from backstage by a hidden "great man." No one in the audience, he says, "is ignorant of his being there, or supposes that the puppets are not

mere sticks of wood, and he himself the sole mover; but as this (though every one knows it) doth not appear visibly, *i.e.* to their eyes, no one is ashamed of consenting to be imposed upon" (III.xi).

15. I adopt the concept of "residual," "emergent," and "dominant" cultures from Raymond Williams's "Base and Superstructure in Marxist Cultural Theory," *Problems in Materialism and Culture*, 40–42.

16. Sophia's conversation with Honour in this scene (book 7, chapter 7) has specific parallels with the conversation between Julia and her maid Lucetta in *Two Gentlemen of Verona*, II.vii; and see also the discussion of the plan to run away between Rosalind and Celia in I.iii of *As You Like It*. Sophia's bold venture out into the world to protect her love for Tom from parental intervention might also be placed in the context of the "Female Warrior" plots which Dugaw has shown to be of persistent interest in this period. These plots most characteristically involve women dressing as men. Furthermore, the Duchess of Mazarin, with whom Fielding earlier compared Sophia (156), was reputed to have escaped from the control of her tyrannical husband disguised in male clothes.

17. As noted in Chapter 5 (n. 2), the phrase "women on top" has been used by Natalie Zemon Davis to evoke an older set of cultural expectations about female nature—expectations that centered on woman's natural lust and urge for disorder. Scheuermann alludes to this older set of expectations about female nature when she comments on the passage about Sophia's "Bravery": "Where has the idea of fierceness come from in this passage? . . . The idea comes from an underlying stereotype of the Amazon" (239).

18. Carlton, "*Tom Jones*," 369.

19. Ibid., 361, 369, 371.

20. Carlton says that "Locke's first law of nature [that of self-interest] prepares us to understand Sophia's role in the novel's political allegory," and glosses her declaration to her aunt that marriage to Blifil "is the only Instance in which I must disobey both yourself and my Father" with the comment, "Sophia speaks here like a good Lockean: to obey her father and marry the despicable Blifil would mean violating the first law of nature" ("*Tom Jones*," 367). But this comment evades the question of why it is only in this particular instance, faced with competing models of romantic and arranged marriage, that Sophia's "self-interest" must triumph over her generally self-sacrificing spirit of obedience to her father; and motives of self-interest are treated with such suspicion and irony throughout *Tom Jones* that it makes one uneasy to explain its heroine's decision simply in their terms.

Carlton's treatment of the tavern discussion of the Jacobite revolt (366) seems to me strained in something of the same way: Fielding's satire suggests not simply that the participants in this discussion speak from *mistaken* views of their personal self-interest, but that they should not be debating a cause of national significance in such terms at all.

21. Although Battestin confidently asserts early in *Henry Fielding*

that Fielding "was unshakable in his principles as a good Whig of the sound Lockean stamp" (115), he later complicates his picture of Fielding's political roots and influences. He reiterates that Fielding "was a staunch Whig in politics," but adds: "his idea of the social order was drawn, as the Preface to the *Enquiry* makes clear, from much older sources—from Plato and the 'Greek Philosophy,' and, closer to home, from 'the Constitutions of *Alfred*,' whom Bolingbroke (and hence Lyttelton and Dodington) romanticized as Britain's most enlightened king. . . . Fielding was profoundly conservative as a social thinker. Indeed, as M. R. Zirker concludes in the most authoritative study of the subject, he 'accepted unquestioningly a hierarchical, static society nearly feudal in some of its outlines'" (514).

Battestin thus observes the incoherence, the irreducible multiplicity of orientations, within Fielding's thought, a multiplicity that cannot be dissolved by any artificial distinction between "political" and "social" visions.

22. Both historians and literary critics have argued that a struggle between the ideologies of arranged and of companionate marriages is central to the plot of *Tom Jones*. Stone writes, "In *Tom Jones* . . . Fielding set out the two views of marriage, the old and the new. . . . In this novel Fielding presents somewhat ideal stereotypes of the two extremes in attitudes to marriage, and the plot revolves around the clash between the two" (279); see also Carlton, "*Tom Jones*," 365–68; and Scheuermann, 249–54.

23. In the opening pages of "The Eighteenth Brumaire of Louis Bonaparte," Karl Marx makes famous use of images of ghosts to describe the past's presence within the present, or the way that "the tradition of all the dead generations weighs like a nightmare on the brain of the living." As "The Eighteenth Brumaire" goes forward, these images are employed variously, to express a range of contrasting effects with which the rhetoric, the institutions, the ideals, the ideas, of the past may be conjured or may appear unbidden within the dynamic unfolding of present conflicts. In particular, Marx contrasts the functions of the past-made-present in the French revolutions of 1789–1814 and of 1848–51: the "awakening of the dead" in the earlier revolutionary period "served the purpose of glorifying the new struggles, not of parodying the old; of magnifying the given task in imagination, not of fleeing its solution in reality" (97–98).

In focusing on *Tom Jones*'s "ghosting hours," I mean to recall Marx's resonant use of these images, but not to locate the nature of the "ghostly revivals" depicted by Fielding within the specifics of Marx's argument.

24. See Natalie Zemon Davis, 126.

25. Carlton, "Mitigated Truth," 404.

26. See *The English Hero*, ed. Folkenflik, for several relevant essays on changing models of male heroism in the eighteenth century, including J. Paul Hunter's "Fielding and the Disappearance of Heroes" (116–42).

27. Carlton, "Mitigated Truth," 406.

28. *Dictionary of National Biography*, 428–30. Ironically, Fielding's

paper-war enemy, Samuel Foote, turned Swift's contemptuous device on Fielding himself in April 1748, announcing in *The Daily Advertiser* that the real Henry Fielding, author of *Joseph Andrews*, was long since dead (Battestin, *Henry Fielding*, 437–38).

29. Battestin comments on Fielding's identification with and emulation of Swift at a number of points in *Henry Fielding*, saying at one that Swift was a man "whose works [Fielding] admired and delighted in more than those of any other contemporary author" (405; see also 274, 276, 396, 514, 544, 555, 559). In Fielding's obituary for Swift in *The True Patriot* (November 5, 1745) he calls him "a genius who deserves to be ranked among the first whom the World ever saw" (quoted in *Henry Fielding*, 405).

30. Battestin, *Henry Fielding*, 441, 451.

31. See, for instance, *A Dialogue between a Gentleman of London . . . and an Honest Alderman*, in *Jacobite's Journal*, 47. The threat was real: as Coley notes, the Jacobite invasion spawned the near-panic of "Black Friday" (December 6, 1745). The bank's notes fell to a discount; a run began; and later in December, the Bank's directors felt compelled to call in 20 percent from those who had subscribed to the last subscription (47 n. 2; and see Clapham, *The Bank of England*, vol. 1, 233–34).

Thompson places the loss and recovery of Sophia's bank-note in a more general historical context, focusing not on the particular crisis in credit precipitated by the Jacobite rebellion, but on the gradual and uneven evolution of monetary systems in eighteenth-century England and on the anxiety that that evolution provoked. He argues that through the workings of *Tom Jones*'s "monetary subplot," "Fielding domesticates cash transactions and commodities by inscribing them in a traditionally fixed, hierarchical (and agricultural) economy, where real property is the essential model for all other types of property, especially currency" (23). I find his argument very suggestive, but I believe that the specific confrontation between political positions represented by the Jacobite revolt complicates his picture of Fielding as a spokesperson for straightforwardly "conservative desires."

32. In *The True Patriot and Related Writings*, 72–73. See also British Museum print 2686, which presents "Publick Credit" threatened by "Popery."

33. Suggestively, Fielding allows Allworthy to recognize and recover his own lost bank-bills from Black George only when he meets with Nightingale in an effort to advance the cause of companionate over arranged marriage (920–21).

Chapter 7

1. Relevant passages in Filmer and Locke (whom I again take as merely representative figures in this widespread debate) include: Filmer, *Patriarcha*, 77; "Observations on Mr. Hobbes's *Leviathan*," 245; and *The An-*

archy of a Limited or Mixed Monarchy, 287 (all in *Patriarcha and Other Political Works*); and Locke, 166, 212, 322, 329, 331.

In *Anarchy*, for example, Filmer argues, "where subjection of children to parents is natural, there can be no natural freedom. If any reply, that not all children shall be bound by their parents' consent, but only those that are under age: it must be considered, that in nature there is no *nonage*; if a man be not born free, she doth not assign him any other time when he shall attain his freedom" (287). Similarly, in *Patriarcha*, he grumbles that "Suarez . . . saith that 'Adam had fatherly power over his sons whilst they were not made free.' Here I could wish that the Jesuit had taught us how and when sons become free. I know no means by the law of nature" (77).

In "Of Paternal Power," Locke comments specifically on the temporary nature of a tutor's authority when he says, "Some other must govern [a son], and be a Will to him, till he hath *attained to a state of Freedom*, and his Understanding be fit to take the Government of his Will. But after that, the Father and Son are equally *free* as much as Tutor and Pupil after Nonage; equally Subjects of the same Law together, without any Dominion left in the Father" (*Second Treatise*, chapter 7, para. 59).

Fielding makes his own position on this issue explicit, *Jacobite's Journal*, 316.

2. Although he here speaks of his own authority as schoolmaster rather than as parent, Thwackum later emphasizes his allegiance to a patriarchalist view of a father's absolute right to obedience (859); Fielding strengthens the connections between schoolmasters, fathers, and inflated claims to power when he equates the voice of a schoolmaster with that of a tyrant (601).

3. *The Oxford English Dictionary* confirms that "the hinder parts of the body; the buttocks" was one available meaning for the term "posteriors" in the eighteenth century. Indeed, the first example it provides for such a usage involves the same context as Fielding's pun: "A poor pedantick schoolmaster, sweeping his living from the posteriors of little children" (1619).

4. Eve Kosofsky Sedgwick argues that such interconnections of heterosexual arrangements, homoerotic or "homosocial" bonds, and institutions of property and language are in fact structurally central in English culture and literature; see her *Between Men: English Literature and Male Homosocial Desire*.

5. See Partridge, *Dictionary of Slang*, who dates the first use of "Roger" as a term for the penis around 1650; and Farmer and Henley, vol. 6.

6. See the Norton *Tom Jones*, ed. Baker, 201 n. 1, and Frederick W. Hilles's "Art and Artifice in *Tom Jones*," reprinted in that edition, 928–29; also Battestin, *Tom Jones*, 263 n. 1.

7. See above, 31–32.

8. *The First Treatise*, 141 (book 1, chapter 1, para. 1).

9. In *The Jacobite's Journal*, see 203, 285–86, 296, 340, 344, 357. The rhetoric is pervasive in other anti-Jacobite writings. One example among a great number: the author of *Old England, or The Constitutional Journal* asks why Englishmen would want to exchange pure religion and liberty for "Idolatry" and "Slavery" under the Pretender (no. 129; Oct. 5, 1745).

10. See *The Jacobite's Journal*, 246–48, 248–49, 256–61, 270–71, 299–300. Kropf discusses Fielding's sustained concern with educational theories and the general influence of Locke's educational writings on him.

11. Stone, 217, and Locke quoted from *Educational Writings of John Locke* in Stone, 440–41.

12. Early in *Tom Jones*, Tom vows that he will never make Thwackum "any other Answer than with a Cudgel, with which he hoped soon to be able to pay him for all his Barbarities" (142); later, when he hears how irreverent the King's soldiers are in speaking of their officers, it makes him think of "the Custom which he had read of among the *Greeks* and *Romans*, of indulging, on certain Festivals and solemn Occasions, the Liberty to Slaves, of using an uncontrouled Freedom of Speech towards their Masters" (369).

The horror expressed in *The Jacobite's Journal*, as in other Whig writings, at the Tory mobs' horsewhipping of the Duke of Bedford also seems to express a fear that physical discipline may be used to overturn social order as well as to enforce it. See below on this incident, and on the connection Fielding suggests between the mobs' verbal and physical abuses of "their Betters."

13. Fielding had expressed anti-Semitism in a different context in his early satires of Jewish stockjobbers and usurers (noted in Battestin, *Henry Fielding*, 528).

14. Shadwell, II.ii; quoted in Stone, with other examples, 440 and 732 n. 92.

15. *The Children's Petition* (London, 1669), quoted in Stone, 439–40.

16. See *The Jacobite's Journal*, 116, 126, 173–76, 210, 372–74, 384, 391, 396. Suggestively, Fielding had portrayed *himself* as a badly fed ass, pulling the cart of the Opposition's political aspirations, in *The Opposition: A Vision* (1741).

17. A number of eighteenth-century graphic satires use images of the exposed male buttocks to ridicule their political opponents. Most of these satires, at least during Walpole's era, are directed against the new Whig order rather than against Tories or suspected Jacobites (see note 19). A print late in the century, "Progress of a Scotsman" (1794), jokes in particular about Highland dress by depicting a Scotsman in a kilt with his bare rear end exposed beneath it (Lewis Walpole Library).

18. Whereas Fielding here identifies the conventions of satire themselves with castration, he had earlier used metaphors of castration to de-

scribe the *censorship* or restraint of satire. In his anonymous *Some Thoughts on the Present State of the Theatres*, he complained about managers' anxious editing of authors' plays, saying that "this Caution has (to my Knowledge) struck out many beautiful and justifiable Strokes of Satire, from some Performances which have been, after Castration, exhibited"; in an essay for *The Craftsman* (July 2, 1737), he argues that government paranoia may require managers to subject even classic works in repertory to "considerable Castrations and Amendments" before they can be performed (quoted in Battestin, *Henry Fielding*, 218, 236).

19. Though insinuations of homoeroticism or of specifically anal eroticism had a special force when directed against Lord Hervey, graphic satires of Walpole's ministry (or of the Whig "conspiracy" of bribes and favors more generally) frequently centered on images of exposed male buttocks. In the one essay involving an illustration in Fielding and Ralph's collected *Champion*, Fielding describes a device by which a minister may interpose himself between the king and the people; the graphic illustration of this device depicts the people bringing their petitions for the king to the gigantic bare rear end of the effigy in which the minister sits (May 31, 1740, 2: 282).

"Idol-worship or the way to preferment" (1740) also depicts Walpole from behind, pulling his pants down and with his legs forming an archway through which political aspirants—after doing him proper homage—may pass; the famous "Festival of the Golden Rump" (1737) gives us a view of King George as a naked satyr on a pedestal, seen from behind, with Queen Caroline and Walpole apparently administering a ceremonial enema to his prominent buttocks. Other prints use visual puns on the political terms "the Broad-bottom Coalition" or a "rump" parliament to debunk politics' claims to dignity (see British Museum catalog [ed. Stephens], entries 2613, 2621, 2797).

See also my discussion of both verbal and visual depictions of Lord Hervey in "Politics and Sexuality in Portraits of John, Lord Hervey."

20. See Coley's introduction to *The Jacobite's Journal*, liii and liii n. 4.

21. Similarly, in *The Covent-Garden Journal* (as in the *Enquiry*), Fielding complains that the mob has appropriated the force of mock-epic and farcical forms, turning them to their own insurrectionary ends, making the hangings at Tyburn, for example, into festivals of bold defiance of government authority (March 28, 1752, and July 18, 1752; discussed in Battestin, *Henry Fielding*, 547–48).

22. The most famous piece of commendation offered in *The Jacobite's Journal* is a letter praising *Clarissa*, the second work of a writer whose first novel Fielding had so mercilessly satirized. But this praise is not entirely unqualified: Fielding subtly ironizes the letter-writer when he makes him begin (within the politically alarmist pages of the *Journal*) by confessing that he knows nothing of politics, and sanguinely enjoys his fortune "without

any Apprehensions" of unrest or rebellion (119). In *Tom Jones*, Fielding seeks to create a form that will combine an explicit political agenda with the "deep Penetration into Nature," the imaginative "Power to raise and alarm the Passions," for which his correspondent praises Richardson.

Chapter 8

1. The recovery of Amelia's inheritance and the events leading up to it occupy only about 20 pages in a 530-page work, and they depend very little on anything that precedes them in the long train of events occupying the rest of the book.

2. I here follow Nancy Armstrong's lead in *Desire and Domestic Fiction*, where she argues that "the domestic novel antedated—was indeed necessarily antecedent to—the way of life it represented" and that "domestic fiction helped to produce a subject who understood herself in the psychological terms that had shaped fiction" (9, 23).

Traditionally, while the delicate and decarnalized "new woman" described by Watt has been seen as emerging in the eighteenth century, the full-blown domestic heroine, presiding as the "angel of the house" both in life and in literary works, has appeared as a distinctively *Victorian* figure. Recent work on this late-eighteenth-century and nineteenth-century paradigm by Mary Poovey and others has greatly deepened our sense of her ideological functions and contradictions (see Poovey's *The Proper Lady* and *Uneven Developments*). Vivien Jones, on the other hand, sees the "dominant ideology of middle-class femininity" as already established early in the eighteenth century and as remaining, "in its essential features . . . fairly constant throughout the period" (7).

3. As noticed by Battestin in "The Problem of *Amelia*" (630–31). In "The Prison and the Dark Beauty of *Amelia*," Peter LePage argues that the prison provides the "unifying symbol" of *Amelia*, linked as it is to the other forms of confinement that so dominate Booth's experience in London.

4. James Nelson, for example, argued in 1756 for the importance of constant maternal attention and affection, and for the advantages of breast-feeding by a child's own mother, but he commented that he was not "insensible how little Probability there is that my Advice herein will be follow'd by Persons in high Life" (*An Essay on the Government of Children*, 47–50). See Stone, 269–73. Hill's *On the Management and Education of Children* will be discussed below.

5. Rawson, 93–94.

6. In an unpublished essay, "Mysteries of Conduct: Gender and Narrative Structure in Fielding's *Amelia*," Andrew Elfenbein argues that this scene may be viewed as "Fielding's fantasy of revenge on the masculine woman" (30). I am grateful to Mr. Elfenbein for sharing this essay with me in manuscript.

7. Rawson, 93–94.

8. Most famously—and most elaborately—developed and exploited, of course, in *Tristram Shandy*, the first volumes of which appeared in the same decade as *Amelia*.

9. Samuel Foote linked Amelia's injured nose to sexual license when he appended a frontispiece to his comedy *Taste*, which depicted the bust of Praxiteles' Venus of Paphos without a nose; as did Smollett when he described Fielding, riding an ass, as approaching "a draggle-tailed Bunter, who had lost her Nose in the Exercise of her Occupation" and addressing her as "the adorable *Amelia*" (cited in Battestin, *Henry Fielding*, 534–35).

10. See Battestin's introduction to *Amelia*, xvi–xxi, and his *Henry Fielding*, 540–51 (also 146, 254, 288).

11. In a very interesting discussion of the problem of fathers in Fielding's fiction, Sitter comments that, in general, "Fielding's fathers are relics. Much of the time they are venerable relics, whose lack of contact with modernity is part of their Edenic charm; but finally they remain ancestral antiques, representatives of another era whose function in this one is questionable and whose quaintness is unmistakeable" (*Literary Loneliness*, 199). He goes on to note that in *Amelia*, specifically, Fielding incorporates elements from his father's as well as his own life into the character of Booth; and proposes that this contributes to the "problems of attitude and tone" in that novel (200).

Cruise observes more generally that in many early eighteenth-century novels "fathers fail to prosper or are completely absent." He interprets this narrative pattern in the context of Locke's successful refutation of Filmer's *Patriarcha* and the new structures of authority that came to predominate in this period. "The government of fathers," as he puts it, ". . . had yielded to the government of sons." Though his discussion centers on *Joseph Andrews*, he comments that "in *Amelia*, Fielding's reliance on a weakened narrator may be read as a concession to anti-patriarchalism" (253–55). I find his discussion extremely suggestive; and I agree with his sense that, within any sharp opposition between "patriarchalism" and "commercialism," Fielding's position can only be described as a compromised one. To the extent, however, that Cruise identifies Fielding with a political position of "patriarchalism," compromised only by an unwilling implication in "commercial ideology," I feel that Fielding's active opposition to Jacobite ideology strains the terms of his characterization (256).

12. Battestin, *Henry Fielding*, 94, 97–98, 177–78.

13. This feature of the novel has been emphasized and illuminated for me both by Andrew Elfenbein's "Mysteries of Conduct" and by conversations with Barbara M. Benedict. I do not agree with Rogers that in the marriage of the Booths, "apparently with no sense of incongruity, Fielding pairs a perfect woman with a weak, self-indulgent man" (258).

14. It is striking, for example, that in the chapter entitled "The His-

tory of Mr. Trent," we are given more information about this minor character's family and past life than we ever receive about Booth in the course of the novel (465–71).

15. Idle hours in "Country Quarters" replace occasions for valor on the battlefield; the presumption of the uneducated "Block-head" replaces the rapier wit of a Restoration spark; "loitering in a Coffee House" or mere sotting stands in for the competitive verbal exchange of sophisticated male gatherings; and the adventurous plotting of sexual conquest now takes aim at "a Set of harmless ignorant Country Girls."

16. Sherburn, "Fielding's *Amelia*," 149.

17. On this controversy, see Battestin's footnotes to *Amelia*, 135, 364, and 367.

18. In his Preface to the *Enquiry*, Fielding develops the analogy between social and physical constitutions employed as a "Pun" in the passage above; he there suggests how important the term "Constitution" is to him as a way to conceive of principles underlying a whole social order. "Now in this Word, *The Constitution*, are included the original and fundamental Law of the Kingdom, from whence all Powers are derived, and by which they are circumscribed; all legislative and executive Authority; all those municipal Provisions which are commonly called *The Laws*; and, *lastly*, the Customs, Manners, and Habits of the People" (quoted by Battestin, who discusses Fielding's use of the term in the Preface and elsewhere, in *Henry Fielding*, 515–16).

19. I am indebted to conversations with Cathy Shuman for drawing out the importance of this notion of the domestic woman's transcendence of class relations.

20. As noted by Battestin, 436 n. 1 and 437 nn. 1, 2, and 3.

21. In this way, the example above does not appear typical—although Eve Kosofsky Sedgwick has taught us to see cuckoldry as itself a phenomenon centered on intimate and rivalrous relations between men.

22. Amelia comforts Booth by telling him that "however other Friends may prove false and fickle to him, he hath one Friend, whom no Inconstancy of her own, nor any Change of his Fortune, nor Time, nor Age, nor Sickness, nor any Accident can ever alter" (175). The language of her avowal draws on that of the marriage ceremony in the Book of Common Prayer and so supports her claim for the permanence of their love by associating it with religion, while she describes Booth's male friendships as subject to the vicissitudes of time.

23. 180–98. Bender asserts that in *Amelia*, "we find significant movement towards the transparency of the later realist novel," as the narrator's "contrivance and control" are deemphasized and thus concealed, although he also reads the novel (and its mode of narration) as fraught with evident contradictions because of its "situation on the threshold of reformist discourse" (180–81).

My understanding of *Amelia*'s narrative peculiarities has benefited from Elfenbein's discussion in "Mysteries of Conduct" of what he calls "reverse narration," a more specific type of inconsistent narration than the one I describe.

24. These fluctuations in Fielding's treatment of Mrs. James are presented in more detail, and analyzed in greater depth, by Elfenbein (2–11). John Coolidge and Michael Irwin also discuss the problem of unstable character depiction in *Amelia*, though they both explain it, generally, as a result of Fielding's attempt to present characters with a new degree of moral complexity. Wanko provides a different approach to the problem of inconsistent characterization in *Amelia*: she focuses on the moral quandary created for a reader who is asked to emulate the trusting Amelia, but who is also subjected by the novel's narrative techniques to a series of sharp disillusionments about individual characters.

25. Castle discusses this strange episode in *Amelia* in depth and with great acuity, arguing that it in fact transforms the plot and narrative method of the novel and establishes "a new dispensation." She concludes that this new dispensation affects, most significantly, Fielding's treatment of Amelia herself, who is thereafter shadowed with an "unprecedented moral fluidity" (*Masquerade and Civilization*, 223–42).

26. Some readers have admired this quality, while others have complained about its effects, particularly upon *Amelia*. See my discussion above (109–10) of Henry Knight Miller's and J. Paul Hunter's view that Fielding's willingness to sustain "unresolved dualities" is a crucial source of strength and subtlety in his fiction. Battestin, on the other hand, treats Fielding's ambivalence as an artistically damaging rather than enriching influence on his novels when he proposes that the "ambivalency of Fielding's own attitude toward the new psychology" is one source for the "awkwardness" of *Amelia*—or for the sense in which it presents us with a "problem" ("The Problem of *Amelia*," 634–35).

27. Battestin, "The Problem of *Amelia*," 616–17 and 632–35. See also Mulford, who describes Booth as struggling with the "confused juxtaposition" of a wider variety of philosophies, including those of the Stoics, Hobbes, Mandeville, and Shaftesbury and the Latitudinarians. In her view, this struggle explains Booth's "inconsistent action and belief" but also makes plausible his ultimate "conciliation with Barrow" (21–28).

28. See Battestin, *Amelia*, 256 n. 1 and 511 n. 1, and "The Problem of *Amelia*."

29. Discussed by Battestin, "The Problem of *Amelia*," 622–23.

30. And Battestin indicates that Harrison here follows Cockburn's similar protection of the ancient world from the accusations he levels against dueling (366 n. 3).

31. In his discussion of the 1789–95 French Revolution, Marx called

attention to the important function of this kind of "ruse" in the process of historical change, commenting that this kind of revolution needs to "draw its poetry from the past"—to "anxiously conjure up the spirits of the past . . . and borrow from them names, battle cries and costumes in order to present the new scene of world history in this time-honored disguise and this borrowed language" ("The Eighteenth Brumaire," 97–99).

32. Sitter discusses the importance of Harrison's role as symbolic father-figure (*Literary Loneliness*, 196–202).

33. In *Joseph Andrews*, Adams's excursus on the greatness of Homer emphasizes his characterization of various male heroes (Achilles, Agamemnon, Ajax, Diomedes, Nestor, Ulysses); but then it too comes to focus on Homer's portrayal of Andromache. Adams comments: "If he [Homer] hath any superior Excellence to the rest, I have been inclined to fancy it is in the Pathetick. I am sure I never read with dry Eyes, the two Episodes, where *Andromache* is introduced, in the former lamenting the Danger, and in the latter the Death of *Hector*. The Images are so extremely tender in these, that I am convinced, the Poet had the worthiest and best Heart imaginable" (199).

34. Published in London, 1754; reprinted in the *Marriage, Sex, and the Family in England, 1660–1800* series. All further references to this work will be by page number in this facsimile edition, cited parenthetically in the text.

35. Stone, 322–23.

36. Although the man in the first scenario avoids being whipped by offering his punishers a bribe, the connection drawn in *The Jacobite's Journal* between childhood whipping and homoerotic desire suggests that there may be some association implied between these two scenes, which are presented in rapid succession, like related elements in a dream.

37. We might think back to Pulteney's metaphor of homosexual relations to describe Robert Walpole's and Lord Hervey's political alliance (see 21 above and my "Politics and Sexuality in Portraits of John, Lord Hervey"); or to Fielding's joke (placed in the ironized Mrs. Grace's mouth) about a "copulation of ministers" in *The Jacobite's Journal* (discussed at 194–95 above).

38. In the preface Fielding contributed to Sarah Fielding's *Familiar Letters* in 1747, he had sketched in broad outline the female ideal he would embody later in Amelia. There, he concluded "that the Consummation of a Woman's Character, is to maintain the Qualities of Goodness, Tenderness, Affection and Sincerity, in the several social Offices and Duties of Life" (quoted in Battestin, *Henry Fielding*, 416).

39. See Plumb, "The New World of Children in Eighteenth-Century England," as well as the work of Stone and Ariès.

40. References either to Amelia's supervision of her children or to her

arrangement for someone else to look after them occur on a large number of pages, and with accelerating frequency as the novel goes on. See 169, 170, 186, 263, 315, 320, 343, 384, 419, 433, 478, 479, 488, 496, 501.

41. E.g., *On the Management*, 2, and *An Essay on the Government*, Dedication.

42. Several of Fielding's contemporaries claimed that his scornful disapproval of female classical learning had in fact caused friction between himself and his sister Sarah, whose want of "Learning" he had treated as a deficiency in his preface to *David Simple*, but who subsequently mastered Latin and Greek—to Henry's annoyance, according to some (Battestin, *Henry Fielding*, 380–81).

43. Battestin describes the sometimes friendly, sometimes antagonistic, relations between Fielding and Hill in 1751 to 1753. Hill praised *Tom Jones* extravagantly and imitated it in his own novels, but he actually proved one of *Amelia*'s detractors; and he and Fielding engaged in a mock-paper-war that somehow became a war in earnest (*Henry Fielding*, 526, 530–31, 537, 555–57, 561–63, 573).

44. See Battestin, *Henry Fielding*, as cited in note 43.

45. See Abelove for "some speculations" on the new enforcement of heterosexual norms that would develop in the course of "the long eighteenth century."

46. As Battestin notes, "the celebrated Delphin Classics were produced at the command of Louis XIV for the instruction of the Grand Dauphin, each volume being therefore inscribed with the phrase, 'in usum serenissimi Delphini' " (528 n. 4). He also notes that the Delphin editions were of the Latin classics only, so that Mrs. Atkinson's and Dr. Harrison's exchange in this scene about "the Delphin *Homer*" and "the Delphin *Aristotle*" simultaneously provides one more jab of ridicule at female learning and underlines the partialness with which the body of classical learning is transmitted in modern re-renderings.

Epilogue

1. The thematics of "entrapment and restraint" described by Melinda Alliker Rabb as central to the *Journal* (76) are closely related to the situation of paralysis I emphasize here. Along with the obvious, physical forms of entrapment experienced by Fielding in his voyage to Lisbon, Rabb notes that time itself comes to seem one more "means of entrapment" for him, as a "pattern of hurry and delay manipulates the sense of time in the *Journal*" and as "the ship's retarded progress suggests that human endeavor falters against the relentless march of time" (81–82).

2. "[The seamen] acknowledged [the captain] to be their master while they remained on shipboard, but did not allow his power to extend to the shores, where they had no sooner set their foot, than every man be-

came *sui juris*, and thought himself at full liberty to return when he pleased." *The Journal of a Voyage to Lisbon*, 99. All further citations of the *Journal* will be given by page number parenthetically in the text.

3. Rawson compares Fielding's description of Mrs. Francis to Pamela's portrait of the "man-like" Mrs. Jewkes, which Fielding had already imitated (with characteristic alterations) in his description of Mrs. Slipslop in *Joseph Andrews* (56–65). Rabb points out that a close comparison may also be drawn between Mrs. Francis and Fielding's own Mrs. Tow-wouse (87), who, as we have seen, stages a scene of "petticoat government" at Joseph's first stopping-place on the road.

4. As Rabb acutely observes, the relation between public and private matters is a source of continual tension within the *Journal*. She comments, "in a way," the *Journal* itself "is a result of their antagonism." Fielding writes the *Journal* in order to provide for his family, and he must do so because his private fortune, his personal health, and his prospects of continued life have all decayed as he labored to advance the public good.

Rabb points out the disproportion claimed by Fielding between the good he has rendered the public and the compensation he has received for his sacrifice and efforts: "Parliament dispenses 600 pounds 'to demolish the then reigning gangs' of London robbers, although only 200 pounds reaches Fielding. In exchange, he returns a small miracle: 'not only no such thing as a murder, but not even a street-robbery [was] commited.' But the reader discovers there is no satisfactory system with which to measure the value of such an achievement; there is only 200 pounds of 'the dirtiest money upon earth' " (82–83). The broadly drawn satiric sketch of Mrs. Francis, with her fantastically expanding powers to undermine systems of value and equitable exchange, strangely mirrors, then, in individual female form, the institutions of public life that have failed to reward Fielding fairly at home.

5. Battestin, *Henry Fielding*, 597–604.

6. Letter to John Fielding from Junqueira, quoted in Battestin, *Henry Fielding*, 599.

Bibliography

Abelove, Henry. "Some Speculations on the History of Sexual Intercourse during the Long Eighteenth Century in England." *Genders* 6 (1989): 125–30.

Ackroyd, Peter. *Dressing-Up—Transvestism and Drag: The History of an Obsession*. New York: Simon and Schuster, 1979.

Agnew, Jean-Christophe. *Worlds Apart: The Market and the Theater in Anglo-American Thought, 1550–1750*. New York: Cambridge University Press, 1986.

Allen, Walter. *The English Novel: A Short Critical History*. London: Phoenix House, 1954.

Alter, Robert. *Fielding and the Nature of the Novel*. Cambridge, Mass.: Harvard University Press, 1968.

Althusser, Louis. *For Marx*. Trans. Ben Brewster. London: Verso, 1979.

Ariès, Philippe. *The Hour of Our Death*. Trans. Helen Weaver. New York: Alfred A. Knopf, 1981.

Armstrong, Nancy. *Desire and Domestic Fiction: A Political History of the Novel*. New York: Oxford University Press, 1987.

Armstrong, Nancy, and Leonard Tennenhouse, eds. *The Ideology of Conduct: Essays in Literature and the History of Sexuality*. New York: Methuen, 1987.

Ash, Peter. "The First Auctioneer: Origin of Sales by Auction of Real Property." *Estates Gazette* Centenary Supplement (May 3, 1958): 33–37.

Baker, Sheridan. "*The Female Husband*: Fact and Fiction." *PMLA* 74 (1959): 213–24.

Bakhtin, Mikhail M. *The Dialogic Imagination: Four Essays by M. M. Bakhtin*. Trans. Caryl Emerson and Michael Holquist. Ed. Holquist. Austin: University of Texas Press, 1981.

Barish, Jonas. *The Antitheatrical Prejudice*. Berkeley: University of California Press, 1981.

Battestin, Martin C. Introduction. *Amelia*. By Henry Fielding. Ed. Battestin. xvi–lxi.

———. "Fielding and 'Master Punch' in Panton Street." *Philological Quarterly* 45 (1966): 191–208.

———. "Fielding's Changing Politics and *Joseph Andrews*." *Philological Quarterly* 39 (1960): 39–55.

———. Introduction. *Joseph Andrews* and *Shamela*. By Henry Fielding. Ed. Battestin. v–xl.

———. "Lord Hervey's Role in *Joseph Andrews*." *Philological Quarterly* 42 (1963): 226–41.

———. *The Moral Basis of Fielding's Art: A Study of* Joseph Andrews. Middletown: Wesleyan University Press, 1959.

———. "Pictures of Fielding." *Eighteenth-Century Studies* 17 (1983): 1–13.

———. "Pope's 'Magus' in Fielding's *Vernoniad*: The Satire of Walpole." *Philological Quarterly* 46 (1967): 137–41.

———. "The Problem of *Amelia*: Hume, Barrow, and the Conversion of Captain Booth." *ELH* 41 (1974): 613–48.

———. Introduction. *Tom Jones*. By Henry Fielding. Ed. Bowers. xvii–lxi.

———. "Tom Jones and 'His *Egyptian Majesty*': Fielding's Parable of Government." *PMLA* 82 (1967): 68–77.

Battestin, Martin C., with Ruthe R. Battestin. *Henry Fielding: A Life*. New York: Routledge, 1989.

Bender, John. *Imagining the Penitentiary: Fiction and the Architecture of Mind in Eighteenth-Century England*. Chicago: University of Chicago Press, 1987.

Benjamin, Walter. "Paris, Capital of the Nineteenth Century." In *Reflections: Essays, Aphorisms, Autobiographical Writings*. Trans. Edmund Jephcott. Ed. Peter Demetz. New York: Harcourt Brace Jovanovich, 1978.

Blanchard, Frederic. *Fielding the Novelist: A Study in Historical Criticism*. New Haven: Yale University Press, 1926.

Boswell, James. *Life of Johnson*. Ed. R. W. Chapman. Intro. Pat Rogers. New York: Oxford University Press, 1980.

Boucé, Paul-Gabriel, ed. *Sexuality in Eighteenth-Century Britain*. Totowa, N.J.: Manchester University Press, 1982.

Braudy, Leo. *Narrative Form in History and Fiction: Hume, Fielding, Gibbon*. Princeton: Princeton University Press, 1970.

Bray, Alan. *Homosexuality in Renaissance England*. London: Gay Men's Press, 1982.

A Brief Account of the Life and Family of Miss Jenny Cameron, the Reputed Mistress of the Pretender's Eldest Son. Containing Many very singular Incidents. London, 1746.

Bronson, Bertrand. *Facets of the Enlightenment: Studies in English Literature and Its Contexts*. Berkeley: University of California Press, 1968.

Brooks, Douglas. "Richardson's *Pamela* and Fielding's *Joseph Andrews*." *Essays in Criticism* 17 (1967): 158–68.

Brown, Homer Obed. "*Tom Jones*: The 'Bastard' of History." *boundary 2* 7 (1979): 201–33.

Brown, Laura. *Alexander Pope*. Oxford: Blackwell, 1985.

———. *English Dramatic Form, 1660–1760: An Essay in Generic History*. New Haven: Yale University Press, 1981.

———. "Reading Race and Gender: Jonathan Swift." *Eighteenth-Century Studies* 23 (1990): 424–43.

Butler, Judith. *Gender Trouble: Feminism and the Subversion of Identity*. New York: Routledge, 1990.

Butler, Melissa A. "Early Liberal Roots of Feminism: John Locke and the Attack on Patriarchy." *The American Political Science Review* 72 (1978): 135–50.

Campbell, Jill. "'The Exact Picture of His Mother': Recognizing Joseph Andrews." *ELH* 55 (1988): 643–64.

———. "Politics and Sexuality in Portraits of John, Lord Hervey." *Word & Image* 6 (1990): 281–97.

———. "'When Men Women Turn': Gender Reversals in Fielding's Plays." In *The New Eighteenth Century*, ed. Nussbaum and Brown. 62–83.

Carlton, Peter J. "The Mitigated Truth: Tom Jones's Double Heroism." *Studies in the Novel* 19 (1987): 397–409.

———. "*Tom Jones* and the '45 Once Again." *Studies in the Novel* 20 (1988): 361–73.

Carson, James P. "Commodification and the Figure of the Castrato in Smollett's *Humphry Clinker*." *The Eighteenth Century: Theory and Interpretation* 33 (1992): 24–46.

Cassady, Ralph, Jr. *Auctions and Auctioneering*. Berkeley: University of California Press, 1967.

Castle, Terry. *Clarissa's Ciphers: Meaning and Disruption in Richardson's Clarissa*. Ithaca: Cornell University Press, 1982.

———. *Masquerade and Civilization: The Carnivalesque in Eighteenth-Century English Fiction and Culture*. Stanford: Stanford University Press, 1986.

———. "Matters Not Fit to Be Mentioned: Fielding's *The Female Husband*." *ELH* 49 (1982): 602–22.

———. "The Spectralization of the Other in *The Mysteries of Udolpho*." In *The New Eighteenth Century*, ed. Nussbaum and Brown. 231–53.

Charke, Charlotte. *A Narrative of Mrs. Charlotte Charke*. 2d ed. Intro. Leonard R. N. Ashley. Gainesville: Scholars' Facsimiles & Reprints, 1969.

Cibber, Colley. "The Contretemps; or, Rival Queans" (anon.). Included in *The Dramatic Works of Colley Cibber, Esq.* (5 vols.). Vol. 4. 1777. Reprint. New York: AMS Press, 1966.

Cixous, Hélène. "Castration or Decapitation?" Trans. Annette Kuhn. *Signs* 7 (1981): 41–55.

————. "The Laugh of the Medusa." Trans. Annette Kuhn. *Signs* 1 (1976): 875–99.

Clapham, Sir John. *The Bank of England*. 2 vols. Cambridge: Cambridge University Press, 1958.

Cleary, T. R. *Henry Fielding: Political Writer*. Waterloo, Ontario: Wilfrid Laurier University Press, 1984.

Clinton-Baddeley, V. C. *The Burlesque Tradition in the English Theater After 1660*. London: Methuen, 1952.

Coley, W. B. "Henry Fielding and the Two Walpoles." *Philological Quarterly* 45 (1966): 157–78.

"The Contretemps; or, Rival Queans" (anon.). Reprinted in *The Dramatic Works of Colley Cibber, Esq.*

Coolidge, John. "Fielding and 'Conservation of Character.'" In *Fielding: A Collection of Critical Essays*, ed. Paulson. 158–76.

Craik, T. W. "Fielding's 'Tom Thumb' Plays." *Augustan Worlds*. Ed. J. C. Hilson et al. New York: Harper and Row, 1978. 165–74.

Crean, J. P. "The Stage Licensing Act of 1737." *Modern Philology* 35 (1938): 249–52.

Cross, Wilbur L. *The History of Henry Fielding*. 3 vols. New Haven: Yale University Press, 1918.

Cruise, James. "Fielding, Authority, and the New Commercialism in *Joseph Andrews*." *ELH* 54 (1987): 253–76.

The Daily Gazetteer (1746), collected in *The Fool*. London, 1748.

Damrosch, Leopold. *God's Plot and Man's Stories: Studies in the Fictional Imagination from Milton to Fielding*. Chicago: University of Chicago Press, 1985.

Davis, Lennard J. *Factual Fictions: The Origins of the English Novel*. New York: Columbia University Press, 1983.

Davis, Natalie Zemon. *Society and Culture in Early Modern France*. Stanford: Stanford University Press, 1975.

Dickson, P. G. M. *The Financial Revolution in England: A Study in the Development of Public Credit 1688–1756*. New York: St. Martin's, 1967.

Doody, Margaret Anne. *A Natural Passion: A Study of the Novels of Samuel Richardson*. Oxford: Clarendon, 1974.

Douglas, Ann. *The Feminization of American Culture*. New York: Avon Books, 1978.

Dubro, James R. "The Third Sex: Lord Hervey and His Coterie." *Eighteenth-Century Life* 2 (1976): 89–95.

Dudden, F. Homes. *Henry Fielding: His Life, Work, and Times*. Hamden: Archon, 1966.

Dugaw, Dianne. *Warrior Women and Popular Balladry, 1650–1800*. New York: Cambridge University Press, 1989.

Eagleton, Terry. *The Rape of Clarissa: Writing, Sexuality, and Class Struggle in Samuel Richardson.* Minneapolis: University of Minnesota Press, 1982.

Early, Alice K. *English Dolls, Effigies, and Puppets.* London: Batsford, 1955.

Eaves, T. C. Duncan, and Ben D. Kimpel. "Two Names in *Joseph Andrews.*" *Modern Philology* 72 (1975): 408–9.

Edwards, Thomas R. *Imagination and Power: A Study of Poetry on Public Themes.* London: Chatto & Windus, 1971.

Elfenbein, Andrew. "Mysteries of Conduct: Gender and Narrative Structure in Fielding's *Amelia.*" Department of English, University of Minnesota, Minneapolis. Photocopy.

"An Epistle to *John James H--dd-g--r*, Esq.; On the Report of *Signior F-r-n-lli's* being with Child." London: E. Hill, 1736.

Epstein, Julia, and Kristina Straub, ed. *Body Guards: The Cultural Politics of Gender Ambiguity.* New York: Routledge, 1991.

Erskine-Hill, Howard. "The Significance of Gay's Drama." In *English Drama: Forms and Development: Essays in Honor of Muriel Clara Bradbook*, ed. Marie Axton and Raymond Williams. New York: Cambridge University Press, 1977.

Fabricant, Carole. "Binding and Dressing Nature's Loose Tresses: The Ideology of Augustan Landscape Design." *Studies in Eighteenth-Century Culture* 8 (1979): 109–35.

———. "Pope's Portraits of Women: The Tyranny of the Pictorial Eye." In *Women and Men: The Consequences of Power*, ed. Dana V. Hiller and Robin Ann Sheets. Cincinnati: University of Cincinnati Office of Women's Studies, 1977.

Farmer, John S., and W. E. Henley. *Slang and Its Analogues, Past and Present.* 1904. Reprint. Millwood, New York: Kraus Reprint Co., 1974.

The Female Rebels: Being Some Remarkable Incidents of the Lives, Characters, and Families of the Titular Duke and Dutchess of Perth, the Lord and Lady Ogilvie, and of Miss Florence M'Donald. Containing Several Particulars of those Remarkable Persons not hitherto published. Edinburgh, reprinted London, 1747.

Fielding, Henry. *The Complete Works of Henry Fielding.* Ed. William Ernest Henley. 16 vols. New York: Croscup & Sterling, 1902.

———. *Amelia.* Ed. Martin C. Battestin. Intro. Fredson Bowers. Middletown: Wesleyan University Press, 1983.

———. *The Author's Farce.* Ed. Charles B. Woods. Lincoln: University of Nebraska Press, 1966.

———. *The Champion.* 2 vols. London: H. Chapelle, 1743.

———. *The Covent Garden Journal.* Ed. Gerard Edward Jensen. 2 vols. New Haven: Yale University Press, 1915.

———. *The Criticism of Henry Fielding.* Ed. Ioan Williams. London: Routledge & Kegan Paul, 1970.

———. "An Enquiry into the Cause of the Late Increase of Robbers, [etc.]." In *The Works of Henry Fielding*, ed. Browne. Vol. 10.

———. "An Essay on the Knowledge of the Characters of Men." In *Miscellanies, Volume One*, ed. Miller.

———. *The Female Husband and Other Writings*. Ed. Claude E. Jones. English Reprint Series No. 17. Liverpool: Liverpool University Press, 1960.

———. *The Grub-Street Opera*. Ed. Edgar V. Roberts. Lincoln: University of Nebraska Press, 1968.

———. *The Historical Register for the Year 1736* and *Eurydice Hissed*. Ed. William W. Appleton. Lincoln: University of Nebraska Press, 1967.

———. *The History of Tom Jones: A Foundling*. Ed. Fredson Bowers. Intro. and commentary Martin C. Battestin. 2 vols. Middletown: Wesleyan University Press, 1975.

———. *The History of Tom Jones: A Foundling*. Ed. Sheridan Baker. Norton Critical Edition. New York: W. W. Norton, 1973.

———. *The Jacobite's Journal and Related Writings*. Ed. W. B. Coley. Oxford: Clarendon Press, 1974.

———. *Jonathan Wild*. Ed. David Nokes. New York: Penguin Books, 1982.

———. *Joseph Andrews*. Ed. Martin C. Battestin. Intro. Fredson Bowers. Middletown: Wesleyan University Press, 1967.

———. *Joseph Andrews* and *Shamela*. Ed. Martin C. Battestin. Boston: Houghton Mifflin, 1961.

———. *The Journal of a Voyage to Lisbon*. Ed. Harold E. Pagliaro. New York: Nardon, 1963.

———. "A Journey from This World to the Next." In *Miscellanies, Volume Two*, ed. Amory and Goldgar.

———. *The Masquerade*. By "Lemuel Gulliver." London: J. Roberts, 1728.

———. *Miscellanies, Volume One*. Ed. Henry Knight Miller. Intro. Fredson Bowers. Oxford: Clarendon Press, 1972.

———. *Miscellanies, Volume Two*. Ed. Hugh Amory. Intro. and commentary Bertrand A. Goldgar. New York: Oxford University Press and Wesleyan University Press, 1993.

———. *New Essays by Henry Fielding: His Contributions to the Craftsman (1734–1739) and Other Early Journalism*. Ed. Martin C. Battestin. With a stylometric analysis by Michael J. Farringdon. Charlottesville: University Press of Virginia, 1989.

———. "Of the Remedy of Affliction for the Loss of Our Friends." In *Miscellanies, Volume One*. Ed. Miller.

———. *The Opposition. A Vision*. London, 1741.

———. *The Tragedy of Tragedies*. Ed. James T. Hillhouse. New Haven: Yale University Press, 1918.

———. *The True Patriot and Related Writings*. Ed. W. B. Coley. Middletown: Wesleyan University Press, 1987.

————. *The Vernoniad.* "Done into English, From the original Greek of Homer." London: Charles Corbett, 1741.

————. *The Works of Henry Fielding.* Ed. James P. Browne. 11 vols. London: Bickers, 1903.

Filmer, Sir Robert. *Patriarcha and Other Political Works.* Ed. Peter Laslett. New York: Garland Publishing, 1984.

Folkenflik, Robert, ed. *The English Hero, 1660–1800.* Newark: University of Delaware Press, 1982.

The Fool. London, 1748. Reprinting *The Daily Gazetteer.*

Foucault, Michel. *The History of Sexuality: An Introduction.* Trans. Robert Hurley. New York: Pantheon Books, 1978.

Frank, Judith. "Chance Hits the Mark: Exchange and the Gift in *Joseph Andrews.*" Department of English, Amherst College, Amherst, Mass. Photocopy.

————. "Literacy, Desire, and the Novel: From *Shamela* to *Joseph Andrews.*" *Yale Journal of Criticism* 6 (1993): 157–74.

Gallagher, Catherine. "Embracing the Absolute: The Politics of the Female Subject in Seventeenth-Century England." *Genders* 1 (1988): 24–39.

Gallagher, Catherine, and Thomas Laqueur, eds. *The Making of the Modern Body: Sexuality and Society in the Nineteenth Century.* Berkeley: University of California Press, 1987.

Garber, Marjorie. *Vested Interests: Cross-Dressing and Cultural Anxiety.* New York: Routledge, 1992.

Gay, John. *The Beggar's Opera.* Ed. Peter Elfred Lewis. Edinburgh: Oliver & Boyd, 1973.

Girard, René. *Deceit, Desire, and the Novel: Self and Other in Literary Structure.* Trans. Yvonne Freccero. Baltimore: Johns Hopkins University Press, 1966.

Goldberg, Homer. *The Art of* Joseph Andrews. Chicago: University of Chicago Press, 1969.

Golden, Morris. "Public Context and Imagining Self in *Tom Jones.*" *Papers on Language and Literature* 20 (1984): 273–92.

Goldgar, Bertrand A. *Walpole and the Wits: The Relation of Politics to Literature, 1722–42.* Lincoln: University of Nebraska Press, 1976.

Graeme, Alan. "The Mystery Woman of the '45." *The Scots Magazine,* April 1931: 17–28.

Gray, Harold. *Theatrical Criticism in London to 1795.* New York: Columbia University Press, 1931.

Greenblatt, Stephen. "Invisible Bullets: Renaissance Authority and Its Subversion." *Glyph* 8 (1981): 40–61.

Guillory, John. "Dalila's House: *Samson Agonistes* and the Sexual Division of Labor." *Rewriting the Renaissance: The Discourses of Sexual Difference in Early Modern Europe*. Ed. Margaret W. Ferguson, Maureen Quilligan, and Nancy J. Vickers. Chicago: University of Chicago Press, 1986. 106–22.

Hagstrum, Jean. *Sex and Sensibility: Ideal and Erotic Love from Milton to Mozart*. Chicago: University of Chicago Press, 1980.

Hahn, H. George. *Henry Fielding: An Annotated Bibliography*. Metuchen, N.J.: Scarecrow Press, 1979.

———. "Main Lines of Criticism of Fielding's *Joseph Andrews*, 1925–1978." *The British Studies Monitor* 10 (1981): 4–17.

Halsband, Robert. *Lord Hervey: Eighteenth-Century Courtier*. Oxford: Clarendon, 1973.

Haraway, Donna J. *Simians, Cyborgs, and Women: The Reinvention of Nature*. New York: Routledge, 1991.

Harding, Sandra. *The Science Question in Feminism*. Ithaca: Cornell University Press, 1986.

Hatfield, Glenn W. *Henry Fielding and the Language of Irony*. Chicago: University of Chicago Press, 1968.

Heriot, Angus. *The Castrati in Opera*. London: Secker and Warburg, 1956.

Hervey, Lord John. *Lord Hervey's Memoirs*. Ed. Romney Sedgwick. New York: Macmillan, 1963.

Highfill, Philip H., Jr., Kalman A. Burnim, and Edward A. Langhans. *A Biographical Dictionary of Actors, Actresses, [Etc.] in London, 1600–1800*. Vol. 8. Carbondale: Southern Illinois University Press, 1982.

Hill, John. *On the Management and Education of Children*, by "Juliana-Susannah Seymour." London, 1754. Reprint. New York: Garland Publishing, 1985.

Hilles, Frederick W. "Art and Artifice in *Tom Jones*." In *Tom Jones* (Norton Critical Edition), ed. Baker. 916–32.

The History of the Rebellion in the Years 1745 and 1746, from a Manuscript Now in the Possession of Lord James Stewart-Murray. Ed. Henrietta Tayler. Oxford: Oxford University Press, 1944.

The History of the Rise, Progress, and Extinction of the Rebellion in Scotland in the Years 1745 and 1746. 2nd ed. London, 1747.

Holland, Peter. *The Ornament of Action: Text and Performance in Restoration Comedy*. New York: Cambridge University Press, 1979.

Hollander, John. *The Figure of Echo: A Mode of Allusion in Milton and After*. Berkeley: University of California Press, 1981.

"Honeycombe, Charles." "Of the Effects of Romances on the Youthful Mind . . ." *The Royal Female Magazine—or the Ladies General Repository of Pleasure and Improvement* 1 (1760): 7–11.

Howard, Susan K. "The Intrusive Audience in Fielding's *Amelia*." *Journal of Narrative Technique* 17 (1987): 286–95.

Hume, Robert D. *Henry Fielding and the London Theatre, 1728–1737*. Oxford: Clarendon Press, 1988.

Hunter, J. Paul. *Before Novels: The Cultural Contexts of Eighteenth-Century English Fiction*. New York: W. W. Norton, 1990.

———. "Fielding and the Disappearance of Heroes." In *The English Hero, 1660–1800*, ed. Folkenflik. 116–42.

———. *Occasional Form: Henry Fielding and the Chains of Circumstance*. Baltimore: Johns Hopkins University Press, 1975.

Hutchens, Eleanor N. "O Attic Shape! The Cornering of Square." In *A Provision of Human Nature*, ed. Kay. 37–44.

Ireland, John. *Hogarth Illustrated from his own Manuscripts*. London, 1798.

Irwin, Michael. *Henry Fielding: The Tentative Realist*. Oxford: Clarendon Press, 1967.

Irwin, W. R. "Satire and Comedy in the Works of Henry Fielding." *ELH* 13 (1946): 168–88.

Jenkins, Owen. "Richardson's *Pamela* and Fielding's 'Vile Forgeries.'" *Philological Quarterly* 44 (1965): 200–210.

Jewett, William. "Exemplarity and the Problem of Narcissism in Fielding's *Joseph Andrews*." Graduate course presentation, Yale University, 1984.

Johnson, Barbara. *The Critical Difference*. Baltimore: Johns Hopkins University Press, 1980.

Johnson, Maurice. *Fielding's Art of Fiction: Eleven Essays on* Shamela, Joseph Andrews, Tom Jones, *and* Amelia. Philadelphia: University of Pennsylvania Press, 1961.

Johnson, Samuel. "Life of Milton." In *Samuel Johnson: Selected Poetry and Prose*. Ed. Frank Brady and W. K. Wimsatt. Berkeley: University of California Press, 1977.

Jones, Vivien, ed. *Women in the Eighteenth Century: Constructions of Femininity*. New York: Routledge, 1990.

Kay, Donald. *A Provision of Human Nature: Essays on Fielding and Others in Honor of Miriam Austin Locke*. University: University of Alabama Press, 1977.

Kearney, Anthony. "Tom Jones and the Forty-five." *Ariel* 4 (1973): 68–78.

Keller, Evelyn Fox. *Reflections on Gender and Science*. New Haven: Yale University Press, 1985.

Kermode, Frank. "Richardson and Fielding." *Cambridge Journal* 4 (1950): 106–14.

Kern, Jean B. *Dramatic Satire in the Age of Walpole 1720–1750*. Ames: Iowa State University Press, 1976.

Kernan, Alvin. *Printing Technology, Letters, and Samuel Johnson*. Princeton: Princeton University Press, 1987.

Kowaleski-Wallace, Beth. "Shunning the Bearded Kiss: Castrati and the Definition of Female Sexuality." *Prose Studies* 15 (1992): 153–70.

Kramnick, Isaac. *Bolingbroke and His Circle: The Politics of Nostalgia in the Age of Walpole*. Cambridge: Harvard University Press, 1968.

Kreissman, Bernard. *Pamela-Shamela: A Study of the Criticisms, Burlesques, Parodies, and Adaptations of Richardson's* Pamela. Lincoln: University of Nebraska Press, 1960.

Kropf, C. R. "Educational Theory and Human Nature in Fielding's Works." *PMLA* 89 (1974): 113–20.

Lanham, Richard A. *A Handlist of Rhetorical Terms: A Guide for Students of English Literature.* Berkeley: University of California Press, 1969.

Laqueur, Thomas. *Making Sex: Body and Gender from the Greeks to Freud.* Cambridge, Mass.: Harvard University Press, 1990.

Lenman, Bruce. *The Jacobite Risings in Britain, 1689–1746.* London: Methuen, 1980.

Lenta, Margaret. "Comedy, Tragedy and Feminism: The Novels of Richardson and Fielding." *English Studies in Africa* 26 (1983): 13–25.

LePage, Peter. "The Prison and the Dark Beauty of *Amelia.*" *Criticism* 9 (1967): 337–54.

Lewis, Peter. *Fielding's Burlesque Drama: Its Place in the Tradition.* Edinburgh: Edinburgh University Press, 1987.

Liu, Alan. "The Power of Formalism: The New Historicism." *ELH* 56 (1989): 721–71.

Locke, John. *Two Treatises of Government.* Ed. Peter Laslett. New York: Cambridge University Press, 1988.

Loftis, John. *Comedy and Society from Congreve to Fielding.* Stanford: Stanford University Press, 1959.

Lucian. *The Dialogues of the Dead.* Trans. M. D. Macleod. Cambridge, Mass.: Harvard University Press, 1961.

McCrea, Brian. "Fielding's Role in *The Champion*: A Reminder." *South Atlantic Bulletin* 42 (1977): 19–24.

———. *Henry Fielding and the Politics of Mid-Eighteenth-Century England.* Athens: University of Georgia Press, 1981.

Macey, Samuel L. "Fielding's *Tom Thumb* as the Heir to Buckingham's *Rehearsal.*" *Texas Studies in Literature and Language* 10 (1968): 405–14.

McIntosh, Mary. "The Homosexual Role." *Social Problems* 16 (1968): 182–92.

Mack, Maynard. *The Garden and the City: Retirement and Politics in the Later Poetry of Pope, 1731–1743.* Toronto: University of Toronto Press, 1969.

———. "*Joseph Andrews* and *Pamela.*" In *Fielding: A Collection of Critical Essays,* ed. Paulson. 52–58.

McKendrick, Neil, John Brewer, and J. H. Plumb. *The Birth of a Consumer Society: The Commercialization of Eighteenth-Century England.* Bloomington: Indiana University Press, 1982.

McKeon, Michael. "A Defense of Dialectical Method in Literary History." *Diacritics* 19 (1989): 83–96.

———. *The Origins of the English Novel 1600–1740*. Baltimore: Johns Hopkins University Press, 1987.

Maresca, Thomas E. *Epic to Novel*. Columbus: Ohio State University Press, 1974.

Marshall, David. *The Figure of Theater: Shaftesbury, Defoe, Adam Smith, and George Eliot*. New York: Columbia University Press, 1986.

Marx, Karl. "The Eighteenth Brumaire of Louis Bonaparte." In *Karl Marx and Frederick Engels, Selected Works*. New York: International Publishers, 1968.

Maus, Katharine Eisaman. "'Playhouse Flesh and Blood': Sexual Ideology and the Restoration Actress." *ELH* 46 (1979): 595–617.

Miller, Henry Knight. *Essays on Fielding's Miscellanies. A Commentary on Volume One*. Princeton: Princeton University Press, 1961.

Milton, John. *Complete Poems and Major Prose*. Ed. Merritt Y. Hughes. Indianapolis: Odyssey, 1957.

———. *The Poems of John Milton*. Ed. John Carey and Alastair Fowler. Longman edition. New York: W. W. Norton, 1968.

Moers, Ellen. *Literary Women: The Great Writers*. Garden City: Anchor, 1975.

Monod, Paul Kleber. *Jacobitism and the English People, 1688–1788*. New York: Cambridge University Press, 1989.

Montrose, Louis Adrian. "The Elizabethan Subject and the Spenserian Text." In *Literary Theory/Renaissance Texts*, ed. Patricia Parker and David Quint. Baltimore: Johns Hopkins University Press, 1986.

———. "*A Midsummer Night's Dream* and the Shaping Fantasies of Elizabethan Culture: Gender, Power, Form." In *Rewriting the Renaissance: The Discourse of Sexual Difference in Early Modern Europe*, ed. Margaret Ferguson and Maureen Quilligan. Chicago: University of Chicago Press, 1986.

Moore, Robert Etheridge. "Dr. Johnson on Fielding and Richardson." *PMLA* 66 (1951): 162–81.

Morrissey, L. J. "Fielding's First Political Satire." *Anglia* 90 (1972): 325–48.

———. *Henry Fielding, a Reference Guide*. Boston: G. K. Hall, 1980.

Mulford, Carla. "Booth's Progress and the Resolution of *Amelia*." *Studies in the Novel* 16 (1984): 20–31.

Nelson, James. *An Essay on the Government of Children*. 1756. Reprinted in facsimile. New York: Garland Publishing, 1985.

Nichols, John, and George Steevens. *The Genuine Works of William Hogarth; Illustrated with Biographical Anecdotes*. London: Longman, 1810.

Nicholson, Linda J. *Gender and History: The Limits of Social Theory in the Age of the Family*. New York: Columbia University Press, 1986.

Nicoll, Allardyce. *A History of Early Eighteenth-Century Drama*. Cambridge: Cambridge University Press, 1925.

Noble, Yvonne. "Sex and Gender in Gay's *Achilles*." In *John Gay and the*

Scriblerians, ed. Peter Lewis and Nigel Wood. New York: St. Martin's Press, 1988.

Nussbaum, Felicity. *The Autobiographical Subject: Gender and Ideology in Eighteenth-Century England.* Baltimore: Johns Hopkins University Press, 1989.

———. *The Brink of All We Hate: English Satires on Women, 1660–1750.* Lexington: University Press of Kentucky, 1984.

———. "Heteroclites: The Gender of Character in the Scandalous Memoirs." In *The New Eighteenth Century,* ed. Nussbaum and Brown. 144–67.

Nussbaum, Felicity, and Laura Brown, eds. *The New Eighteenth Century; Theory, Politics, English Literature.* New York: Methuen, 1987.

Old England, or The Constitutional Journal. 1745.

O'Neill, John H. "Sexuality, Deviance, and Moral Character in the Personal Satire of the Restoration." *Eighteenth-Century Life* 2 (1975): 16–19.

Oppé, A. P. *The Drawings of William Hogarth.* London: Phaidon Press, 1948.

Orgel, Stephen. *The Illusion of Power: Political Theater in the English Renaissance.* Berkeley: University of California Press, 1975.

Osland, Dianne. "Tied Back to Back: The Discourse Between the Poet and Player and the Exhortations of Parson Adams in *Joseph Andrews.*" *The Journal of Narrative Technique* 12 (1982): 191–200.

Ovid. *Metamorphoses.* Trans. Frank Justus Miller. Loeb Classical Library. Cambridge, Mass.: Harvard University Press, 1977.

Partridge, Eric. *Dictionary of Slang and Unconventional English.* New York: Macmillan, 1961.

———. *Shakespeare's Bawdy.* London: Routledge, 1947.

Pateman, Carole. *The Sexual Contract.* Cambridge, UK: Polity Press, 1988.

Paulson, Ronald. *Breaking and Remaking: Aesthetic Practice in England, 1700–1820.* New Brunswick: Rutgers University Press, 1989.

———. *Hogarth: His Life, Art, and Times.* 2 vols. New Haven: Yale University Press, 1971.

———. *Hogarth's Graphic Works.* 2 vols. New Haven: Yale University Press, 1965.

———. "Models and Paradigms: *Joseph Andrews,* Hogarth's *Good Samaritan,* and Fénelon's *Télémaque.*" *Modern Language Notes* 91 (1976): 1161–85.

———. "The Pilgrimage and the Family: Structures in the Novels of Fielding and Smollett." In *Tobias Smollett: Bicentennial Essays Presented to Lewis M. Knapp,* ed. Rousseau and Boucé. 57–78.

———. *Popular and Polite Art in the Age of Hogarth and Fielding.* Notre Dame: University of Notre Dame Press, 1979.

———. *Satire and the Novel in Eighteenth-Century England.* New Haven: Yale University Press, 1967.

———. "Satire, Poetry, and Pope." *English Satire.* Papers read at a Clark Library Seminar, Jan. 15, 1972. Los Angeles: William Andrews Clark Memorial Library, University of California, 1972.

————, ed. *Fielding: A Collection of Critical Essays*. Englewood Cliffs: Prentice-Hall, 1962.

Paulson, Ronald, and Thomas Lockwood, eds. *Henry Fielding: The Critical Heritage*. New York: Barnes & Noble, 1969.

Perry, Ruth. *The Celebrated Mary Astell: An Early English Feminist*. Chicago: University of Chicago Press, 1986.

Peschel, Enid Rhodes, and Richard Peschel, M.D. "Medicine and Music: The Castrati in Opera." *Opera Quarterly* 4 (1986): 21–38.

"Phillips, Teresia Constantia." *The Happy Courtezan: Or, the Prude demolish'd*. London: J. Roberts, 1735.

Plumb, J. H. "The New World of Children in Eighteenth-Century England." *Past and Present* 67 (1975): 64–93.

————. *Sir Robert Walpole*. 2 vols. London: Cresset, 1956 and 1960.

Pollak, Ellen. *The Poetics of Sexual Myth: Gender and Ideology in the Verse of Swift and Pope*. Chicago: University of Chicago Press, 1985.

Poovey, Mary. *The Proper Lady and the Woman Writer: Ideology as Style in the Works of Mary Wollstonecraft, Mary Shelley, and Jane Austen*. Chicago: University of Chicago Press, 1984.

————. *Uneven Developments: The Ideological Work of Gender in Mid-Victorian England*. Chicago: University of Chicago Press, 1988.

Pope, Alexander. *The Poems of Alexander Pope*. Twickenham Edition. 11 vols. Gen. ed. John Butt. New Haven: Yale University Press, 1961.

Prebble, John. *Culloden*. London: Secker and Warburg, 1961.

Pulteney, William. *A Proper Reply to a late Scurrilous Libel; intitled, Sedition and Defamation display'd*, by "Caleb D'Anvers." London, 1731.

Quennell, Peter. *Caroline of England: An Augustan Portrait*. New York: Viking, 1940.

Rabb, Melinda Alliker. "Confinement and Entrapment in Henry Fielding's *Journal of a Voyage to Lisbon*." *Studies in the Literary Imagination* 17 (1984): 75–89.

Rackin, Phyllis. "Androgyny, Mimesis, and the Marriage of the Boy Heroine on the English Renaissance Stage." *PMLA* 102 (1987): 29–39.

Ralph, James. *The Touch-Stone*. 1728. Facsimile. Ed. Arthur Freeman. New York: Garland, 1973.

Rawson, C. J. *Henry Fielding and the Augustan Ideal Under Stress: "Nature's Dance of Death" and Other Studies*. Boston: Routledge & Kegan Paul, 1972.

Ray, James. *A Compleat History of the Rebellion, From its first Rise in 1745, To its total Suppression at the glorious Battle of Culloden, in April 1746*. 4th ed. 1753.

Reilly, D. R. *Portrait Waxes: An Introduction for Collectors*. London: Batsford, 1953.

Richardson, Samuel. *Pamela; or, Virtue Rewarded*. Ed. T. C. Duncan Eaves and Ben D. Kimpel. Boston: Houghton Mifflin, 1971.

Richetti, John J. "The Portrayal of Women in Restoration and Eighteenth-

Century English Literature." In *What Manner of Woman: Essays on English and American Life and Literature*, ed. Marlene Springer. New York: New York University Press, 1977.

———. "Representing an Under Class: Servants and Proletarians in Fielding and Smollett." In *The New Eighteenth Century*, ed. Nussbaum and Brown. 84–98.

Rogers, Katherine M. "Sensitive Feminism vs. Conventional Sympathy: Richardson and Fielding on Women." *Novel* 9 (1976): 257–71.

Rogers, Pat. "The Breeches Part." In *Sexuality in Eighteenth-Century Britain*, ed. Boucé. 244–58.

Rose, Mark. "The Author as Proprietor: *Donaldson v. Becket* and the Genealogy of Modern Authorship." *Representations* 23 (1988): 51–85.

Rothstein, Eric. "The Framework of *Shamela*." *ELH* 35 (1968): 381–402.

Rousseau, G. S. "Pineapples, Pregnancy, Pica, and *Peregrine Pickle*." In *Tobias Smollett: Bicentennial Essays Presented to Lewis M. Knapp*, ed. Rousseau and Boucé. 79–109.

———. "The Pursuit of Homosexuality in the Eighteenth Century: 'Utterly Confused Category' and/or Rich Repository?" *Eighteenth-Century Life* 9 (1985): 133–68.

Rousseau, G. S., and Paul-Gabriel Boucé, eds. *Tobias Smollett: Bicentennial Essays Presented to Lewis M. Knapp*. New York: Oxford University Press, 1971.

Rudolph, Valerie C. "People and Puppets: Fielding's Burlesque and the 'Recognition Scene' in *The Author's Farce*." *Papers on Language and Literature* 11 (1975): 31–38.

Sabor, Peter. "*Amelia* and *Sir Charles Grandison*: The Convergence of Fielding and Richardson." *Wascana Review* 17: 3–18.

———. "*Joseph Andrews* and *Pamela*." *British Journal for Eighteenth-Century Studies* 1 (1978): 169–81.

Sacks, Sheldon. *Fiction and the Shape of Belief: A Study of Henry Fielding, with Glances at Swift, Johnson, and Richardson*. Berkeley: University of California Press, 1966.

Scheuermann, Mona. "Fielding's Images of Women." *The Age of Johnson* 3 (1990): 231–80.

Schilling, Bernard. *The Comic Spirit: Boccaccio to Thomas Mann*. Detroit: Wayne State University Press, 1965.

Schochet, Gordon J. *Patriarchalism in Political Thought: The Authoritarian Family and Political Speculation and Attitudes, Especially in Seventeenth-Century England*. Oxford: Basil Blackwell, 1975.

Schonhorn, Manuel. "Fielding's Ecphrastic Moment: Tom Jones and His Egyptian Majesty." *Studies in Philology* 78 (1981): 305–23.

Scott, Joan Wallach. *Gender and the Politics of History*. New York: Columbia University Press, 1988.

Scouten, Arthur H., ed. *The London Stage, 1660–1800*. Vol. 1. Carbondale: Southern Illinois University Press, 1961.

Sedgwick, Eve Kosofsky. *Between Men: English Literature and Male Homosocial Desire.* New York: Columbia University Press, 1985.

Shadwell, Thomas. *The Virtuoso.* Ed. Marjorie Hope Nicolson and David Stuart Rodes. Lincoln: University of Nebraska Press, 1966.

Sherbo, Arthur. "Fielding's Dogs." *Notes & Queries* 17 (1970): 302–3.

———. *Studies in the Eighteenth-Century English Novel.* East Lansing: Michigan State University Press, 1969.

Sherburn, George. "*The Dunciad*, Book IV." *University of Texas Studies in English* (1944): 174–90.

———. "Fielding's *Amelia*: An Interpretation." In *Fielding: A Collection of Critical Essays,* ed. Paulson. 146–57.

Sheriff, John K. *The Good-Natured Man: The Evolution of a Moral Ideal, 1660–1800.* University: University of Alabama Press, 1982.

Sitter, John E. *Literary Loneliness in Mid-Eighteenth-Century England.* Ithaca: Cornell University Press, 1982.

———. "Mother, Memory, Muse and Poetry After Pope." *ELH* 44 (1977): 312–36.

———. *The Poetry of Pope's* Dunciad. Minneapolis: University of Minnesota Press, 1971.

Smallwood, Angela J. *Fielding and the Woman Question: The Novels of Henry Fielding and Feminist Debate, 1700–1750.* New York: St. Martin's Press, 1989.

Smith, Hilda L. *Reason's Disciples: Seventeenth-Century English Feminists.* Urbana: University of Illinois Press, 1982.

Spacks, Patricia Meyer. *An Argument of Images: The Poetry of Alexander Pope.* Cambridge, Mass.: Harvard University Press, 1971.

———. *Desire and Truth: Functions of Plot in Eighteenth-Century English Novels.* Chicago: University of Chicago Press, 1990.

———. "Female Changelessness; Or, What Do Women Want?" *Studies in the Novel* 19 (1987): 273–83.

———. *The Female Imagination.* New York: Knopf, 1975.

———. *Gossip.* Chicago: University of Chicago Press, 1986.

———. *John Gay.* New York: Twayne, 1965.

Spilka, Mark. "Comic Resolution in Fielding's *Joseph Andrews.*" *College English* 15 (1953): 11–19.

Stapleton, Michael. *A Dictionary of Greek and Roman Mythology.* New York: Hamlyn, 1978.

Staves, Susan. "A Few Kind Words for the Fop." *SEL* 22 (1982): 413–28.

Stephanson, Raymond. "The Education of the Reader in Fielding's *Joseph Andrews.*" *Philological Quarterly* 61 (1982): 243–58.

Stephens, Frederick George, ed. *The Catalogue of Political and Personal Satires Preserved in the Department of Prints and Drawings in the British Museum.* Vol. 3.1, 1734–50. London: British Museum Publications, 1978.

Stephens, Sir Leslie, and Sir Sidney Lee, eds. *The Dictionary of National Bi-*

ography, from the Earliest Times to 1900. Vol. 15. London: Oxford University Press, 1949.

Stoler, John A., and Richard D. Fulton. *Henry Fielding: An Annotated Bibliography of Twentieth-Century Criticism, 1900–1977.* New York: Garland, 1980.

Stone, Lawrence. *The Family, Sex and Marriage in England 1500–1800.* New York: Harper & Row, 1977.

Straub, Kristina. *Sexual Suspects: Eighteenth-Century Players and Sexual Ideology.* Princeton: Princeton University Press, 1992.

Summers, Joseph. *The Muse's Method: An Introduction to* Paradise Lost. Cambridge, Mass.: Harvard University Press, 1962.

Swedenborg, H. T., Jr. *The Theory of the Epic in English, 1650–1800.* University of California Publications in English. Vol. 15. Berkeley: 1944.

Taylor, Dick, Jr. "Joseph as Hero in *Joseph Andrews.*" *Tulane Studies in English* 7 (1957): 91–109.

Thompson, James. "Patterns of Property and Possession in Fielding's Fiction." *Eighteenth-Century Fiction* 3 (1990): 21–42.

Tompkins, Jane P. "Sentimental Power: *Uncle Tom's Cabin* and the Politics of Literary History." *Glyph* 8 (1981): 79–102.

Trumbach, Randolph. "London's Sapphists: From Three Sexes to Four Genders in the Making of Modern Culture." In *Body Guards: The Cultural Politics of Gender Ambiguity,* ed. Epstein and Straub. 112–41.

———. "London's Sodomites: Homosexual Behavior and Western Culture in the Eighteenth Century." *Journal of Social History* 11 (1977): 1–33.

———. *The Rise of the Egalitarian Family: Aristocratic Kinship and Domestic Relations in Eighteenth-Century England.* New York: Harcourt Brace Jovanovich, 1978.

———. "Sodomitical Subcultures, Sodomitical Roles, and the Gender Revolution of the Eighteenth Century: The Recent Historiography." *Eighteenth-Century Life* 9 (1985): 109–21.

Utter, Robert Palfrey, and Gwendolyn Bridges Needham. *Pamela's Daughters.* New York: Macmillan, 1936.

Veeder, William. *Mary Shelley and Frankenstein: The Fate of Androgyny.* Chicago: University of Chicago Press, 1986.

Wanko, Cheryl. "Characterization and the Reader's Quandary in Fielding's *Amelia.*" *Journal of English and Germanic Philology* 90 (1991): 505–23.

Warner, William B. "Realist Literary History: McKeon's New Origins of the Novel." *Diacritics* 19 (1989): 62–81.

Warren, Leland E. " 'This Intrepid and Gallant Spirit': Henry Fielding's Sentimental Satiric Voyage." *Essays in Literature* 9 (1982): 43–54.

Watt, Ian. *The Rise of the Novel: Studies in Defoe, Richardson, and Fielding.* Berkeley: University of California Press, 1957.

———. "Serious Reflections on *The Rise of the Novel.*" *Novel* 1 (1968): 207–18.

Weinbrot, Howard D. "*The New Eighteenth Century* and the New Mythology." *The Age of Johnson* 3 (1990): 353–403.

Weinstein, Arnold. *Fictions of the Self: 1550–1800.* Princeton: Princeton University Press, 1981.

Welsh, Alexander. *Strong Representations: Narrative and Circumstantial Evidence in England.* Baltimore: Johns Hopkins University Press, 1992.

White, Eric Walter. *A History of English Opera.* London: Faber & Faber, 1983.

Wilding, Michael. "The Last of the Epics: The Rejection of the Heroic in *Paradise Lost* and *Hudibras.*" In *Restoration Literature: Critical Approaches,* ed. Harold Love. London: Methuen, 1972.

Williams, Aubrey. "Literary Backgrounds to Book Four of *The Dunciad.*" *PMLA* 68 (1953): 806–13.

Williams, Murial Brittain. *Marriage: Fielding's Mirror of Morality.* University: University of Alabama Press, 1973.

Williams, Raymond. *Problems in Materialism and Culture: Selected Essays.* London: Verso, 1980.

Williamson, Marilyn L. *Raising Their Voices: British Women Writers, 1650–1750.* Detroit: Wayne State University Press, 1990.

Wilson, John Harold. *All the King's Ladies: Actresses of the Restoration.* Chicago: University of Chicago Press, 1958.

Wittreich, Joseph. *Feminist Milton.* Ithaca: Cornell University Press, 1987.

Woods, Charles B. "Captain B----'s Play." *Harvard Studies and Notes in Philology and Literature* 15 (1933): 243–55.

Wright, Thomas. *Caricature History of the Georges; or, Annals of the House of Hanover.* London: Chatto & Windus, 1898.

Zaretsky, Eli. *Capitalism, the Family, and Personal Life.* New York: Harper & Row, 1986.

Zirker, M. R. *Fielding's Social Pamphlets.* University of California English Studies, No. 31. Berkeley and Los Angeles, 1966.

Index

In this index an "f" after a number indicates a separate reference on the next page, and an "ff" indicates separate references on the next two pages. A continuous discussion over two or more pages is indicated by a span of page numbers, e.g., "57–59." *Passim* is used for a cluster of references in close but not consecutive sequence.

Abelove, Henry, 254n27, 281n8

Adams (in *Joseph Andrews*), 75, 88, 97–106, 109–16, 122–23, 126, 129

Aeneid (Virgil), 98, 183f

Affectation, 12f, 25ff, 41–49 *passim*, 54, 56, 129

Alexander in India (Lumpugnani), 189

Alter, Robert, 73, 93, 270n3, 279n3

Althusser, Louis, 255n39

Amazons, 10, 21, 50, 134, 138, 140, 144, 170, 210

Andrews, Fanny (in *Joseph Andrews*), 71, 74, 82–88, 100, 109, 113–14, 116f, 127

Antitheatricality, 25–27, 86, 88f, 101, 105

Apollo, 165

Appleton, William, 263n39

Armstrong, Nancy, 4, 134, 148, 163, 253n13, 293n2

Astell, Mary, 284n18

Atkinson, Mrs. (in *Amelia*), 207–9

Auction, 36–37

Bakhtin, Mikhail, 274n10

Barrow, Isaac, 229

Battestin, Martin C., 3, 15, 52–53, 212–13, 228, 275n11, 278n11, 288n21, 289n29, 298n46

Beaux, 6–12 *passim*, 21, 42, 50, 53ff, 62, 72, 73–74, 99, 258n9, 264n52, 273n24, n25. *See also* Didapper, Beau

Bender, John, 226, 295n23

Benjamin, Walter, 203, 232

Blanchard, Frederic, 251n8

Blondel, Augustus, 124

Booby, Lady (in *Joseph Andrews*), 61, 68f, 82, 91–94

A Brief Account of the Life and Family of Miss Jenny Cameron, 142, 154–57, 171, 191

Broschi, Carlo (Farinelli), 28–39 *passim*, 55, 57, 261n27, 262n34, Figs. 3, 4, 5

Brown, Homer Obed, 70f, 126f, 280n27, n29

Brown, Laura, 40, 155n29, 267n68

Burlesque, 20, 107, 208–9, 248, 257n4, 272n23. *See also* Genre

Butler, Judith, 5f, 13, 20, 253n18, 254n23, 257n6, 265n55

Butler, Melissa A., 145f, 284n20

Cameron, Jenny, 133, 141f, 154–57, 171f, 285n29

Carlton, Peter J., 4, 132f, 135, 172–73, 175, 213, 282n5, 287n20

Caroline, Queen of England, 11, 19, 21f
Carson, James P., 260n24
Castle, Terry, 14, 50, 56, 255n33, n37, 257n5, 258n11, 278n11, 296n25
Castrati, 6, 10f, 21, 28–35, 37, 42–44, 57, 59, 62, 74, 75–77, 84–85, 86, 115, 130, 180, 189–90, 245–46, 258n8, 260n24, 261n25, n26, 273n4. *See also* Broschi, Carlo; Castration
Castration, 29–30, 193, 260n24, 292n18. *See also* Castrati
Cavalier, *see under* Masculinity
Champion, 16, 41–42, 43, 50, 53ff, 58, 114, 268n85
Character and historical contradictions, 2, 8, 135f, 170–78, 205–6, 212–26, 236, 243
Characterization, 15, 64–65, 112, 115, 120–22, 124
Charke, Charlotte, 26f, 37, 56–57, 268n82, n86
Chesterfield, Lord, 44
Child-rearing, 136, 207, 235–39 *passim. See also* Corporal punishment; Maternal relations
Christianity, 133, 175, 205, 216, 228–29, 230, 239, 243. *See also* Masculinity: male heroism; *Paradise Lost*; Virtue
Cixous, Hélène, 128–29
Classical education, 182, 184, 199f, 229–35 *passim*, 241. *See also* Child-rearing
Class identity, 68, 153, 206, 218f, 221, 223, 229, 269n2
Clinton-Baddeley, V. C., 257n4
Cock, Christopher, 27, 37–40, 103
Coley, W. B., 198
Collier, Margaret, 248
Commercial society, 9, 23, 33, 210. *See also* McKendrick, Neil
Common Sense (Opposition newspaper), 44
Companionate marriage, 10, 136, 170, 288n22. *See also* Heterosexuality

Corporal punishment, 76, 136, 156f, 182, 186–93, 197, 199, 235, 291n12
Cross-dressing, 11, 25, 27, 253n20, 264n46. *See also* Cross-gender casting; Gender: inversion
Cross-gender casting, 2, 7, 11, 18, 20, 26f, 45, 256n3, 257n4, 259n19, n20
Cruise, James, 294n11
Cumberland, Duke of, 140f, Figs. 10, 12, 13, 14
Cuzzoni, Francesca, 84f, Fig. 3

Davis, Natalie Zemon, 154, 282n2, 287n17
Dialogues of the Dead (Lucian), 53, 267n76
Didapper, Beau (in *Joseph Andrews*), 71–75, 78f, 90
Dildo, 36, 57f
Directory for Midwives (Nicholas Culpepper), 124
Doctrine of imagination, 12, 124–25. *See also* Maternal relations
Domesticity, 136, 163, 206f, 224, 229. *See also* Femininity; Private sphere
Don Quixote (Cervantes), 96
Dreams, 203–5
Dueling, 175, 205, 213–17, 230–32. *See also* Masculinity: male heroism
Dugaw, Dianne, 255n31, n32, n34
Dunciad (Pope), 11, 32, 47, 262n32

Eagleton, Terry, 252n11
Echo, 14, 89, 90–94, 101
Elegy, 64, 111, 116, 121–22. *See also* Genre
Elfenbein, Andrew, 226, 293n6
Epic, 2, 63f, 98f, 103, 106f. *See also* Genre; *Paradise Lost*
"An Epistle to *John James H--dd--g--r, Esq.*," 33–35, 55, 244
Epistolary form, 95, 112
Excise bill (1733), 48
"An Extract of a Letter from a Lady at Preston," 139

Farinelli, *see* Broschi, Carlo
Fashion, 26, 42–44, 82, 210

The Female Rebels, 137–38, 142, 147–
54, 162, 171f, 181, 211, 232
Femininity: female heroism, 11, 204–
11 *passim*, 237; female authority,
21–23, 211, 241, 244, 248; female
reproduction, 33f, 164–66; female
Jacobitism, 138–39, 148–54, 170,
171–72, 285n28; Whig femininity,
142, 147, 178–79; New Woman,
148, 150, 154, 170–174, 282n2,
293n2. *See also* Maternal relations;
Virtue
Fielding, Henry: life of, 1–2, 163, 212,
242–47; "ambivalence" of, 2, 109–
10, 228, 296n26; attitude toward
satire, 13–14, 31–32, 35, 57, 64, 76–
77, 83, 90–106 *passim*, 111, 178,
182, 190, 194–200, 275n14; face of,
15f, 52–53, Figs. 1, 8, 9
Fielding, Henry, works: *Amelia*, 7,
131, 136, 204–41, 243, 246; *The
Author's Farce*, 26, 32–33, 45, 47,
72, 107, 210, 262n32; *Champion* essays, 16, 41–42, 53ff, 58, 114,
268n85; *Covent Garden Tragedy*, 26,
47, 245; "An Essay on the Knowledge of the Characters of Men," 25,
46; *Eurydice*, 22, 43, 47, 83, 247,
266n67; *Eurydice Hissed*, 47–48; *The
Female Husband*, 55–60; *The Grub-
Street Opera*, 21, 83; *The Historical
Register*, 26–35 *passim*, 36–44, 67;
*History of the Present Rebellion in
Scotland*, 179; *The Intriguing Chambermaid*, 31–32, 76, 189; *The Jacobite's Journal*, 132f, 136–49 *passim*,
158, 164, 168, 171f, 176, 182f, 185f,
190, 191–200, 211, 235, 276n20;
Jonathan Wild, 114, 125, 245,
279n22, 286n14; *Joseph Andrews*, 7,
14, 32, 59–60, 61–130, 164, 182,
199, 220, 247; *Journal of a Voyage to
Lisbon*, 7, 125–26, 212, 241, 243–
48; "A Journey from This World to
the Next," 107, 120; *Juvenal's Sixth
Satire* (translation), 39ff; *Love in
Several Masques*, 21, 23f; *The Masquerade*, 12–13, 21, 34, 50–52, 54–

55, 138, 165f; *The Modern Husband*,
21; "Of the Remedy of Affliction
for the Loss of Our Friends," 120,
280n26; *Pasquin*, 21, 26, 33, 44ff,
72, 83; *Shamela*, 24–25, 30, 112;
Tom Jones, 1, 7, 14–15, 131–33,
135–36, 144, 158, 160–81, 183–91,
195, 199f, 204, 211, 220, 246; *Tom
Thumb*, 1–2, 19, 47, 72, 107, 209,
245, 256n3, 257n4, 266n65; *Tragedy
of Tragedies*, 22, 47, 83 (*see also* Tom
Thumb). *See also individual characters
by name*
Fielding, John, 246
Filmer, Sir Robert, 12, 143, 145f, 185,
190, 283n17, 290n1
Flogging, *see* Corporal punishment
Foote, Samuel, 294n9
Foucault, Michel, 10

Gandy, Henry, 146
Garber, Marjorie, 20, 253n20, 257n6,
259n20
Garrick, David, 15, 180
Gay, John, 11
Gender: and critical dualism of Field-
ing/Richardson, 2–5, 110; and difference, 5–7; inversion, 7, 19–28
passim, 39, 45, 54, 59, 62f, 70ff, 80–
83, 138, 153f, 158, 168, 173, 231,
241, 243, 254n27; historicity of, 8–
12, 163; adoptive quality of, 12,
135, 166; as performative, 13, 20;
impersonation, 35–36, 44, 55–59,
141; and authority, 164, 239. *See
also* Cross-gender casting; Femininity; Masculinity
Genre, 1, 63–65, 88, 91, 96, 98–99,
100, 107f, 274n1. *See also* Burlesque; Elegy; Fielding, Henry: attitude toward satire; Satire
George II, King of England, 10, 19,
21f
Ghosts: and status of feminine identity, 16, 24, 44, 46–48, 59, 119,
243, 247, 266n65; as emblems of
historical change, 16, 173–74, 176f,
205, 288n23

Girard, René, 265n52
Glorious Revolution, 9, 143–44, 146, 148, 177
Goldsmith, Oliver, 11
Graeme, Alan, 283n16

Hagstrum, Jean, 271n17, 273n25, 276n23
Hamilton, Mary ("George"), 56–58
The Happy Courtezan, 30–31, 34
Haraway, Donna, 5f
Harding, Sandra, 6
Heidegger, John, 12f, 15, 50–55, 59, 267n70, Figs. 4, 6, 7
Hervey, Lord, 11, 21, 25, 45, 72f, 78, 94, 103, 195, 273n25
Heterosexuality, 10, 132, 136, 157, 163, 184, 221, 223f
Hill, John ("Mrs. Seymour"), 233–35, 240
Hilles, Frederick W., 189
Hillhouse, James T., 257n4
Hogarth, William, 15, 22, 30, 32–33, 50ff, 261n27
Holland, Peter, 268n86
Hollander, John, 94
Homoeroticism, 136, 157f, 165, 182f, 189–91, 195, 292n19, 297n36. *See also* Homosexuality; Homosocial relationships; Masculinity
Homosexuality, 34, 42, 56, 235f, 241, 254n27
Homosocial relationships, 10, 221, 223ff, 235f
Hume, David, 228f
Hunter, J. Paul, 4, 61, 87, 95, 121, 269n1, n5, 270n5, 271n14, 273n25, n26, 274n7, 275n12, n13, 277n3
Hutchens, Eleanor N., 131f
Hyacinthus, 165

Iliad (Homer), 98, 103, 231
In Rufinum (Claudian), 229
Ireland, John, 30

Jacobite rebellion of 1745, 7, 12, 132, 135, 137, 154, 162, 164, 289n31;

Whig propaganda against, 14, 134, 137–39, Figs. 10–17
Jacobitism, 51, 132–33, 135; propaganda supporting, 140, Fig. 14; propaganda against, Figs. 10–13, 16, 17
Jewett, William, 273n25
Johnson, Maurice, 62–63, 84, 93, 269n2, n5, 277n4
Johnson, Samuel, 107, 266n60
Jones, Miss (actress), 209
Jones, Vivien, 293n2
Juvenal (*Sixth Satire*), 39–41, 99

Kern, Jean B., 258n9
Kowaleski-Wallace, Beth, 261n26
Kramnick, Isaac, 9

Laqueur, Thomas, 254n27
Lenman, Bruce, 282n6
Lenta, Margaret, 252n11
Life of Cicero (Middleton), 72, 78, 94
Liu, Alan, 256n42
Locke, John, 12, 142–46 *passim*, 173, 185, 190–91, 283n17, 284n20, n23, 287n20, 290n1
Lottery, 263n40
Lovat, Lord, 53, 267n76
Lyttleton, 44, 178

MacDonald, Flora, 150f, 152f
Macey, Samuel L., 257n4
McIntosh, Mary, 254n27
McKendrick, Neil, 9, 42
McKeon, Michael, 252n12, 253n13, 255n38, 270n4
Mancini, Hortense (Duchess of Mazarin), 169
Maresca, Thomas E., 251n9, 271n17
Marriage Hater Matched (Thomas D'Urfey), 103
Marshall, David, 121
Marx, Karl ("The Eighteenth Brumaire"), 288n23, 296n31
Masculinity: 166, 175, 212; Whig masculinity, 4, 7, 11f, 134, 138, 140–47 *passim*, 151–52, 158, 193; "cavalier" masculinity, 4, 133, 151,

155, 157f, 175f, 205, 213f, 219, 230, 243; compromised masculinity, 11, 20ff, 63, 69–71, 73–77, 110–16 *passim*, 124, 126, 166, 193–94, 205, 209, 220f, 243–49; male heroism, 53–54, 114f, 133ff, 175–76, 205, 242; military honor, 213, 219, 230; masculine authority, 233, 239. *See also* Homoeroticism; Homosocial relationships

Masks, 12, 14f, 48, 51–52, 131, 196

Masquerade, 49–51, Figs. 4, 6. *See also* Affectation; Fielding, Henry, works: *The Masquerade*

Maternal relations, 10f, 33f, 36, 54f, 123–25, 128, 164–66, 199, 207, 238

Maus, Katherine Eisaman, 268n86

Mediated desire, 74, 95, 188, 265n52

Middleton, Conyers (*Life of Cicero*), 72, 78, 94

Miller, Henry Knight, 110, 121, 126

Misrecognition, 122–23, 126, 220, 222–23, 224, 226

The Modish Couple, 266n59

Monod, Paul Kleber, 283n11

Monticello (castrato), 189

Montrose, Louis, 168

Moore, Robert Etheridge, 252n11

Morrissey, L. J., 257n4

Murphy, Arthur, 15

Narcissism, 273n25

Narcissus, 85–86, 88

Narrative disjunction, 206, 221, 225–26

Nelson, James, 293n4

New Woman, *see* Femininity

Novel: rise of, 2–5, 252n13; novelistic narrative and political prose, 134–35, 163–64, 181. *See also* Epistolary form; Genre

Ogilvy, Lady, 150–51, 152, 282n6

Old England, 52

On the Management and Education of Children, 207, 232–35, 239

Opposition satire, 1, 10, 21, 25, 44, 195

Orgel, Stephen, 167

Orpheus and Eurydice (Rich), 53

Pamela (Richardson), 7, 14, 59, 61–62, 67–71, 77, 81–82, 94f, 111f, 115, 269n2, 280n28

Paradise Lost (Milton), 14, 64, 79–83, 89, 90–91, 95–108 *passim*, 117

Partridge (in *Tom Jones*), 140, 176–79

Partridge, John, 177–78

Pateman, Carole, 284n20

Patriarchalism, *see* Filmer, Sir Robert

Paulson, Ronald, 15, 121, 261n27, 274n6, n9, 276n21

Pedagogy and discipline, 182, 185, 189–93, 197, 199

Perth, Duchess of, 149, 150–51, 152, 282n6

"Petticoat government," 19, 21, 24f, 38, 83, 133f, 137f, 151, 209, 211, 245, 247, 262n32

Phillips, Teresia Constantia, 30f, 262n29

Pitt, William, 178

Plumb, J. H., 9

Pollak, Ellen, 255n20, 264n49

Pope, Alexander, 11, 21, 32, 47, 262n32

Priapus, 55, 76, 85

Private sphere, 163f, 166, 170, 179f

Prynne, William, 259n20

Pulteney, William, 21

Puppets, status of men as, 7, 48–51, 114f, 245

Pygmalion, 85f

Queen Common-sense (in *Pasquin*), 44–47

Rabb, Melinda Alliker, 298n1, 299n3, n4

Rackin, Phyllis, 279n21

Rawson, Claude, 209, 299n3

Reflections on Theatrical Expressions in Tragedy, 30, 33

Re-translation, 209f. *See also* Genre

Richardson, Samuel, 1–2, 24, 100,
107f, 120, 122, 171, 252nn11–13,
292n22; in critical dualism with
Fielding, 2–5, 110f, 252n11
"Roasting-Squire" (in *Joseph An-
drews*), 77, 90, 100f
Roderick Random, 191
Rogers, Katherine M., 294n13
Rothstein, Eric, 258n14
Rousseau, G. S., 134
Royal Female Magazine, 117–18

Satire, 10, 12f, 21f, 40, 90. *See also*
Fielding, Henry: attitude
toward satire; Genre; Opposition
satire
Schilling, Bernard, 62, 77
Schochet, Gordon J., 285n25
Scott, Joan Wallach, 5ff
Sedgwick, Eve Kosofsky, 290n4
Seymour, Juliana-Susannah ("Mrs.
Seymour"), 233–35, 240
Shakespeare, William, 171, 277n3.
Works: *As You Like It*, 171, 287n16;
Macbeth, 113, 277n4, n5; *Othello*,
220; *Two Gentlemen of Verona*, 171,
287n16
Sherbo, Arthur, 61
Sherburn, George, 213
Sitter, John E., 255n30, 266n61,
294n11
Slipslop (in *Joseph Andrews*), 75, 91–
94, 112
Smallwood, Angela J., 3, 10
Stage Licensing Act, 1, 16, 26
Stone, Lawrence, 207, 254n27, 281n8,
284n20, n23

Stuart, Charles Edward, 137, 140f,
151–52, 153f, 158, 283n13, 285n28,
Figs. 12–15, 17
Summers, Montagu, 276n23
Swift, Jonathan, 177–78

Taylor, Dick, Jr., 63, 84, 86f, 269n2,
270n8, 272n22, 273n27
Theatricality, 25–27, 46, 56, 167–
69
Thompson, James, 289n31
Thwackum, Mr. (in *Tom Jones*),
161, 183–90
Trott-Plaid, John (in *The Jacobite's
Journal*), 139–40, 193–96, Fig. 11
Trumbach, Randolph, 263n39
Turner, Daniel, 124
Tyrrell, James, 145

Virtue, 24, 38–48 *passim*, 54, 57, 59,
67, 69
The Virtuoso (Shadwell), 192

Walpole, Sir Robert, 1, 9, 22, 25, 27,
48, 138, 193, 210, 262n33, 292n19
Warner, William, 253n13
Watt, Ian, 4, 81f, 103, 120–21, 134,
148, 171, 282n2
Weinbrot, Howard D., 260n24,
263n39
Western, Sophia (in *Tom Jones*), 161–
70 *passim*, 171–74, 180
Witchcraft, 246
Woods, Charles B., 262n33
Woodward, Dr., 25

Library of Congress Cataloging-in-Publication Data

Campbell, Jill.
  Natural masques : gender and identity in Fielding's plays and
novels / Jill Campbell.
     p. cm.
Includes bibliographical references and index.
ISBN 0-8047-2391-5 (cl.) ISBN 0-8047-2520-9 (pbk.)
  1. Fielding, Henry, 1707–1754—Knowledge—Psychology.
2. Masculinity (Psychology) in literature.   3. Femininity
(Psychology) in literature.   4. Identity (Psychology) in literature.
5. Gender identity in literature.   6. Sex role in literature.
I. Title.
PR3458.P8C36   1995
823'.5—dc20   94-33011   CIP